Enhancing Adobe Acrobat DC Forms with JavaScript

Jennifer Harder

Apress®

Enhancing Adobe Acrobat DC Forms with JavaScript

Jennifer Harder
Delta, British Columbia, Canada

ISBN-13 (pbk): 978-1-4842-2892-0 ISBN-13 (electronic): 978-1-4842-2893-7
DOI 10.1007/978-1-4842-2893-7

Library of Congress Control Number: 2017954339

Cover image designed by Freepik

Managing Director: Welmoed Spahr
Editorial Director: Todd Green
Acquisitions Editor: Natalie Pao
Development Editor: James Markham
Technical Reviewer: Dan Carr
Coordinating Editor: Jessica Vakili
Copy Editor: Mary Behr
Compositor: SPi Global
Indexer: SPi Global
Artist: SPi Global

Distributed to the book trade worldwide by Springer Science+Business Media New York, 233 Spring Street, 6th Floor, New York, NY 10013. Phone 1-800-SPRINGER, fax (201) 348-4505, e-mail orders-ny@springer-sbm.com, or visit www.springeronline.com. Apress Media, LLC is a California LLC and the sole member (owner) is Springer Science + Business Media Finance Inc (SSBM Finance Inc). SSBM Finance Inc is a **Delaware** corporation.

For information on translations, please e-mail rights@apress.com, or visit www.apress.com/rights-permissions.

Apress titles may be purchased in bulk for academic, corporate, or promotional use. eBook versions and licenses are also available for most titles. For more information, reference our Print and eBook Bulk Sales web page at www.apress.com/bulk-sales.

Any source code or other supplementary material referenced by the author in this book is available to readers on GitHub via the book's product page, located at www.apress.com/978-1-4842-2892-0. For more detailed information, please visit www.apress.com/source-code.

Printed on acid-free paper

Contents at a Glance

Contents

About the Author

Jennifer Harder has worked in the graphic design industry for over 10 years. She has a degree in Graphic Communications and is currently teaching Acrobat, InDesign, and Dreamweaver courses at Langara College. As a freelancer, Jennifer frequently works with Adobe PDFs and checks them before they go to print or are uploaded to the Web. She enjoys talking about Adobe software and her interests include writing, illustration, and working on her websites.

About the Technical Reviewer

Dan Carr is a veteran software developer and UX designer specializing in vanilla JavaScript, web components, React, and Node. During a decade of consulting with Adobe, Dan produced articles, tutorials, and product features for Dreamweaver, Flash, Flex, and Authorware. Life currently finds him enjoying the weather in Westside Los Angeles.

Acknowledgments

For their patience and advice, I would like to thank the following people, for without them I could never have written this book:

- My parents, for encouraging me to read large computer textbooks that would one day inspire me to write my own book.
- My Dad, for reviewing the first draft before I sent a proposal.
- My program coordinator, Raymond Chow, at Langara College, who gave me the chance to teach evening courses when others would not give me that opportunity or believe that I had anything worthy to contribute.
- My printing boss, Eddie, at Pender Copy Ltd., who knows how much work it is to put together a large document and how much effort I put into working with Adobe software.

At Apress, I would like to thank Natalie and Jessica for showing me how to lay out a professional textbook and pointing out that even when you think you've written it all, there's still more to write. Also thanks to Jim Markham and the technical reviewers Dan Carr and Karl Kremer for taking the time to test my files and for providing encouraging comments. And thanks to the rest of the Apress team for printing this book and making my dream a reality. I am truly grateful and blessed.

Introduction

Welcome to the first step in an exciting journey I call *Enhancing Adobe Acrobat DC Forms with JavaScript.*

My journey into learning about Adobe software began 17 years ago when I started college. I took a two-year Graphic Communications course in Vancouver, BC. While learning about how to set up documents for print layout using QuarkXPress and later Adobe InDesign, I created PDF files. At that point, I only saw the PDF as a transition from one file format to the next production step, from layout to the printing press. It never crossed my mind what else could be done with PDF files in Adobe Acrobat.

Several years after graduating, while doing freelance work for one of my clients, I began to investigate the features of Acrobat to discover what else the program had to offer. In 2008, I decided to learn more about web design and improve my layout skills in Adobe software. After finishing three certificates in Web Design at Langara College Continuing Studies, I realized that I wanted to help students learn more about Adobe software. There were times through the journey when I read different computer books and felt, "OK I've finished this tutorial or project, but how does this relate to the real world and what I'm trying to accomplish?" In 2011, I became a Teaching Assistant at Langara College and this gave me the opportunity to write my own course on introducing students to Adobe Acrobat. While writing it, I realized there was a lot more that could be said about Acrobat than what I could present in three-evening course. At that point, I was looking at one icon in the Acrobat menu that perplexed me. It was called JavaScript.

JavaScript in Acrobat? What is this doing here? The only JavaScript that I knew about at that point was through building websites. I had built a few basic template forms using LiveCycle Designer, MS Word, and Acrobat, but I had never used JavaScript in the Acrobat program. So I began to wonder how JavaScript could improve my forms.

So, this is when and how the idea began for developing a book for students on the topic of Acrobat and JavaScript. After years of research, looking at Adobe and Acrobat forums, and studying the questions and concerns users had when trying to add JavaScript to Acrobat, I came to the following conclusions:

- Users are looking for simple solutions to programing an Acrobat form that they will use in real-world situations. Many are looking for the same answers.

- When documentation is not written in a simplified manner, the average user becomes intimidated. They will shy away from using the JavaScript menu and eventually give up and ignore the tool. To them, JavaScript coding is like a foreign language, and the average person who has not taken web design lessons does not have a clue what it means or where the code should be inserted, since the form field's property dialog boxes look nothing like a web page.

- At some point, it's important to share with others what you have learned about Acrobat and JavaScript and not keep your thoughts to yourself. That's what leads to innovative ideas. However, these thoughts need to be organized so that the user can find the solution quickly and be able to comprehend it.

Shortly after compiling my notes, Adobe introduced the latest version Acrobat DC. I saw that the layout of the program had changed and now there was no book to show the user how to add JavaScript in this new format. I completed the first draft of my Advanced Adobe course and had it approved by my Program Coordinator at the college. In 2016, I realized I could reach a wider audience if the book was published and so I approached Apress. They saw my vision, and that is how this book came to be in your possession.

Understanding How Acrobat DC and Its Forms Work with JavaScript

If you are currently using Adobe Acrobat Pro XI or older, it's time to upgrade to the new Acrobat DC Pro. You can either acquire Adobe Acrobat DC as a stand-alone program through Adobe or get a Creative Cloud subscription and enjoy all the exciting Adobe programs for a monthly fee. Refer to these links and check if your computer's operating system meets the system requirements needed for the upgrade:

```
https://helpx.adobe.com/creative-cloud/system-requirements.html
https://helpx.adobe.com/acrobat/system-requirements.html
```

Make sure to follow the online instructions and tutorials for installing and working with Acrobat and Creative Cloud.

If you are new to Adobe Acrobat DC, I encourage you to first read the book *Adobe Acrobat DC Classroom in a Book* by Brie Gyncild and Lisa Fridsma. This book will give you a basic overview of the new Acrobat DC features as well as form basics in Chapter 10. However, that book does not go into detail regarding forms when working with JavaScript. I consider my book to be the part 2 for intermediate and advanced users to take their forms to the next level.

Adobe Acrobat DC will allow you to add form fields to any PDF file, as I will explain further in Chapter 1. It can even work with pre-existing form fields that were created in Adobe InDesign CC when the file was exported as an interactive PDF. However, it's important that your client views and interacts with the forms in Acrobat DC Pro, Standard, or Acrobat Reader. Other PDF readers, like Mac Preview, have been known to corrupt the JavaScript programing, so keep this in mind when you email the forms.

Another possibility is that the user may have disable the use of JavaScript under Edit ➤ Preferences Categories JavaScript.

See Figure I-1 for how your JavaScript preferences should appear.

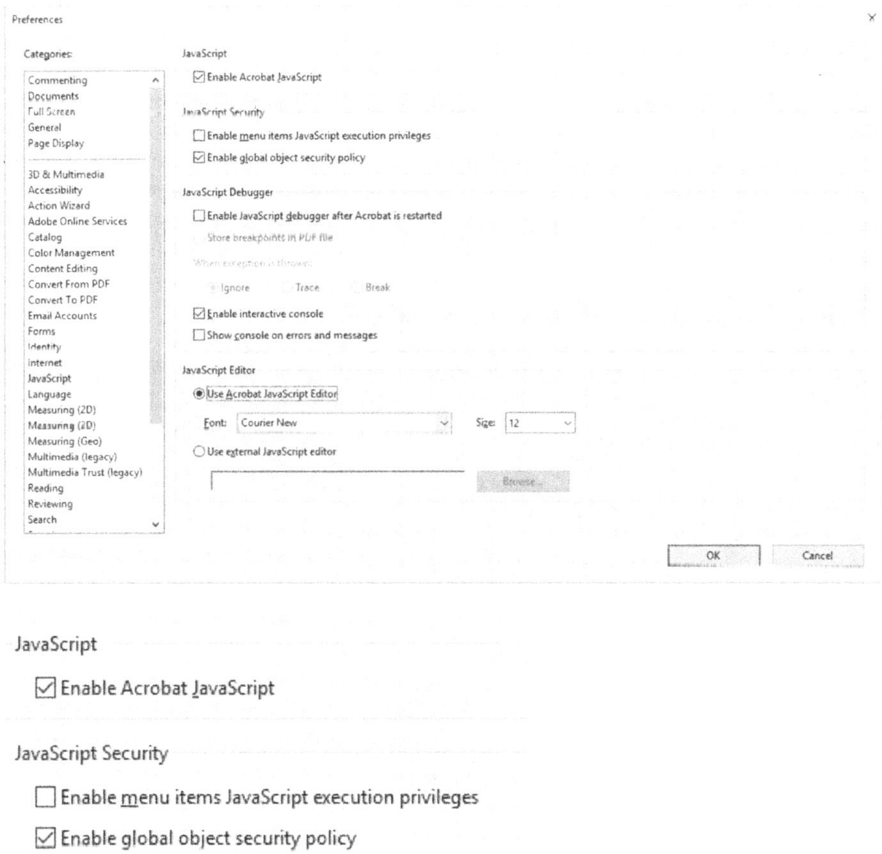

Figure I-1. *Acrobat DC's Preferences menu for enabling and disabling JavaScript and security features*

The following is an explanation from the Adobe website on some of the settings. See `https://helpx.adobe.com/acrobat/using/javascripts-pdfs-security-risk.html` for more information.

- **Enable Acrobat JavaScript**: Uncheck to disable JavaScript completely or restrict JavaScript through APIs.
- **Enable menu items JavaScript execution privileges**: Enables executing JavaScript by clicking menu items. When off, privileged JavaScript calls can be executed through the menu. Executing non-privileged JavaScript calls through menu items is not blocked whether this box is checked or not.

- **Enable global object security policy**: Allows JavaScript globally through APIs, or trusts specific documents containing JavaScripts.

The debugger and the JavaScript Editor options will be looked more closely in Chapter 5.

Note that you will not be working with any JavaScript that could create a security risk so you can leave this area at the default settings for these chapters as you work with the files you download.

In most cases, Adobe Acrobat DC will auto-detect in a PDF where form fields can be added in a form, but it's not a perfect science. It's up to you as the author to edit and test your forms for errors as you build them and add your JavaScript code.

What to Expect from this Book

Enhancing Adobe Acrobat DC Forms with JavaScript covers up-to-date, real working examples that you can easily download, practice with, and edit to suit your own projects. Using screenshots from Adobe Acrobat DC, users of previous versions will also be able to utilize these techniques. This book also shows work-arounds and solutions to various form issues you might encounter. JavaScript does not need to be scary. Feel empowered by it and improve your PDF documents!

What You'll Learn

You'll learn the following from this book:

- How to create calculations, rating forms, and QR code stamps using the form elements
- Simplified field notation and basic JavaScript for Acrobat
- How to use buttons for navigation
- How to create complex forms that include dropdown and list boxes in combination with other form fields
- Action Wizard and JavaScript
- Improved form navigation and printing of forms
- Various types of alerts and custom validations to improve client-entered data

PART 1

Basic Form Improvements

CHAPTER 1

A Fundamental Forms Primer

Creating the right form before you add JavaScript to your PDF fields takes time and careful planning. Therefore, it's important that you become familiar with each of the form tools and the properties that are associated with them. This chapter provides a quick overview of forms, fields, properties, and tabs that will serve as the basis for future chapters. If you are already comfortable with these topics, feel free to jump ahead to Chapter 2.

Forms Review

Each form field has within it properties that can be accessed by right-clicking on the form field. The properties of that form field are organized by a use of tabs. Each form field has slightly different properties and therefore different tabs.

Throughout this book you will be working on lessons with a variety of different PDF forms and documents for a fictitious company called The Tourmaline Mining Corporation.

Each chapter (except for Chapters 1 and 5) comes with JavaScript in a `.txt` file and PDF files that you can open and compare. You can either view the final PDF file or use the start PDF file and follow along with the notes in these chapters. You can find the files at `www.apress.com/9781484228920`.

Note Please be aware that the PDF files used with this book should only be opened in Adobe Acrobat Pro or Acrobat Reader XI or DC and not in Mac Preview or any other PDF creation/reader program. Other PDF readers have been known to corrupt the JavaScript code within the Acrobat PDF files and then the calculations fail to work.

Upon opening Acrobat DC, make sure to check your preferences at Edit Preferences ➤ Forms. They should be set to the default settings shown in Figure 1-1.

J. Harder, *Enhancing Adobe Acrobat DC Forms with JavaScript*,
DOI 10.1007/978-1-4842-2893-7_1

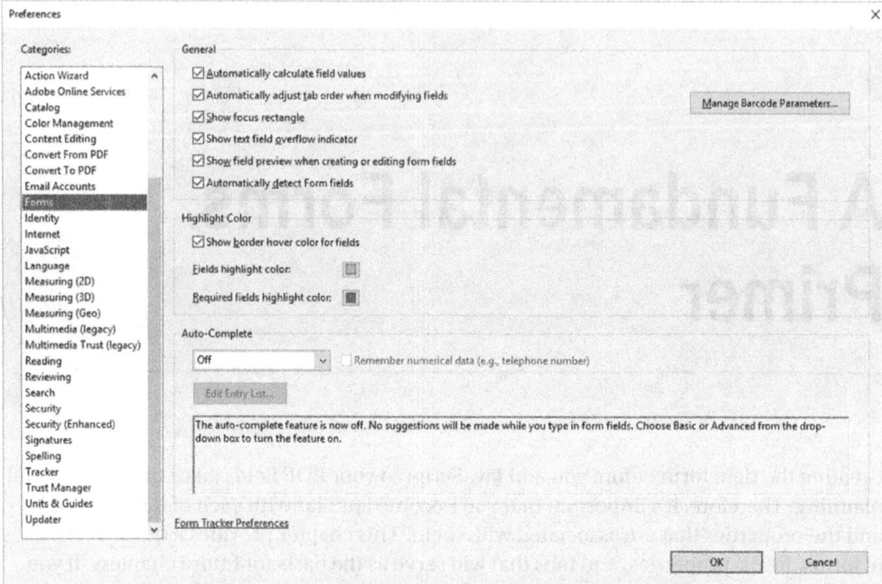

Figure 1-1. *Default settings for the Forms tool*

The book assumes that you are familiar with filling in basic forms or have used PDF forms in the past. If you are unsure of how to use the Prepare Form tool (shown in Figure 1-2) and its auto-detection of fields in Acrobat DC, this section provides a refresher.

Draw out your form either by hand or create it in MS Word, Adobe Illustrator, or Adobe InDesign, and decide what steps you want the form to do and accomplish. Then plan how to execute your goals. Is what you want the form to do possible? Do you need to simplify the form? Or do you need to learn more about the topic of forms to create what you want?

Except for the program of Adobe InDesign, you cannot assemble the form's interactive fields outside of Acrobat, so you need to make a PDF to do that. Until you are ready to make the PDF, continue to assemble the form in your layout program until it looks the way it should. Then create the PDF. Once you have the final PDF, open it in Acrobat DC and follow these steps to add interactivity:

1. Click Tools ➤ Prepare Form Tool.
2. While in the tool, choose your file and make sure that form field auto-detection is ON. Do not check "This document requires signatures" (Figure 1-2).

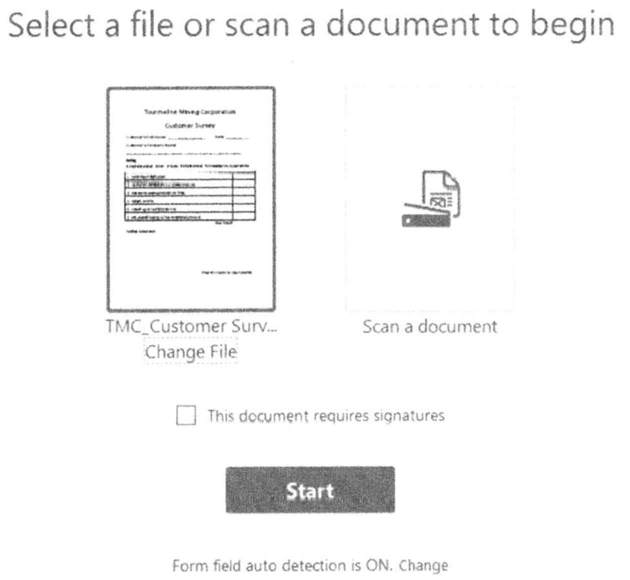

Figure 1-2. *The Prepare Form tool when you first create a new form*

3. Click Start. Acrobat will scan the file for fields; if it detects any, it will create the field. However, it is not perfect in its detection, so you may have to add, delete, or edit some fields afterward.
4. Once you have added your fields, save the file as a new PDF. The new PDF is now an interactive form. Refer to Figure 1-3.

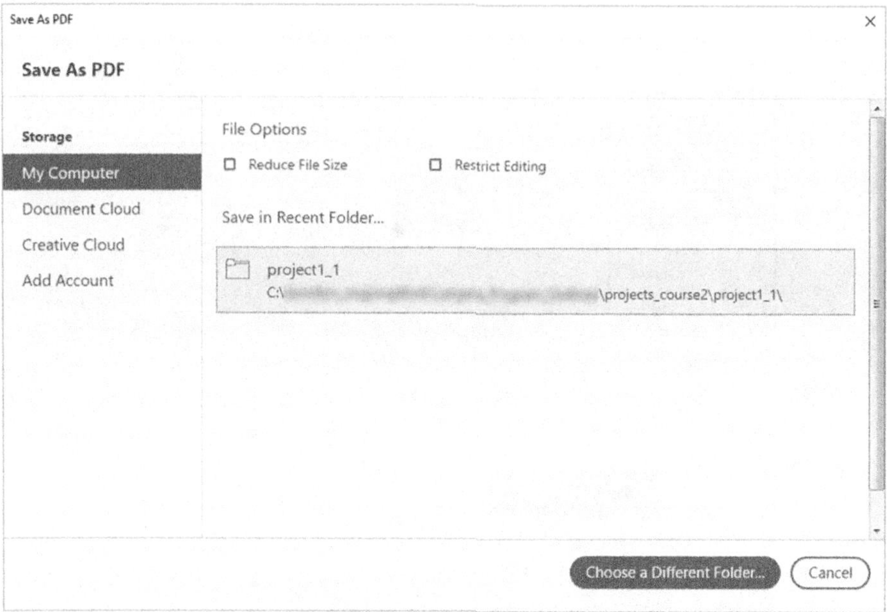

Figure 1-3. *Saving the new PDF form in a folder after auto-detection is completed*

You can now begin adding your formatting and actions to the properties of each field. Test it, and ask others to try it on their computer, before you send it to your clients. Always keep a backup on a disk or USB drive in case something happens to your main computer. Also make a printout of the PDF and all code in case you need to refer to it later for another project.

Once the fields are in the form, you can open the fields any time with the Prepare Form tool; you do not need to run the auto-detection again for that form.

You can exit the Prepare Form area partially by toggling the Preview/Edit button in the upper right (Figure 1-4). To exit the Prepare Form tool completely, you must click the X in the upper right (Figure 1-4).

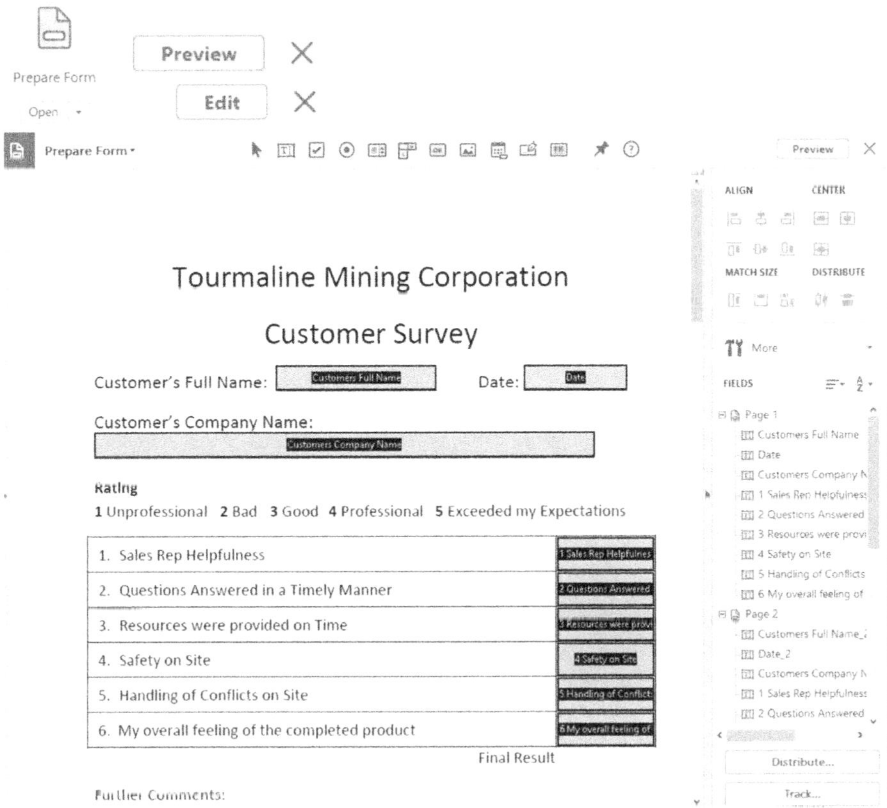

Figure 1-4. *The Prepare Form tool and the tools for adding and working with the fields. Note the Preview/Edit toggle and Exit (X) buttons in the upper right. Also note the view of a form while in Edit mode.*

For more information on basic forms or basic form creation, check out the following links before you proceed any further in this book:

- `https://helpx.adobe.com/acrobat/using/pdf-form-field-properties.html`
- `https://helpx.adobe.com/acrobat/using/pdf-forms-basics.html#pdf_forms_basics`
- `https://helpx.adobe.com/acrobat/using/creating-distributing-pdf-forms.html#creating_and_distributing_pdf_forms`
- `https://helpx.adobe.com/acrobat/using/pdf-form-field-basics.html#pdf_form_field_basics`

Other form tools, such as the Align and Distribute options, are found in the pane on the right-hand side and in the More dropdown menu (Figure 1-5). I will go into more detail about the JavaScript area in later in the book. Refer to the previous web links for more details.

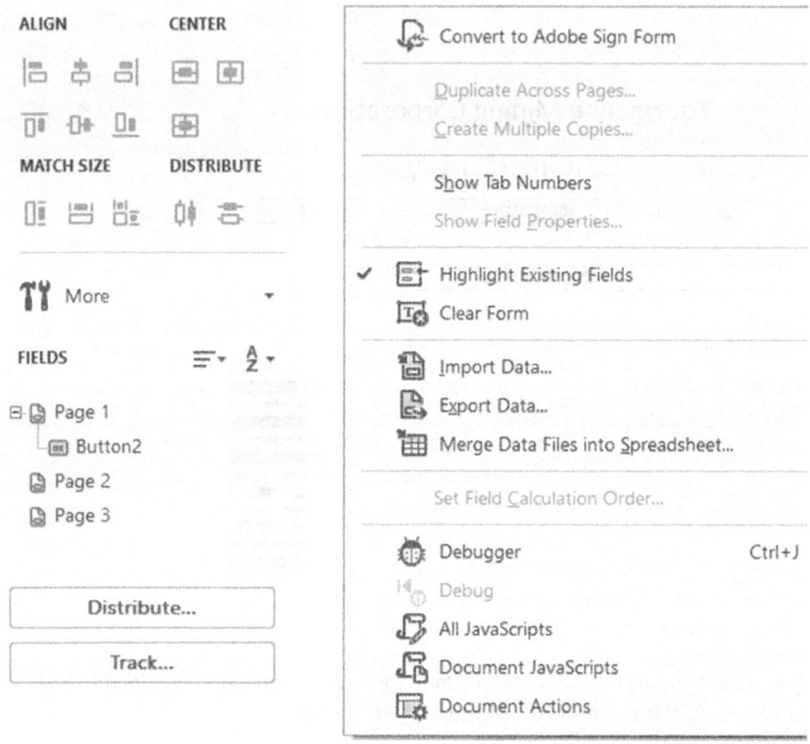

Figure 1-5. *Additional options found in the right-hand pane of the Prepare Form tool*

Fields Refresher

Fields can be blank and inactive, or they can contain a script that, upon entering or clicking a trigger, sets the action in motion. For example, they can execute a menu item or import form data. In Acrobat, the Forms Menu tool area contains all the field options listed below plus the Selection tool. These fields can be used in any form, while the Selection tool is just an arrow that allows you to select, size, and move them around.

- **Selection tool**: Select, size, and move fields.
- **Text box**: Type name or numbers into field.
- **Check box**: Select multiple options of an item.

- **Radio button**: Select one option from a group: yes or no.
- **List box**: Select one or multiple items in a list.
- **Dropdown list**: Select an option from a list.
- **Button**: Initiates an action like reset or submit.
- **Image field (new)**: Same as button, only with some JavaScript added (more on this topic later).
- **Date field (new)**: Same as text field, but pre-formatted to date. It can operate as a date picker.
- **Digital signature**: Electronically sign with your signature.
- **Barcode**: For a product barcode reader.

These items are also shown in Figure 1-6. To access them, select Tools ➤ Prepare Form and then choose a document. The icons will then appear at the bottom.

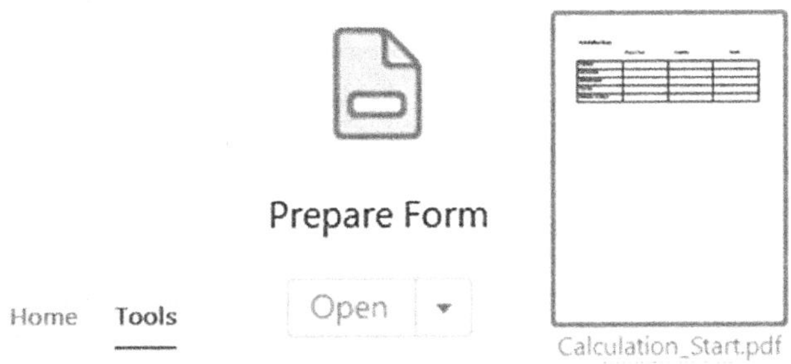

***Figure 1-6.** Form tools available when working with a PDF from in Adobe Acrobat DC. You can access them by going to the Tools tab and selecting the Prepare Form tool.*

■ **Note** If you require a custom QR Code, you can create one in InDesign CC 2014 or higher. QR Codes are like barcodes, and we will look at them more closely in Chapter 3.

Properties Refresher

Each form field contains properties that can be easily accessed while you are in form editing mode. Simply right-click the field you want to edit and choose Properties (Figure 1-7). Then select the property you want to work with in the various tabs that will appear in the dialog box.

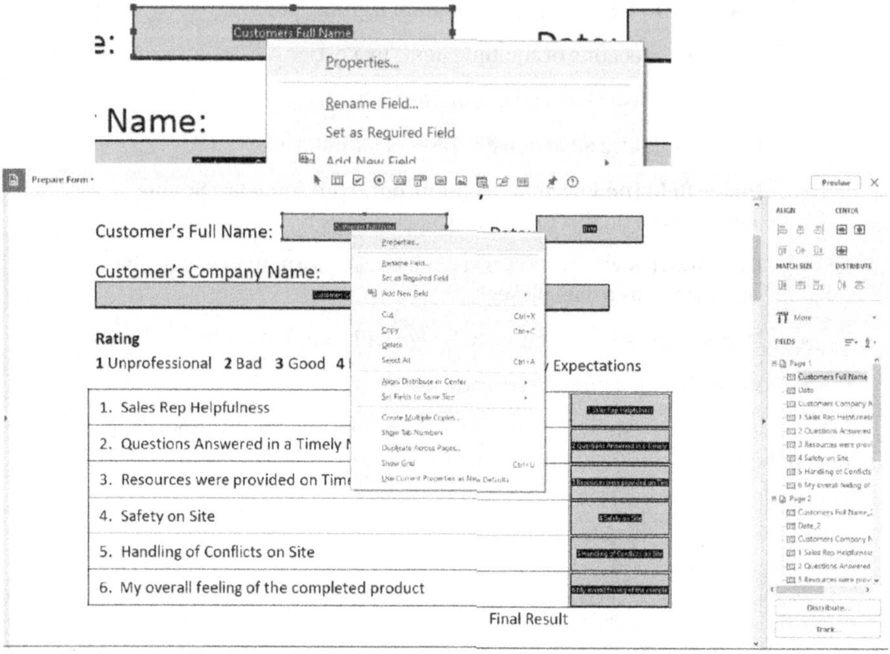

Figure 1-7. Right-click a field to reveal its properties

Various properties can be set for each field depending upon which field is chosen because the amount of properties varies. The properties are organized into sections using tabs. Refer here to Figures 1-8 through 1-15. Properties can be typed in, checked, or unchecked. The settings are applied as soon as you exit the field and move to another field in the Properties dialog box or by clicking the Close button. However, the settings are not fully saved until you save the PDF file.

To review, to work with the form fields, you must be in the Prepare Forms tool in Edit mode. You will know you are in Edit mode because the Preview button toggle is in the upper-right and the name of each field will appear. You can now either edit one field at a time or multiple fields.

Use the Selection tool and either click one field or mark several and then right-click and choose Properties from the menu.

■ **Note** If you select several fields at once, you may not have access to all tabs depending on the type of fields selected. If you have selected several fields, what you type in the tab properties will apply to all fields selected.

You will now be inside the form's properties dialog box. Now you can change properties within each tab; when you are done, click the Close button to close the dialog box and save your PDF file to confirm the changes.

The following sections provide a cursory look at the properties associated with the form fields listed earlier in the chapter.

Text Box Field Properties and New Date Field Properties

The text field and date field have eight tabs to organize their properties. The only difference between a text field and a date field is that the format category for a date field is preset to Date while the format category for a text field is preset to None. Note that the heading of the dialog box for both is "Text Field Properties." Refer to Figure 1-8.

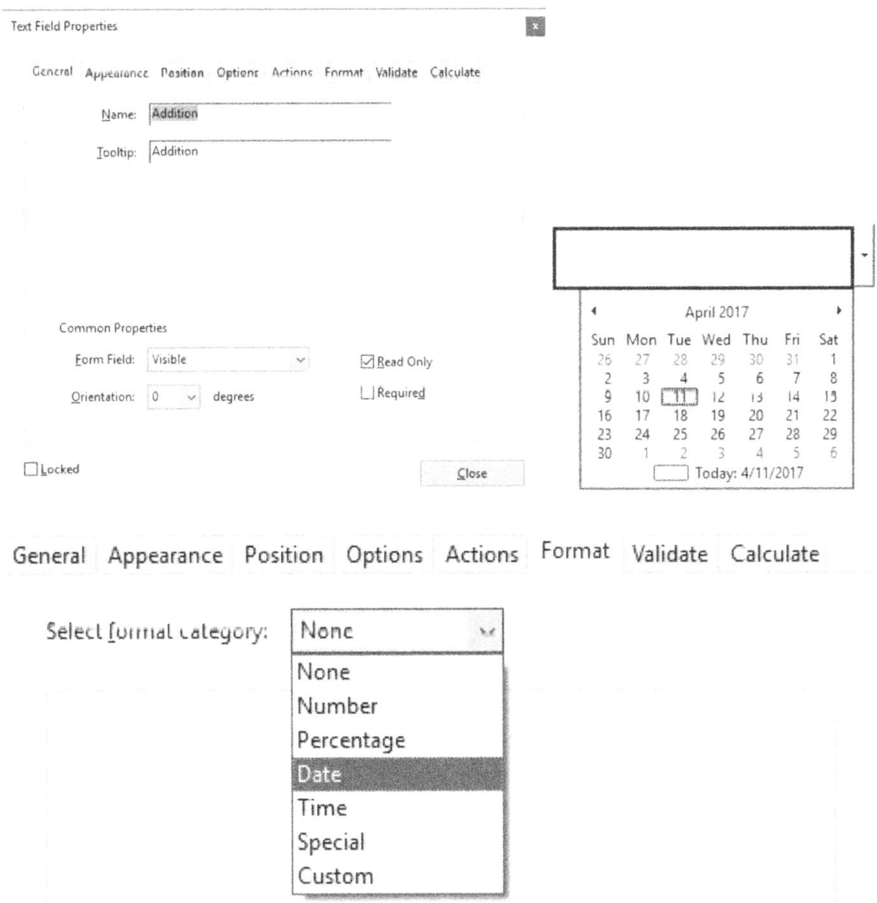

Figure 1-8. *Text field and date properties*

Dropdown Properties

The Dropdown Properties dialog box also has eight tabs to organize the properties. The tabs have the same names as the text field properties and contain many equivalent properties; however, if you compare the Options tab on the Text Field Properties dialog box to the Options tab on the Dropdown Properties dialog box, it will look different because dropdown menus are meant to hold multiple export values while a text field can only hold one default value.

While it is an option, the Calculate tab is rarely used with the Dropdown menu. Refer to Figure 1-9.

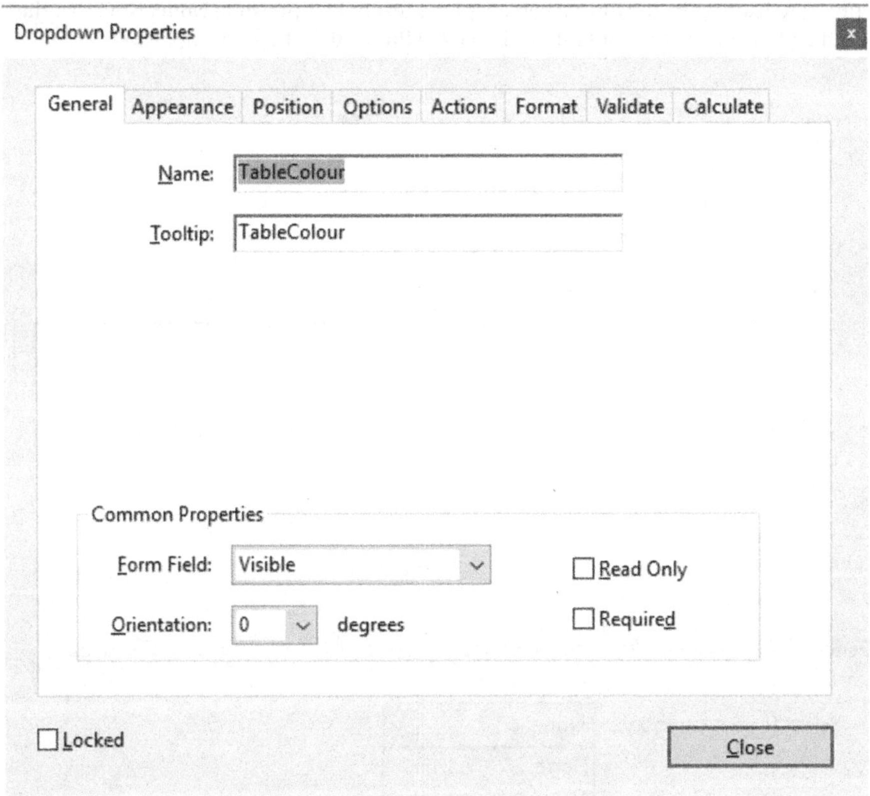

Figure 1-9. *Dropdown Properties dialog box*

List Box Properties

List box properties act like dropdown menus. However, there are only six tabs to organize the properties. Like dropdown menus, they can have multiple export values. Unlike dropdown menus, you can select more than one value at a time. Refer here to Figure 1-10.

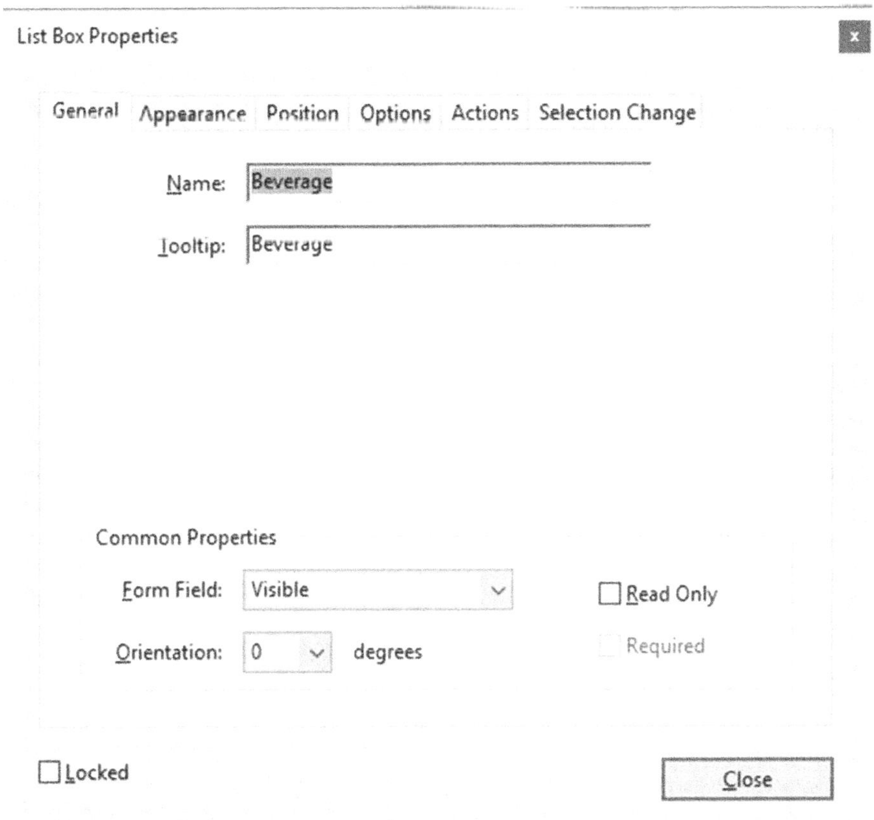

Figure 1-10. *List Box Properties dialog box*

Check Box Properties

The Check Box Properties dialog box has five tabs to organize the properties. A check box can either be checked on or off. You cannot enter text into a check box; however, you can give it a word or number value. Like all other properties, you can alter its appearance and color (via the Appearance and Option tabs). Check boxes can act separately or in groups. Refer to Figure 1-11.

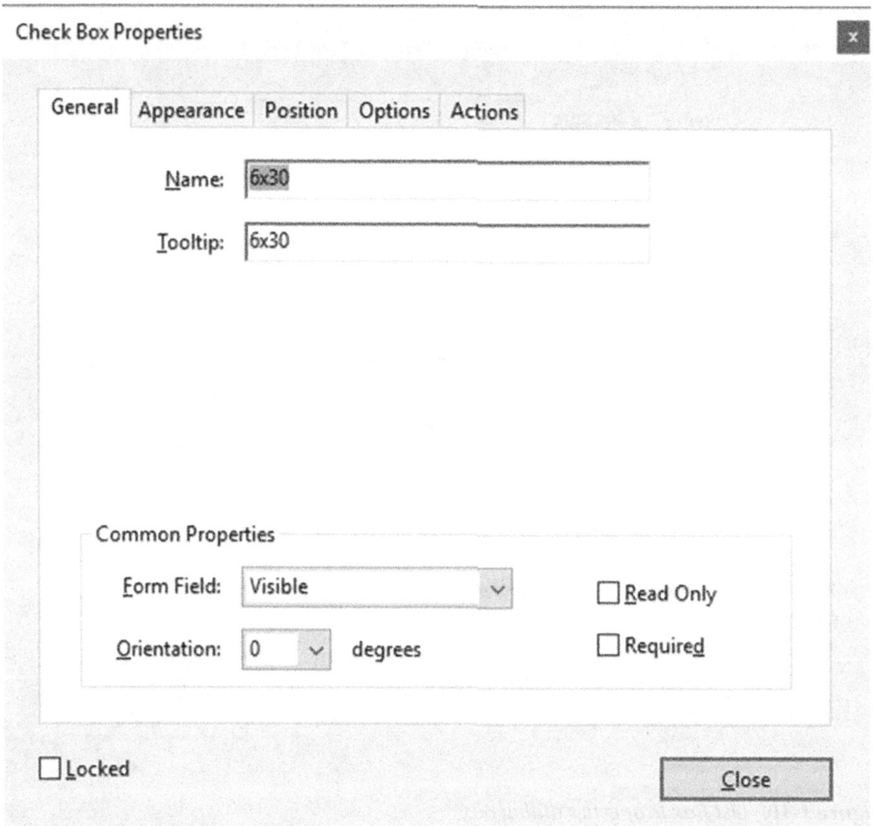

Figure 1-11. *Check Box Properties dialog box*

Radio Button Properties

The Radio Button Properties dialog box, like the check box dialog box, has five tabs to organize the properties. A radio button must come in pairs that can either be checked on or off. While one is on, the other is off. You cannot enter text into a radio button; however, you can give it a word or number value. Like all other properties, you can alter its appearance and color (Appearance and Option tabs). You can have more than one group of radio buttons, but there must always be at least two in the group. Refer to Figure 1-12.

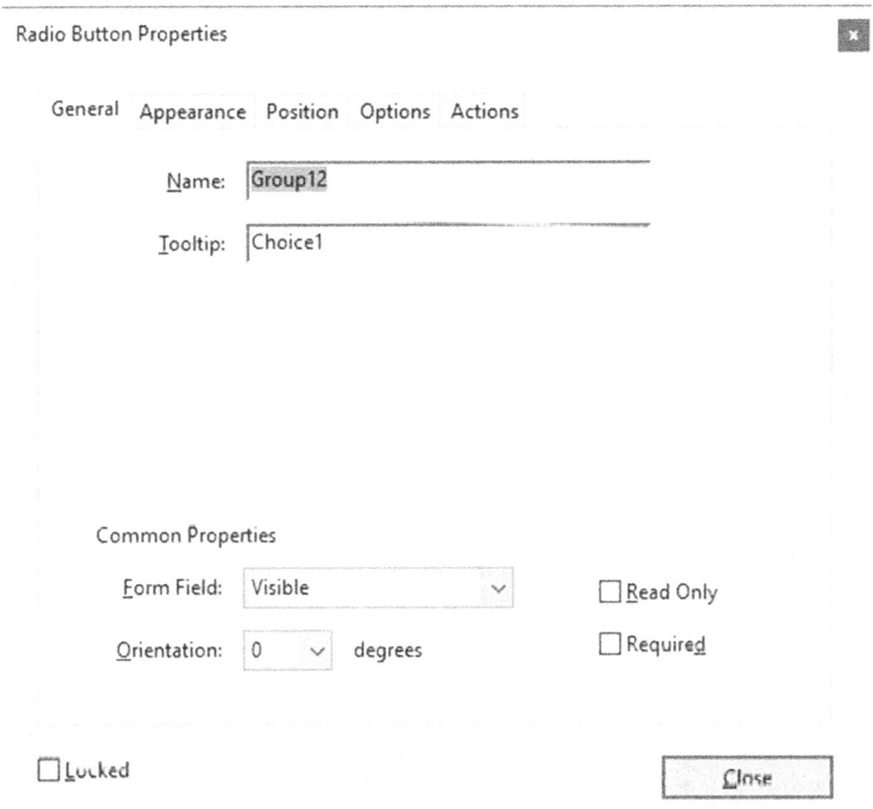

Figure 1-12. *Radio Button Properties dialog box*

Button Properties and Image Properties

Button properties and image properties are identical except that image properties have a small bit of code in the Actions tab to allow the importing of an image. See Chapter 17 for details. Both contain five tabs and the tabs each have identical properties. Unlike buttons, images can have more than two states and they operate independently. Refer to Figure 1-13.

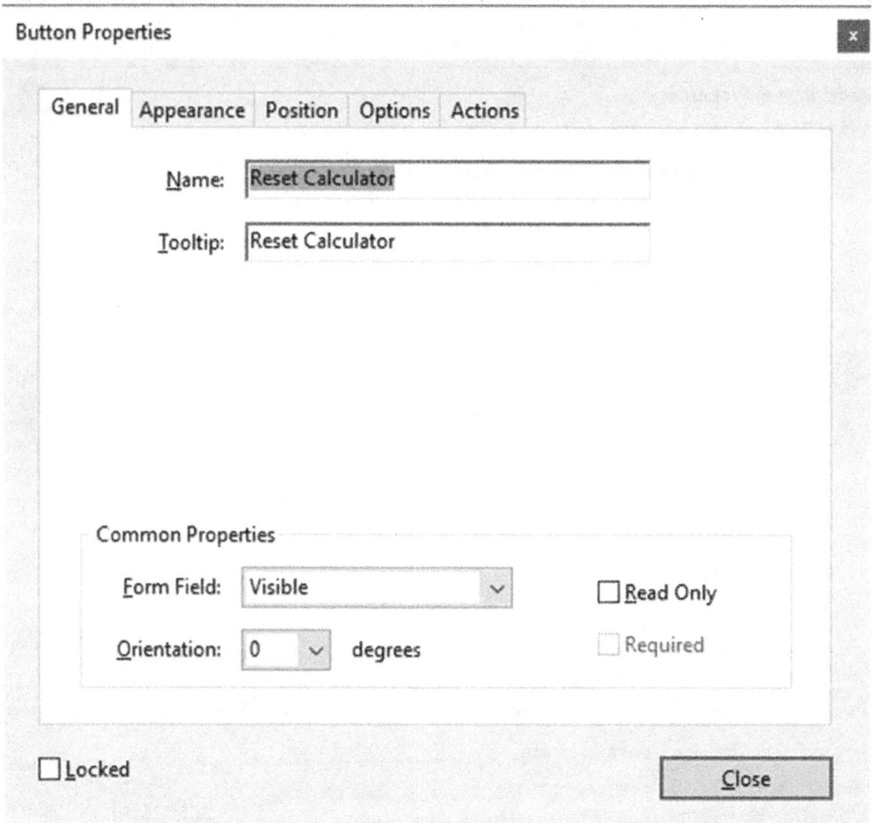

Figure 1-13. Button Properties dialog box

Digital Signature Properties

Digital signatures are used for signing electronic PDF forms with a client's digital signature, which is stored on their computer. The digital signature field appears like the text field; however, it only has five tabs to organize its properties and is specifically designated for signature only. Chapter 19 offers more details on digital signatures. Refer here to Figure 1-14.

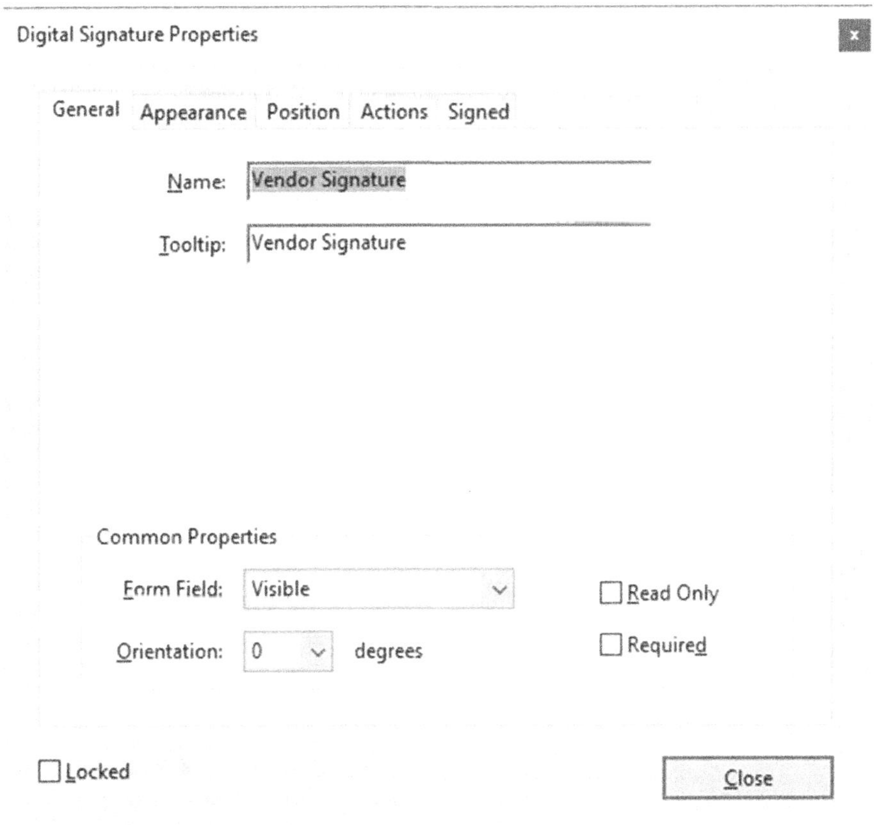

Figure 1-14. *Digital Signature Properties dialog box*

Barcode Properties

The barcode field properties are organized under five tabs. A barcode's main purpose is to create a scannable barcode that relates to the information that is entered into the various fields around it. Chapter 19 offers more details on barcodes. Refer here to Figure 1-15.

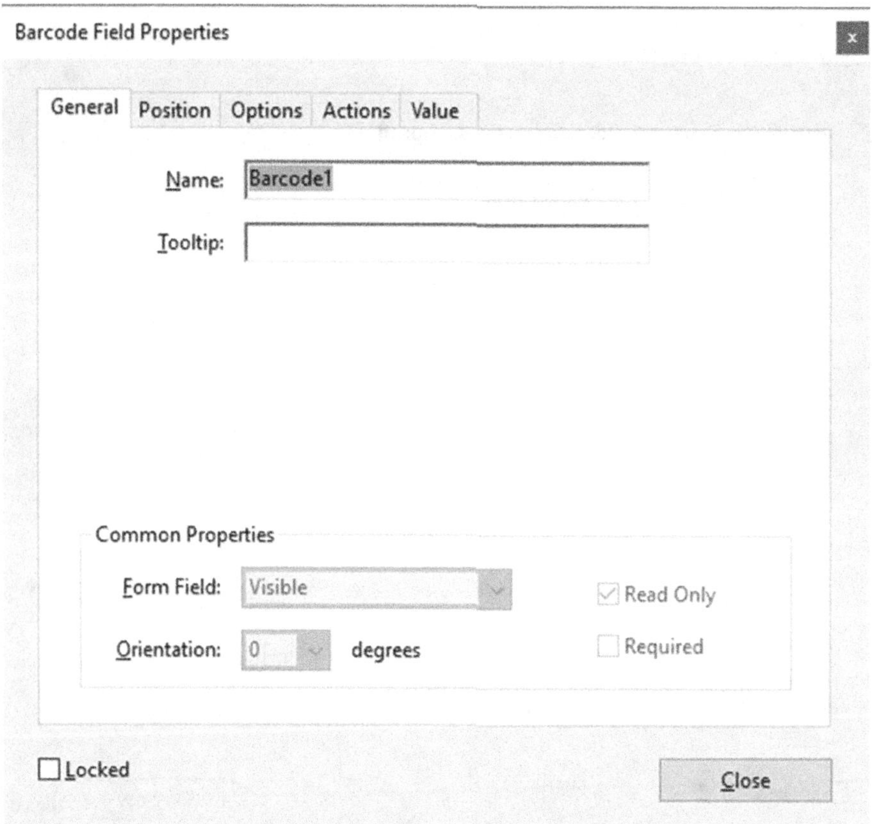

Figure 1-15. *Barcode Field Properties dialog box*

Tabs Refresher

As mentioned, all form fields have similar tabs, as listed here.

In the General tab,

- **Name**: The name of the field.
- **Tooltip**: This adds a type of accessibility text to the field so that people with visual impairments can scan over the field and know the purpose of the field.

- **Common properties**: Form field whether visible, hidden, or printable visible or hidden. Not available to barcodes.
- **Orientation**: Adjusts the angle of the field. Not available to barcodes.
- **Read only**: You can read the text within but not alter it. Not available to barcodes.
- **Required**: This field is required to complete the form. Not available to buttons, image fields, and barcodes.

In the Appearance tab (not available to barcodes),

- **Border and colors**:
  - **Border color**: Color of the border surrounding the field.
  - **Line thickness**: The thickness of the border: thin, medium, or thick.
  - **Fill color**: The fill color of the field.
  - **Line style**: The style of the line going around the field: solid, dashed, beveled, inset, underline.
- **Text**: Font size (not available to signatures), text color, and font (not available to check boxes or radio buttons).

In the Position tab,

- **Units**: Units of measurement of the size and position of the field(s): Points, picas, millimeters, centimeters, inches.
- **Position units**: Left, right, top, bottom, width, and height.
- Check "Do not change height and with when changing position." if you do not want the size of the box to alter during movement with the Selection tool. Unchecking it may cause the form field to scale.

In the Options tab (not available to digital signatures and only for text and date fields),

- **Alignment**: Aligns text left, center, or right.
- **Default value**: Temporary or default text for field.
- **Field for file selection**: Used to select a file's text link info. Not available for the date field.
- **Password**: Creates *** to mask the actual text. Not available for the date field.
- **Check spelling**: Indicates if there is a spelling error when checked.

- **Multi-line**: Allows you to enter more than one line of text in the field. Not available for the date field.
- **Scroll long text**: If there is more text than the field can handle, a scroll bar appears.
- **Allow rich text formatting**: Allows users to make the text bold or italic. Not available for the date field.
- **Limit of characters**: The amount characters allowed in a field.
- **Comb of characters**: Creates a divider between characters so they are easier to read later and compare (see Chapter 4).

For list boxes and dropdown menus only:

- **Item**: Enter the item name.
- **Export value**: Enter its export value letter or numbers.
- **List item**: Lists all the items.
- **Add, Delete, Up, Down buttons**: Add, remove, or alter an item's order in the list.
- **Sort items**: Sort alphabetically.
- **Allow user to enter custom text**: Allow the user to enter their own text. Not available for list boxes.
- **Check spelling**: Indicates if there is a spelling error when checked. Not available for list boxes.
- **Commit selected value immediately**: When selected, the value may interact with another field's value.
- **Multiple selection**: Lets you select multiple items in a list box only.

For check boxes and radio buttons only:

- **Style**: Check, circle, cross, diamond, square, Star.
- **Export value**: Value of field. For check box only.
- **Radio button choice**: Same as export value.
- **Check box is checked by default**: Appears checked when the form opens.
- **(Radio) button is checked by default**: Appears filled when the form opens.
- (Radio) buttons with the same name and choice are selected in unison.

For buttons and image fields:

- **Layout**: Adds a layout for the icon and label (see Chapter 4).
- **Advanced button**: Creates a more advanced layout for the Icon button (see Chapter 4).
- **Behavior alters the states of the button**: None push, outline, invert (see Chapter 4).
- **Icon and label state**:
    - **State**: How the button appears in up, down, and rollover states.
    - **Label**: The text name on the button.
- **Icon**: A thumbnail of the chosen icon.
    - **Choose icon**: Allows you to choose an icon.
    - **Clear**: Clears the icon from the field.

For barcodes only:

- **Symbiology**: Distinct types of barcodes available.
- **Compress data encoding barcode**
- **Decode condition**: Custom and manage barcode parameters, such as how the barcode will be decoded by some device.
- **Settings**: Setting of that barcode.

In the Action tab (for all form fields; more info in Chapters 4 and 5),

- **Add an action**: Select what triggers the action when the field is entered.
- **Select action**: What kind of action is triggered.
- **Add button**: Adds the action.
- **Up button**: Moves the action in its order.
- **Down button**: Moves the action in its order.
- **Edit button**: Edits the action in the JavaScript Editor.
- **Delete button**: Deletes the action.

In the Format tab (the Text, Date Field, and Dropdown menus; refer to Chapters 6 and 7 for a detailed explanation),

- **None**: For text and numbers with no true numeric value.
- **Number**: Formats the numbers with or without decimal places, currency symbol, location, and negative style.

- **Percentage**: Formats the percentage.
- **Date**: Formats the type of date.
- **Time**: Formats the type time.
- **Special**: ZIP code, phone number, social security number, and arbitrary mask.
- **Custom**: Create custom scripts called Format and Key Stroke.

In the Validate tab (Text, Date Field, and Dropdown menus),

- **Field value is not validated**: Does not require validation.
- **Field value is in range**: Numbers 1-5.
- **Run a custom validation script.**

In the Calculate tab (Text, Date Field, and Dropdown menus),

- Value is not calculated.
- **Value is the (sum, product, average, minimum, maximum) for the following fields**: Pick a button to choose the fields.
- **Simplified field notation**: Edit allows you to enter a script in the JavaScript Editor.
- **Custom calculation script**: Edit allows you to enter it in the JavaScript Editor.

In the Selection Change tab (list box only),

- Do nothing (if no action is required).
- **Execute this script**: Add a custom script. Edit allows you to enter it in the JavaScript Editor.

In the Signed tab (Digital Signature field only; refer to Chapter 19),

- Nothing happens when signed.
- **Mark as read-only**: All fields or only certain ones. Pick button to choose the fields.
- **This script executes when the field is signed**: Edit allows you to enter in the JavaScript Editor.

In the Value tab (Barcode field only; refer to Chapter 19 for more info),

- **Encoding using tab delimitated or XML**: Pick button to choose the fields.
- Include field names.
- **Custom calculation script**: Edit allows you to enter in the JavaScript Editor.

Found with all tabs and fields:

- **Locked**: When selected, prevents any further changes to any form field properties until unlocked.
- **Close**: This button closes the form field's Properties dialog box. If you are changing the properties of multiple fields, you can leave the Properties dialog box open. Click each field to change its properties. And then click the Close button.

The following are the tabs you'll find in most of the fields. Figure 1-16 shows the tabs found in the Text Field Properties dialog box.

Figure 1-16. *The tabs that contain the properties*

Bear in mind that the properties can differ depending upon the type of field chosen. For example, the Options tab properties are different for a text field versus a barcode or a radio button (Figure 1-17).

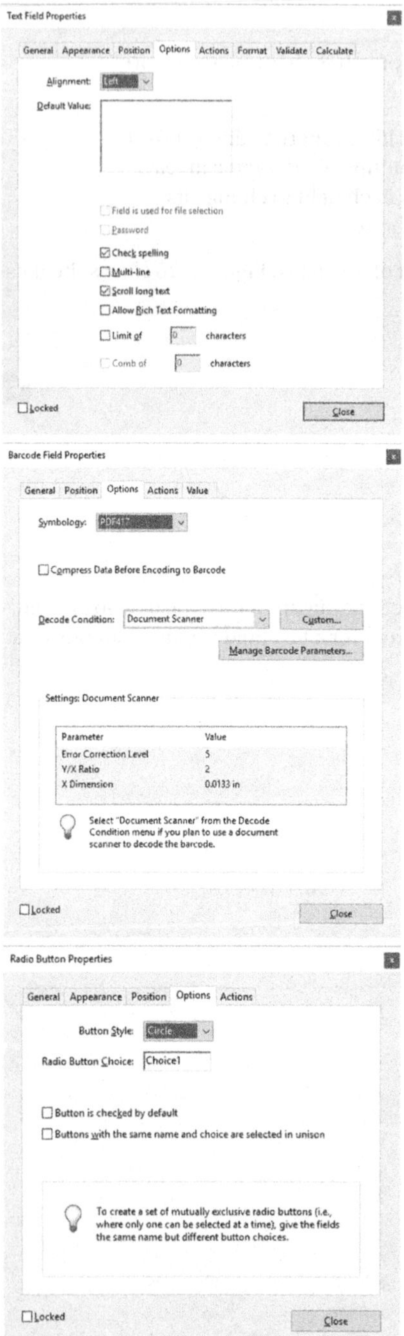

Figure 1-17. *Three fields (text field, bar code, and radio) that have different properties in their Options tab*

Summary

This chapter covered the basics of form fields, their tabs, and the properties within those tabs. The next chapter will be an introduction to the basic actions that you can apply to fields.

CHAPTER 2

Introduction to Actions

Now that you have reviewed the basic form properties, you will begin your study of JavaScript by taking a closer look at several types of automatic or preprogramed actions that can be applied within various tabs within each field. In this chapter, you'll be working with forms and you'll discover how actions can be applied.

Getting Started

If you want to work along in this lesson or review the final result, download the Chapter 2 files from `www.apress.com/9781484228920`. The file with the label "Start" is the file without the code and the file with the label "End" is the final result. You will also find folders with original MS Word and PDF files if you would like to edit them plus a folder containing the original scripts if you would like to add them to your own PDF forms.

Note To view the properties of a field, you must select the Prepare Form tool. Only then can you right-click or double-click on a field to review its properties. If you are creating your form from an original PDF that contains no form fields, refer to the "Forms Review" section in Chapter 1.

You can apply actions to all form fields. Actions, as you will see in more detail in Chapter 4 and later chapters, can trigger off various events such as alert boxes or cause a field to display a final calculation or a button to reset fields in a form. However, some actions work better with certain form fields than others.

For instance, applying an action to a radio button might give you some very select calculations but if you want to add up those values, using check boxes or text fields would probably be a better option.

If there are fields on the page, you can open and view their properties by clicking the Prepare Form tool and either right-clicking the field and choosing Properties from the menu or double-clicking the field itself. The text fields contain no information in the Actions tab and are blank. However, as you'll see shortly, other tabs within the field and other field types do contain information that will cause an event to occur. See Figure 2-1.

J. Harder, *Enhancing Adobe Acrobat DC Forms with JavaScript*,
DOI 10.1007/978-1-4842-2893-7_2

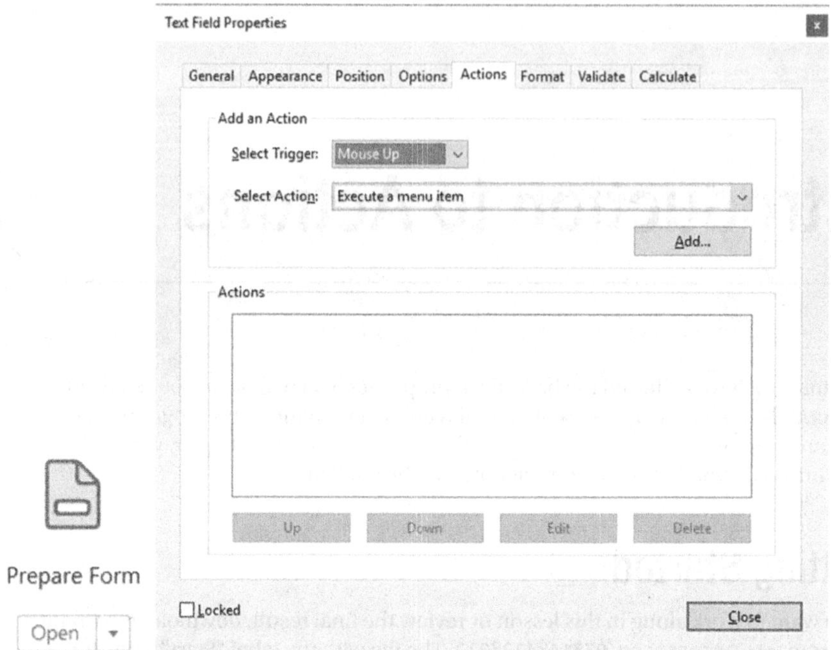

Figure 2-1. *The Action tab in the Text Field Properties dialog box*

Here you can see one of the many areas where you can add actions and a trigger, which I will discuss in more detail shortly.

Rating Forms Value Averaging and Sum: Working with Text Fields

Let's look at several ways to use a combination of text boxes, radio buttons, and check boxes to do averaging and summing.

Let's say you want to create a survey to see if your clients have any concerns about your customer service or interactions. You can create a rating form that helps you determine where you need to improve. On page 1 of the Customer Survey PDF example shown in Figure 2-2, in the final "End" form the fields in this survey are formatted with a setting of Number rather than None so that the client cannot enter in letters, only numbers.

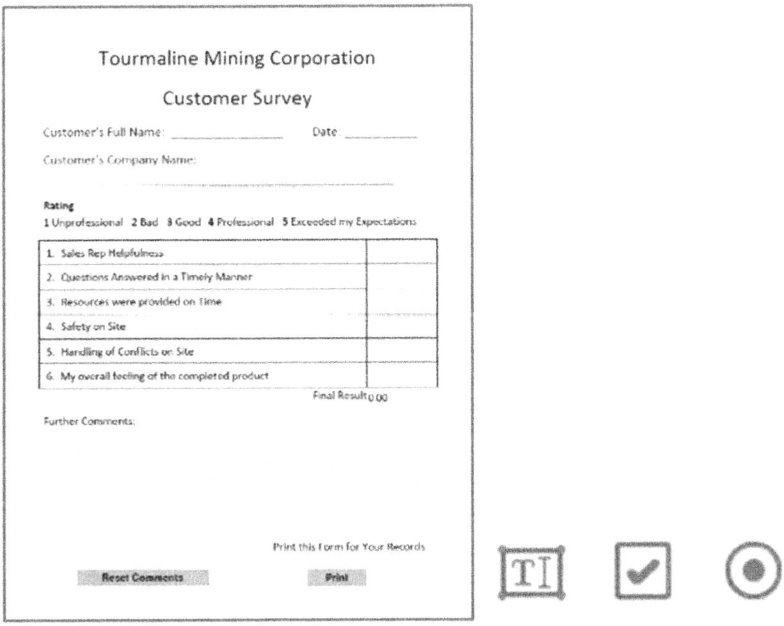

Figure 2-2. *Example of a customer survey form and the Form Tools used*

To insure a client puts the correct information into a field, it is important to limit their options. You can change the formatting by selecting from the "Select format category" dropdown menu.

Figure 2-3 provides an example of the formatting used in the Format tab of the Text Fields Properties dialog box.

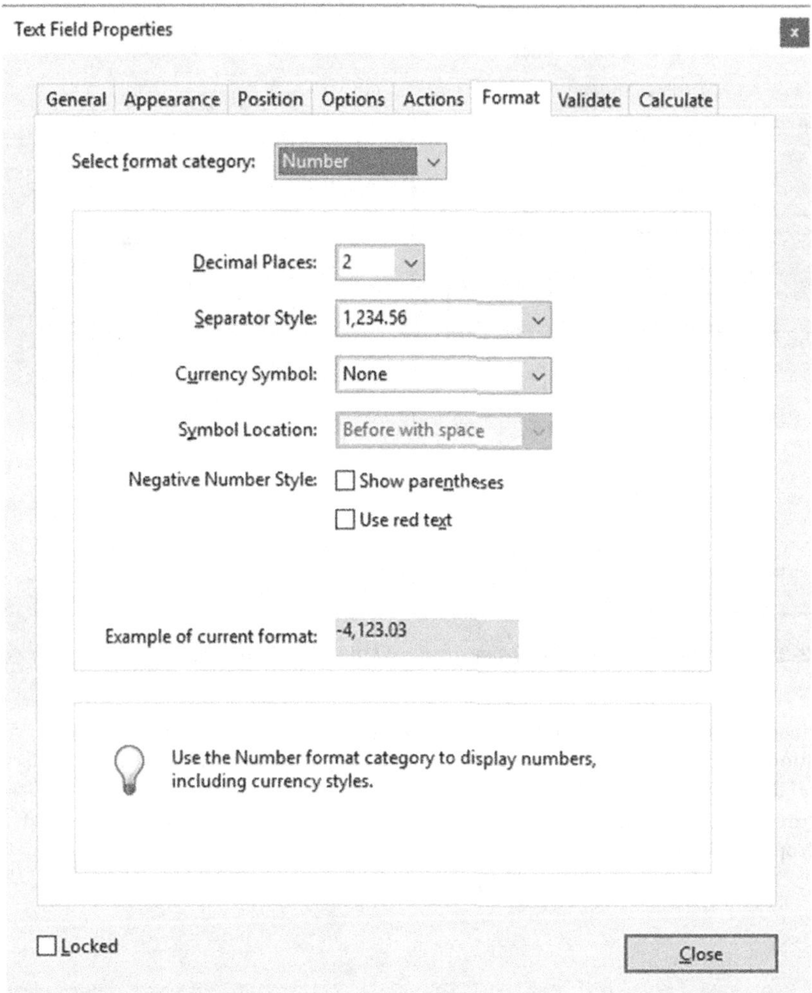

Figure 2-3. *The formatting for each of the text fields on page 1 of the Customer Survey file*

The Validate Tab

You can limit the client's options even further by setting a range of numbers in the same field under the Validate tab. Now the client can only enter numbers that range from 1 to 5. If they enter a 6 or higher, a warning will occur. Figure 2-4 shows the warning.

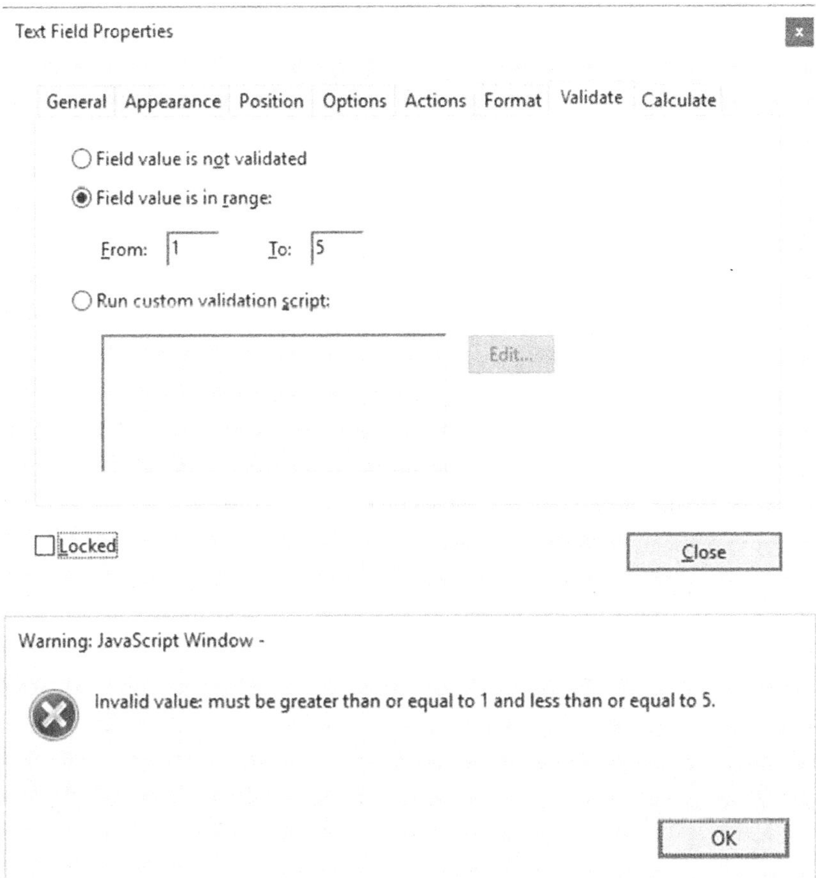

Figure 2-4. *The Validate tab of each of the text fields on page 1 with the values set from 1-5 to limit the range input*

If you inspect the Calculate tab for the Grand Total or Final Result field on page 1 of the project (and as in Figures 2-5 and 2-6), you can see how the field will receive data from other fields using the "Value is ________ of the following fields" and picking "Average" plus the various text fields that this field will gather information from.

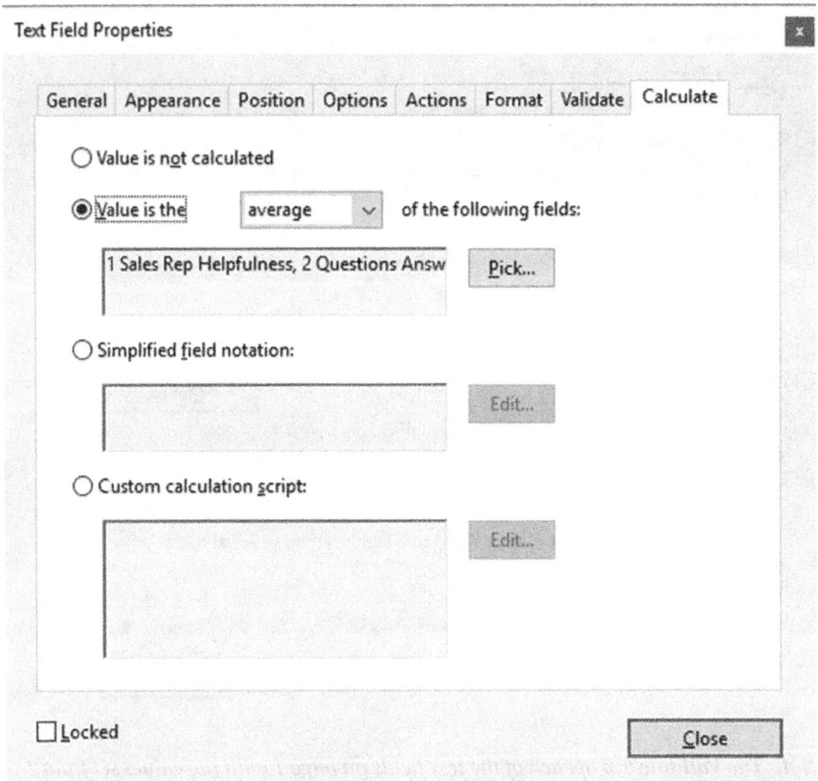

Figure 2-5. *The Calculate tab for the final result*

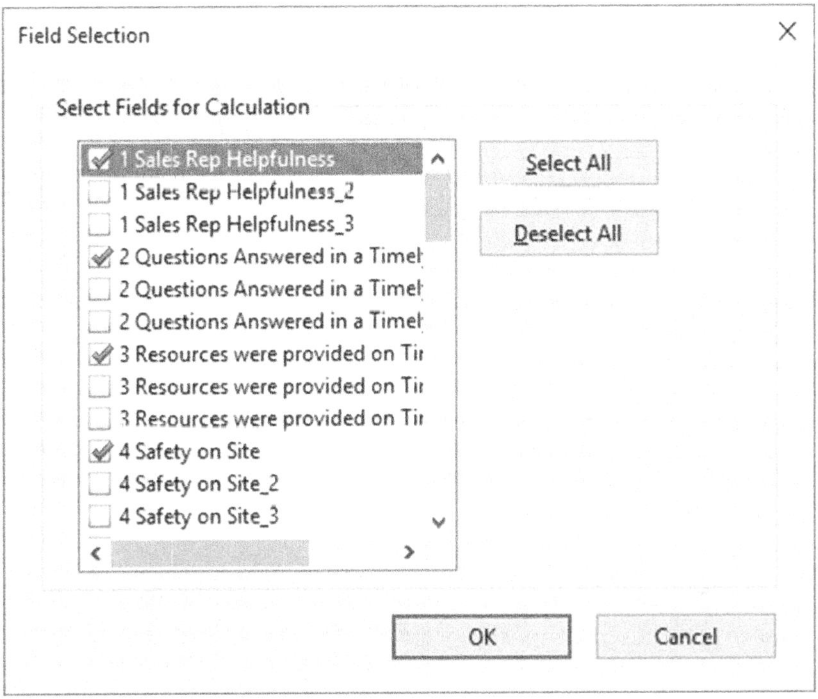

Figure 2-6. *The Field Selection dialog box*

To access other fields and their data for this final field, click the Pick button to access field selection. Select only the fields you want to calculate. When done, click OK. You can also select or deselect all fields. This will allow you to make your selections faster, rather than checking off or on all the fields one at a time.

■ **Tip** If you have trouble selecting the check box, you can highlight it and press the space bar on your keyboard. This toggles the check box on or off.

The Final Result text field is set to read-only in the General tab so that a client cannot alter the final result.

Page 2 of Project: The Calculate Tab for the Grand Total Using Sum

The only difference between this form and the one on page 1 is that the Final Result value in the Calculate tab was changed to sum (+). Refer to Figure 2-7.

■ **Note** I selected only fields on page 2. If I need fields from other pages to complete the calculation, such as page 1 or 3, I would pick these fields as well. Form calculations can be on as many pages within the PDF document as required.

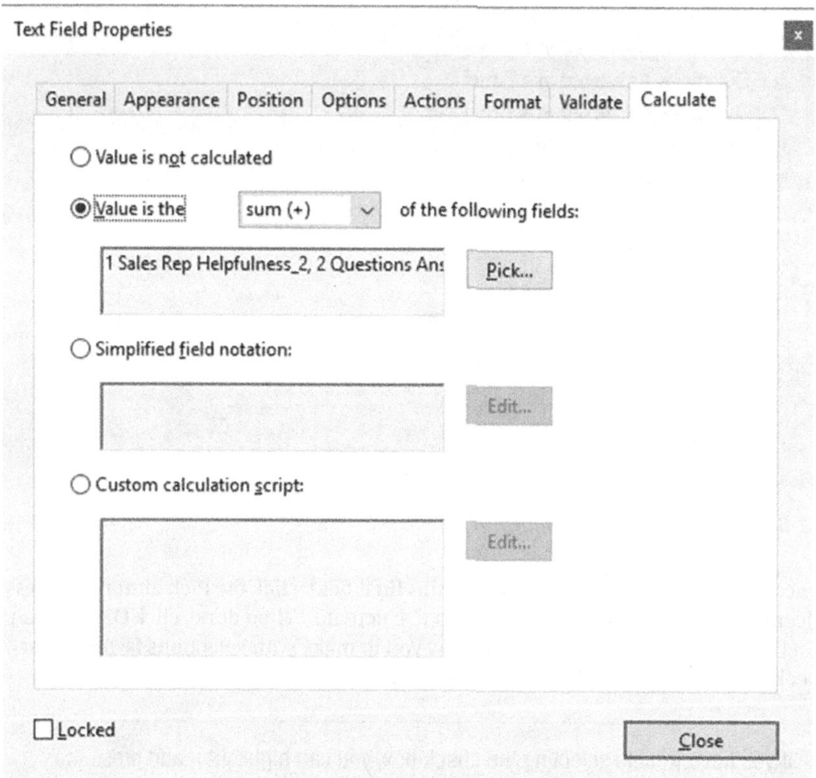

Figure 2-7. *The Calculate tab for the final result on page 2*

■ **Alternate Dropdown Rating** If you skip past page 3 down to page 4 of this example, you can see how, with this same form, you can replace some of the text fields with dropdown menus to rate. While similar to text fields, I find this method a suitable alternative if you want your client to use very specific values. Also, it eliminates the need for validation on each dropdown because the values are already set. To set an export value for a dropdown menu, you need to set the value for each menu item in the Options tab. Refer to Figures 2-8 and 2-9.

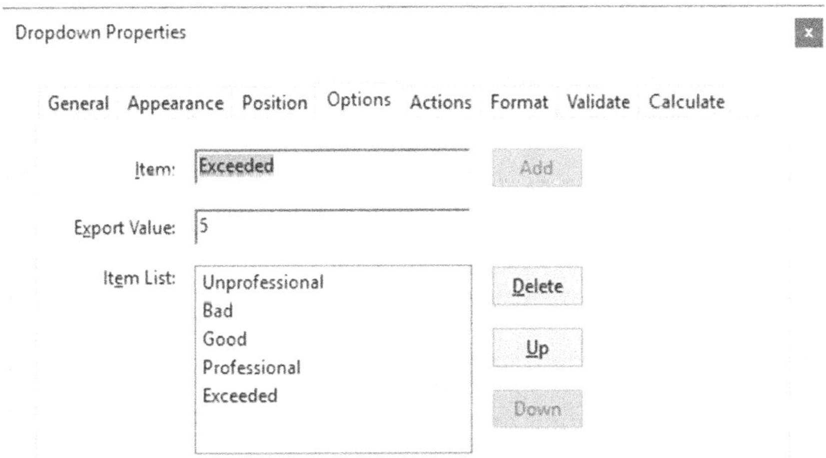

Figure 2-8. The Dropdown Properties dialog box for the selections on page 4 of the customer survey

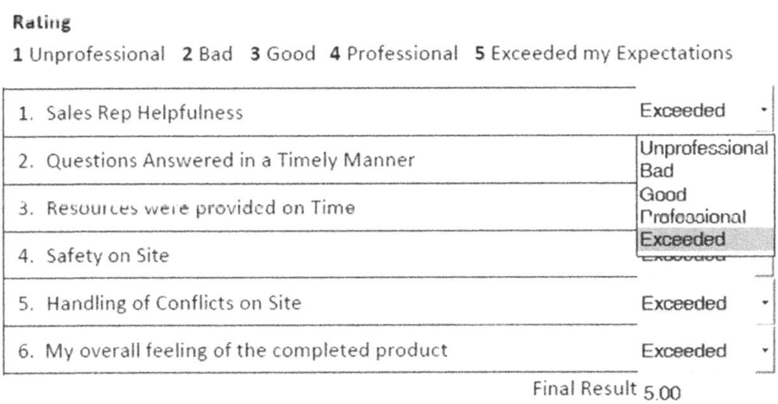

Figure 2-9. One of the dropdown fields extended

On Page 4 you can see how by choosing a word that has a numeric value applied to it, the Final Result field takes that information and adds it to what is already calculated.

Sum and Averaging Using Check Boxes or Radio Buttons with Text Fields

While text fields and dropdowns are useful for surveys on pages 1, 2, and 4, sometimes radio buttons and check boxes will do a more efficient job. Look at Page 3 of the PDF file as shown in Figure 2-10.

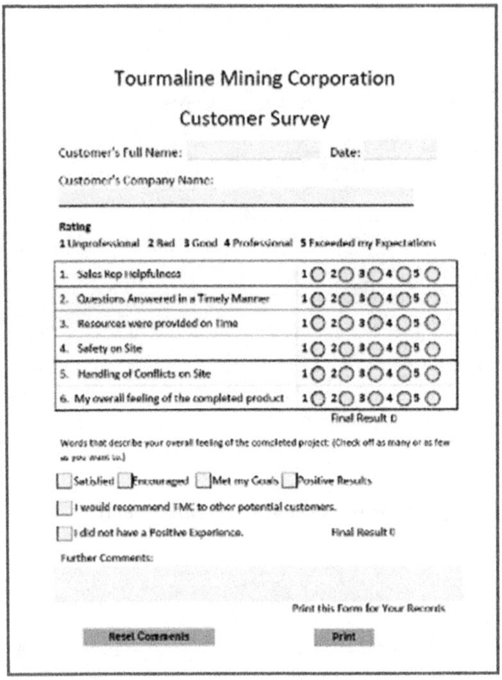

Tourmaline Mining Corporation

Customer Survey

Customer's Full Name: Date:

Customer's Company Name:

Rating

1 Unprofessional 2 Bad 3 Good 4 Professional 5 Exceeded my Expectations

1. Sales Rep Helpfulness	1 ○ 2 ○ 3 ○ 4 ○ 5 ○
2. Questions Answered in a Timely Manner	1 ○ 2 ○ 3 ○ 4 ○ 5 ○
3. Resources were provided on Time	1 ○ 2 ○ 3 ○ 4 ○ 5 ○
4. Safety on Site	1 ○ 2 ○ 3 ○ 4 ○ 5 ○
5. Handling of Conflicts on Site	1 ○ 2 ○ 3 ○ 4 ○ 5 ○
6. My overall feeling of the completed product	1 ○ 2 ○ 3 ○ 4 ○ 5 ○

Final Result 0

Words that describe your overall feeling of the completed project: (Check off as many or as few as you want to.)

☐ Satisfied ☐ Encouraged ☐ Met my Goals ☐ Positive Results

☐ I would recommend TMC to other potential customers.

☐ I did not have a Positive Experience. Final Result 0

Further Comments:

Print this Form for Your Records

Reset Comments Print

Figure 2-10. *Page 3 of the customer survey*

Using Radio Buttons on Page 3 of the Project

In the Options tab, the choices can be set to any number value (1, 2, 3, or even negative numbers if required). Figures 2-11 and 2-12 display how this is entered in the dialog boxes.

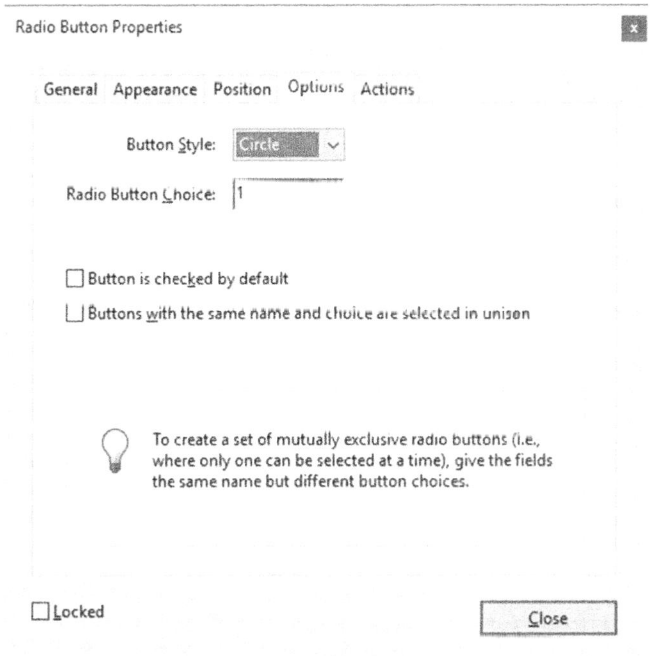

Figure 2-11. *Radio button properties in the Option tab on page 3 of the customer survey*

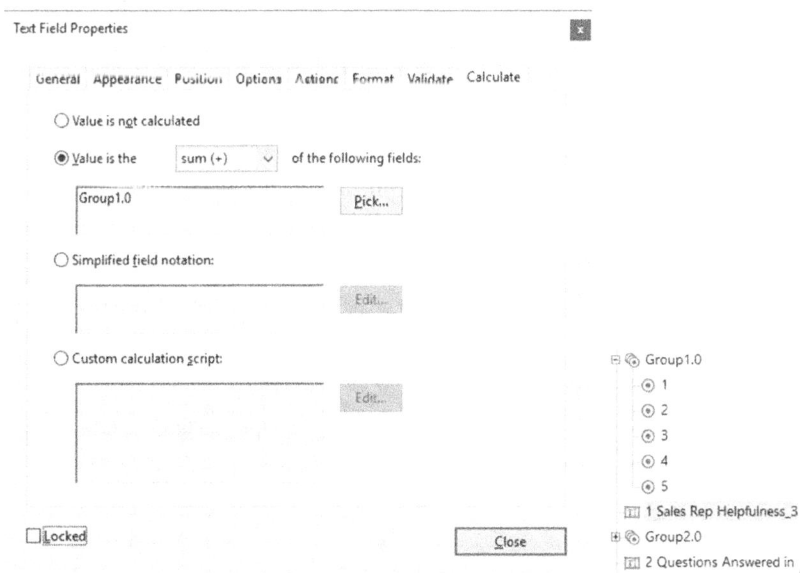

Figure 2-12. *Text field properties in the Calculate tab with the radio group selected on page 3 of the customer survey and how the group of buttons appears in the Prepare Form Preview fields on the right-side bar list*

A text field is then used to calculate the sum of the radio group, as in Figure 2-13. To operate correctly, radio buttons must always be in groups of two or more.

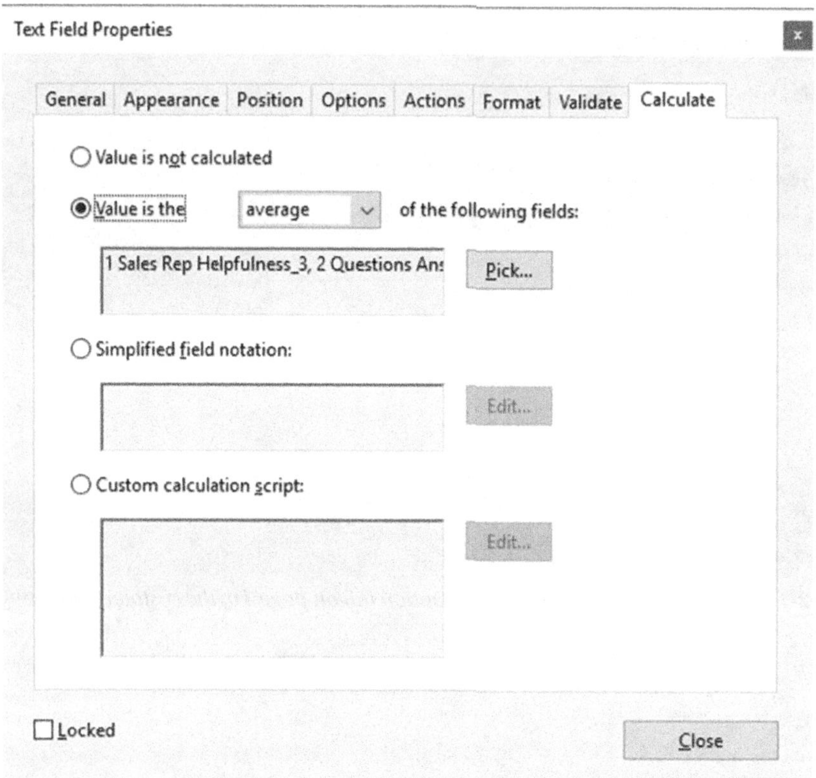

Figure 2-13. *Text field properties in the Calculate tab on page 3 of the customer survey*

The Final Result text box is used to calculate the average rating of the other text boxes linked to the radio button groups.

Using Check Boxes on Page 3 of the Project

Figure 2-14 shows how similar values can be entered into the Options tab of a Check Box Properties dialog box.

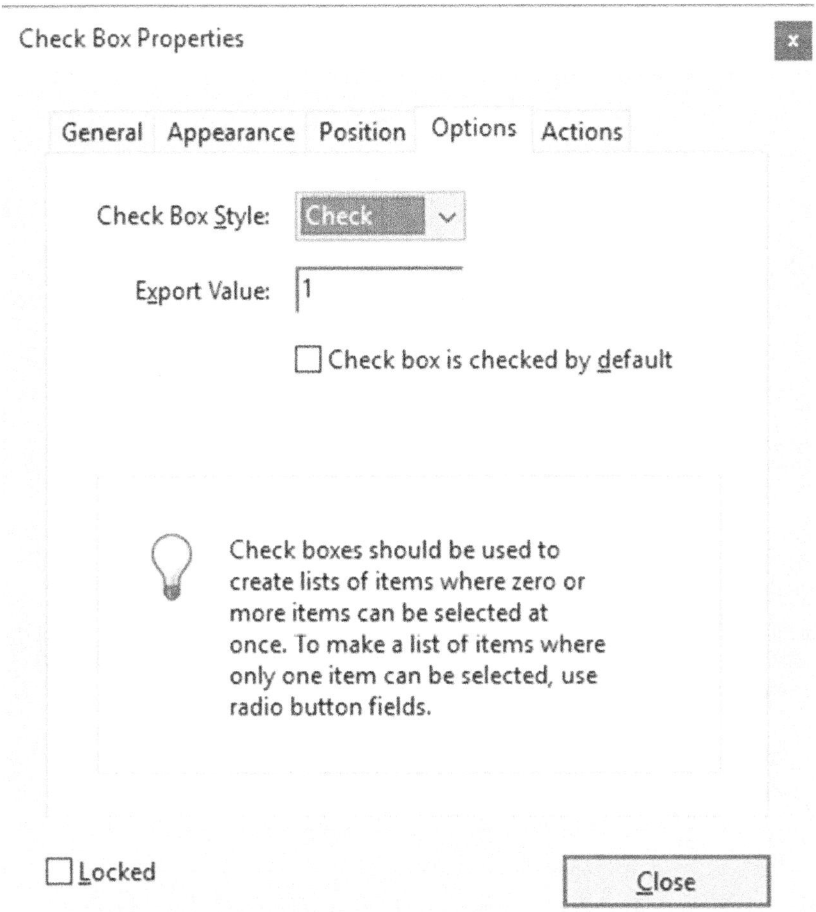

Figure 2-14. *The Options tab of the Check Box Properties dialog box on page 3 of the customer survey*

Check boxes can be used in a comparable way in the Options tab and given an export value of 1, 2, 3... or even negative numbers for a negative rating.

The Final Result text field can sum up the check boxes values. See Figure 2-15.

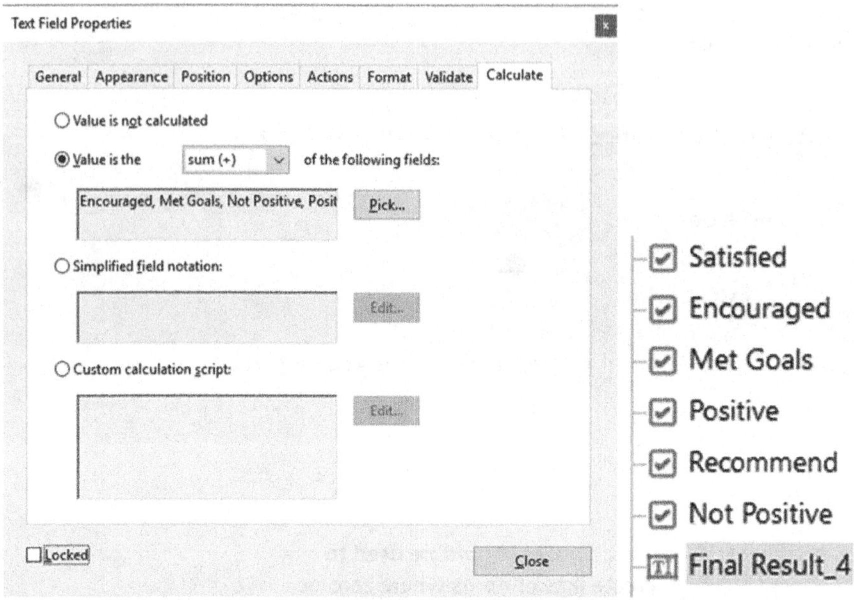

Figure 2-15. *An example of the Calculate tab with the check boxes selected on page 3 of the PDF and how the check boxes appear not grouped in the Prepare Form Preview Fields on the right-side bar list*

■ **Note** The check boxes can operate independently and don't need to be grouped.

Basic Action Button Triggers for Reset Buttons and Printing Buttons

There are many basic actions that can be added to buttons, as you'll see in Chapter 4 and later. However, for this lesson let's focus on two that are used quite frequently in forms: the Reset and Print actions.

Reset Button

If a client makes a mistake in several fields or wants to clear the entire form rather than highlight and press the Delete or Backspace key for each field, it is helpful to add a Delete button to your form. Figure 2-16 displays what this action looks like in the Action tab.

***Figure 2-16.** Button properties in the Actions tab*

All fields or only the comments can be reset by a button; it's your choice.

1. Make sure the select trigger is set to Mouse Up.
2. Select the action of "Reset a Form" from the Select Action menu.
3. Click the Add button to add the action.
4. Then click the Edit button at the bottom of the Properties box to select which fields you would like to reset, as in Figure 2-17. When done, click OK.

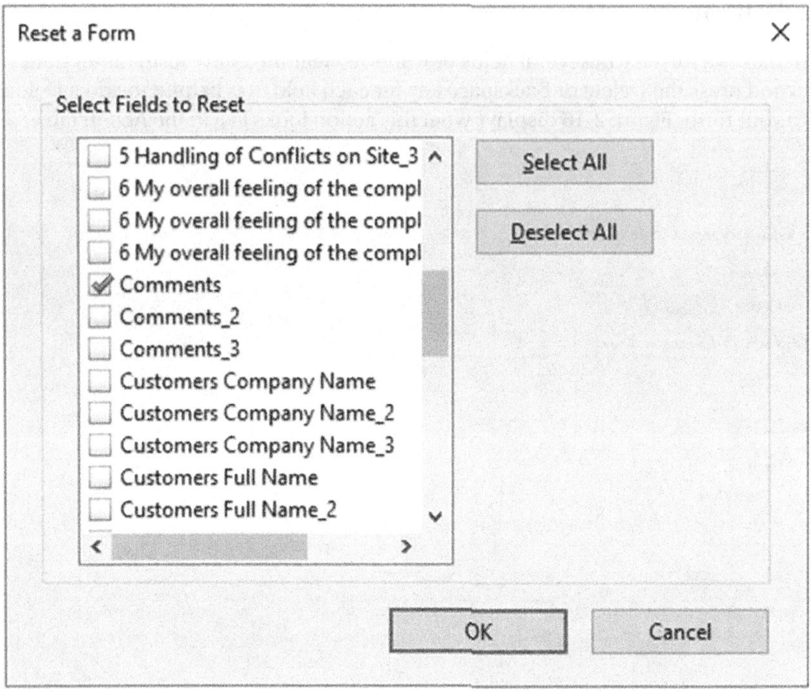

Figure 2-17. *The Reset a Form options in the Actions tab*

Print Form Button

Add the File ➤ Print action if you want to create a Print button for the whole document. Refer to Figure 2-18 and to page 1 of the project's PDF file to review this action.

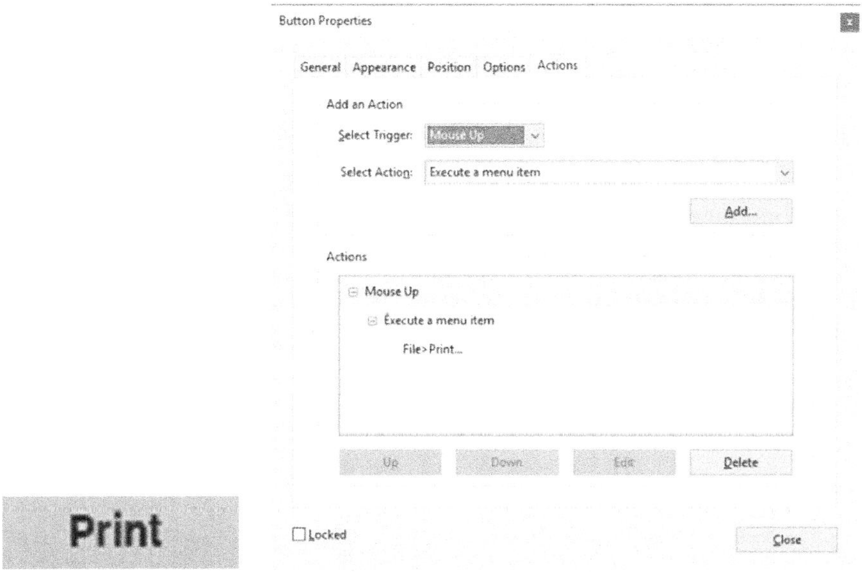

Figure 2-18. The File ➤ Print options in the Actions tab

However, if you need only a specific page to print, you need to add a JavaScript instead. To see a preview of this, refer to pages 2 and 4 of the PDF file and to Figure 2-19. I'll discuss this more in later chapters.

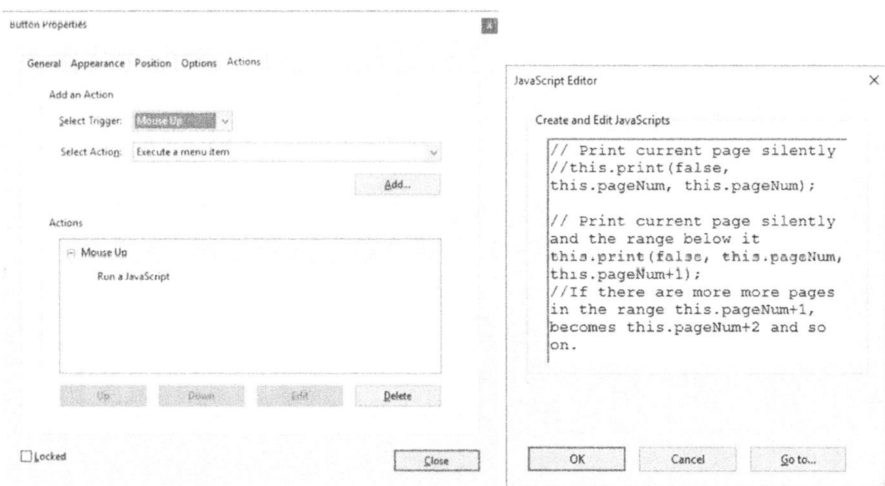

Figure 2-19. Adding JavaScript in the Actions tab

When you are done viewing the form, click the X in the upper right-hand corner of the preview to close the Prepare Form tool.

Summary

As you saw in this chapter, you can use the Prepare Form tool and its respective properties in a variety of ways to create various customer rating surveys to suit your needs. By looking through the tabs, you can also see that many of the form fields have similar properties, while others have properties that only relate to that specific field. As you progress though the lessons you will discover how knowing which types of fields to use will be important as the forms become more complex.

CHAPTER 3

Creating a QR Code Custom Stamp

You've all probably opened and viewed a PDF file. And the program that made that possible was most likely Adobe Acrobat Reader or Acrobat Pro DC. For many computer users, Reader has become the industry standard simply because it is a freeware program that anyone can download for Mac or PC platforms.

When you are reviewing the file with your client, Acrobat DC allows you to view and add comments to a PDF document.

Acrobat also allows you to create barcodes and QR codes with the Prepare Form tool. However, the information generated in the barcode and QR code only applies to the surrounding form fields and not to specific text elsewhere in the document (see Figure 3-1). Currently, with the Comment tool you cannot generate a custom QR code, so this chapter shows you a way to get around this situation.

Note If you want to work along in this lesson or review the final result, download the Chapter 3 files from `www.apress.com/9781484228920`. You will find the original Adobe InDesign, QR image, and PDF files if you would like to edit them.

To view the properties of a field, you must select the Prepare Form tool. Only then can you right-click or double-click on a field to review its properties.

J. Harder, *Enhancing Adobe Acrobat DC Forms with JavaScript*,
DOI 10.1007/978-1-4842-2893-7_3

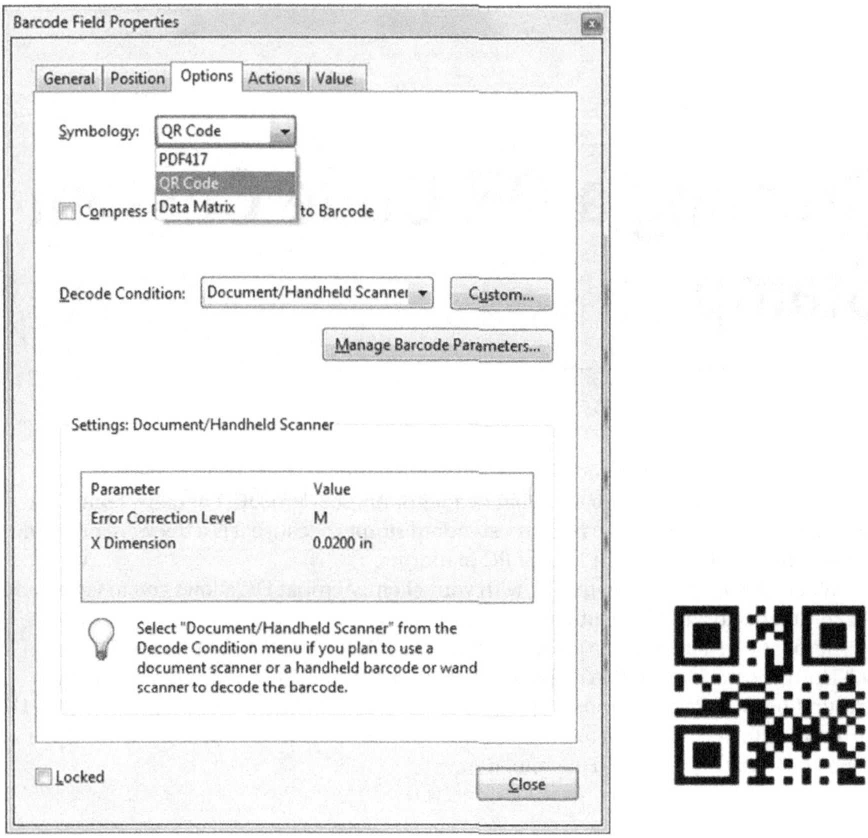

Figure 3-1. *The Barcode Field Properties dialog box with an example of a created QR code*

Customizing Your QR Code Stamp

It's become popular to place a QR code on business cards, resumes, and newsletters; these codes can be read by smartphones. However, Acrobat only allows you to create a QR code that applies to forms. For your resume or letterhead, you might want a QR code to only contain the URL of your company website or just some text. The solution is to build your own custom QR code stamp that you can place in your online PDFs for clients to view. The following exercise will show you how.

■ **Note** If you plan to use the QR code for professional print material, always place it into the original document (MS Word or Adobe InDesign CC 2014 or later) rather than using the Acrobat Stamp tool. While the stamp image will print out fine on your home computer, it may not print out when sent to some professional printers depending on if the layout requires altering. See details on how to do this in the "Final Thoughts" section at the end of the chapter.

QR Code Creation

Either create a QR code using InDesign CC 2014 or later, software that allows you to generate a QR code, or ask a graphic designer in your company to create one for you. Copy the image into a program like Adobe Photoshop and save the file as a greyscale JPEG 200px by 200px with a 72ppi being an appropriate size. Test it with your smartphone app to make sure it works correctly. See Figure 3-2.

Figure 3-2. *A generated QR code*

Open the PDF file in which you plan to add the QR code in Acrobat Reader or Pro DC via File ➤ Open. Refer to Figure 3-3.

Figure 3-3. *The File menu*

Select the PDF file you want to open.
Select the Stamp button in the Tools menu. Refer to Figure 3-4.

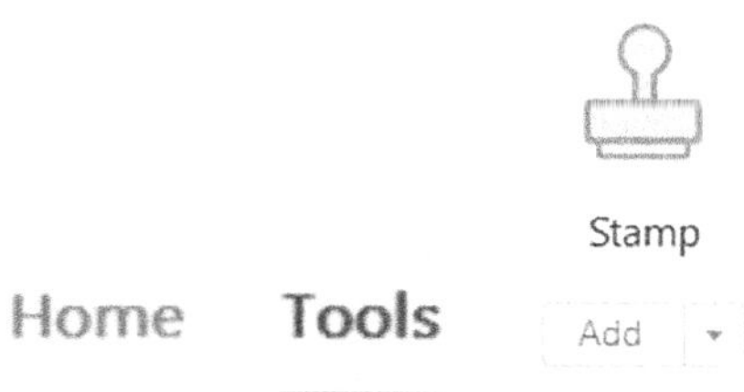

Figure 3-4. *The Stamp tool*

Select the Custom Stamps option. Choose Create. Refer to Figure 3-5.

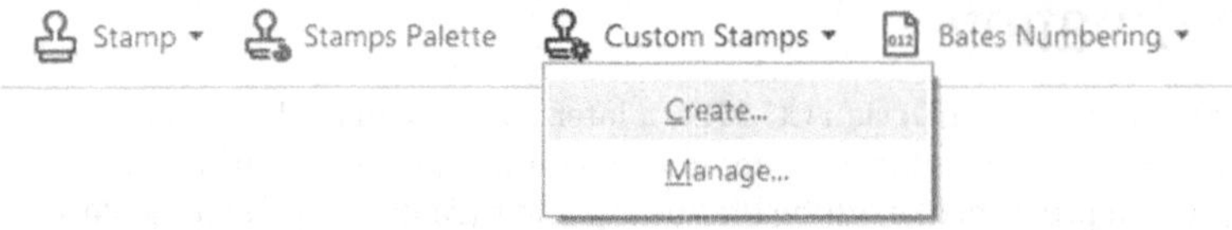

Figure 3-5. The Stamp Tool menu

Create the custom stamp. When you choose this option, you will be presented with the Select Image for Custom Stamp dialog box. Click the Browse button to locate your file. Refer to Figure 3-6.

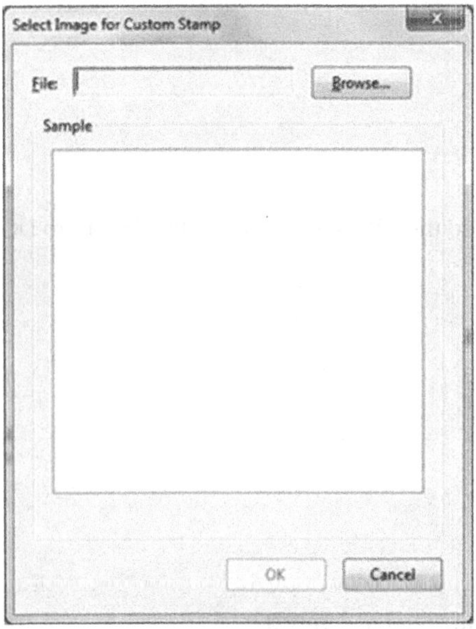

Figure 3-6. The Select Image for Custom Stamp dialog box

In Acrobat Pro DC, you can browse and use several different file formats including JPEG, TIFF, GIF, and PNG. Refer to Figure 3-7.

Figure 3-7. Browse for the QR code

In this case, choose a JPEG graphic of the QR code that you or your graphic designer have already created.

Click the Open button and you will be returned to the previous dialog box. Refer here to Figure 3-8.

Figure 3-8. *The Select Image for Custom Stamp dialog box with a QR code visible*

If you like how the image looks, click OK. Otherwise, browse for another image. You may need to make minor adjustments in a program like Photoshop for spacing needs to reduce or increase the size. If you do, make sure to keep the shape square and don't distort the QR code. Click OK to proceed to the next dialog box.

Before you can use the custom stamp, Acrobat wants you to choose a folder category for your stamp and give it a name. You can either create a new folder by typing a name in or choose from current folders that are available in the Category dropdown menu. Refer here to Figure 3-9.

Figure 3-9. *The Create Custom Stamp dialog box*

You have the option to down-sample the stamp to reduce the file size. In the case of the QR, I might uncheck this to preserve quality. In this case, the file is only 45KB, which is not large. When you are done, click OK.

Using the Stamp Tool

The stamp is created. You can go to your file folder in the Stamp dropdown menu and choose your new custom stamp. Refer to Figure 3-10.

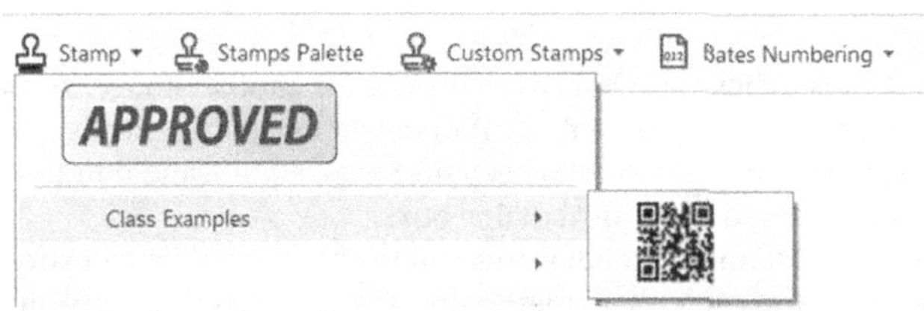

Figure 3-10. *Created QR code stamp in the Stamp menu*

At this point, a dialog box may appear that will request an initial identity setup. This is so the client will know who made this approval stamp for security reason. You do not have to fill in all the boxes. When you're done, click the Complete button. You should only do this identity setup once for your new stamp. If you do not see this box, it may mean that you or someone else already set this area up. Refer to Figure 3-11. You can check this under Edit ➤ Preferences ➤ Categories: Identity and adjust your information there.

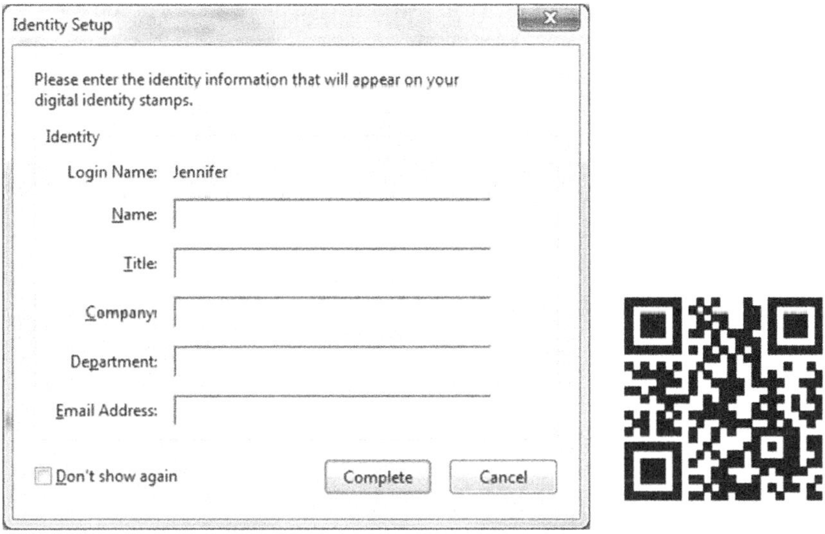

Figure 3-11. *Identity setup for new stamps*

The mouse cursor will now turn into the stamp. You can move it around on the page until you find where you want to place the stamp. Click the mouse button and the stamp will be set. If you don't like where it is set, you can move it around. The mouse turns into four arrows. If you hold down the mouse icon on the stamp, you can move the stamp around, twist, or scale it.

If for some reason you need to delete the stamp later, you can go to the Custom Stamps ➤ Manage box and remove it from your custom list. Refer here to Figure 3-12.

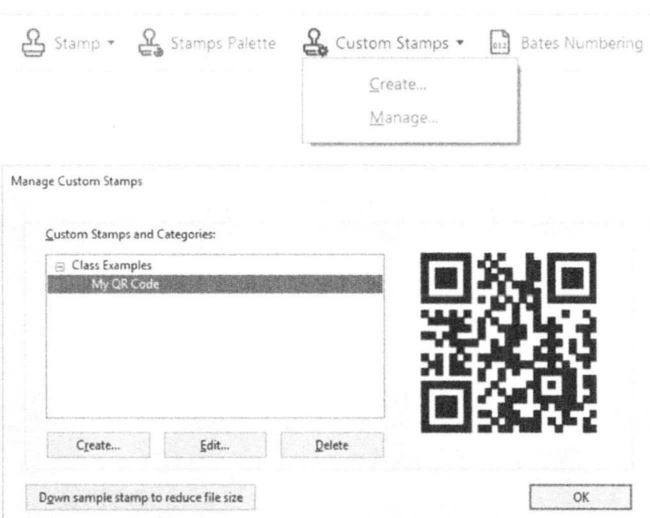

Figure 3-12. *The Stamp Tool menu and the Manage Custom Stamps dialog box*

Custom QR stamps as in Figure 3-13 can also have comments attached. You can attach a comment in the Comment tool section.

Figure 3-13. *The Comment tool*

Now your comments list has a stamp comment. In here you can add further information about the stamp by double-clicking it to add to a comment. If you need to delete the QR code stamp, just select it and press the Delete button on the keyboard or right-click and select Delete.

You can add this QR code stamp to as many places in the document as required. When you're done, save the file and email to a client or post it on your website.

If you need to print the document, choose the "Document and Stamps" option in the Print dialog box. Refer here to Figure 3-14. If you just choose the Document option only, the QR code stamp will not print.

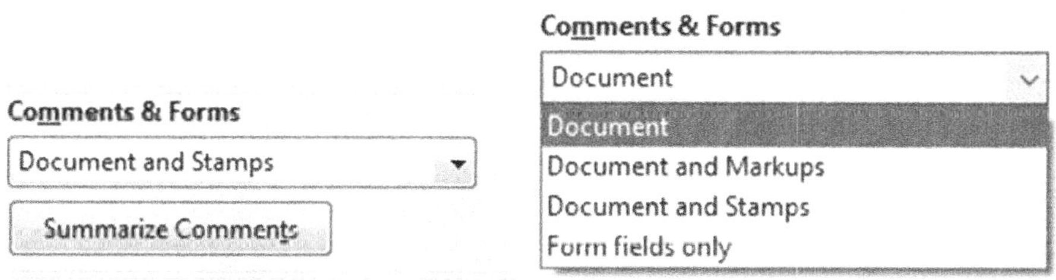

Figure 3-14. *Print settings for stamps. Choosing "Document and Stamps" will insure that the QR code stamp prints.*

Final Thoughts: QR Code for Professional Printing

If you plan to send your resume or a newsletter to a company and you want to ensure that the QR code will print out regardless of the print document settings, I recommend typing your resume/newsletter in a program like MS Word, and then choosing the location where you want to place your QR code. Then in the above menu, choose Insert ➤ Picture. Refer here to Figure 3-15.

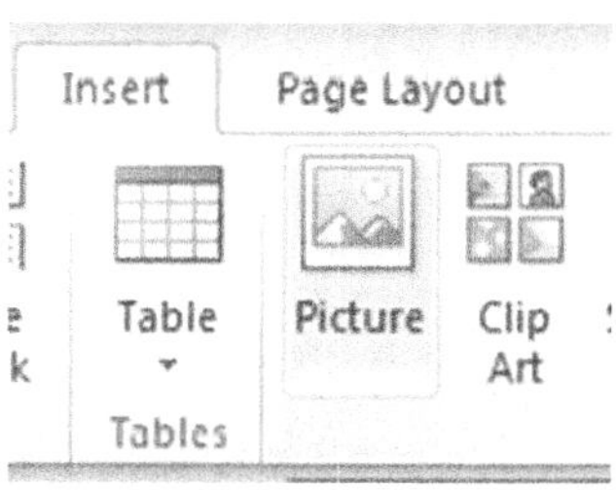

Figure 3-15. *Insert an image in MS Word*

Locate your JPEG image and then click the Insert button. The image will be inserted. Finally, click Save as or print your file as a PDF. This will ensure that the QR code is embedded in the document and will print with the rest of your resume.

Summary

In this chapter, you learned how you can turn a QR code into a custom stamp that you can use in a form or any PDF document. The stamp can also be modified and scaled.

Creating the QR code in this manner, rather than just as a form field, allows for a wider range of possibilities.

For more information about how to create a QR code in Adobe InDesign CC 2014 or later visit, `https://helpx.adobe.com/indesign/using/generate-qr-code.html`.

Summary

CHAPTER 4

Buttons, Navigation, Form and Non-Form Actions

In Chapter 2, you saw a few simple examples of actions you could create with buttons. Now you will focus on a few more. This chapter will cover

- A review of the Action tab's properties in various fields and non-form items
- Looking at built-in triggers and actions that require no coding
- Applying what you discover to buttons for page navigation
- How to use button icons rather than just text
- How a button can become a help icon to show or hide information in an order form
- How a check box can show or hide information in combination with a reset button

---

Note If you want to work along in this lesson or review the final result, download the Chapter 4 files from `www.apress.com/9781484228920`. The file with the label "Start" is the file without the code and the file with the label "End" is the final result. You will also find folders with original MS Word and PDF files if you would like to edit them and a folder containing the original images if you would like to add them to your own PDF forms.

To view the properties of a field you must select the Prepare Form tool. Only then can you right-click or double-click a field to review its properties.

If you are creating your form from an original PDF that contains no form fields, refer to the "Forms Review" section in Chapter 1.

J. Harder, *Enhancing Adobe Acrobat DC Forms with JavaScript*,
DOI 10.1007/978-1-4842-2893-7_4

Creating a Button Icon

Not all buttons have to be just text; you can also have text and an image or just an image that you created in a program like Adobe Photoshop or GIMP. As in the QR code stamp example in Chapter 3, the file can be many formats including a JPEG, GIF, or PNG.

The icon for the button is placed in the Options tab when you click the Choose Icon button (Figure 4-1).

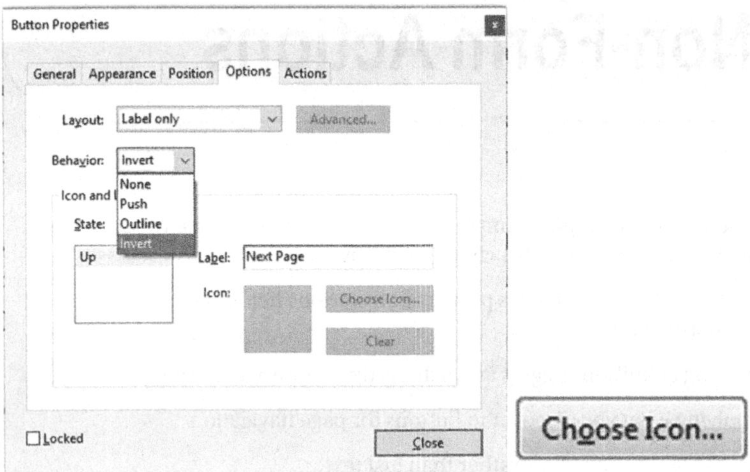

Figure 4-1. The Option tab with the Choose Icon button

Choose the layout setting of the icon only or have the icon on top or in another location if you want to use the icon in combination with text (known as a label).

The layout options are

- Label only (this setting will not allow you to add an icon)
- Icon only
- Icon top, label bottom
- Label top, icon bottom
- Icon left, label right
- Label left, icon right
- Label over icon

The Advanced button will allow you to adjust the placement of the icon precisely (refer to Figure 4-2).

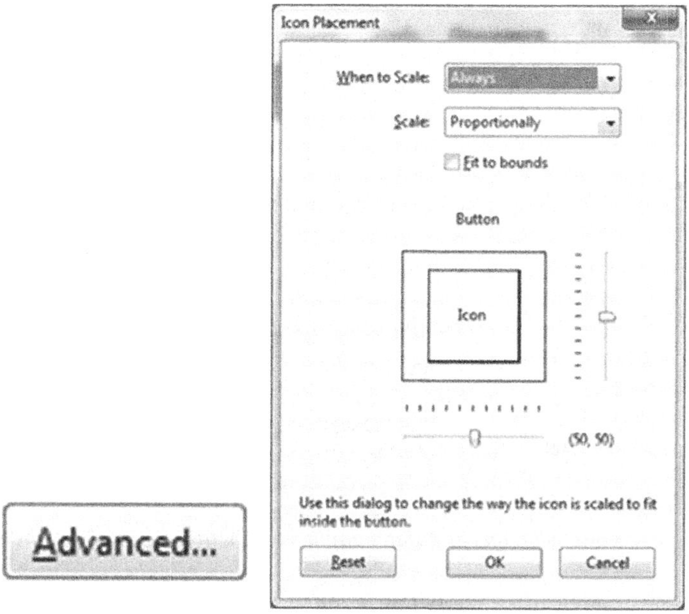

Figure 4-2. *Clicking the Advanced button in the Options tab opens the Icon Placement dialog box*

Example of a Button as a Label Only

Figure 4-3 is an example of a button with only a label applied, as found in the Newsletter file. This button's label says Next Page because you want the user to go to the next page when they click the button. The label is a helpful hint so that the user will know what will happen when the button is clicked. These types of buttons can be used in any document that contains three or more pages.

Figure 4-3. *Label-only button*

■ **Note** The current state is Up based on the behavior of the button.

A behavior like push will give other options; instead of one icon or label you could add three. See Figure 4-4 for some of the options.

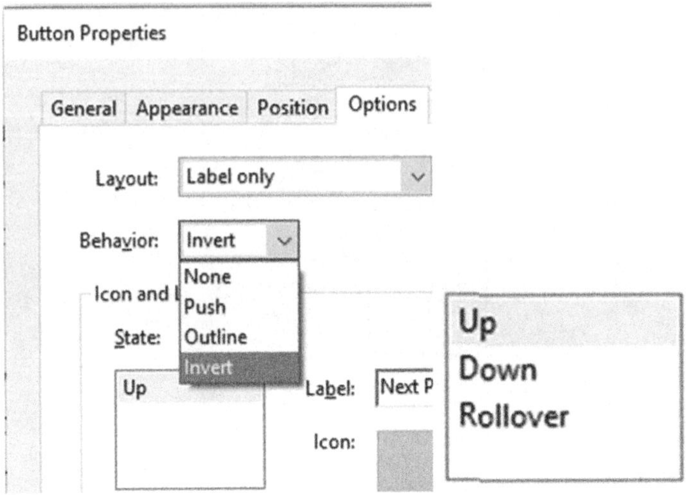

Figure 4-4. *Example of various behaviors and states applied to a button*

Figure 4-5 shows an example of a three-button group that has an icon image and some actions applied to them. Without actions, these buttons would function independently and not interact with each other.

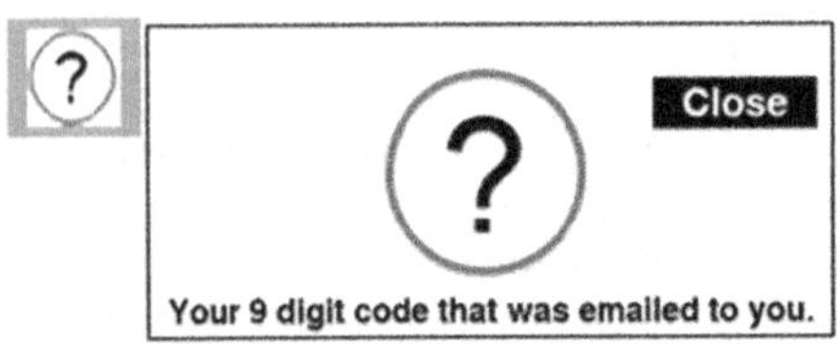

Figure 4-5. *Example button group with different show and hide fields applied to each button in the Order Form PDF*

If you enter each of the buttons properties, you will see, as in Figure 4-6, various hide and show actions.

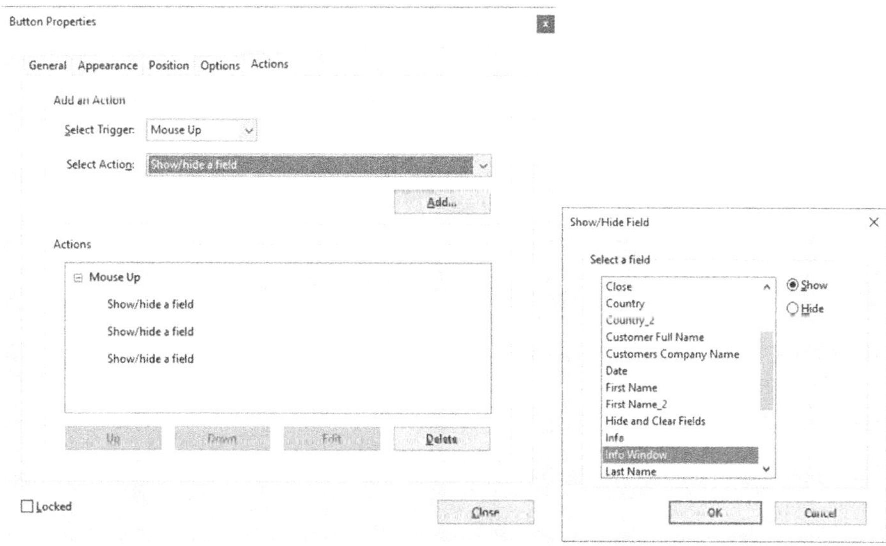

Figure 4-6. *Example button group with show and hide fields applied*

All actions can be

- Added using the Add button
- Rearranged using the Up and Down buttons
- Edited using the Edit button
- Deleted using the Delete button

Note With the Show/Hide action you need to apply the action to each field one at a time. Some actions, like Reset, allow you to apply the actions to more than one field or collectively. Refer to Figure 2-17 of Chapter 2.

Non-Form Properties Actions

The following sections take a quick look at the kinds of properties you can apply actions to that are not part of forms.

Pages

For this example, refer to the Newsletter Navigation PDF file and see Figure 4-7.

Figure 4-7. *Accessing the page thumbnails*

Under View ➤ Show/Hide ➤ Navigation Panes ➤ Page Thumbnails you will find on the left-hand side of Acrobat all the page thumbnails of your current document.

Select one of the pages in the Thumbnail section and from the dropdown choose Page Properties at the bottom of the options list to access this dialog box (refer to Figure 4-8).

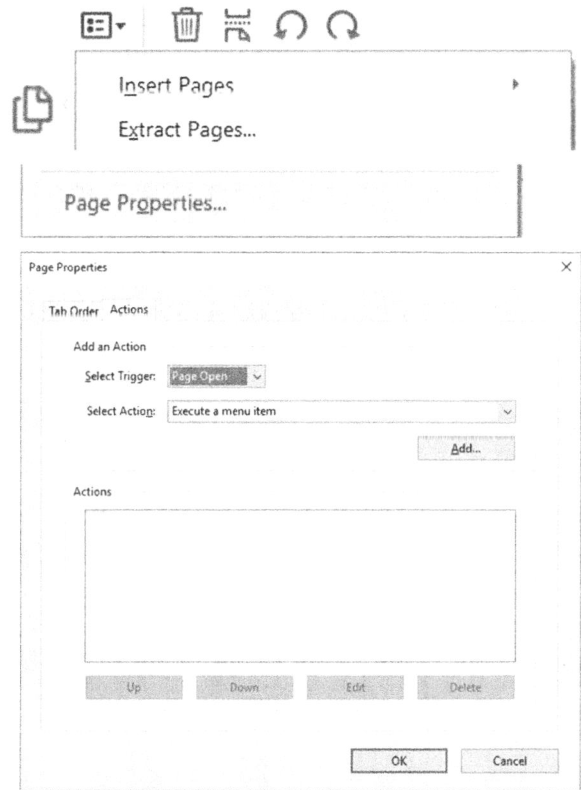

Figure 4-8. *The Page Properties option in the Action tab*

Pages can have actions applied for improved navigation. Remember that you can access this area on the left side of Acrobat in the Page Thumbnail section. Alternately, you can right-click on a thumbnail and choose Page Properties from the list.

Bookmarks

For this example, refer to the Newsletter Navigation PDF file.

Under View ➤ Show/Hide ➤ Navigation Panes ➤ Bookmarks you will find on the left-hand side of Acrobat all the bookmarks of your current document (refer to Figure 4-9).

Figure 4-9. *Bookmarks found in the Newsletter file in the Navigation Panes area*

Select one of the bookmarks and from the Options menu at the bottom of the list choose Properties. This will allow you to add or view the actions for the bookmark (refer to Figure 4-10).

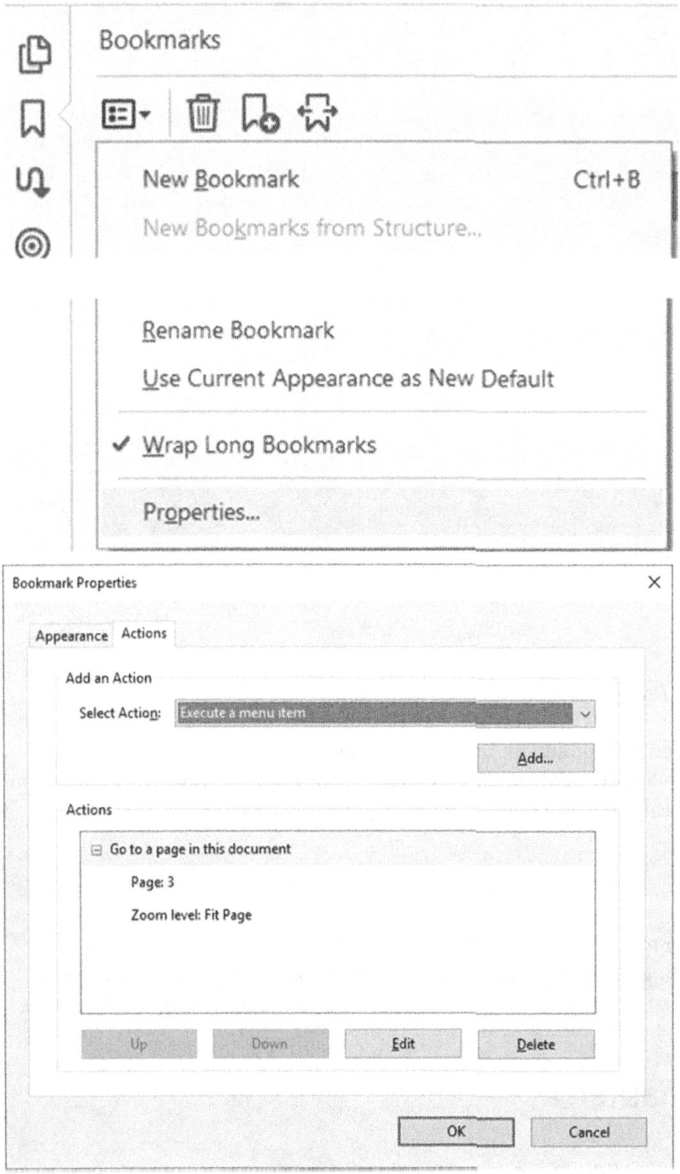

***Figure 4-10.** Bookmark properties in the Action tab*

Remember that you can access this area on the left side of Acrobat in the Bookmark Thumbnail section. Alternately, you can right-click on a bookmark and choose Properties from the list.

Web Hyperlinks

For this example, refer to the Newsletter Navigation PDF file.

You can access this area under Tools ➤ Edit PDF ➤ Link ➤ Add or Edit Web or Document Link if a link already exists. Then right-click the link and choose Properties from the list. (refer to Figure 4-11).

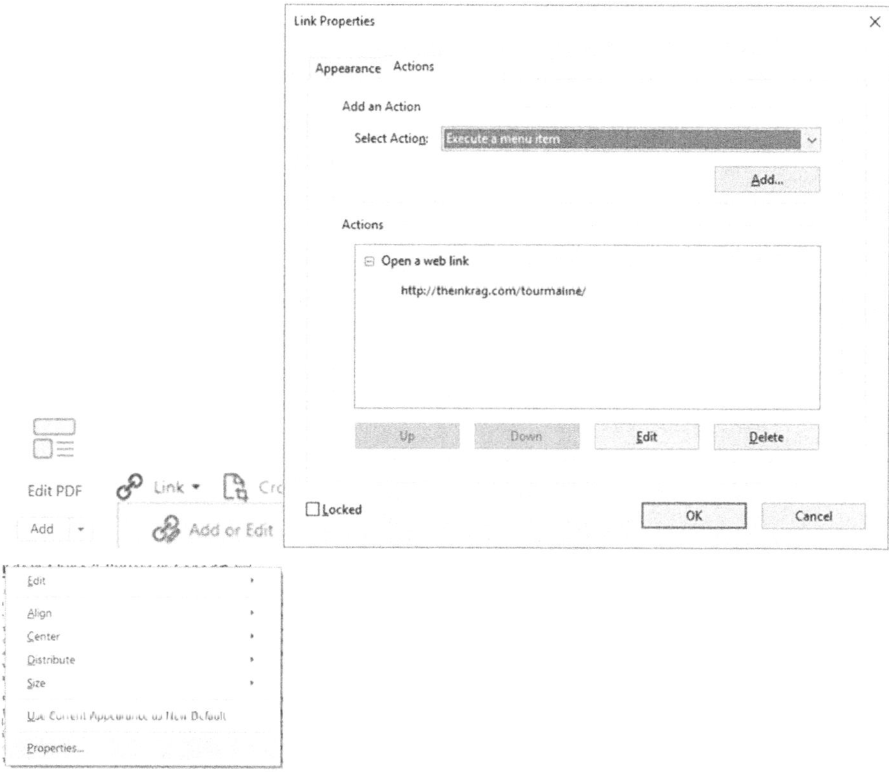

Figure 4-11. *Accessing link properties in the Action tab*

Alternately, outside of the Edit PDF tool, you can Select the link by right-clicking the link and choosing Edit Link from the list (refer to Figure 4-12).

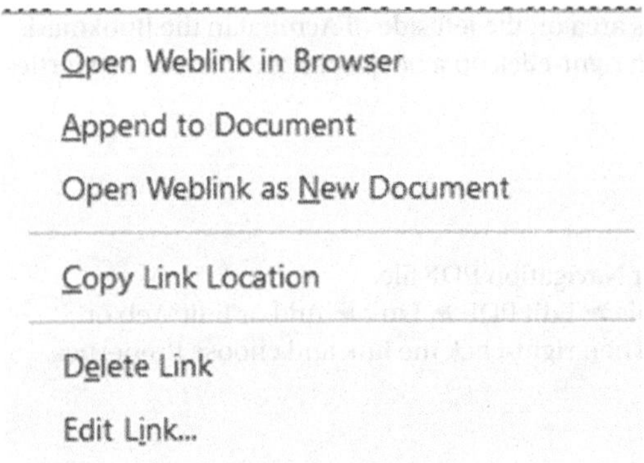

Figure 4-12. *Accessing the link properties in the Action tab outside of the Edit PDF tool*

Rich Media Non-Form Navigation Buttons

For this example, refer to the Floor Plan Layout PDF file.

Buttons can be added either via the Forms tool or the Rich Media tool (refer to Figure 4-13).

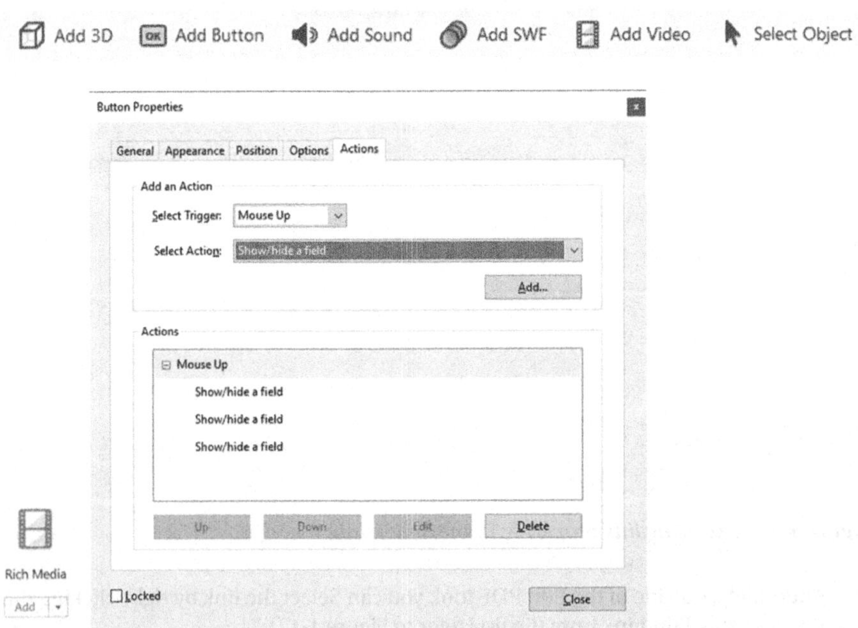

Figure 4-13. *Rich Media Button Properties dialog box in the Action tab*

Non-form button actions can be used for video media, 3D models, navigation, or later for forms while working with the Rich Media tool. However, after you close the file and open it again, to access the buttons properties, you will need to go into the Prepare Form tool to edit the button actions because you lose access after exiting the Rich Media tool.

Layers Basic Actions

For this example, refer to the Floor Plan Layout PDF file.

Under View ➤ Show/Hide ➤ Navigation Panes ➤ Layers you will find on the left-hand side of Acrobat all the layers of your current document (refer to Figure 4-14).

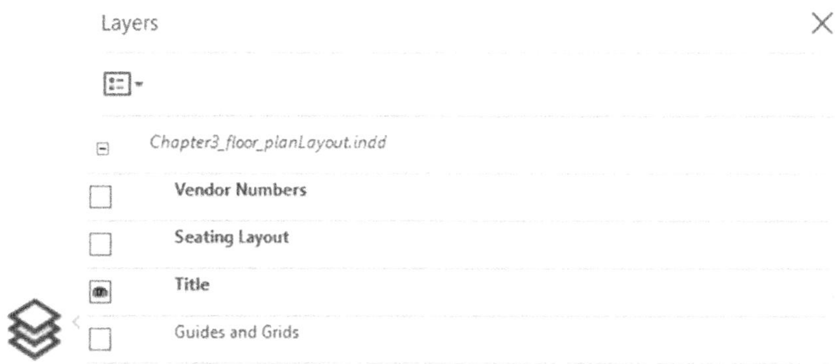

***Figure 4-14.** Access to the layers in the Navigation Panes area*

To access the Layer properties, you can select a layer and from the Options menu and choose Layer Properties from the bottom of the list. Alternately, you can right-click on a layer and choose Properties (refer to Figure 4-15).

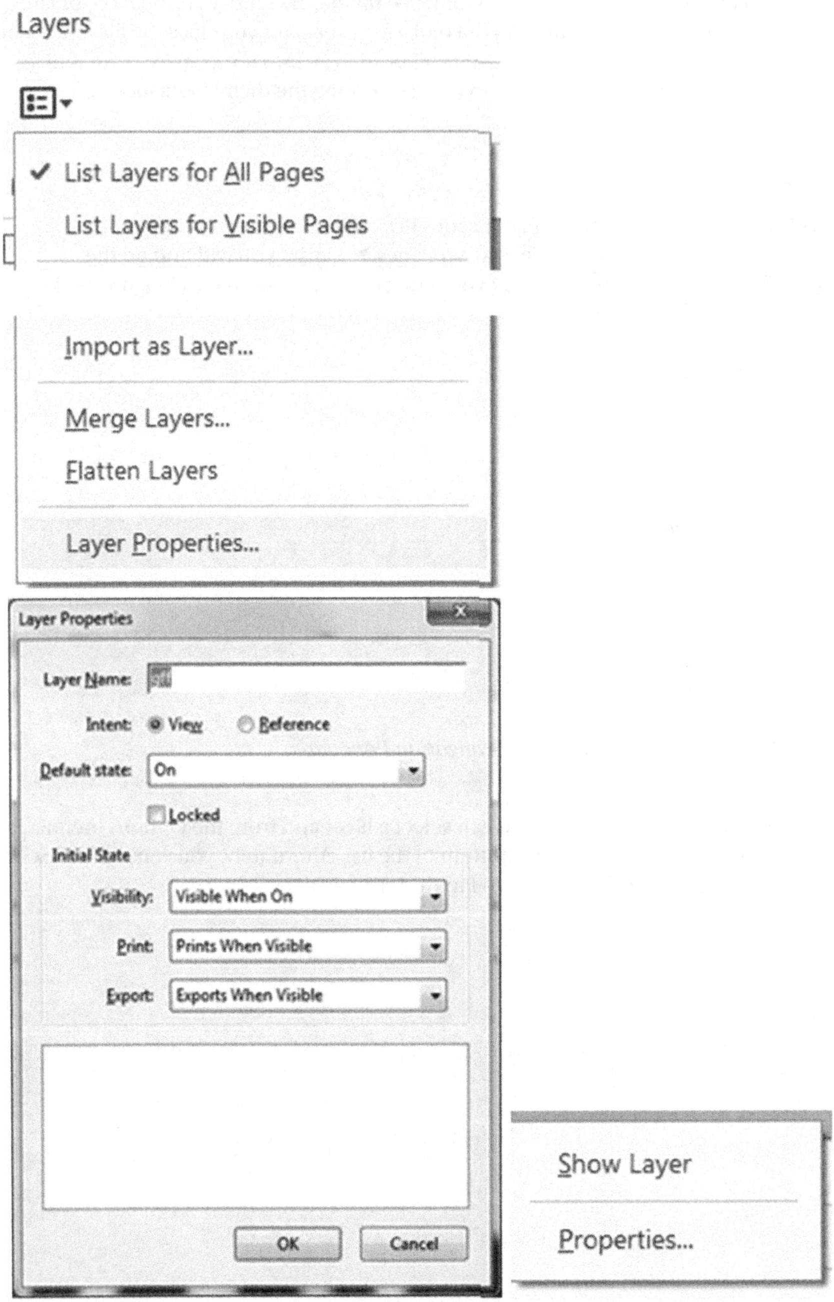

Figure 4-15. *Layer properties as seen in the Floor Plan example when you select a layer and either choose from the Options menu or right-click the layer in the Navigation pane*

- Layer actions have some similarities to Acrobat page transitions.
- Layers can have a default state of on or off.
- Layers are good for use as overlays to show, for example, optional layouts of a room or floor. The layers can be separated and exported out of program such as Adobe InDesign when you create an interactive PDF.
- Unlike other actions, they can be tricky to set up and are best kept to one or two layers.

As you can see, most of these non-form properties can be accessed in the navigation pane/thumbnail area in Acrobat. The same is true for layers.

Triggers for Actions

Before you choose an action, it is important to select a trigger.

Trigger + Select Action = Result You Want

The most common trigger to use in digital forms is Mouse Up, as seen in Figure 4-16.

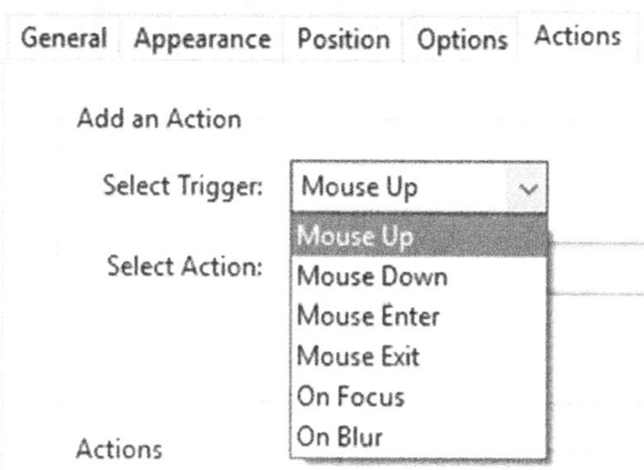

Figure 4-16. *Various action triggers that can be selected*

The following describes this and a few other actions you may encounter:

Mouse Up: When the mouse button is released after a click. This is the most common button trigger because it gives the user one last chance to drag the pointer off the button and not activate the action.

Mouse Down: When the mouse button is clicked (without being released). In most cases, Mouse Up is the preferred trigger.

Mouse Enter: When the pointer enters the field or play area.

Mouse Exit: When the pointer exits the field or play area.

On Receive Focus (media clips only): When the link area receives focus, either through a mouse action or tabbing. Also called **On Focus**.

On Lose Focus (media clips only): When the focus moves to a different link area. Also called **On Blur.**

The exceptions to properties not having an available trigger are bookmarks and hyperlinks.

It is assumed that you will click the link with your mouse or finger and that the action of going to that page or URL will be executed.

Refer to the following Adobe link for more details: `https://helpx.adobe.com/acrobat/using/applying-actions-scripts-pdfs.html`.

Choose an Action That Requires No Code

There are many actions you can choose from. As you can see in Figure 4-17, once you choose a trigger you can add an action to a button that will allow you to move to another page or print all the pages in the document.

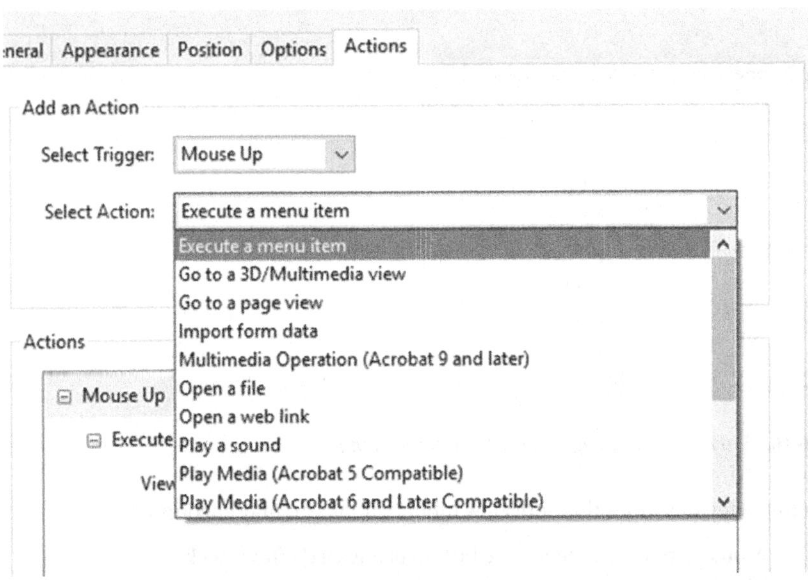

Figure 4-17. *Various actions that can be selected*

You will look at some specific actions shortly. However, take a moment to review some of the actions that are available in this list:

Execute a menu item: Executes a specified menu command as the action.

Go to a 3D/multimedia view: Jumps to the specified 3D view.

Go to a page view: Jumps to the specified destination in the current document.

Import form data: Brings in form data from another file, and places it in the active form.

Multimedia operation (Acrobat 9 and later): Executes a specified action for a multimedia object in the file (such as playing a sound file). The multimedia object must be added to the file before you can specify an action for it.

Open a file: Launches and opens a file. If you are distributing a PDF file with a link to another file, the reader needs the native application of that linked file to open it successfully. (You may need to add opening preferences for the target file).

Open a web link: Jumps to the specified destination on the Internet. You can use HTTP, FTP, and mailto protocols to define your link.

Play a sound: Plays the specified sound file. The sound is embedded into the PDF document in a cross-platform format.

Play media (Acrobat 5, or Acrobat 6 and later compatible): Plays the specified QuickTime or AVI movie that was created as Acrobat 5 or 6-compatible. The specified movie must be embedded in a PDF document.

Read an article: Follows an article thread in the active document.

Reset a form: Clears previously entered data in a form. You can control the fields that are reset with the Select Fields dialog box.

Run a JavaScript: Runs the specified JavaScript. This requires JavaScript to do some custom action.

Set layer visibility: Determines which layer settings are active. Before you add this action, specify the appropriate layer settings.

Show/hide a field: Toggles between showing and hiding a field in a PDF document. This option is especially useful in form fields. For example, if you want an object to pop up whenever the pointer is over a button, you can set an action that shows a field on the Mouse Enter trigger and hides a field on Mouse Exit.

Submit a form: Sends the form data to the specified URL. You may need someone in your IT department to help you test this first (refer to Figure 4-18).

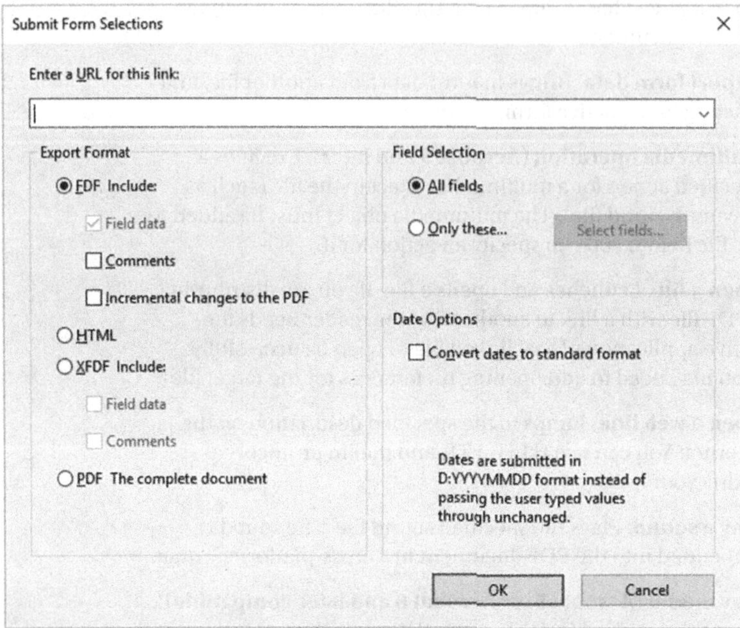

Figure 4-18. *Submit Form Selections dialog box*

It is important to note, in the case of the "Execute a menu item," additional possible variations to the action will appear when the Add button is clicked, such as assorted options for page and document navigation. Figures 4-19 and 4-20 illustrate what options are available.

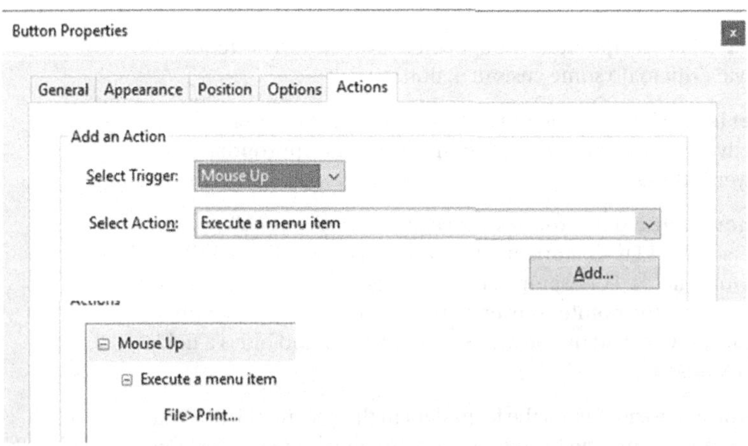

Figure 4-19. *An example of an action added to the Actions tab from the selected action "Execute a menu item"*

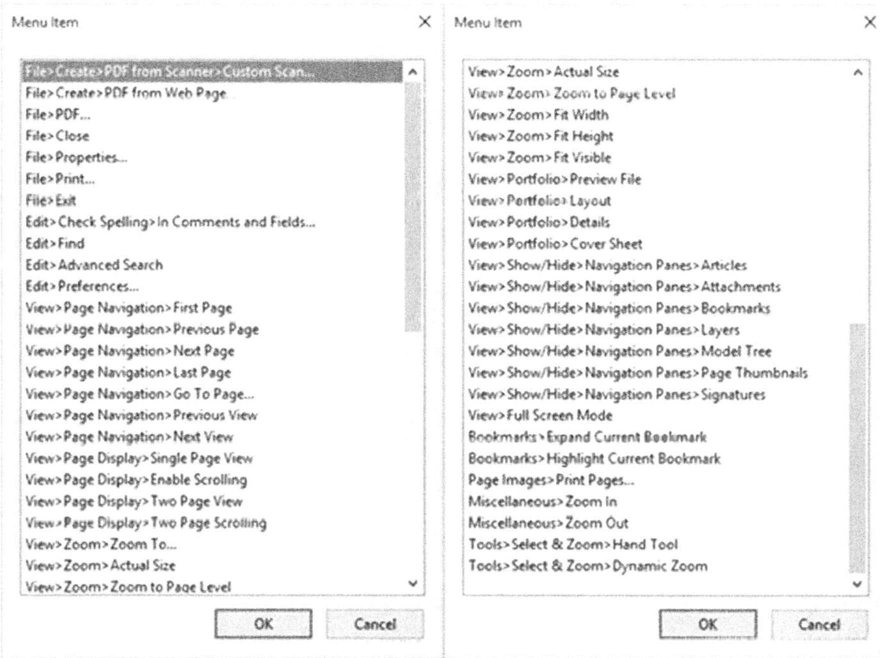

Figure 4-20. *The many different menu options that are available*

In the Actions tab, more than one action can be added using the Add button. One example is to show and hide items on a form; refer to Figure 4-21. It shows some fields and then hides others.

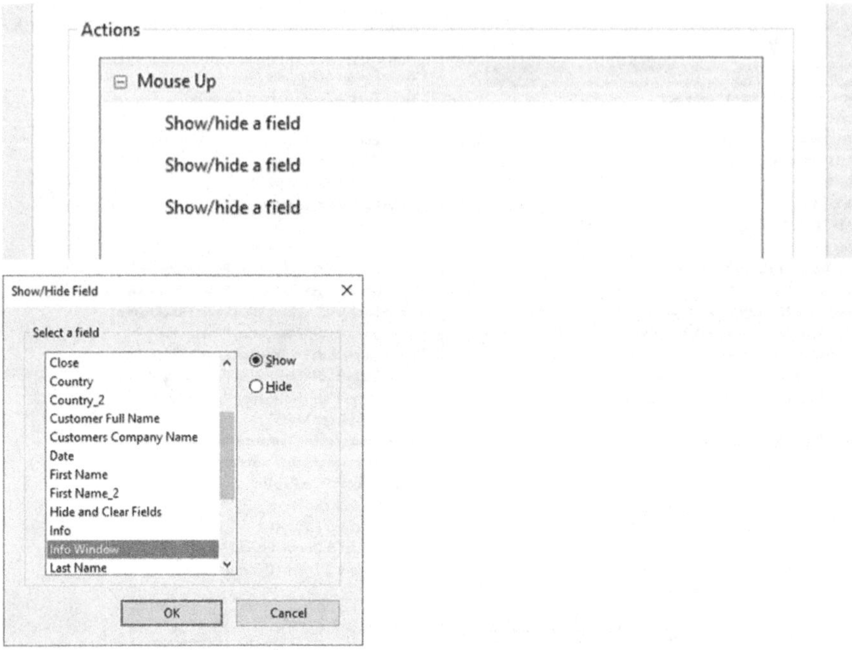

Figure 4-21. *Multiple actions applied to one field*

Newsletter Navigation with Buttons

Open the Newsletter Navigation End file in the Chapter 4 folder. Test the buttons. You can use labels with or without images to enhance the navigation experience. See Figure 4-22 for the buttons with an example of an action applied.

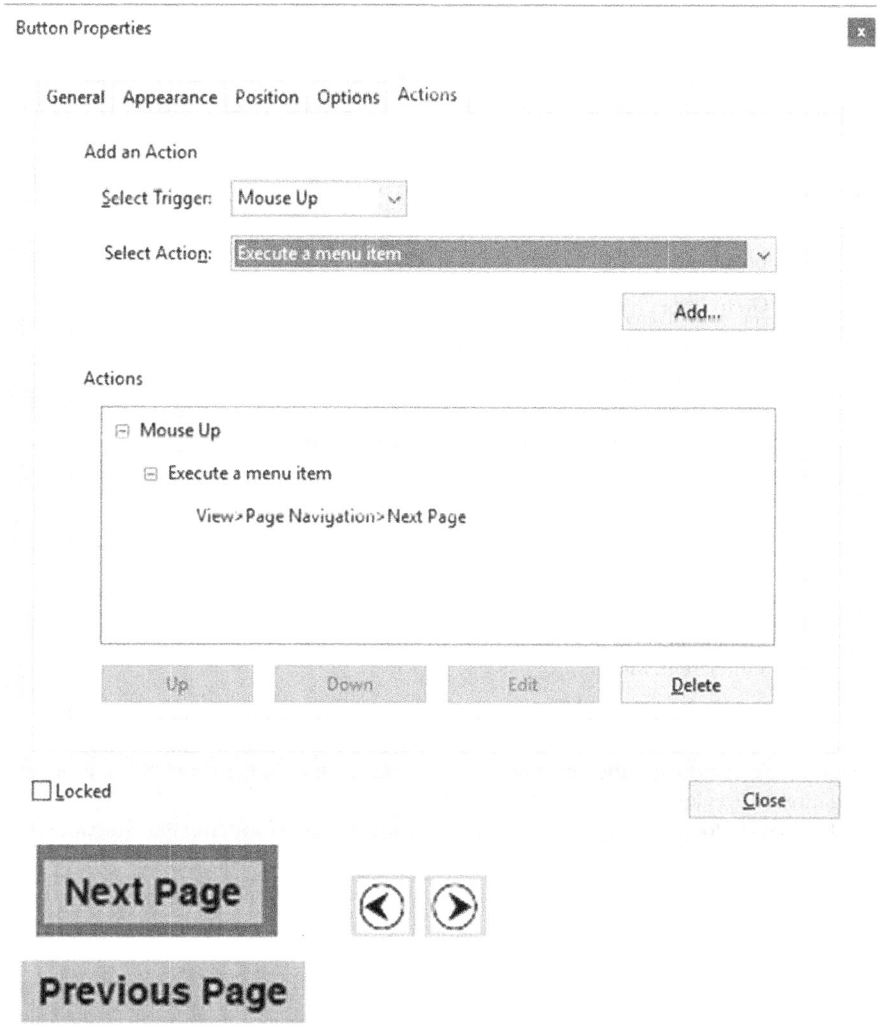

Figure 4-22. *Applying an action to a button to navigate to another page (see pages 1-3 of the Newsletter End file)*

Choose an action of "Execute a menu item" and apply one of the following types of navigation to your button:

View ➤ Page Navigation ➤

- First Page
- Previous Page
- Next Page
- Last Page
- Go to Page
- Previous View
- Next View

As shown back in Figure 4-20, other types of viewing include

- Page Display
- Zoom
- Portfolio
- Show/Hide of Panes
- Full Screen Mode

The Next Page button and the right-pointing arrow icon button in the Newsletter Document have had the action View ➤ Page Navigation ➤ Next Page applied. The Previous Page button and the left-pointing arrow button have had the action View ➤ Page Navigation ➤ Previous Page applied.

To navigate to a file in the same folder or an attachment within the PDF document, see Figure 4-23 with the Go to Form button and the actions applied.

Figure 4-23. *Navigate to a file somewhere on your hard drive or within the PDF file. Refer to page 4 of the Newsletter End PDF.*

With the Go To Form button created, you could do one of the following to open the form:

- Open a file.
- Execute a menu item ➤ View ➤ Show/Hide ➤ Navigation Pane ➤ Attachments.

As mentioned earlier, navigation can be a link or even a bookmark.

In the Newsletter Navigation PDF, you can alter the URL link called "New finds in China." This link can either go to a website or it additionally can have a bookmark that will anchor or jump to that to when clicked. If your bookmark name is no longer the same as the section title because you altered the link action, you can rename the bookmark, as you can see in Figure 4-24. The bookmark has now been renamed and matches the URL or section it is jumping to.

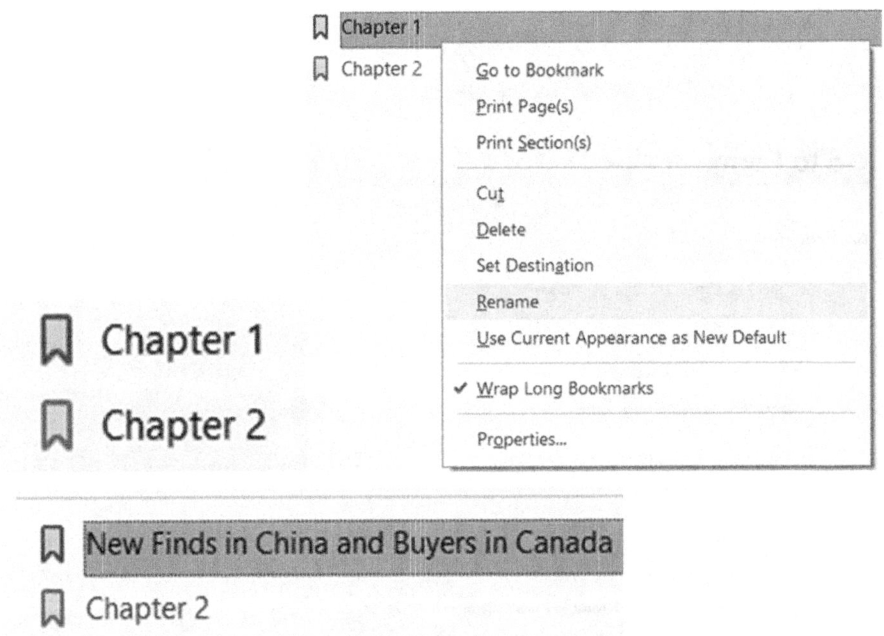

Figure 4-24. *A bookmark can be used a link to a section within a book or to navigate to a URL*

Form Navigation with a Button as Helpful Hint

If a client is unsure what to enter in a field, a hint can be created to give information. Open the TMC Order Form End example to see how this is done.

This example uses "Show/hide a field" to accomplish this. Refer to the button next to the Customer Order Code and Figure 4-25.

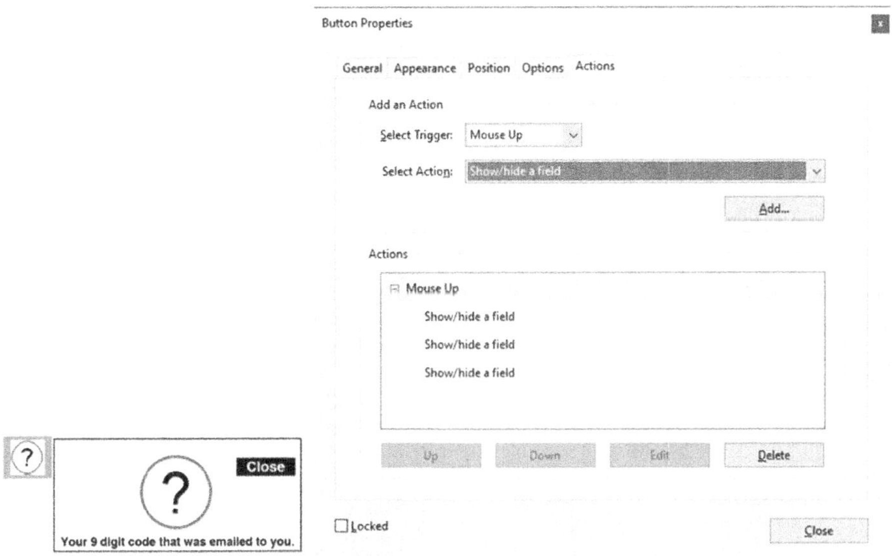

Figure 4-25. Show and hide example

Here is a breakdown of each of the buttons:

- **Info button**: Show-Close, Show-Info Window, Hide-Info (Figure 4-26).

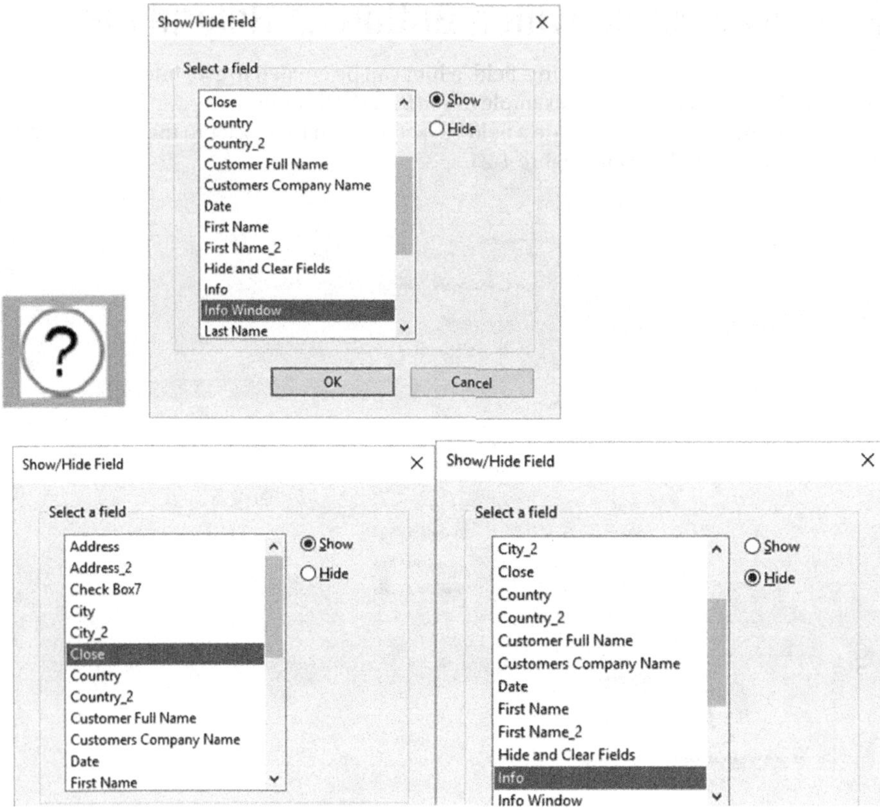

Figure 4-26. *The Info button is visible at first glance*

- **Close button**: Hide-Close, Hide-Info Window, Show-Info (Figure 4-27).

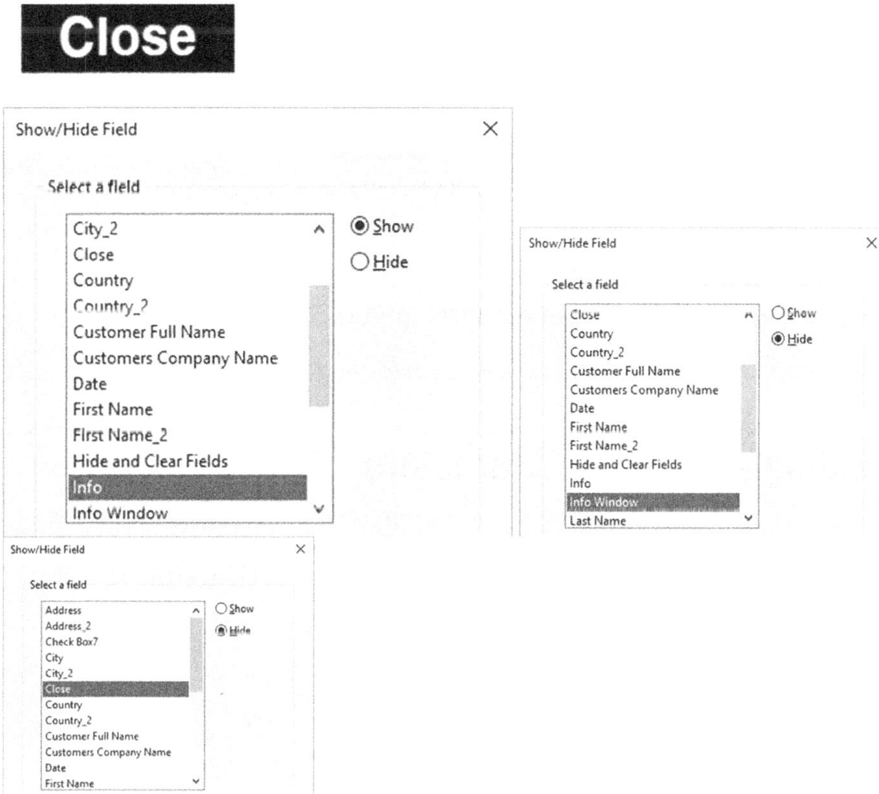

Figure 4-27. *The Close button appears on top of the Info Window button*

- **Info Window button**: No actions applied. Leave Action tabs blank (Figure 4-28).

Figure 4-28. *The Info Window button appears below the Close button*

Adding a Comb of Characters

A comb of characters spreads the user-entered text evenly across the width of the text field. If a border color is specified in the Appearance tab, each character entered in the field is separated by lines of that color. This option is available only when no other check box is selected; refer to Figure 4-29.

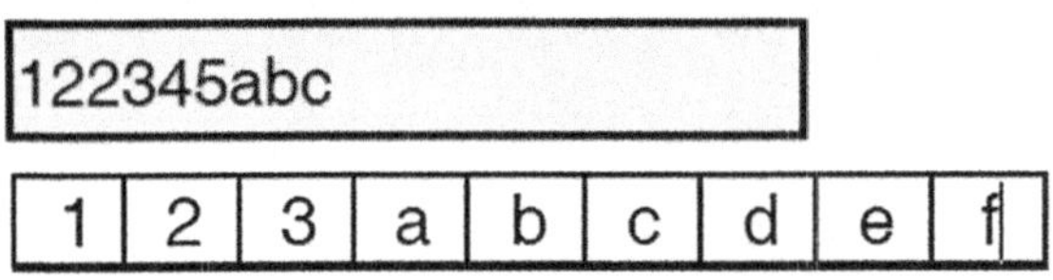

Figure 4-29. *Without and with a comb of characters*

■ **Note** When entering a code, it can helpful to add a comb of characters properties so that the client knows they have entered the correct amount of letters or numbers.

Before Comb and After Comb

Figure 4-30 shows how a text field in the Option tab properties appears before you apply the comb of characters. When you uncheck all other options, only then will the comb of characters be available to alter how many characters will be in it.

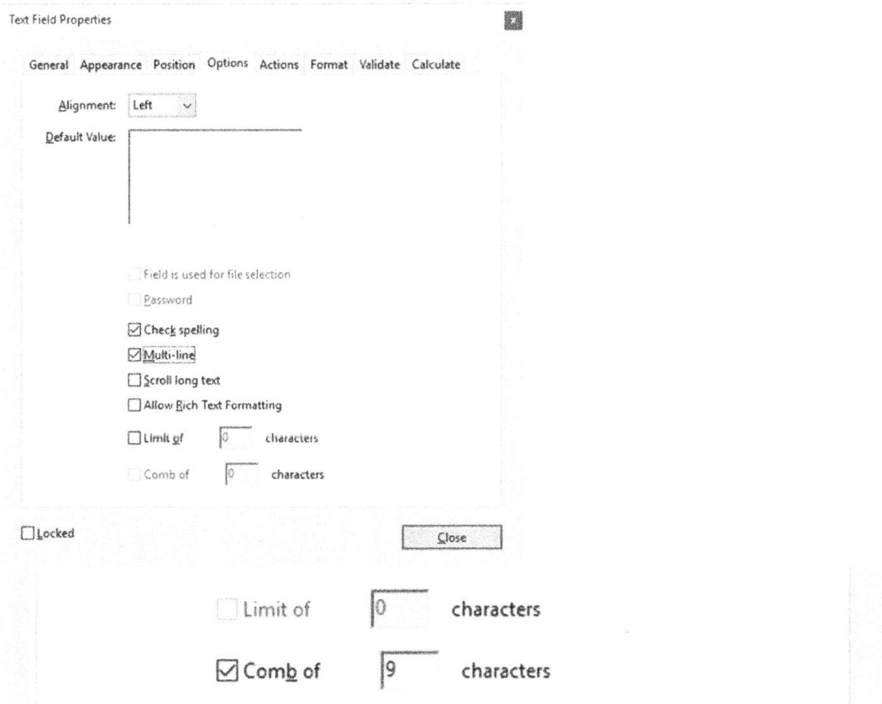

Figure 4-30. *Adding the comb of characters to the text field in the Options tab*

So that the comb of characters displays correctly, go into the Appearance tab and add a border color, line thickness, and line style so that the comb will appear; refer to Figure 4-31.

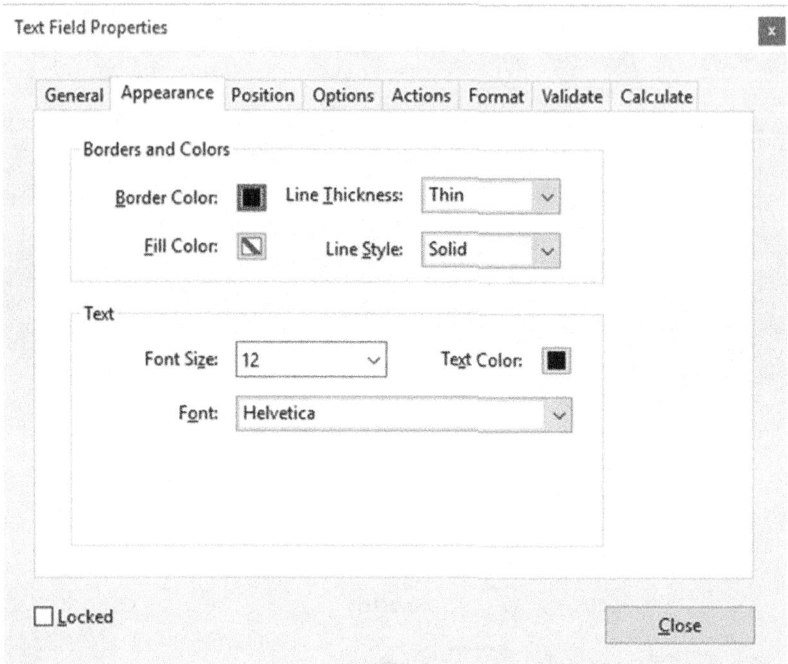

Figure 4-31. *Adjusting the appearance of the comb in the Appearance tab*

There are other ways to help clients when they are unsure what to enter into a field, and we will look at them in later chapters.

More Action Triggers to Show and Hide

Check boxes and buttons can be used in combination to create fields that show or hide. Refer here to the TMC Order Form End file to see the final example and Figures 4-32 and 4-33.

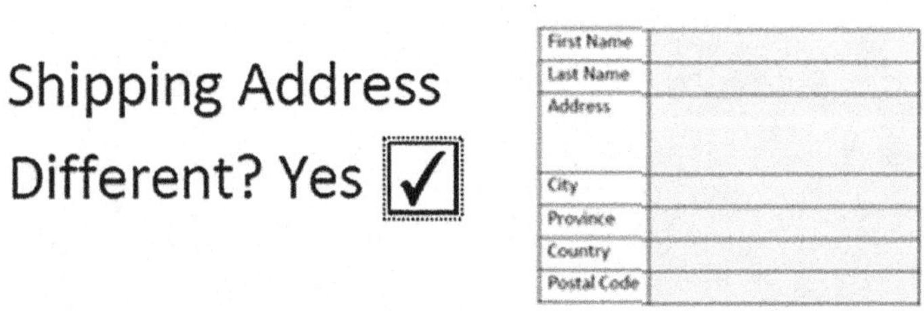

Figure 4-32. *Show and hide a shipping address using a check box*

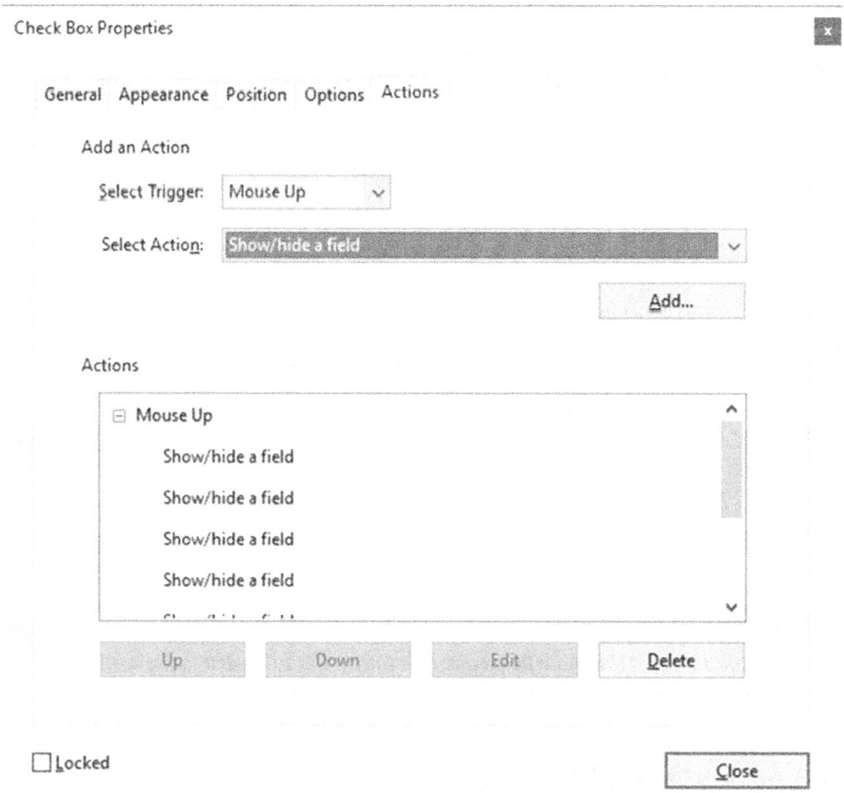

Figure 4-33. *Show and hide a shipping address using a check box*

The settings for the check box actions are
Show Text and Button fields (Figure 4-34):

- First_Name_2
- Last Name 2
- Address_2
- City_2
- Province_2
- Country_2
- Postal Code_2
- Hide and Clear Fields Button

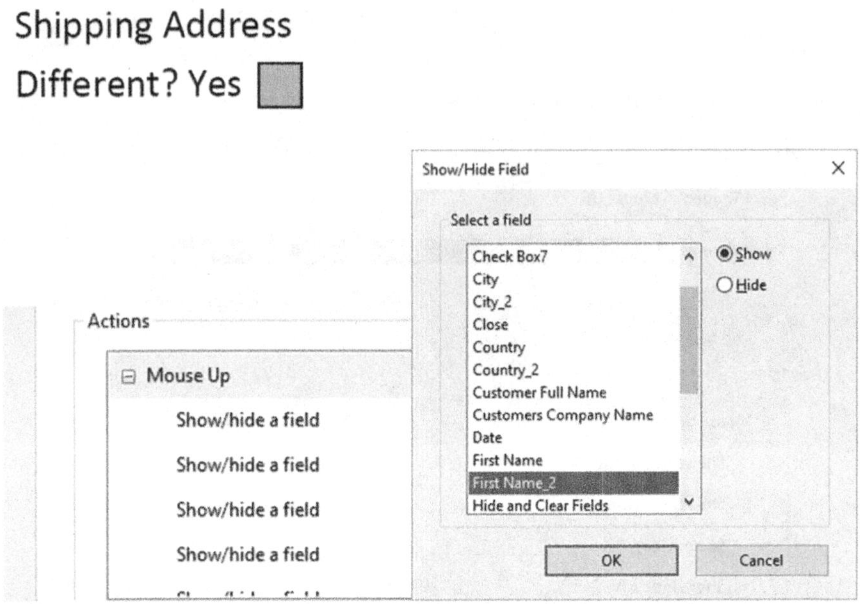

Figure 4-34. *When the check box is click, some fields in the form will show that they were hidden. Since you must set the show fields one at a time, refer to the list to see which field should have the Show setting.*

Hide and Clear Fields Button

This button uses a combination of Reset and Show/Hide. If the shipping address is the same, you don't want to store duplicate data, so you clear the fields that were shown when the check box was checked and hide them again along with the button. Refer to Figure 4-35.

Figure 4-35. *Reset button*

The settings for the button actions are shown in Figure 4-36.

Figure 4-36. *When the button is clicked, some fields in the form will hide that were shown. Since you must set the hide fields one at a time, refer to the list to see which field should have the Hide setting.*

Hide Text and Button fields:

- First_Name_2
- Last_Name_2
- Address_2
- City_2
- Province_2
- Country_2
- Postal Code_2
- Hide and Clear Fields Button

Finally, reset all the fields mentioned in the check box except for the button, which cannot be reset. Refer to Figure 4-37.

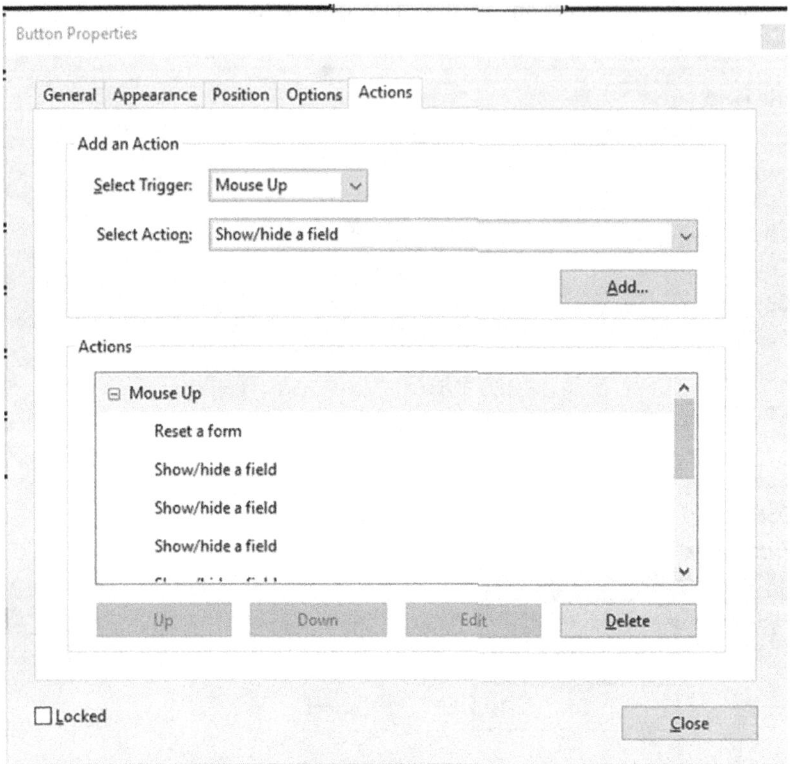

Figure 4-37. *Reset button that clears the information in the fields and hides them again*

Set Layer Visibility

As mentioned earlier, adding and setting layer visibility in a document can be tricky. One of the examples in this chapter is a file of a floor plan, showing how this can be achieved if you have a document with one or more layers. You can either use bookmarks or buttons to show and hide your layers. Refer to Figure 4-38.

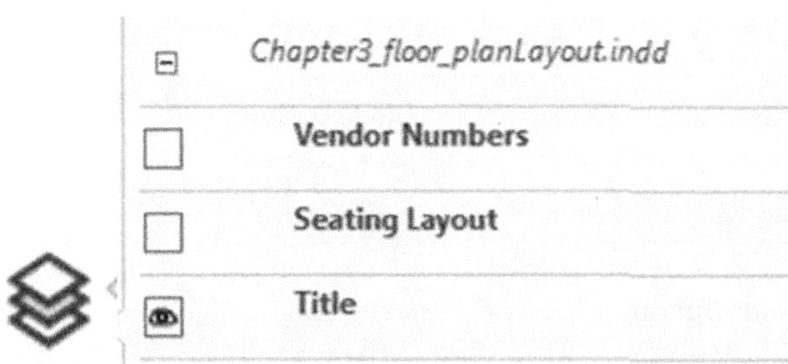

Figure 4-38. *The layers in the floor plan PDF*

■ **Note** In the properties of each layer, I have set only the default mode of the title layer to be on when the document opens; the others are set to Off. Remember that to access the properties of a layer you need to right-click the layer and choose properties.

More details about adding and working with layers can be found at `https://helpx.adobe.com/acrobat/using/pdf-layers.html`.

Using Bookmarks

If you don't want to use buttons, you can alternatively use bookmarks to show and hide layers. See Figure 4-39.

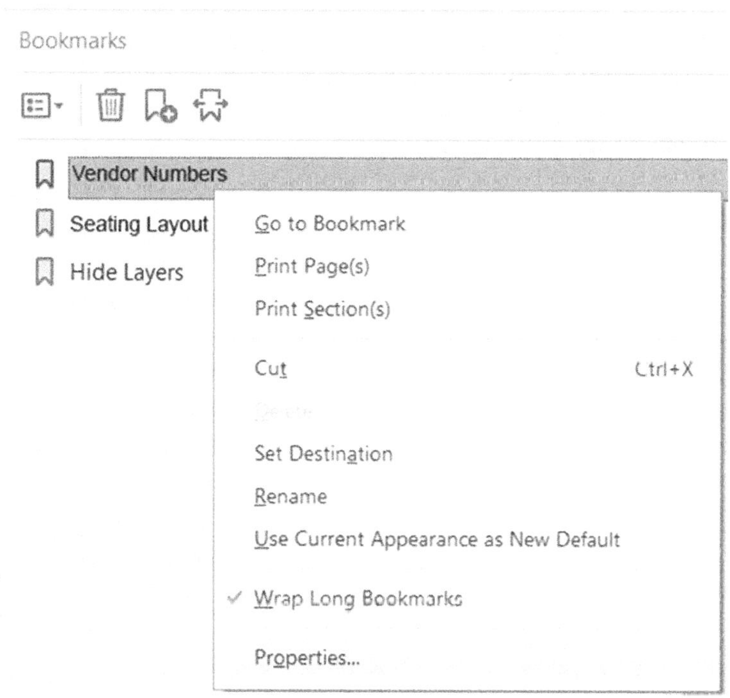

Figure 4-39. *Setting Bookmark properties*

Begin by making sure that the layers you want visible or hidden are on or off to create the correct view for your bookmark.

Once you've created a bookmark, you can right-click it and choose Properties from the menu. The properties will appear. Then select the Actions tab as in Figure 4-40.

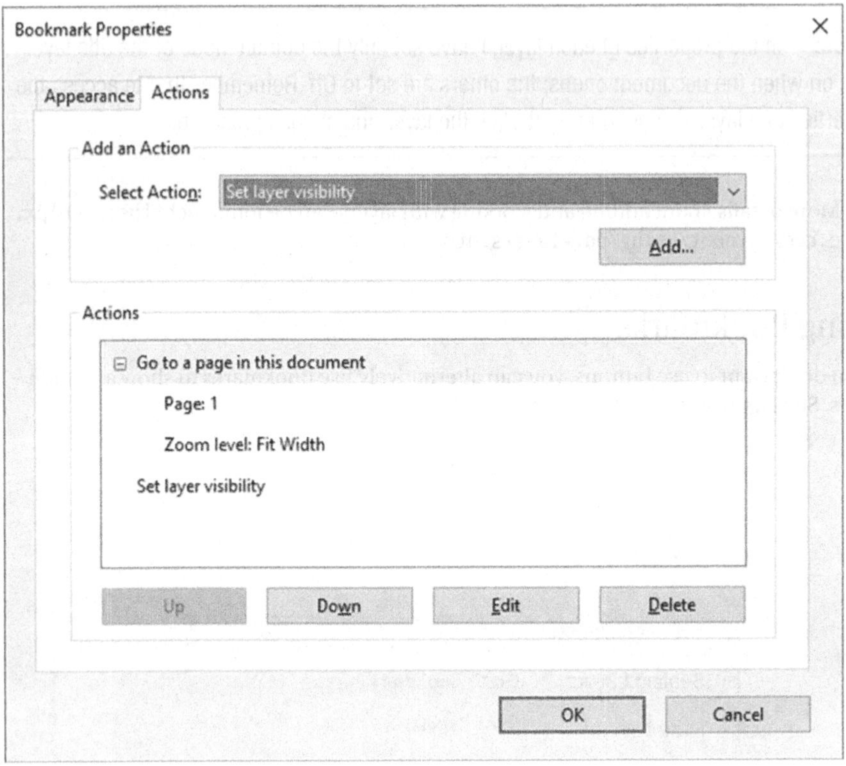

Figure 4-40. *Bookmark Action properties*

Notice that the action "Go to a page in this document" is already added. However, you will need to add the action of "Set layer visibility." Upon clicking Add, an info warning will appear reminding you that whatever the current state the layers are in now will be what this bookmark will display. If you do not like your layer visibility, click Cancel and set your layers to the correct state before choosing OK to add this action.

Now your bookmark should be able to show or hide the layer. As with any action, it can be removed by clicking the Delete button.

Using Buttons

As with bookmarks, buttons can be used as well. Refer to Figure 4-41. However, you may want to hide some buttons along with the layers while some layers are visible to reduce clutter. Also, you may want to reset all the layers to the off or hidden state as well with a button. You can review the file to see what the final effect looks like. The bulleted list below shows what settings were applied to each button. As with the bookmarks, make sure that the layers are in the state you want before you set the layer visibility for each button. Make sure to test your file when you're done.

Figure 4-41. *Example of settings applied to the buttons*

- **Show Floor Plan button**: Set layer visibility, **Show** Vendor Number, and **Show**-Hide Layers Button.
- **Show Vendor Numbers button**: Set layer visibility.
- **Hide Layer button**: Set layer visibility, **Hide** Vendor Number, and **Hide**-Hide Layers Button.
- In the Layers pane, only the title layer is set to on; all other layers are turned off.
- Only turn on layers that you want visible before adding the action of layer visibility to each button. Click OK to confirm setting. Refer to Figure 4-42.

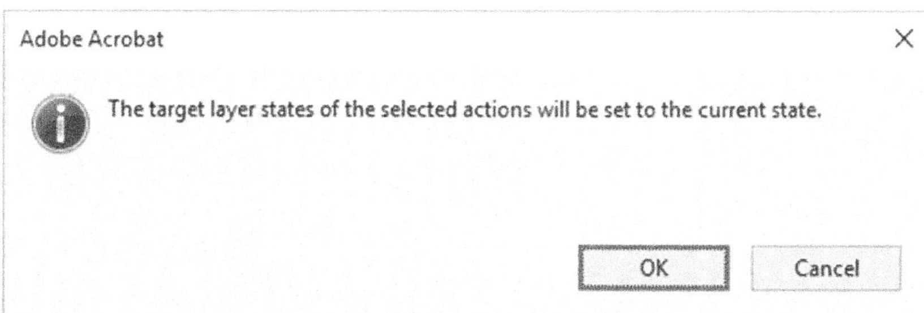

Figure 4-42. *This is the info alert that appears as layer visibility is set*

Once you are finished setting the buttons, return the layers to your default settings, save the file, and close it.

Summary

This chapter covered a lot of topics concerning actions that can be applied to form fields and non-form items like layers, bookmarks, buttons, pages, and links. As you can see, Acrobat offers a lot of options in regard to navigation and controlling how you view or hide fields.

At this point, you haven't added any custom JavaScript. You've only used the settings that come with the Acrobat Actions tab. However, in part 2, you are going to look at running your own JavaScript and how this effects what you input into your form fields.

Before you go any farther in this book, take some time to practice these actions on your own and try adding them to a few of your own projects.

PART 2

Simplified Field Notation and Basic JavaScript

CHAPTER 5

Introduction to Simplified Field Notation and JavaScript

In this chapter, you will first explore simplified field notation (SFN) used in Excel and how it compares to JavaScript. This will set the groundwork for what you can expect in the rest of the book.

The JavaScript that you will be using in the following chapters is only for the form or navigation within a document and is not as advanced as programmer's JavaScript used in software or the Web. That is a whole other topic not discussed in this book. Mostly you will focus on simple math formulas that can be used to improve your forms, and one that clients will use in Reader.

Note This chapter does not reference any files so there are none that need to be downloaded for this lesson.

Getting Started

From the text files (`.txt`) provided in the following lessons, you will copy and paste it into the correct dialog box areas and do very minor modifications to the code.

Some common uses for JavaScript in Acrobat are

- Interaction and addition of watermarks, bookmarks, links, and annotations
- Automatically filling in form fields
- Changing the appearance of information in text fields as the information itself changes
- Navigation of the document, such as zooming in and going to specific pages

J. Harder, *Enhancing Adobe Acrobat DC Forms with JavaScript*,
DOI 10.1007/978-1-4842-2893-7_5

- Printing of the document
- Controlling security settings, signatures, and custom validation
- Assisting the Action Wizard to speed up tasks

The JavaScript entry can be found under the following fields and tabs:

- **Text, Date, and Dropdown menus**: Actions (Execute a JavaScript), Format Custom (Custom Format and Custom Keystroke), Validate, Calculate (Custom Calculation Script)
- **Check Box, Radio Button, Image Field, and Button**: Actions
- **List Box**: Actions and Selection Change
- **Signed**: Actions and Signed change (Execute a Script)
- **Barcode**: Actions and Value (Custom)
- **Main JavaScript Box (Global)/Document JavaScript**

Text Field, Date, and Dropdown Menu Properties

The following sections provide examples of what JavaScript added to these field tabs looks like.

Action Tab

Actions happen upon entering or exiting the field, as seen in Figure 5-1.

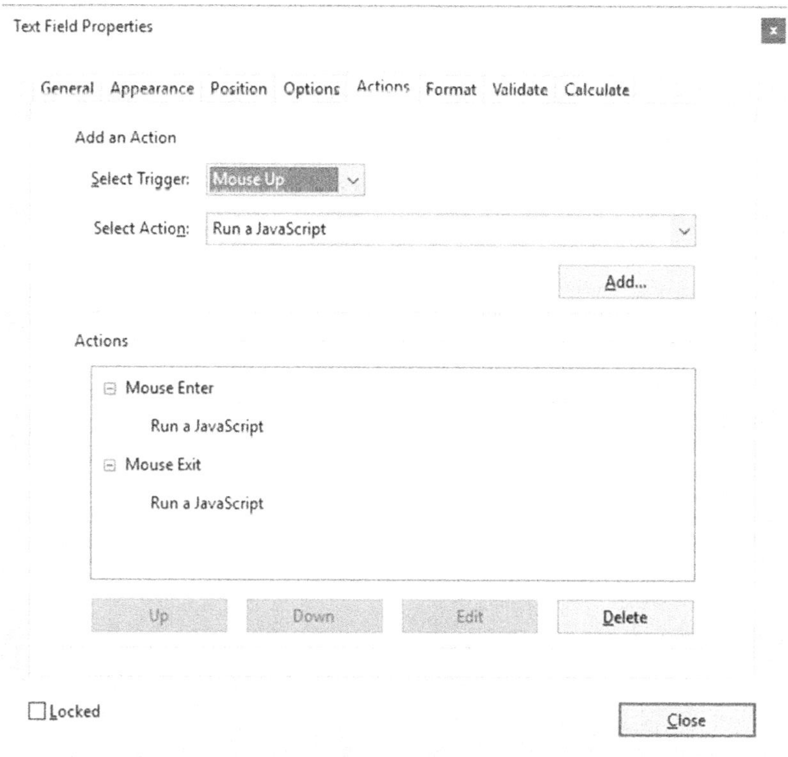

Figure 5-1. *The Action tab in the Text Field Properties dialog box*

Format Tab

A custom format allows changes to text color, as seen in Figure 5-2. A custom keystroke allows events to change within the field when a certain criterion has been reached.

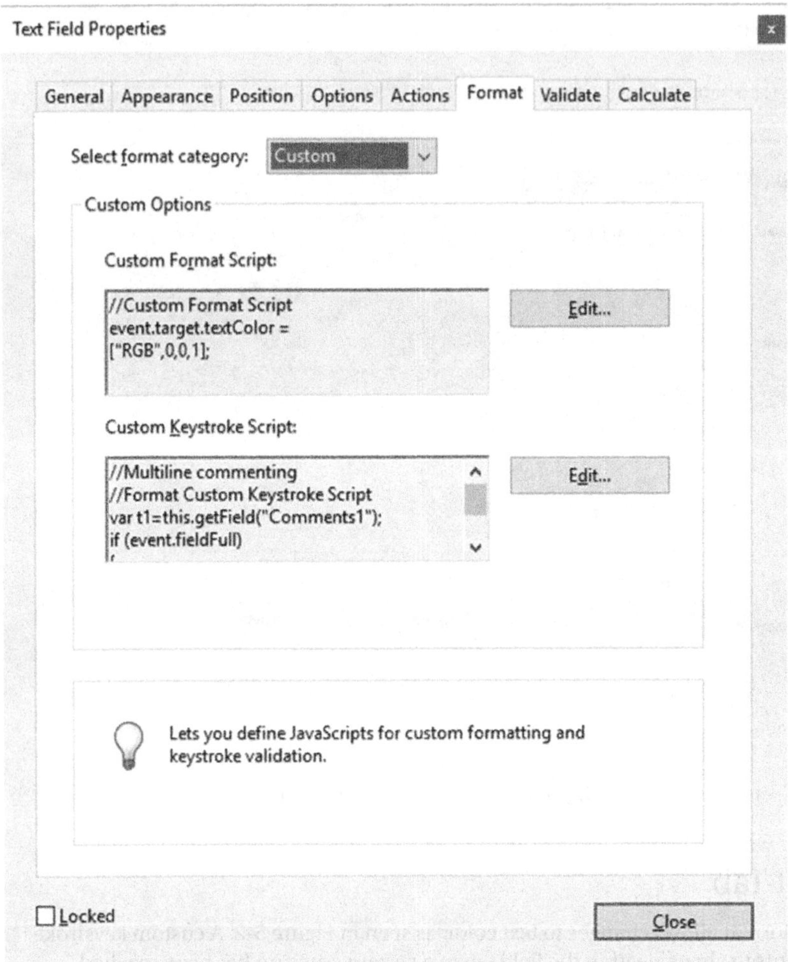

Figure 5-2. The Format tab in the Text Field Properties dialog box

Validate Tab

Similar to a custom format, in the Validate tab certain criteria are checked and must be met before you can proceed, as seen in Figure 5-3.

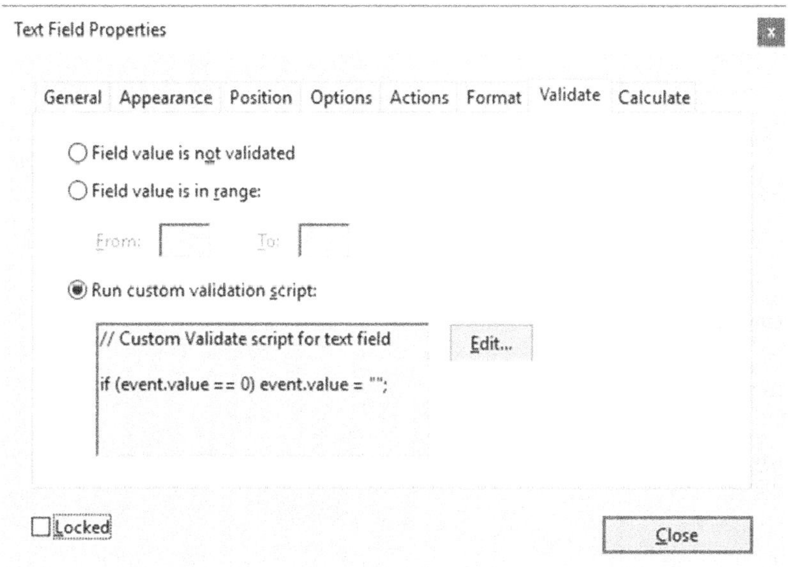

Figure 5-3. *The Validate tab in the Text Field Properties dialog box*

Calculate Tab

The Calculate tab offers custom calculations that can't be done with SFN or Value, as seen in Figure 5-4.

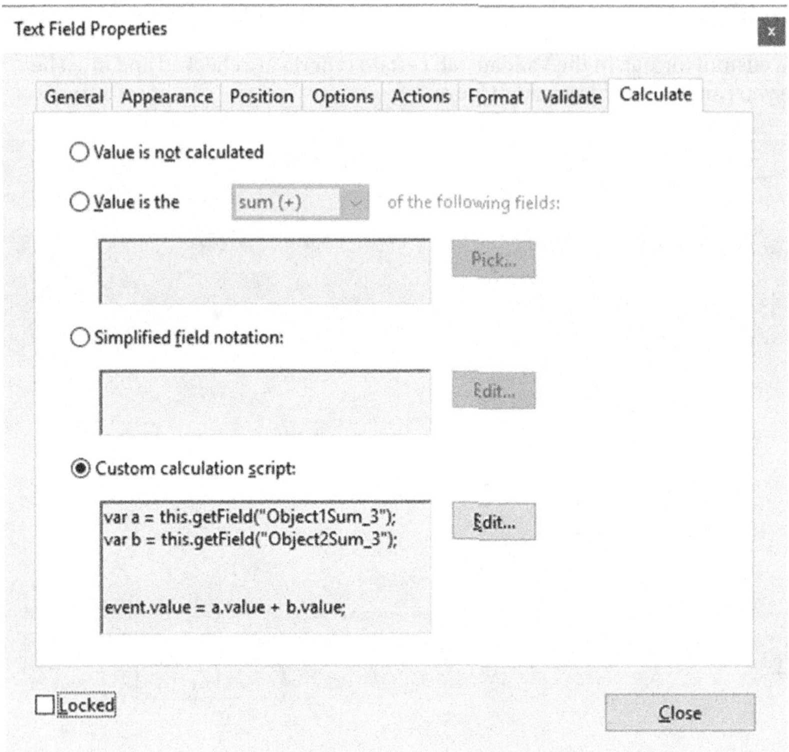

***Figure 5-4.** The Calculate tab in the Field Properties Calculate dialog box*

Check Box, Radio Button, Image Field, and Button Properties

Buttons can also be used as hidden fields if required, as seen in Figure 5-5.

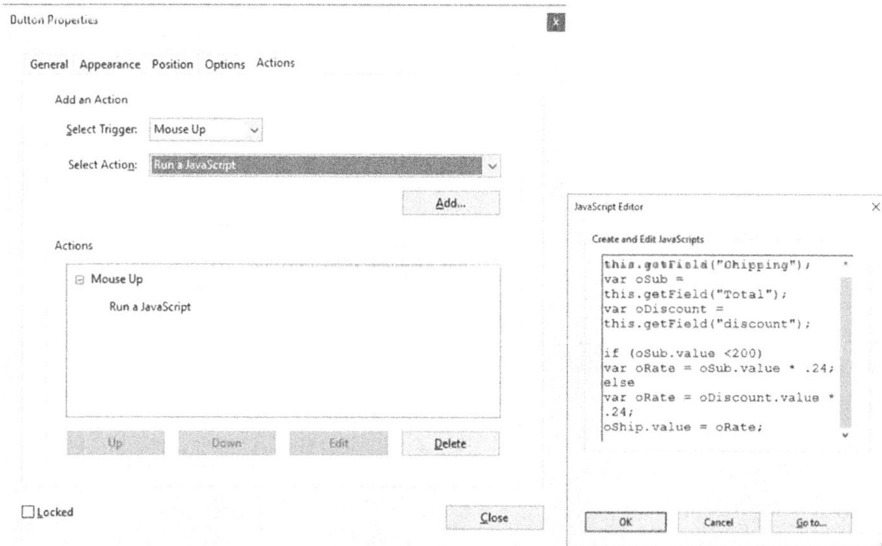

Figure 5-5. *The Action tab in the Button Properties dialog box is the only tab where you can add actions. The same goes for check boxes and radio buttons.*

List Box Properties

Besides the Actions tab, the Selection Change tab is an area for adding a script when you want to change the field that is being selected. Refer to Figure 5-6.

Figure 5-6. *The Actions and Selection Change tabs*

Digital Signature Properties

You can add actions to a digital signature's properties either in Actions or the Signed tab. The Signed tab is like the Validate tab in other fields. Validation occurs when some criteria are met. Refer to Figure 5-7.

Figure 5-7. *The Actions and Signed tabs in the Digital Signature Properties dialog box*

Barcode Properties

As with other fields, you can add actions to barcodes. However, the barcode creates its own value script in the Value tab. Its value depends on what is in the form as a whole in regard to types of fields and their input values. Refer to Figure 5-8.

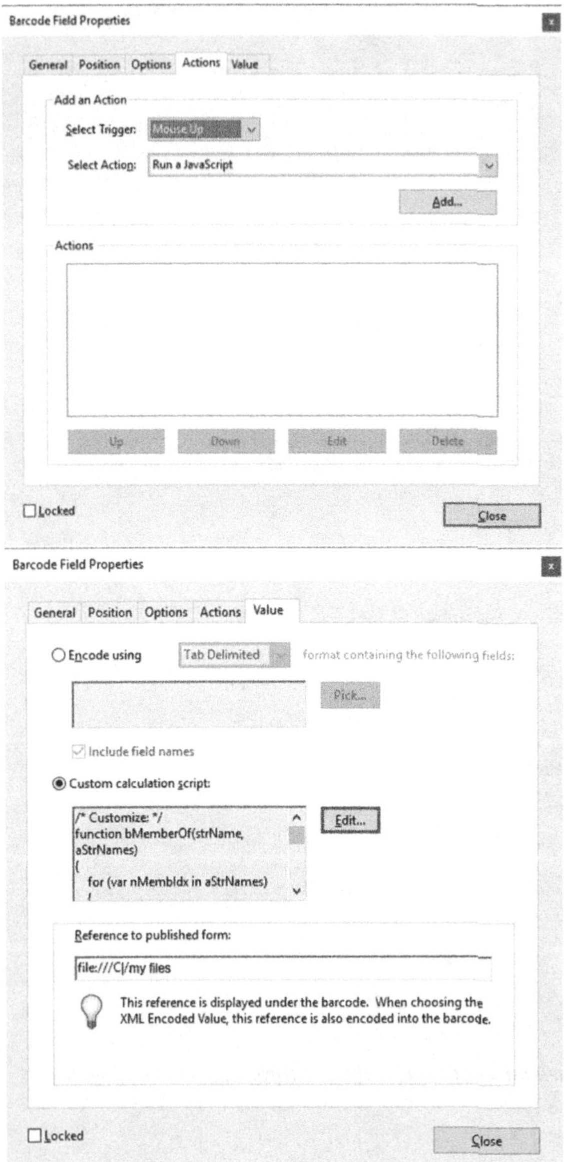

Figure 5-8. *The Action and Value tabs in the Barcode Field Properties dialog box*

Regardless of what type of field you plan to use, all actions and their edits are accessed through the JavaScript Editor box, which holds the script. You can access this editing area when you click the Edit or Add buttons. The Add button is generally seen, as in Figure 5-9, in the Actions tab. The Edit button can also be found in the Actions tab, but is seen in other tabs as well like Format, Validate, and Calculate; they all lead to the JavaScript Editor.

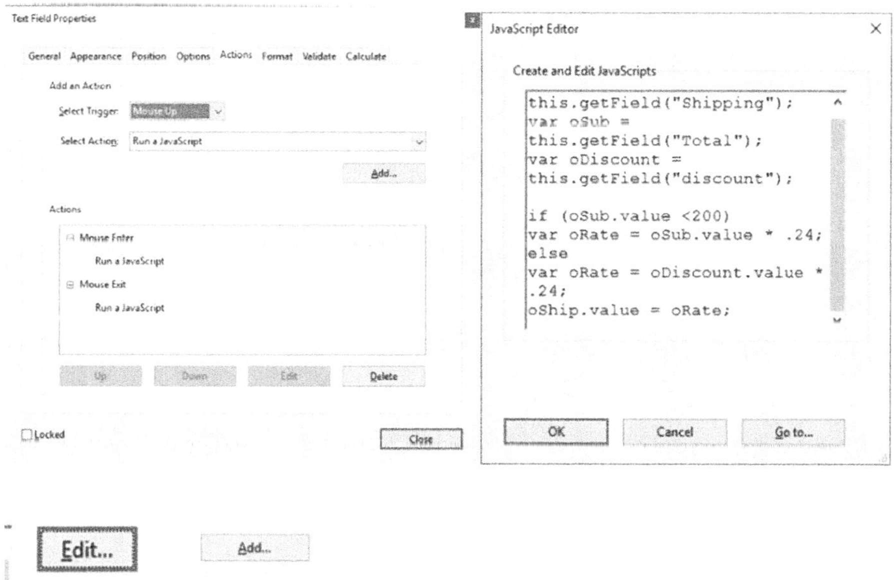

Figure 5-9. Access to the JavaScript Editor through the Edit or Add buttons, which are found in the Actions, Format, Validate, and Calculate tabs

Global Document JavaScript

Now let's look at global document JavaScript. If you have a document open, go to the Tools tab and select the JavaScript tool. You will now be able to view all the subtools, as seen in Figure 5-10.

***Figure 5-10.** JavaScript tool and its submenu items*

Actions that happen globally can affect more than one field. These types of actions will affect many fields throughout the file. Fields can call upon a single global function to reduce typing and size of the document, as seen in Figure 5-11. You will look at this area in more detail in later chapters.

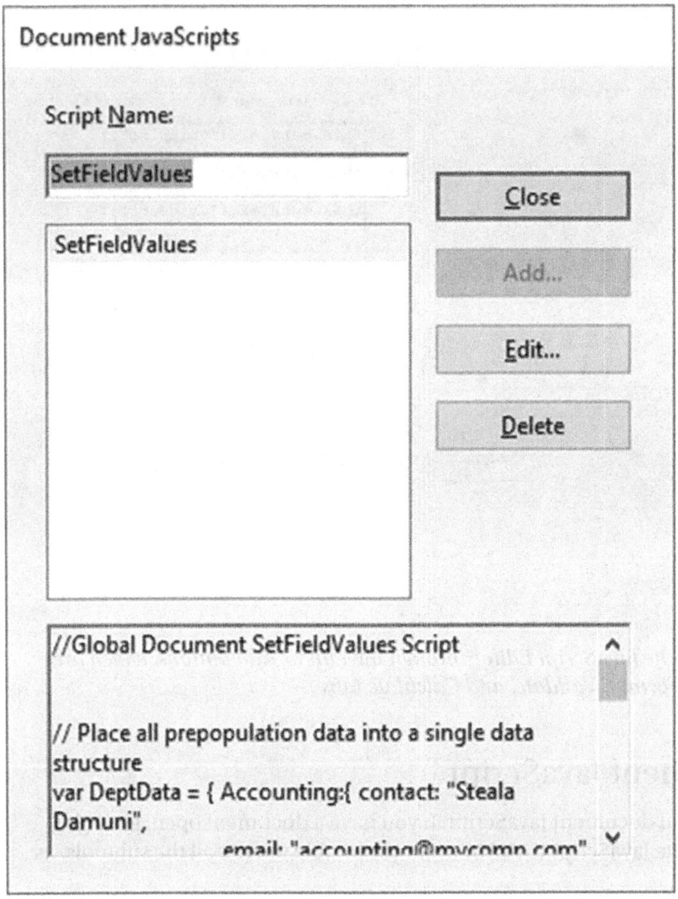

Figure 5-11. *Document JavaScripts dialog box*

Additional actions that are specific to the document can be added using the Document Actions tool, as seen in Figure 5-12.

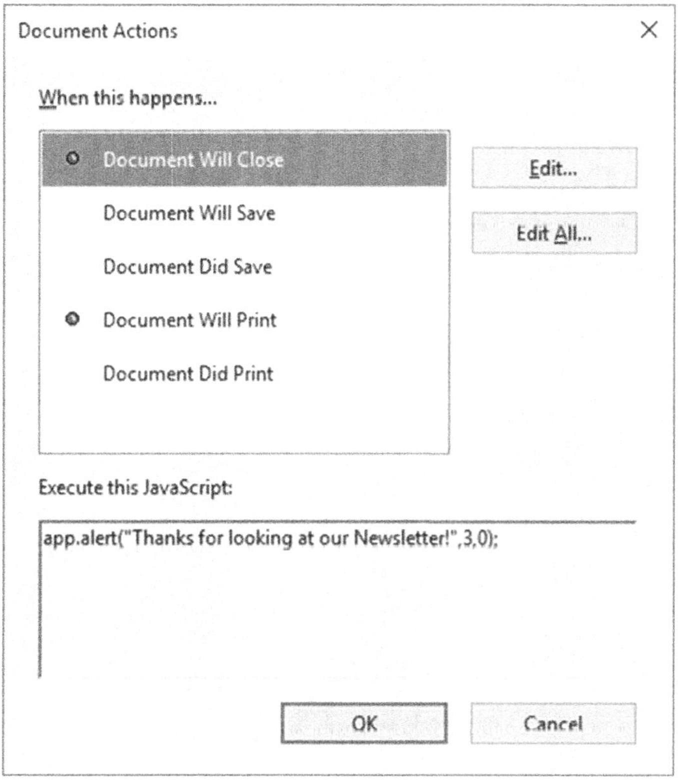

***Figure 5-12.** Document Actions dialog box*

Alerts can be placed here when these following events happen.

■ **Note** You can't add more document actions here without advanced scripting knowledge.

You can also view all your JavaScripts at once under the All JavaScript tool, which opens the JavaScript Editor. Refer to Figure 5-10.

If there are errors, you can use debugger to help you. However, I find it helps to have some knowledge of JavaScript structure and do the editing in a program like Notepad++ or Adobe Dreamweaver where there is more room to type. Editing programs like Dreamweaver also show you clearly with numbers on the left-hand side which line in the code you are on. Acrobat does not have these visual cues, only a text reference in the lower right side of the editor, which I find not useful for detailed code editing. Refer to Figure 5-13.

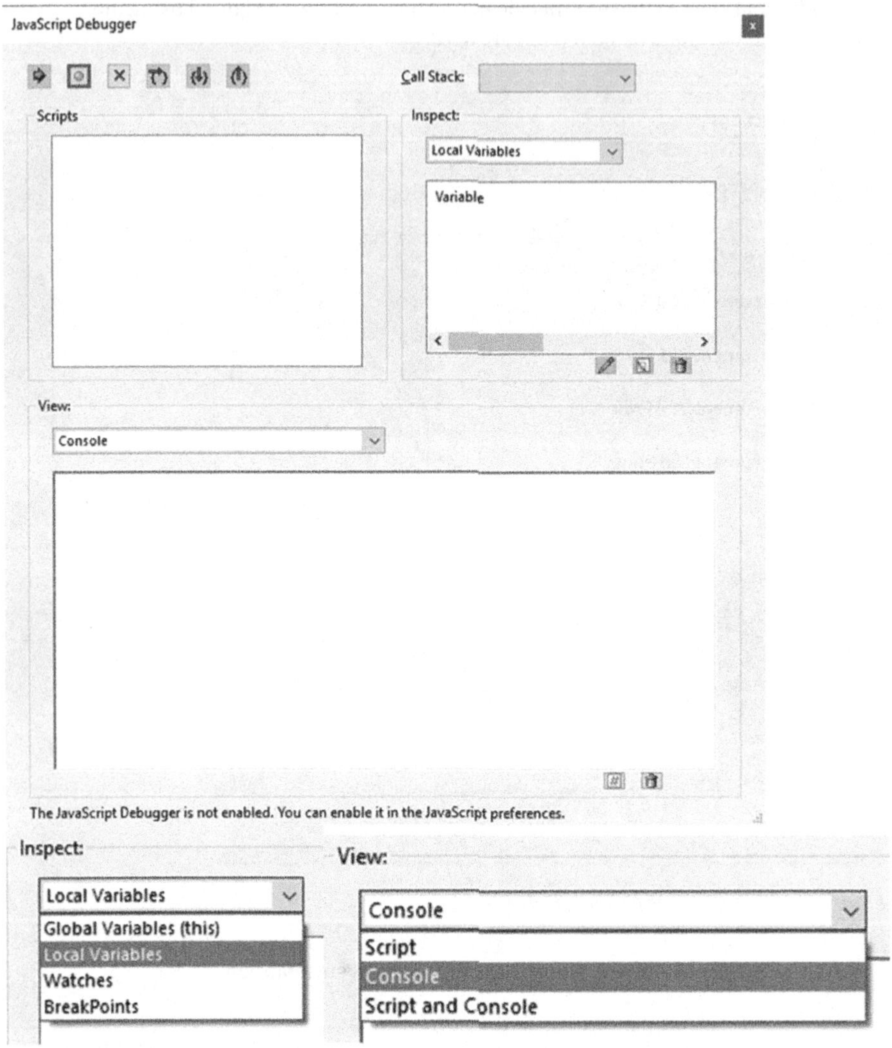

Figure 5-13. *JavaScript Debugger dialog box with settings*

When you've finished typing in your editing program, copy the code back into Acrobat's JavaScript Editor and run the debugger again and test (Figures 5-13 and 5-14) .

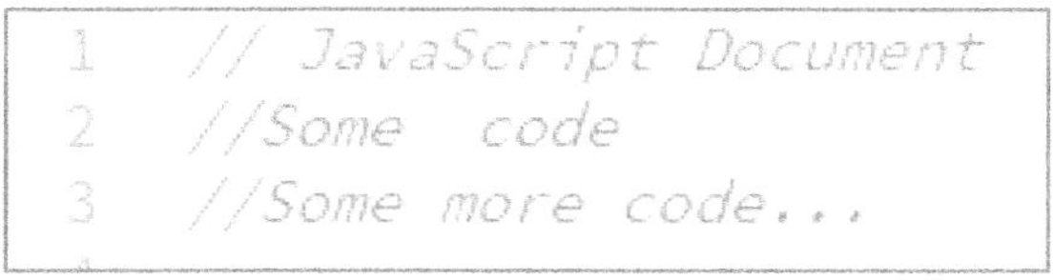


```
//JavaScript Document
//Some code
//Some more code...
```

Ln 1, Col 33

Figure 5-14. *How JavaScript appears in an program like Dreamweaver or Notepad ++ compared to how the code appears in Acrobat DC (no numbered lines)*

Web Links and References

For the full library, refer to version 10 for XI and DC:

`www.adobe.com/devnet/acrobat/javascript.html`

Current known support of JavaScript 1.8.
To learn more about JavaScript, visit `www.w3schools.com/js/`.

Regular Forms vs. E-Sign Forms

The E-Sign form tools are new to Acrobat DC and do contain digital signature fields for the document cloud. While they look similar, they do not operate the same as regular electronic form fields and do not allow for JavaScript. For those reasons, we will not be looking at them in-depth. However, if you would like to learn more about how to use them, read *Adobe Acrobat DC Classroom in a Book* by Brie Gyncild and Lisa Fridsma, especially Chapter 8 on signatures and security. For now, refer to Figure 5-15.

Figure 5-15. *Two types of form field tools found in Acrobat DC*

You can access the E-Sign fields shown in Figure 5-15 if you begin your Prepare Form by checking "This Document requires signatures" (Figure 5-16) and then clicking Start. For your forms in this book, this option should always remain unchecked.

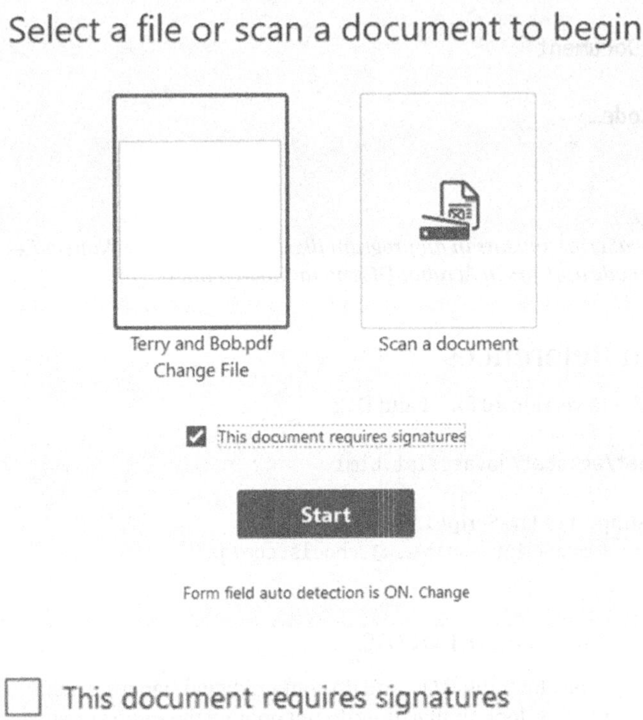

Figure 5-16. *How to create E-Sign forms. For the forms you are working with, keep this unchecked.*

JavaScript and Acrobat on the Document Level

In Acrobat, in order to have a solution you need to follow this equation: Trigger + Select Action = Result You Want

In addition to knowing what's being triggered, you need to know where the results are going to end up. In the case of forms, data or a value is going to be taken from a field (text, dropdown, check box, radio button, etc.) and the collection of that data is going to be deposited into a final field as the result you want. Whether using a value, simplified field notation, or JavaScript, it's important to know the exact name of those fields. If you do not know the exact name, you will not get a result and the form will be useless. To avoid confusion with fields, each must have a unique name.

The exception with naming is radio button groups, which act collectively; however, their groups must have distinct names. With all other fields, there can't be two or more named Sum1 within a form; it should be Sum1 and Sum2 and so on.

Follow along with the form examples provided in order to complete the lessons. The PDFs with the name "End" are the final result.

Summary

JavaScript can be added in a variety of areas; it all depends on what type of form field you plan to use. In the next chapter, you will see how a knowledge of JavaScript can improve forms that you use for creating calculations.

CHAPTER 6

Basic and Complex Calculations

In the first example of JavaScript calculations in this chapter, we will compare three methods: Value, simplified field notation (SFN), and JavaScript as found in the Calculate tab in the Text and Dropdown Menu form fields, as shown in Figure 6-1.

Example	Object 1	Object 2	Total
Sum (+)			
Product (x)			
Subtract (-)			
Divide (/)			
Average			
Minimum			
Maximum			

Figure 6-1. *Inside the Acrobat Calculate Tab Examples PDF file*

While Value is generally the most straightforward way of dealing with calculations for beginner form creators, you will soon discover that there are limitations to Value, so simplified field notation and JavaScript might be better options. This chapter will show the strengths and weaknesses of each method.

J. Harder, *Enhancing Adobe Acrobat DC Forms with JavaScript*,
DOI 10.1007/978-1-4842-2893-7_6

■ **Note** If you want to work along in this lesson or review the final result, download the Chapter 6 files from `www.apress.com/9781484228920`. The file with the label "Start" is the file without the code and the file with the label "End" is the final result. You will also find folders with original MS Word, Excel, and PDF files if you would like to edit them and a folder containing the original scripts if you would like to add them to your own PDF forms.

If you are creating your form from an original PDF, refer to the "Forms Review" section in Chapter 1.

Remember that to view the properties of a field you must select the Prepare Form tool; only then can you right-click or double-click a field to review its properties.

Getting Started

Let's take the addition or sum example, which is common to all methods regardless of which method or option you choose in the Calculate tab. Refer to the Acrobat Calculate Tab PDF file in the folder for this chapter. Refer to Figure 6-2.

***Figure 6-2.** The Calculate tab is common to all three methods we will discuss shortly*

Sum Value

In the Calculate tab, select the "Value is the..." button and pick sum (+) from the dropdown menu. Notice there are field names of some of the fields in the form in the grey area (Figure 6-3).

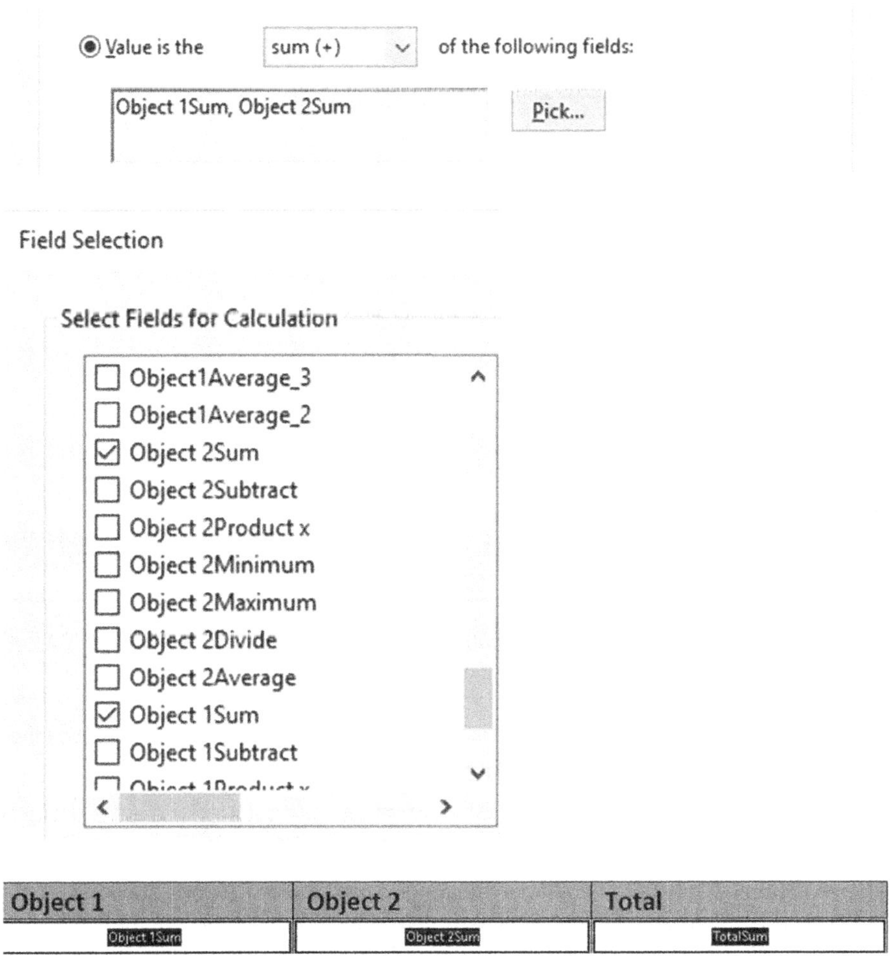

Figure 6-3. *Entering the sum value into the Calculate tab*

In this example and Figure 6-3, you are getting data or value from two fields: Object 1Sum and Object 2Sum. They add together in the field TotalSum to offer a result. These values were entered by selection using the Pick button.

Simplified Field Notation

Now let's look at simplified field notation. Notice in the Calculate tab in Figure 6-4 that the button called Simplified Field Notation is selected.

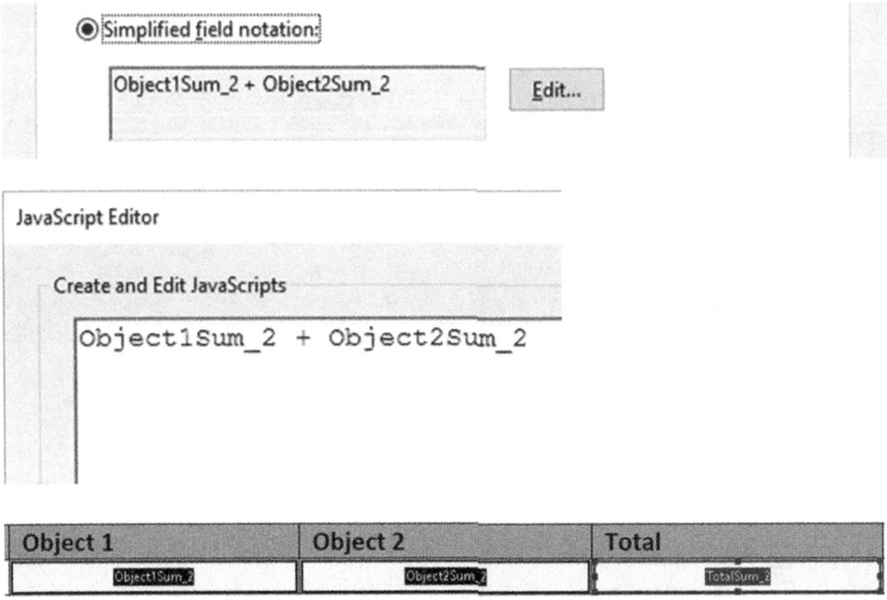

Figure 6-4. *Entering the simplified field notation into the Calculate tab*

■ **Note** With SFN and JavaScript you cannot pick or select your fields; you must type the information directly into the JavaScript Editor. Refer to Figures 6-4 and 6-6.

The second way of accomplishing this is SFN, which is common to a program like Microsoft Excel. While this is similar to the value sum example, there are differences. In the previous sum example, you could have spaces between the words in the fields. However, Object 1Sum in SFN must be written as Object1Sum. There can be no breaks using SFN. This rule is very strict. Any break in the name of the field and it will not calculate. If you need a break, use an underscore (_), as in Object1Sum_2 or use what is known as the camel method where each new word is capitalized, but with no breaks (ObjectSum).

Another difference to SFN is the addition of a plus symbol (+) to show that you are adding these two field values within the field TotalSum_2. If you were multiplying, you would use an asterisk (*), subtraction a minus (-), and division a slash (/). If you've ever taken algebra, you'll be familiar with parentheses (). Whatever occurs within them happens first before the calculation continues. Refer to Figure 6-5.

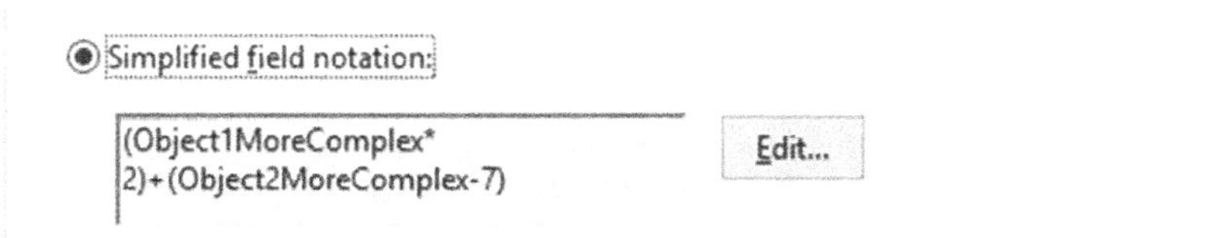

Figure 6-5. *Entering the SFN into the Calculate tab for a more complex calculation*

To type this code into the editor, you must first click the Edit button. Then you can type. When done, click OK to exit.

Here you can see (Object1MoreComplex*2) + (Object2MoreComplex-7) = TotalMoreComplex

If you put numbers into these fields, this should be your answer:

(5*2) + (10-7) = 13

JavaScript Custom Calculation Script

The final method we will look at is a custom calculation script. Figure 6-6 shows the "Custom calculation script" button selected.

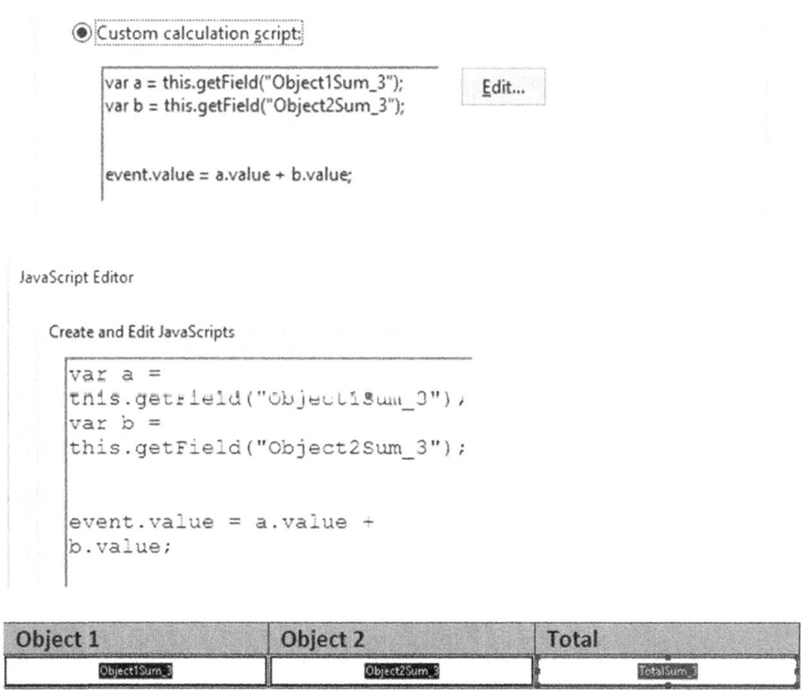

Figure 6-6. *Entering the custom calculation script into the Calculate tab*

To type this code into the editor, you must first click the Edit button. Then you can type. When done, click OK to exit.

In the case of JavaScript, you can again see that there are similarities and differences in the way the code is set up. In order to translate the fields into the language of JavaScript, you need to use variables to hold the fields. Variables act as information containers. In JavaScript, the word `variable` uses the short form `var`. After the word `var` you add a name. In this example, to keep it simple, let's use the name a. This variable called a will now hold whatever value comes into the text field Object1Sum_3. Once a variable is named the first time, it does not need to have the word `var` attached and can be used anywhere in the script as just a. To ensure that the number input will follow through correctly, add `this.getField` which means "get the data in this field." At the end of the variable, use a semicolon (;) to indicate that that is the end of this variable statement. The same is true for the second variable, b.

The final part of the script is

```
event.value = a.value + b.value;
```

It's very similar to the SFN example. However, you need to add the `.value` on the end of each variable to remind Acrobat that you want the value of each and the final value to be added in the final field. The final field, TotalSum_3, is represented by `event.value`. In this final field, the event of the addition taking place is the result. It is important to note that the final field does not need a variable name because of the way Acrobat contains the script within the final field.

Where the naming of variables is concerned, it's OK to have the names longer than one letter, like a. You can give them more meaningful names like age or `sum`. In the final example it would be written like this:

```
event.value = age.value + sum.value;
```

A few other things to remember about variables are

- All JavaScript variables must be identified with unique names.
- Names can contain letters, digits, and underscores.
- Names must begin with a letter.
- Names are case sensitive (y and Y are different variables).
- Reserved words (like JavaScript keywords) cannot be used as names. I would not create a variable like `var event` because `event` is a key JavaScript word used in the final event.
  For example,
  `event.value = age.value + event.value;`
  might not function since `event.value` has already been used once.

Final Thoughts

You have seen three ways in which addition can be done: Value, simplified field notation, and a JavaScript custom calculation script. However, which one is right for your project? Do you need to learn Acrobat JavaScript at all?

In most simple calculation projects, I recommend using Value or SFN in various parts of the form. However, if you take a look at the example, you will see Value and SFN do not equally cover all issues. For Value, you cannot subtract or divide. SFN cannot find minimum or maximum numbers. In this case, you may have to use a combination of both these calculations in your form.

Note JavaScript can do all of these calculation as well as many others. Also, as you will see in Chapter 12, when the JavaScript becomes more complex, it's not always a good idea to mix Values and SFN with JavaScript as this can lead to some fields not responding correctly. Consistent coding methods are crucial for form calculations to run smoothly.

For example,

```
var q = this.getField("Object1Minimum_3");
var r = this.getField("Object2Minimum_3");
event.value=Math.min(q.value,r.value);
```

You can use the JavaScript math formula `Math.min` to get my minimum number similar to the value example. You could use `Math.max` to get the maximum number. There are other math formulas that are not available to us via Value or SFN, but are with JavaScript:

- `Math.abs(x)`: Returns the absolute value of x.
- `Math.acos(x)`: Returns the arccosine of x, in radians.
- `Math.asin(x)`: Returns the arcsine of x, in radians.
- `Math.atan(x)`: Returns the arctangent of x as a numeric value between -PI/2 and PI/2 radians.
- `Math.atan2(y,x)`: Returns the arctangent of the quotient of its arguments.
- `Math.ceil(x)`: Returns x, rounded upwards to the nearest integer.
- `Math.cos(x)`: Returns the cosine of x (x is in radians).
- `Math.exp(x)`: Returns the value of Ex, where E is Euler's number.

- `Math.floor(x)`: Returns x, rounded downwards to the nearest integer.
- `Math.log(x)`: Returns the natural logarithm (base E) of x.
- `Math.PI`: Gives the formula of π.
- `Math.pow(x,y)`: Returns the value of x to the power of y.
- `Math.random()`: Returns a random number between 0 and 1.
- `Math.round(x)`: Rounds x to the nearest integer. Example: Round up a subtotal.
- `Math.sin(x)`: Returns the sine of x (x is in radians).
- `Math.sqrt(x)`: Returns the square root of x.
- `Math.tan(x)`: Returns the tangent of an angle.

From `www.w3schools.com/jsref/jsref_obj_math.asp`.

One final thing, which you could not do in this form without JavaScript is format the number 0. Sometimes on a form you do not want the 0 to be present if no calculation has been added to the first two fields; you just want it blank. Refer to Figure 6-7.

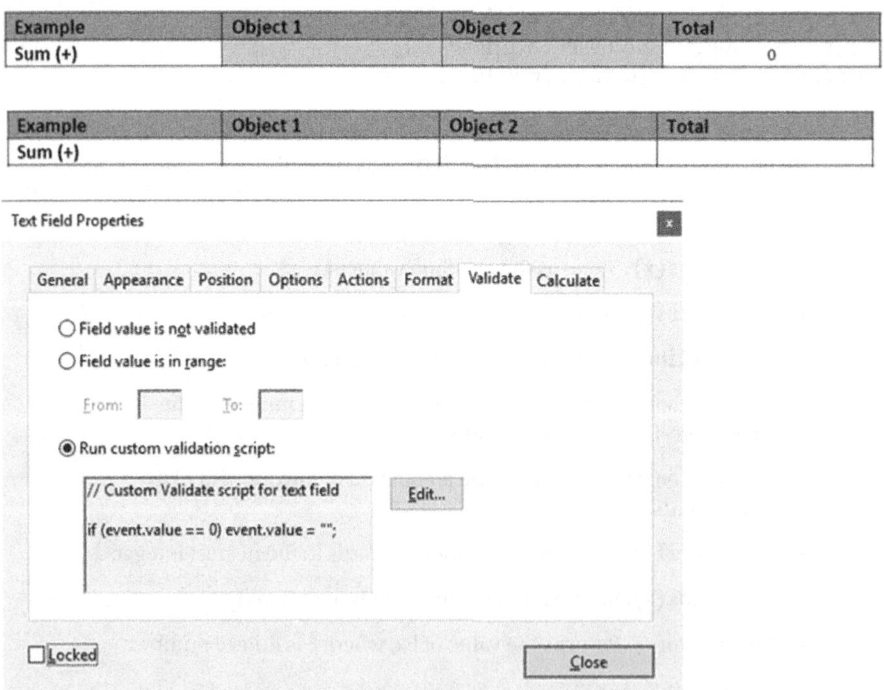

Figure 6-7. *Adding a validation script into the Validate tab of the Total field. Before and after adding the script.*

This looks better.

Along with the Calculate tab script, enter the following into your Validate tab:

```
// Custom Validate script for text field
if (event.value == 0) event.value = "";
```

To start off this script in text field Object1Sum_3, write a comment to remind yourself what you're doing.

A double slash (//) always starts off a comment. They can be written anywhere in JavaScript and will not affect the calculations. Consider them a place for helpful reminders.

Another type of commenting you can use is for longer, paragraph-sized comments:

```
/* This type of comment is for lots of text */
```

However, I generally prefer to use // due to the small space Acrobat provides.

The Final Line of Code

```
if (event.value == 0) event.value = "";
```

This is what is known as a conditional statement and you will look at them in detail later. Essentially it is saying, "if no value or number from the other two fields has been entered (both are blank), then leave the final value field blank as well."

One final item: If you used this script in subtraction or addition with negative numbers and you needed to see the 0, (Example: 5-5=0) you might not see the 0. If you need to see the 0 only when the fields are full, you can use a more complex and stricter validation.

== is not a strict comparison. A result like 5-5=0 might work, but 0-0=0 or 0x5=0 might not work because the validation regards 0 and a blank field as the same thing.

=== is a strict comparison, so now a result like 0-0=0 or 0x5=0 will work because the validation regards 0 and a blank field as not the same thing and will put a 0 in the results field. You could write the following to keep your 0:

```
if (event.value === 0) event.value = "";
```

However, Acrobat seems to act quirky and not get the intended result where the final field is blank if no values are added. So here's the alternate code:

```
//Sum Validation to insure 0 is not missing from an actual calculation
if (a.value !== a.defaultValue && b.value !== b.defaultValue) {
event.value = a.value*1 + b.value*1 ;
} else {
event.value ="" ;
}
```

This code allows you to have the field blank if no numbers are in the other fields and still retain the 0 if the final result is 0. In this case, you used !== (strict not equal) which is similar to strict comparison, ===, but in reverse and checks the current value against the default. If no value is found in both of the other value fields, the `event.value` will remain blank. Notice you used another conditional statement, if/else.

For other operators and comparisons refer to `www.w3schools.com/js/js_comparisons.asp`.

■ **Note** In the subtraction example, in the Calculate Tab Examples End Option 2 Validate PDF, change

```
event.value = a.value*1 + b.value*1 ;
```

to

```
event.value = f.value*1 - g.value*1;
```

For the code to operate correctly the values in the Validate tab must match what is in the Calculate tab.

When you are done viewing the forms, click the X in the upper right-hand corner of the Preview to close off the Prepare Form tool. Refer to the "Forms Review" section in Chapter 1 if you are unsure what this button looks like.

Dropdown Alternatives

As in Chapter 2, for this example, you can replace some of the text fields with dropdown menus to calculate. While similar to text fields, I find this method a good alternative if you want your client to use very specific values, and it eliminates the need for validation on each dropdown because the values are already set. You should not replace the final text field with a dropdown. Even though these Validate and Calculate tabs do work with dropdowns, the end result is really only one value. In Part 3, you will see how to use JavaScript to get more than one result into a dropdown menu when required.

■ **Note** With dropdowns I left the Validation blank because I was using specific numbers. Unlike text fields, there always is a value and never a blank value. Refer to the Calculation Tab Example that contains a Dropdown Menus PDF in the file folder for this chapter.

Summary

In this chapter, you looked at the three ways you can add calculations to your form fields using the Calculate tab.

- Value
- Simplified field notation
- JavaScript

While each example became progressively more complex, a broader range of possibilities opened up as you moved toward JavaScript.

You also saw how adding JavaScript to your Validation tab made it possible to see when the Total field was being utilized and when it was not. Giving clients accurate form information updates is important.

In the next chapter, you will explore how custom JavaScript can affect the Format tab when it comes to

- Number
- Percentage
- Date
- Time

CHAPTER 7

Format Calculations

In this chapter, you'll be working with Number, Percentage, Date, and Time formats using simplified field notation (SFN) and Value. Let's look at where it works and doesn't. You'll also need some JavaScript to assist you.

Like in Microsoft Excel (see Figure 7-1), sometimes you must work with different formats of numbers; you don't always deal with just 1+1. Other formats you might encounter are

- Percentage (98%)
- Date (June 25, 2014)
- Time (8:30 am)

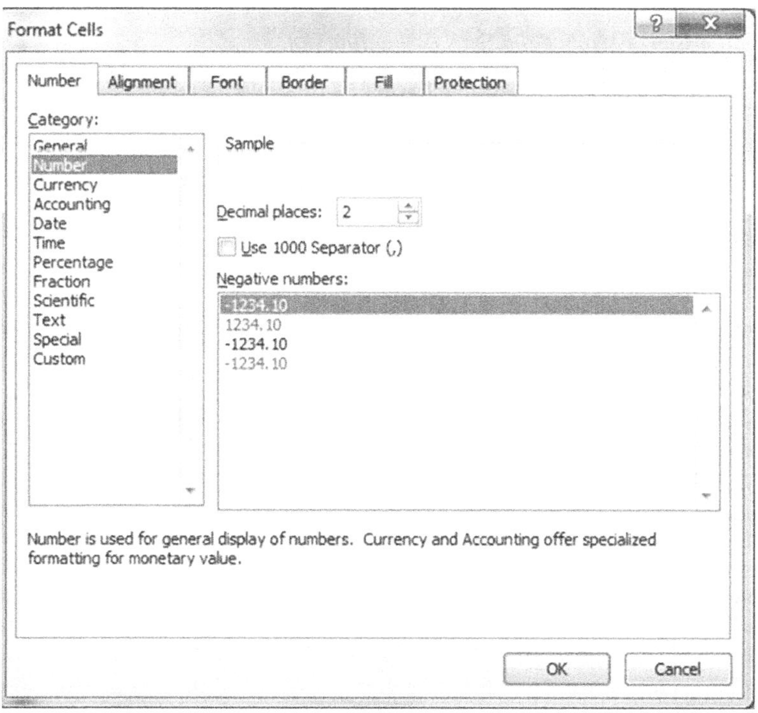

***Figure 7-1.** Formatting cells in MS Excel*

J. Harder, *Enhancing Adobe Acrobat DC Forms with JavaScript*,
DOI 10.1007/978-1-4842-2893-7_7

The same is true when you work in Acrobat.

Text fields and dropdown menus offer the options shown in Figure 7-2.

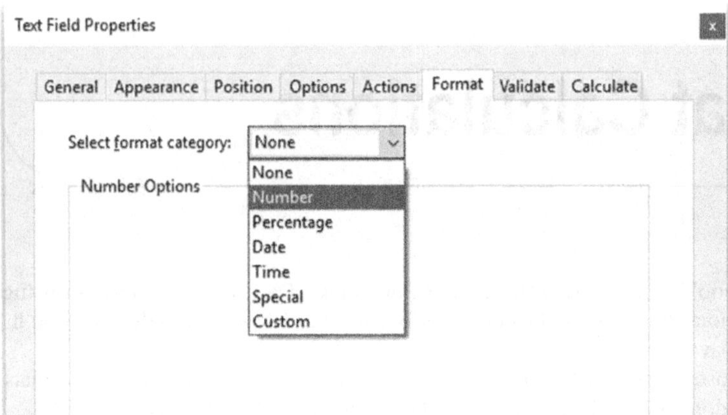

Figure 7-2. *Formatting cells in Acrobat DC*

Table 7-1 compares formatting in Acrobat to Excel.

Table 7-1. *Comparison of Acrobat and Excel Formatting Options*

Acrobat	Excel
None	General, Text
Number	Number, Currency, Accounting, Scientific
Percentage	Percentage
Date	Date
Time	Time
Special	Special
Custom	Custom
Possibly accomplished with Custom or using two separate formatted number fields	Fraction

As you can see, most formatting is similar. None or general is considered a default setting; the field could contain generic numbers or text. However, they would not be used in a calculation.

■ **Note** If you want to work along in this lesson or review the final result, download the Chapter 7 files from `www.apress.com/9781484228920`. The file with the label "Start" is the file without the code and the file with the label "End" is the final result. You will also find folders with original MS Word and PDF files if you would like to edit them and a folder containing the original scripts if you would like to add them to your own PDF forms.

Remember that to view the properties of a field you must select the Prepare Form tool; only then can you right-click or double click a field to review its properties.

Number Formatting

You can accomplish most of your calculations using a combination of Value and SFN. To view, refer to the Format Calculation Tab Example PDF in the file folder for this chapter. Refer to Figure 7-3 as well as the settings in Figures 7-4 and 7-5. For an additional example, refer to the Invoice Form PDF.

Format	Quantity 1	Quantity 2	Total
Number			0.00

***Figure 7-3.** An example of a field formatted with Number*

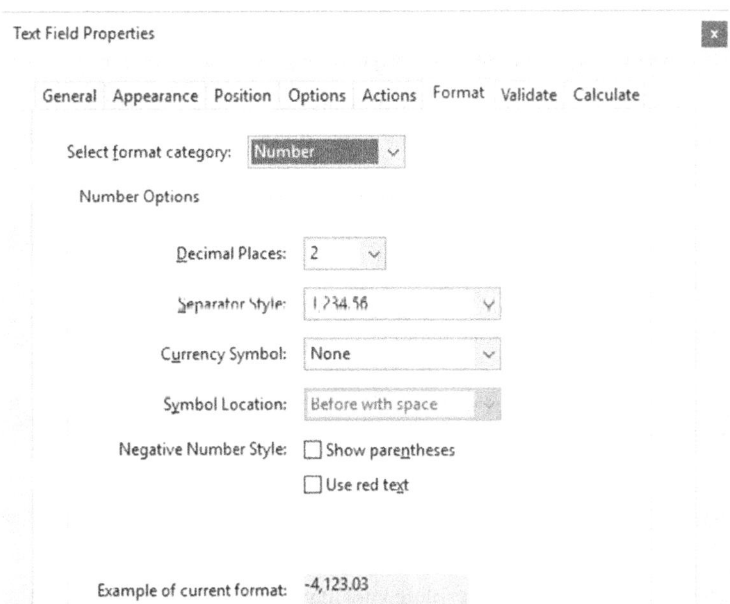

***Figure 7-4.** Settings applied to the fields in the Format tab*

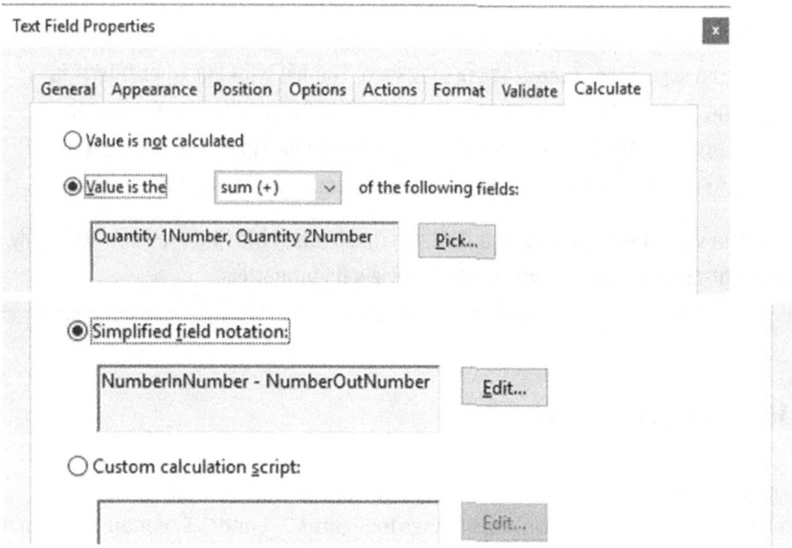

Figure 7-5. *Possible settings applied to the Total field whether it be Value or SNF*

However, as you saw in the math example in Chapter 6, sometimes when doing more scientific calculations (`Math.tan(x)`) you need to use a custom calculation script or JavaScript to assist you.

Formatting with a Percentage

Like Number formatting, Percentage works well with Value and SFN. To view, refer to the Format Calculation Tab Example PDF in the file folder for this chapter. For an additional example, refer to the Invoice Form PDF (Figure 7-6).

Format	Quantity 1	Quantity 2	Total
Number			0.00
Percentage	0.00%	0.00%	0.00

Figure 7-6. *An example of a field formatted with Percentage*

However, keep in mind when you type in 1, Acrobat interprets that to mean 100%, so if you want 1% you need to type in 0.01 and the 1% will appear as the number you entered.

A Workaround for the Percentage

If you are concerned that clients will not understand this formatting, you can add a helpful hint using JavaScript, which you'll explore later. If you don't want to add a helpful hint, another alternative is to improve this formatting. Let's create a custom formatting so that when 1 is pressed only 1% will be entered rather than 100%.

To do this, you need to create a custom format for each percent field that you will be entering percents into. Refer here to Figure 7-7. Fields that will not have data entered, such as the Total, which has been set to read only in the General tab, can be left as the format of Percent.

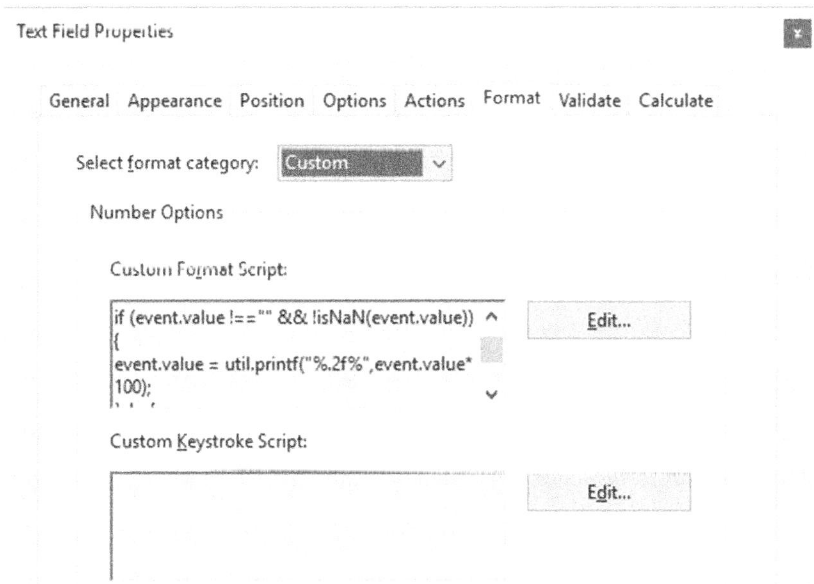

Figure 7-7. *Custom format script rather than Percentage added to the Format tab*

Note that your version may read Number custom or Custom options in the label area but this does not affect the calculations. Under the Format tab, enter the following code using the Edit button:

```
if (event.value !=="" && !isNaN(event.value)){
event.value = util.printf("%.2f%",event.value*100);
}else{
event.value = "";
}
```

Then add a custom validation to the Validate tab. Refer here to Figure 7-8.

```
if (event.value !== "") {
event.value = event.value / 100 ;
}
```

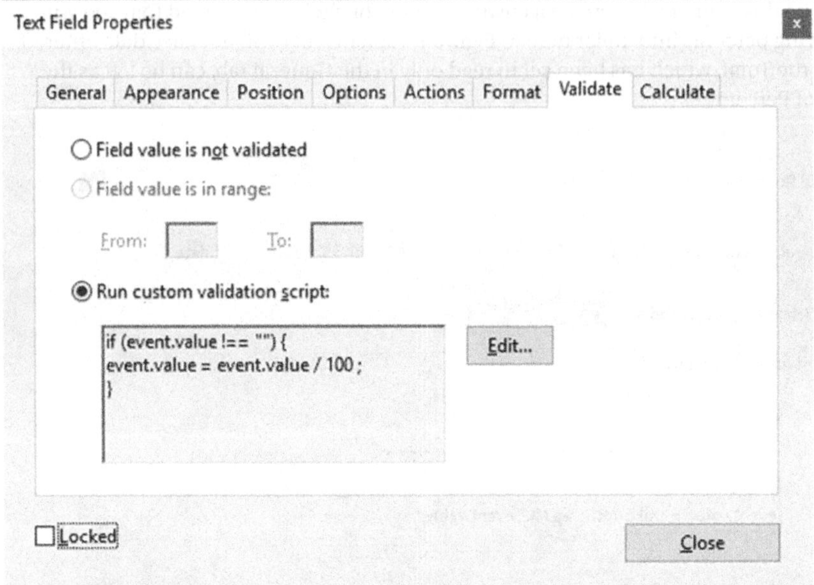

Figure 7-8. *Validation script added to the Validation tab*

Refer to the AcrobatFormTabCalcExamples_AlternatePercentageFormat PDF.

What you have done in this example is tell the field's validation to remain blank if nothing is entered. You then tell the formatting to disregard items that are not numbers. Then you ask it to display in the following manner using the above field calculation: it moves the math decimals so that it understands 1 to mean 1% rather than 100%.

```
event.value = util.printf("%.2f%",event.value*100);
```

The result you get when you enter a number is

```
Addition of Percentage:     1.00%     + 1.00% =     2.00%
```

As mentioned earlier, for the final summing field, you do not need to create any custom script. You can leave it as a percentage format and use either Value or SFN in the Calculate area. Refer here to Figure 7-9.

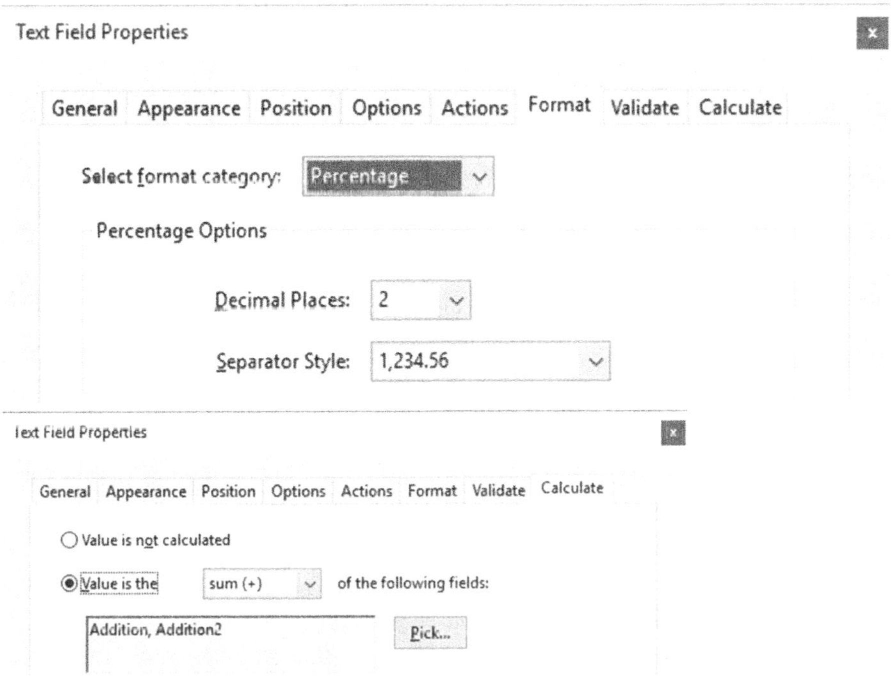

Figure 7-9. *Format tab and Calculate tab for the Total field*

■ **Note** Within the Custom Format and Validate tab is another example (Figure 7-7) of a conditional or if/else statement. If/else statements set a condition. "If" the following conditions are met, do whatever is within the brackets ({}). The other option, "else," in the code above gives the alternative. If "if" does not work, then do the "else," which is whatever is within its brackets. As you shall see later, for longer conditions you will also add additional conditions, "else if," between the if and else if you have more than two options.

Date Formatting

Date formatting is easy to do for one field. To view, refer to the Format Calculation Tab Example PDF in the file folder for this chapter. Refer to here to Figure 7-10.

Format	Number In	Number Out	Total
Number			0.00
Percentage	0.00%	0.00%	0.00
Date	Mar 3, 2015	March 9, 2015	6

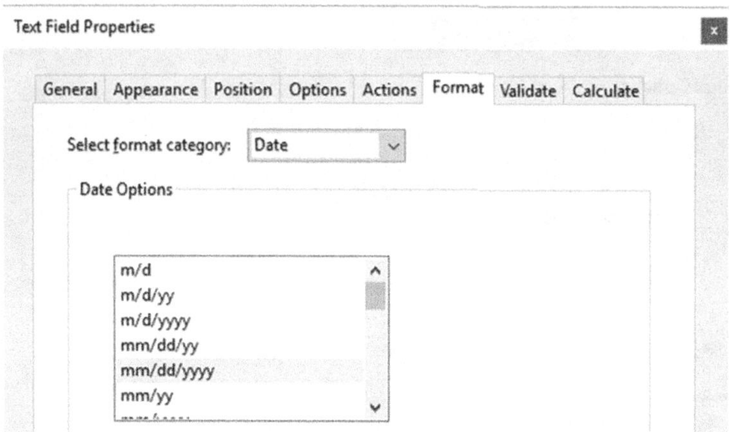

Figure 7-10. Selecting a format of date in the Format tab

However, when it comes to adding or subtracting dates from one another, Value and SFN do not work well.

```
Date:    March 3, 2015     + 1.00 =    4.2015
```

As you can see, this math makes no sense and trying to use two dates can often run into errors; refer to Figure 7-11.

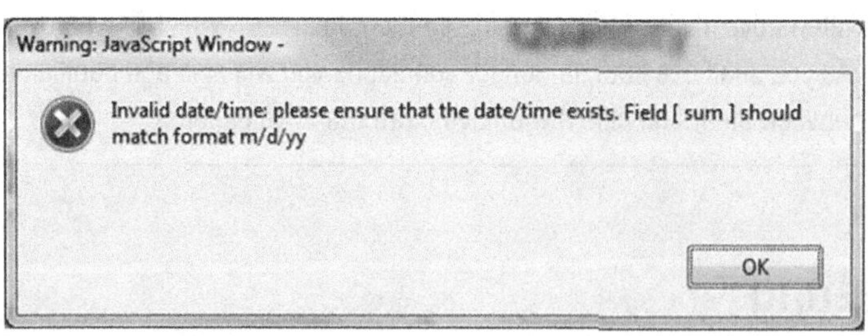

Figure 7-11. Example of an error warning that happens when you try to add two fields that are formatted with dates

Once again you need to look to JavaScript to assist you.

Suppose that you want to create a hotel form that deals with check in and check out dates. Refer to Table 7-2 to see an example.

Table 7-2. Table of Formatted Dates

Format	Number In	Number Out	Total
Date:	Mar 3, 2015	March 9, 2015	6

The Number In or DateStart field is formatted as a date. The Number Out or DateEnd field is formatted as None so it can have both text and a number in it. As mentioned, Acrobat does not like to add or do a calculation on two formatted dates. It prefers to work with one date and None or a Number format. Refer to Figure 7-12.

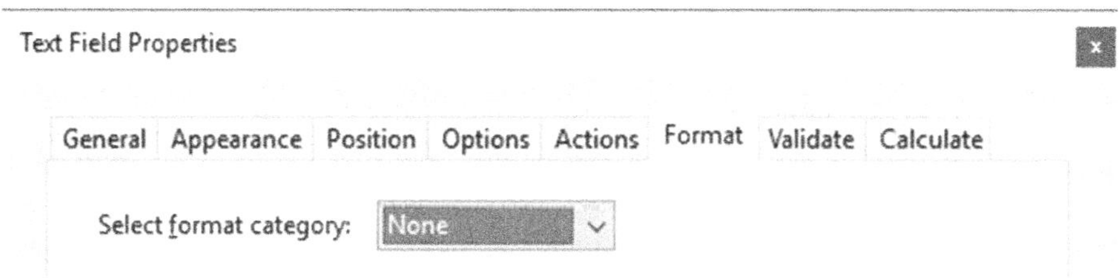

Figure 7-12. *Setting for the DateEnd field in the Format tab*

The Total field is formatted as number; with a custom calculation, it then takes over to complete the formula. Refer to Figures 7-13 and 7-14.

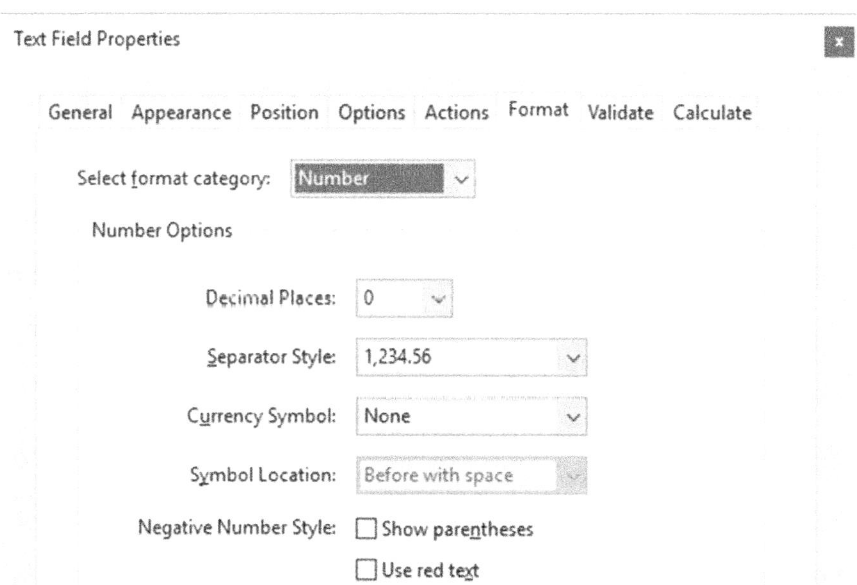

Figure 7-13. *Setting for the Total field in the Format tab*

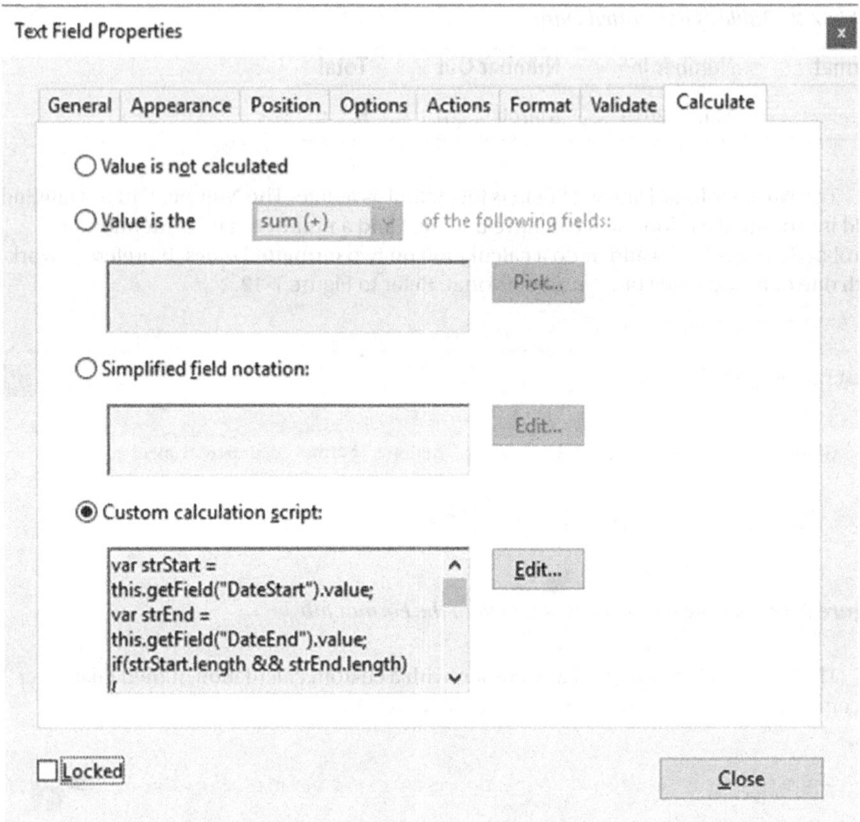

Figure 7-14. *Setting for the Total field in the Calculate tab*

The code is

```
var strStart = this.getField("DateStart").value;
var strEnd = this.getField("DateEnd").value;
if(strStart.length && strEnd.length)
{
  var dateStart = util.scand("mmm d, yyyy",strStart);
  var dateEnd = util.scand("mmm d, yyyy",strEnd);
  var diff = dateEnd.getTime() - dateStart.getTime();
  var oneDay = 24 * 60 * 60 * 1000;
  var days = Math.floor(diff/oneDay)+1;
  event.value = days;
}
else{
  event.value = 0;
}
```

The code grabs the start date and the end date and gets a value from each of them. Those values are then added into a conditional statement that says the solution will either be a number or "else" it will be 0. The if statement makes sure that the values of start date and end date are indeed numbers. Length helps you get a number and the length of each variable (`var strStart` and `var strEnd`) is checked against the formatting "mmm d, yyyy". It's important that this is the same formatting found in the Number In or DateStart field or this calculation will not work.

The `util.scand()` part of the code is a function that can convert any date string by using the date symbols, but it has to know the exact format of the date for this to work. Once this is done for both fields, the end date and start date are recognized as time using the JavaScript `.getTime()` method. This returns a number in milliseconds (Example: 1432672724073) which could be quite long. This is not the answer you want. You want to know how many days. Once the `getTime` of the dateStart is subtracted from the `getTime` of the dateEnd, you then figure out how long one day is and divide that from the result of the two dates.

`Math.floor` then rounds down to the nearest day.

You could not have done this calculation in Acrobat without JavaScript.

■ **Note** I added a +1 to the variable days because this gave me a more accurate number. Example:

```
var days = Math.floor(diff/oneDay)+1;
```

However, if you don't count half days, feel free to remove the `+1`.

Time Formatting

Time formatting is in many ways similar to date formatting. You can even add time to your date depending on what you intend for the field. To view, see to the Format Calculation Tab Example PDF in the file folder for this chapter. Refer here to Figure 7-15.

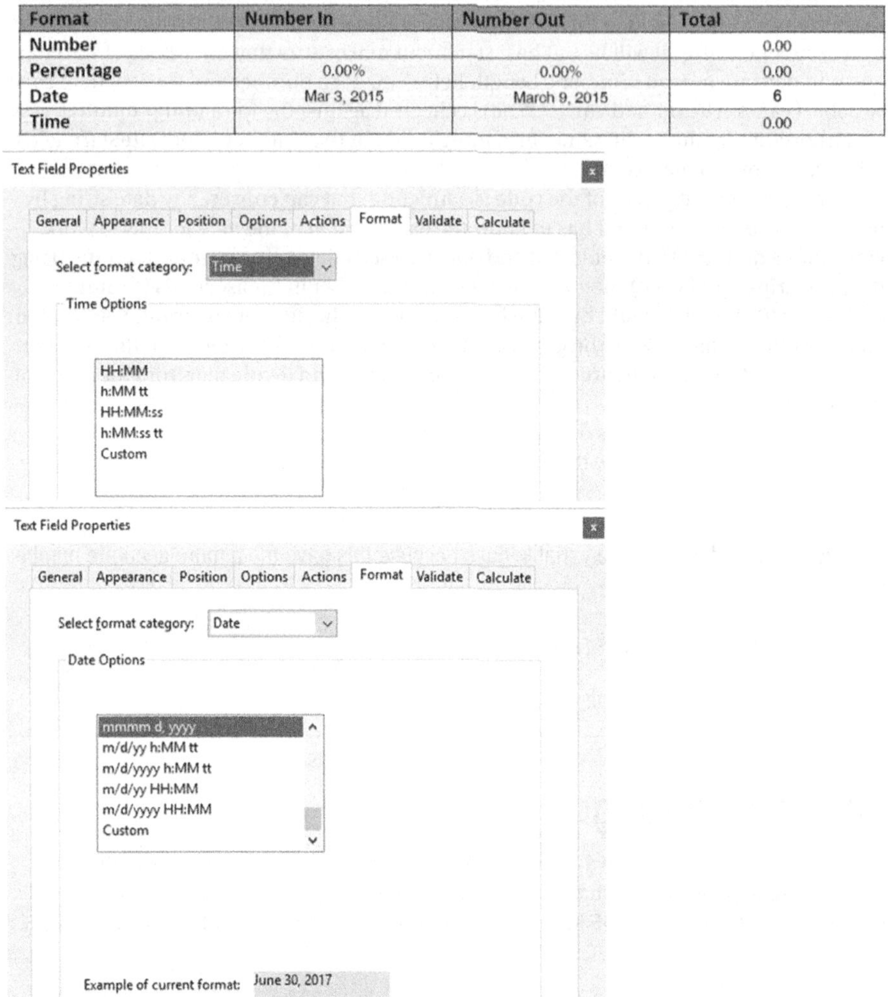

***Figure 7-15.** Comparison of Time and Date formatting in the Format tab*

However, while they're similar, you can use some SFN rather than JavaScript to do a simple subtraction of time.

To see how using a Value does not work well in the calculation area, refer to Tables 7-3 and 7-4.

Table 7-3. *Formatting Total Using Value in the Calculate Tab*

Format	Number In	Number Out	Total
Date:	12:15	27	39.15

Table 7-4. *Formatting Total Using SFN in the Calculate Tab*

Format	Number In	Number Out	Total
Date:	04:30	15:30	11:00

Now let's use SFN.

To make this work correctly, let's say Joe came in at 4:30 a.m. and left at 3:30 p.m. (formatted as 15:30). He therefore stayed a total of 11 hours.

Both NumberInTime and NumberOutTime fields are formatted this way. Refer here to Figure 7-16.

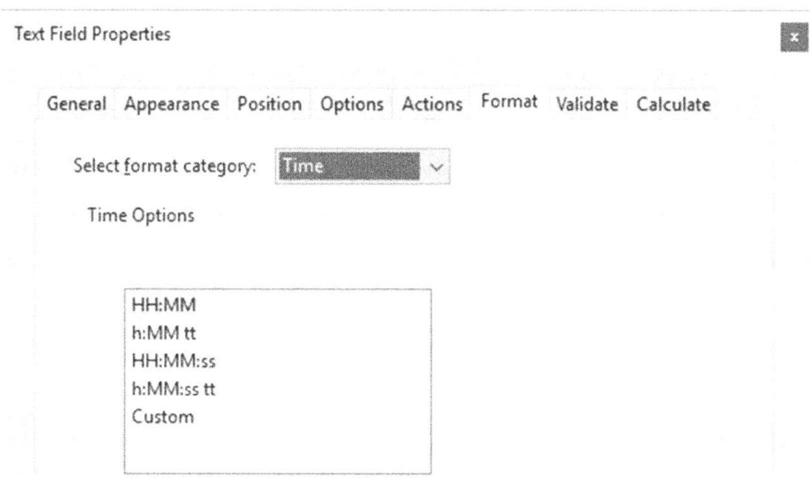

Figure 7-16. *Formatting the in and out fields with Time in the Format tab*

The TotalTime field is then formatted as a number. Refer here to Figure 7-17.

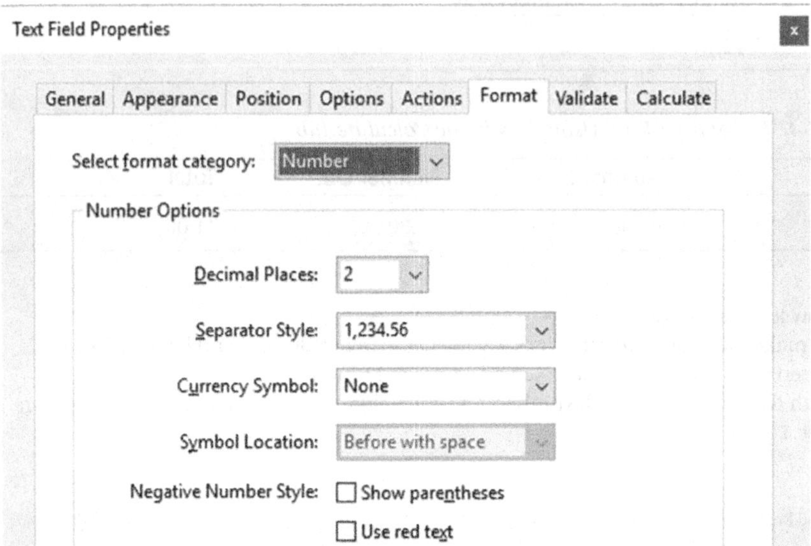

Figure 7-17. *Number format for Total field in the Format tab*

The last thing that is done is the SFN under the Calculate tab. Refer here to Figure 7-18.

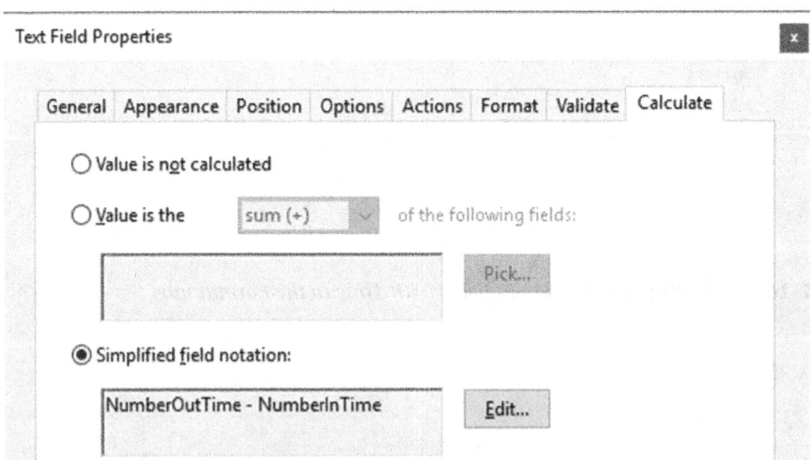

Figure 7-18. *Using SFN in the Total field in the Calculate tab*

NumberOutTime - NumberInTime gives you the number of hours that work was done in the day.

Final Thoughts

As you can see from the above formatting examples, there are times where you can use Value and SFN. However, in some cases they will not give you the results you want. If the calculation becomes complicated or scientific, you may need to look for a custom JavaScript to assist you.

Dropdown Alternatives

As in Chapter 2 and Chapter 6, there is a dropdown alternative in this chapter's folder, if your clients are required to enter very specific values.

Summary

In this chapter, you focused on using the Format tab while working in either text fields or dropdown menus.

You looked at formatting using

- None
- Number
- Percentage
- Date
- Time
- Custom

While Acrobat has some automatic solutions for some formats, in this case you needed to create either a calculation using Value, SFN, or JavaScript to get the results you wanted.

You also looked at how custom formatting interacted with code in the Validate tab. In Part 3, you'll look at the Validate tab in more detail.

In the next chapter, you'll look at how you can add various alerts to your document using JavaScript and add some JavaScript to buttons that will create notes and time stamps.

CHAPTER 8

Various JavaScript Alerts, Notes, and Time Stamps

As you have seen in previous chapters, JavaScript is very useful for forms when you want to do calculations.

However, sometimes you want to accomplish things that are non-form related.

In this chapter, you'll create an alert that welcomes a person when they open your PDF newsletter or catalog, like the one in Figure 8-1.

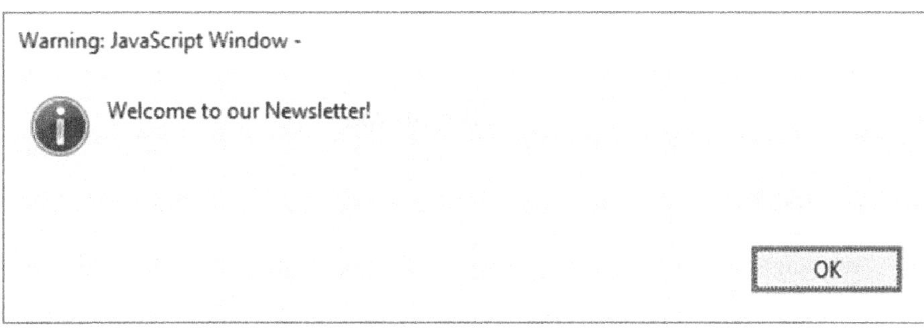

***Figure 8-1.** An informational message that appears when someone opens the Newsletter PDF file*

J. Harder, *Enhancing Adobe Acrobat DC Forms with JavaScript*,
DOI 10.1007/978-1-4842-2893-7_8

■ **Note** If you want to work along in this lesson or review the final result, download the Chapter 8 files from `www.apress.com/9781484228920`. The file with the label "Start" is the file without the code and the file with the label "End" is the final result. You will also find a folder containing the original scripts if you would like to add them to your own PDF forms.

If you are creating your form from an original PDF, refer to the "Forms Review" section in Chapter 1.

Remember that to view the properties of a field, you must select the Prepare Form tool; only then can you right-click or double-click a field to review its properties.

Alert Types

JavaScript has at least four alert types that you can use to alert your clients to an event. It also has four button types that you can choose from. Figure 8-1 shows the info/status type. I chose this because I did not want to scare the person with a warning, which this is not. It is more of greeting.

Table 8-1 provides a breakdown of the alerts.

Table 8-1. *A Table of Alert Types*

#	Icon Type	#	Button Type
0	Error 	0	OK
1	Warning 	1	OK Cancel
2	Question 	2	Yes No
3	Status/Info 	3	Yes No Cancel

In order to achieve this alert, you need to add it *globally*, which means that it is part of the whole document. When the document opens, you want to see this alert.

To do that, you need to go to the JavaScript tool in the Tools menu. Refer to Figures 8-2 and 8-3.

Figure 8-2. *The JavaScript tool*

Create a Document JavaScript

Now you need to choose Document JavaScripts from the JavaScript menu (Figure 8-3). To view, refer to the Newsletter PDF in this chapter's file folder.

Figure 8-3. *The JavaScript Tool menu*

When you first start creating your JavaScript for the document, the console will appear blank. No JavaScripts have been created, so you'll need to follow these steps.

1. Type in a script name. Refer here to Figure 8-4.

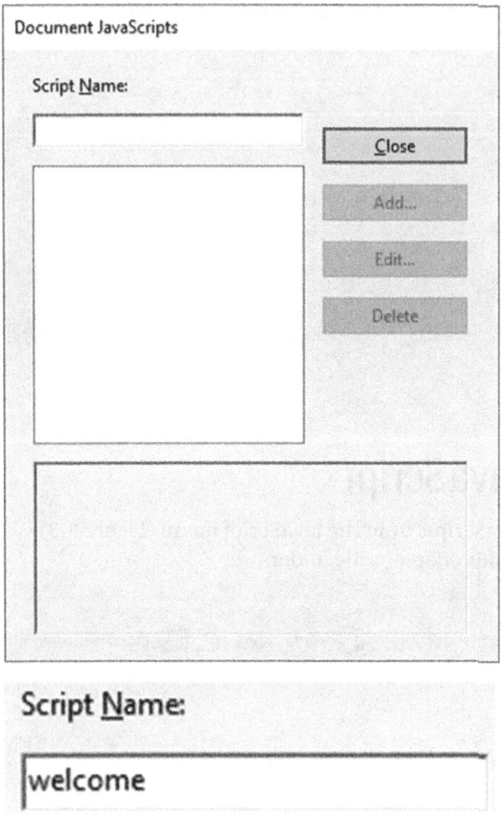

Figure 8-4. *The Document JavaScripts dialog box*

2. Then click the Add button on the right. Refer here to Figure 8-5.

Figure 8-5. *The Add button*

3. Enter the following script:

```
//Welcome Message on start
app.alert("Welcome to our Newsletter!",3,0);
```

The first line with the //, as mentioned earlier, is a comment. It has nothing to do with the function of the code; it is just a reminder of what the code is about.

The real code is this:

```
app.alert("Welcome to our Newsletter!",3,0);
```

It is calling up an alert message. Within this `app.alert()`, you can put your custom text ("Welcome to our Newsletter!" in this example). Then you chose what type of icon and button you want to appear. Refer here to Figure 8-6.

Figure 8-6. *The code and message typed into the JavaScript Editor*

- 3 refers to the Alert Icon type (in this case Status/Info). Refer to Table 8-1.
- 0 refers to the Button type (in this case, the OK button).

Depending upon the type of alert, you might choose other options

4. Click the OK button in the console when done typing.
   Save your work.

Viewer Version and Validation Alert

Let's say you want to make sure that your customer's version of Reader is up-to-date enough to accomplish certain tasks.

You might create your own Viewer validation script such as `viewerVersion`. Refer here to Figure 8-7.

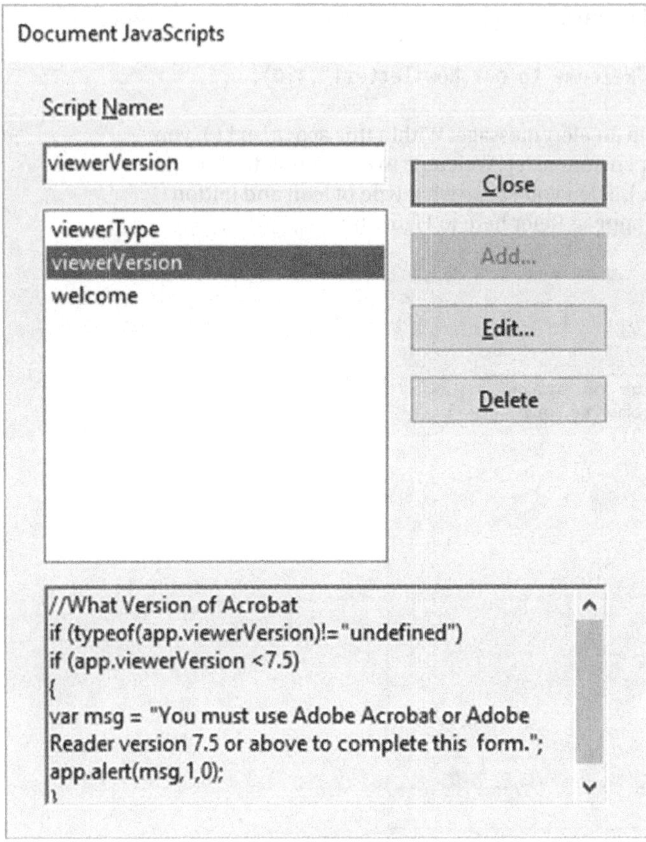

Figure 8-7. *Document JavaScript dialog box displaying three scripts used in the Newsletter PDF*

```
//What version of Acrobat
if (typeof(app.viewerVersion)!="undefined")
if (app.viewerVersion <7.5){
    var msg = "You must use Adobe Acrobat or Adobe Reader version 7.5 or
    above to complete this form.";
    app.alert(msg,1,0);
}
```

This code makes sure that when the document opens in Reader, the code interacts with the client's software and checks itself against the conditional statement and warns the client, using 1 (reference Table 8-1) if the version is earlier than 7.5, that they're going to have difficulty completing this form. The client then knows they need to upgrade.

You could also create a viewerType validation.

```
if (typeof(app.viewerType)!="undefined")

if (app.viewerType == "Reader")
{
var msg = "You must use Acrobat Standard, Acrobat Pro, or Acrobat Pro
Extended to complete this form.";
app.alert(msg,1,0);
}
```

If the client is in Reader and not Acrobat Pro, they might have an issue completing this form due to certain settings that the programmer is aware of. If you are in Acrobat Pro, this error is ignored.

When done, click OK and save your work.

■ **Note** If you think that your client may open their file in a different reader or PDF program, you may need to alter your code to reflect that. Remember that a program like Mac Preview may corrupt the JavaScript in your forms, so run a test of the alert with a client or coworker first.

Document Actions

Other types of global alerts may need to be set up in another area. Let's choose Document Actions. Refer to Figure 8-8.

Figure 8-8. *The JavaScript Tool menu*

In this Newsletter example, you can see two document actions. You know this because there is a dot beside each action that has been created. Refer here to Figure 8-9.

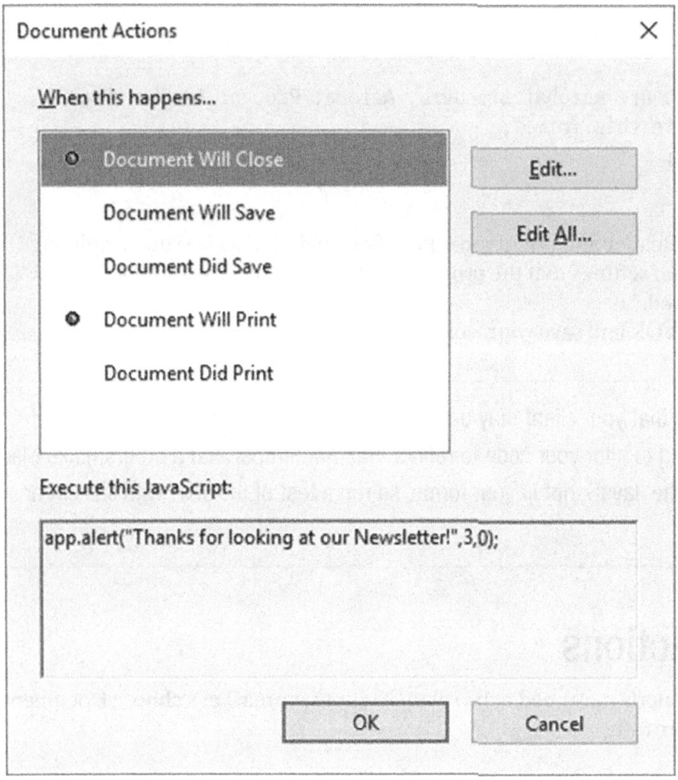

Figure 8-9. *The Document Actions dialog box*

Document Will Close

When the document closes, you might want to add a friendly goodbye to the customer to thank them for taking the time to read the newsletter. Click the Edit button to enter the following code:

```
app.alert("Thanks for looking at our Newsletter!",3,0);
```

Click the OK button when done.

The script is similar to the enter greeting; however, you need to enter it into this section in order for it to work.

Document Will Print

You might enter something like a message before the document prints:

```
var msg = "Hope you found what you were looking for."
app.alert(msg,3,1);
```

■ Note In this case, the message was written as a separate variable, var msg.

I could have written it as one line:

```
app.alert("Hope you found what you were looking for.",3,1);
```

And the same thing would have happened.

However, it is good to know how to write it the other way if you think your message is lengthy or you might use it more than once.

The other options available in this area are

- **Will Save**: Message appears before saving
- **Did Save**: Message appears after saving
- **Did Print**: Message appears after document prints

When you're done, click the OK button and save your work.

You will look further into global document JavaScripts later throughout the following lessons.

Alerts Working with Buttons

Not all alerts have to be global. Sometimes you want an alert only to happen on the push of a button or when you enter text incorrectly into a text box. To view this button, refer to Figure 8-10 and the Newsletter PDF on page 4.

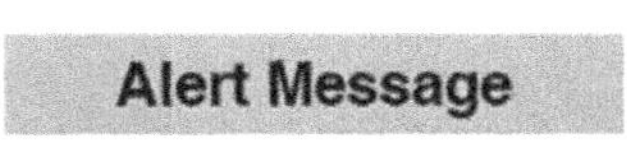

Figure 8-10. *The alert message button found in the Newsletter PDF*

You can create a button either in the Prepare Form area or Rich Media area. Refer here to Figure 8-11.

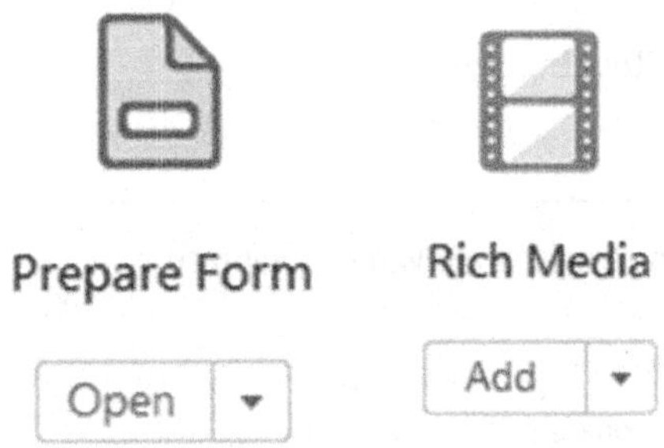

Figure 8-11. *Buttons are found in either the Prepare Form or Rich Media tools.*

You can then add an alert action to the button using a JavaScript in the Button Properties Actions tab. Refer here to Figure 8-12.

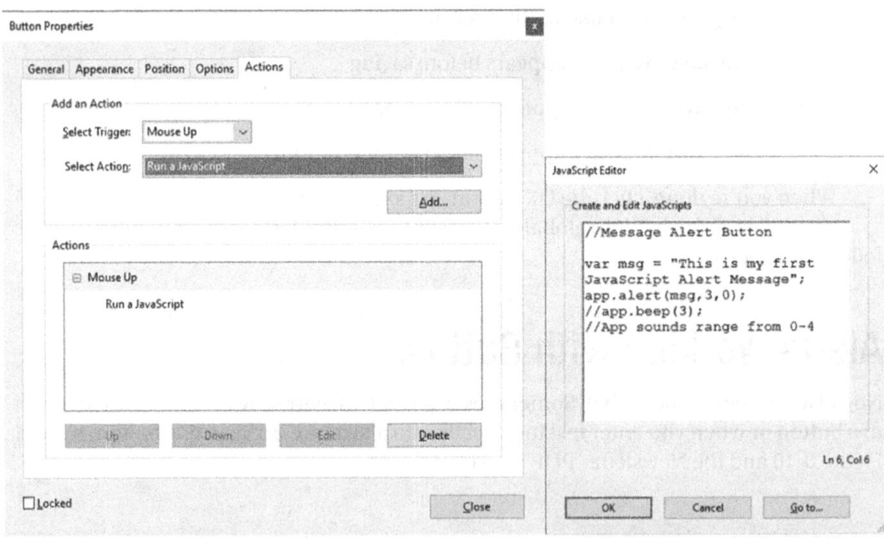

Figure 8-12. *The Action tab in the Button Properties dialog box running a JavaScript action. Text is entered into the JavaScript Editor.*

As before, you set a trigger of Mouse Up and select the action of "Run a JavaScript." Then you click the Add button and add the following text:

```
//Message Alert Button
var msg = "This is my first JavaScript Alert Message";
app.alert(msg,3,0);
```

Click OK to exit the editor, click Close to exit the Button Properties screen, and save your work.

Figure 8-13 shows the alert the button produced when clicked. You will look further into these types of alerts later.

Figure 8-13. *The alert message that was produced when clicked*

Adding a Comment Note, Signature, and Time Stamp

As you can see, buttons are great for alerts, but you can also use them to add both non-form and form items to a page.

For instance, maybe you want to encourage your client to add a comment to a specific page once they are done proofing it. You could add a button. See the Project Comment PDF to follow along. Refer here to Figures 8-14 and 8-15.

Figure 8-14. *A button that will add a comment or sticky note to the page*

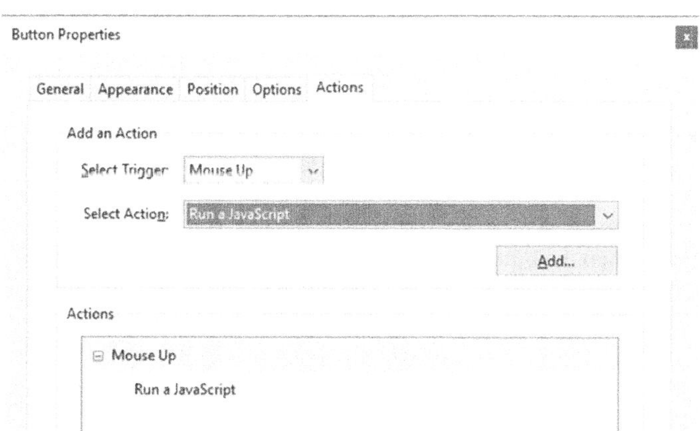

Figure 8-15. *The "Run a JavaScript" action*

Like before, in order to do this you need to run a JavaScript. Click the Add button. Refer here to Figures 8-15 and 8-16.

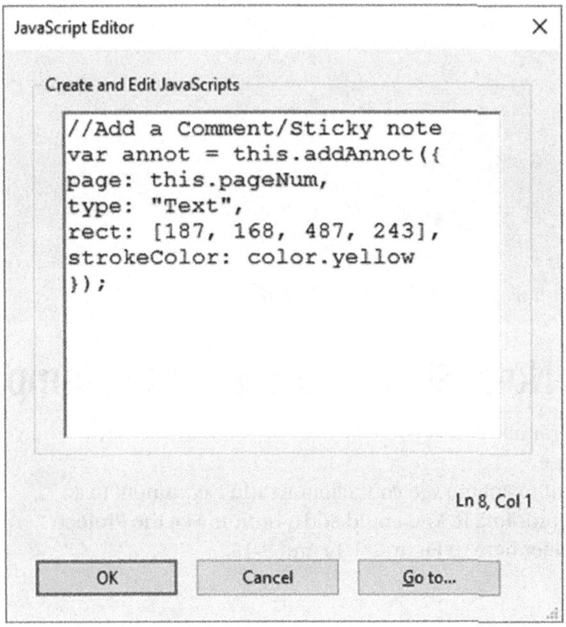

Figure 8-16. *Text entered into the JavaScript Editor*

This time you need to type

```
//Add a Comment/Sticky note
var annot = this.addAnnot({
page: this.pageNum,
type: "Text",
rect: [187, 168, 487, 243],
strokeColor: color.yellow
});
```

Here's what it means. When the button is clicked, it will call upon `addAnnot` or the annotation/comment. A comment sticky note will be added to the page that the button is on, `this.pageNum`.

It will allow you to add text. The type of comment will be set to certain coordinates on the page. This comment will have an icon color of yellow. Refer to Figure 8-17.

Figure 8-17. *Resulting comment when client clicks the button and then enters some text*

The client can then enter their text.

You will consider other types of color formatting later.

Another thing that you can do with a button is use it to add form fields and a time stamp. Refer to the Project Comment PDF and Figure 8-18.

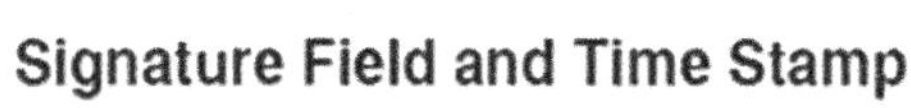

Figure 8-18. *The "Signature Field and Time Stamp" button*

Sometimes you want a button to do two things at once and this is a way of speeding up the process. Again, you run a JavaScript in the Actions tab. Refer here to Figure 8-19.

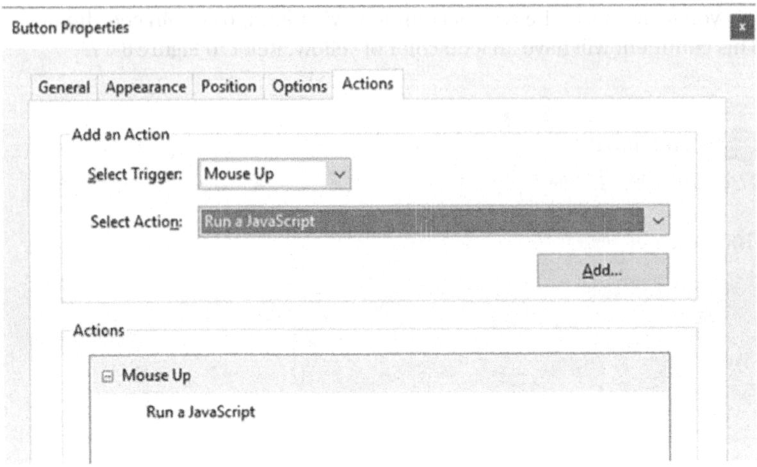

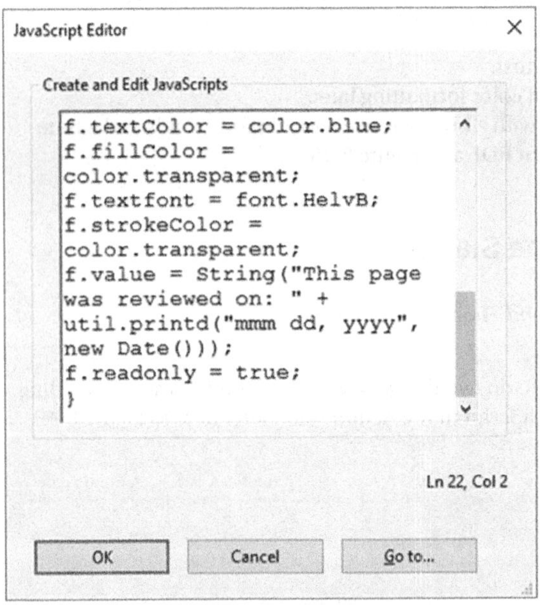

Figure 8-19. *The JavaScript added for the Time Stamp button*

Both scripts are in the same editor. Refer here to Figure 8-20.

Figure 8-20. *Resulting Signature field*

The signature

```
//Adding a signature field automatically
var c = this.addField({
cName: "clientSignature",
cFieldType: "signature",
nPageNum: this.pageNum,
oCoords: [35,74,176,112]
})
```

This first section controls where the signature is being placed. It has been given the name "clientSignature" so that it is identifiable because all fields need a distinct name. The type of field is a signature, which is for signatures only and not for

- Text: Example: `cFieldType`: "text"
- Button: Example: `cFieldType`: "button"
- Dropdown: Example: `cFieldType`: "combobox"
- List Box: Example: `cFieldType`: "listbox"
- Check box: Example: `cFieldType`: "checkbox"
- Radio Button: Example: `cFieldType`: "radiobutton"

Time stamp

This Page was viewed on May 27, 2015

```
//script that creates the text field
{
var r = [200, 200, 400, 300];
var i = this.pageNum;
var f = this.addField(String("completeDate."+i),"text",i,r);
f.textSize = 10;
f.alignment = "right";
f.textColor = color.blue;
f.fillColor = color.transparent;
f.textfont = font.HelvB;
f.strokeColor = color.transparent;
f.value = String("This page was reviewed on: " + util.printd("mmm dd, yyyy",
new Date()));
f.readonly = true;
}
```

Next, the time stamp is added to the page with today's date.

■ **Note** You can format its color to blue and choose a font as well. This text ("This page was reviewed on: Date") is now locked in, because `readonly` was set to true. If you want this text to be edited in some way later, you could have set it to false. This is what is known as a Boolean expression; it can only ever be true or false.

You will look at other reasons to format text and the fields later.

Summary

In this chapter, you added some global alerts to your document and alerts to buttons as well. You also discovered that you can use buttons to create comment/sticky notes, signature fields, and time stamps. As you can see, alerts are useful for non-form documents and adding comments.

In the next chapter, you'll take a look at how alerts can assist you in forms.

CHAPTER 9

Create Help for Clients with Rollover Text and Alerts

In Chapter 4, you learned that you can create a small help menu with the order form using buttons that hide and show. However, if you need your text to be more detailed, this method might not always be the best solution. Luckily, in Acrobat there are a few other methods you can use that can assist you with creating help for your client.

Note If you want to work along in this lesson or review the final result, download the Chapter 9 files from `www.apress.com/9781484228920`. The file with the label "Start" is the file without the code and the file with the label "End" is the final result. You will also find a folder containing the original scripts if you would like to add them to your own PDF forms.

If you are creating your form from an original PDF, refer to the "Forms Review" section in Chapter 1.

Remember that to view the properties of a field you must select the Prepare Form tool; only then can you right-click or double-click a field to review its properties.

J. Harder, *Enhancing Adobe Acrobat DC Forms with JavaScript*,
DOI 10.1007/978-1-4842-2893-7_9

The Rollover Method

Let's look at the rollover method first. Refer here to Figure 9-1.

Figure 9-1. *When you roll over a text field, different information appears in the red text box to give your client a hint*

In this example (see the Rollover End PDF), you can see that when a client moves over a field, the red box in the upper corner of the form provides a helpful hint so that they know what to type if they're not sure. This is very useful when a client needs to know how to type in the correct date format. A hint is always welcomed.

As the client moves out of the field, it becomes blank again until the next field is rolled over. The client now knows what to type and errors are avoided when the form is returned to you.

In this example, the following fields are all controlled by a JavaScript globally and within the fields:

- Customer Full Name
- Date
- Order Code
- Customers Company Name

The red help box, txtHelp, has no JavaScript internally; however, it is referenced globally by all fields.

First, let's take a look at the global or document JavaScripts. In the JavaScript tool, select Document JavaScripts. Refer to Figures 9-2 and 9-3.

Figure 9-2. *The JavaScript tool*

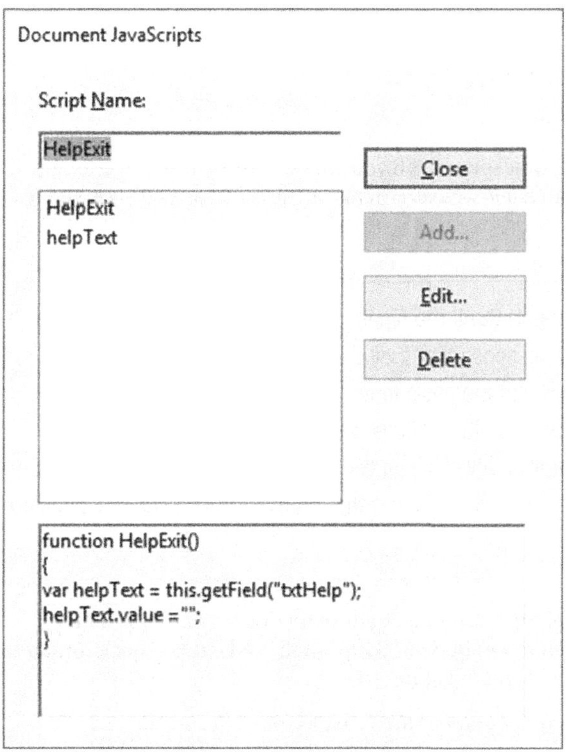

Figure 9-3. *Document JavaScripts*

You can see there are two document JavaScripts.

HelpExit is a global function that controls those fields that will be accessing the red stroked help field, txtHelp.

As the user exits the field, it returns to a blank state.

```
function HelpExit()
{
    var helpText = this.getField("txtHelp");
    helpText.value ="";
}
```

The other JavaScript is helpText; this function contains an array.

```
var gHelpText = [ // Create a variable, gHelpText
    "What's your full name?", //String#0
    "mm/dd/yyyy", //String#1
    "Your customer code is on the form that was emailed to you.", //String#2
    "What's your Company Name?" //String#3
]
```

An array is written with the [] brackets, which you will see more of later. It contains multiple variables or strings within itself. These variable strings can then be accessed by other fields.

■ **Note** JavaScript seems to support the three types of arrays: indexed, objects (a.k.a. associative arrays), and nested (in the sense that they can hold an array within an array). In this chapter, you have been looking at the basic index type which, even though no actual numbers are in the array, based on the order you can still call on a number or string reference from 0-3. In Chapter 12 and 13, you will see examples of more complex associative arrays or objects which deal with words rather than numbers to do the indexing; these array/objects will be nested.

Now let's take a look at one of the fields that needs help: Customer's Full Name.

In the case of the four fields that are showing "help" in the red stroked box, they all have the following two JavaScripts. Refer to Figure 9-4.

- When the mouse or cursor enters, run a JavaScript.
- When the mouse or cursor exits, run a JavaScript.

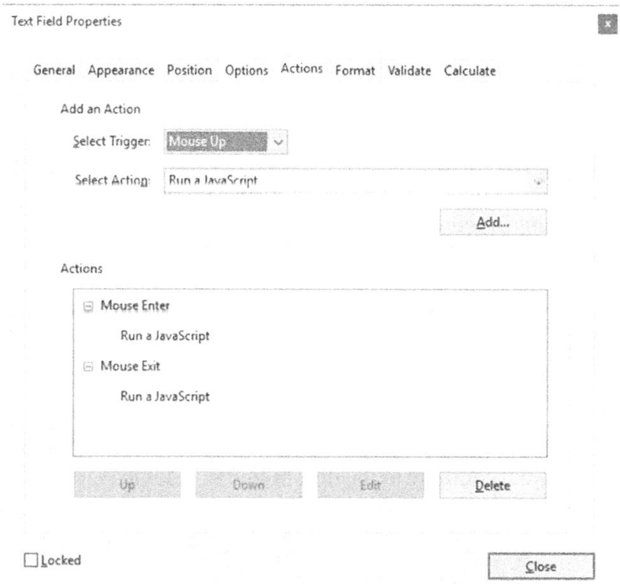

Figure 9-4. *Run a JavaScript on Mouse Enter and Mouse Exit*

Mouse Enter

```
var helpText = this.getField("txtHelp");
helpText.value =gHelpText[0];
```

As the mouse enters the field, JavaScript is asked to access some text from the document JavaScript `helpText` function array `gHelpText`. With arrays, the number 0 always represents the first item in an array, like so:

```
0= "What's your full name?"
1= "mm/dd/yyyy"
2= "Your customer code is on the form that was emailed to you."
3= "What's your Company Name?"
```

And so on, if there were more items in the array.

In the case of the Date field, you can see it is the same except for the number in the array you accessed. This time the Mouse Enter setting is 1. For the Order Code field, it's 2, and for the Customer's Company Name field, it's 3.

```
var helpText = this.getField("txtHelp");
helpText.value =gHelpText[1];
```

Mouse Exit

```
HelpExit();
```

In the case of the mouse exit portion, all actions will be the same for all four fields. When the mouse or cursor exits the red stroked help box, it becomes blank.

Writing global document JavaScript like this can be helpful if for some reason you need to change some code inside this function. Any field that had this function attached would now do the new action rather than you having to go manually through and change each one.

Extra Non-Custom JavaScript Check Box Example

As in the form in Chapter 4, there are the examples of the Shipping Address hide and show text fields. Review this area if you can't remember how it works. However, this area contains no custom JavaScript, so we'll continue to the next example. Refer to Figure 9-5.

Figure 9-5. *Review of Shipping Address check box and button examples*

The Default Text Method

The rollover is a good method for some forms, but on others it may not work well, such as when fields are near the bottom of the page or forms that are two pages or more. As with forms on the Internet, the default text is sometimes found within the actual field. You can add default text to a field in the Options tab. However, when the user clicks that field, the text does not disappear; it remains. You have to select the text first and then delete it. This can become awkward and frustrating to the client who just wants to start typing. Refer to Figure 9-6. Add this to blank text field and test it.

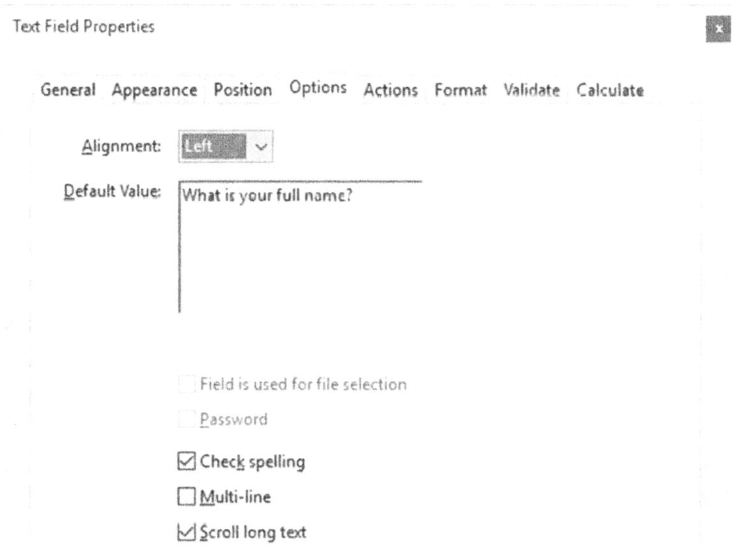

Figure 9-6. *Adding default text to the Text field in the Options tab*

Instead of adding the default text here, you can create a custom format in the Format tab with this script. Refer here to Figures 9-7 and 9-8.

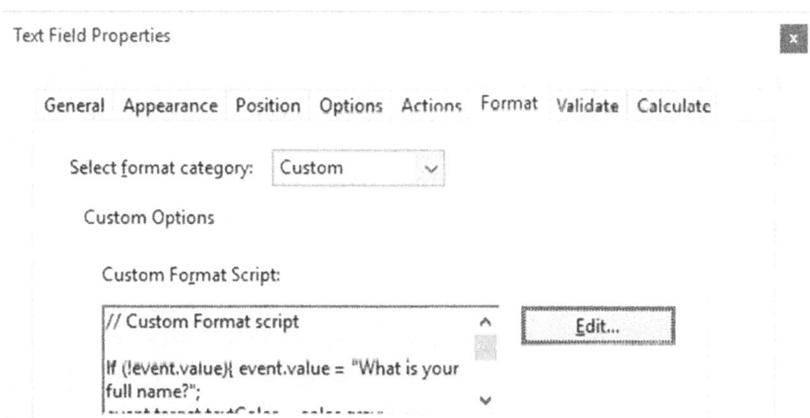

Figure 9-7. *Adding a custom script to the Format tab*

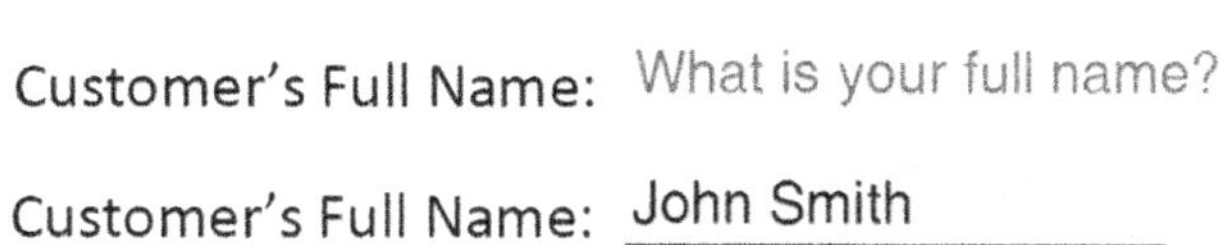

Figure 9-8. *Custom default text (top) and the text entered (bottom)*

See the Text End PDF file for this exercise.

```
// Custom Format script
if (!event.value){
    event.value = "What is your full name?";
    event.target.textColor = color.gray;
}
else{
    event.target.textColor = color.black;
}
```

Figure 9-8 shows the difference.

In this example, the default text is grey as long as nothing is in the field and will disappear when the field is clicked and the new text is typed in. The new text will be black. You can apply this same code to the Customer's Company Name field. No global or JavaScript actions need to be applied.

For some text boxes this is a good method. However, for other boxes that have explanations longer than the field or must also be formatted as a date or number, using this custom format may not be ideal. Let's look at another option for those instances.

■ **Note** `if (!event.value)` becomes a type of Boolean or a true and false statement (if not) when you add the exclamation point. In this case of default text, if there is no value entered in the text field, here is what you should fill it with. Without this exclamation point, the default text will not fill in.

The Alert Method

Is there some other way that the message can move along with the client as they enter fields down the form? Yes, it can be done with alert boxes. Another cool feature of alert boxes is if you set them up correctly, you can enter text into them and the text will then be transferred to the correct form field. Refer to Figure 9-9.

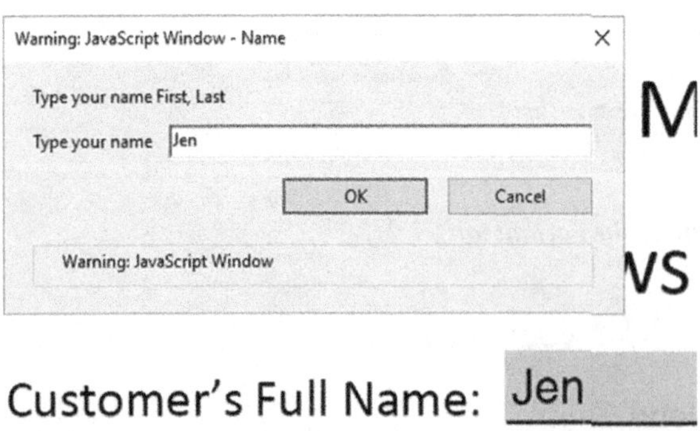

Figure 9-9. *Text is entered into an alert box and is then entered into the field once the user clicks OK and then tabs out of that field*

In this example (see the Alert End PDF file), there is no global document JavaScript so we can skip that area for now.

Again there are four text fields:

- Customer's Full Name
- Date
- Order Code
- Customer's Company Name

This time there is no red-stroked txtHelp field; you will use the alert boxes to do that work.

Customer's Full Name

This time you will only run one JavaScript per field. Do not worry about an exit function because the alert box will take care of that for you, as you shall see. In this case, use On Focus, which activates when anyone clicks into the box. Refer to Figure 9-10.

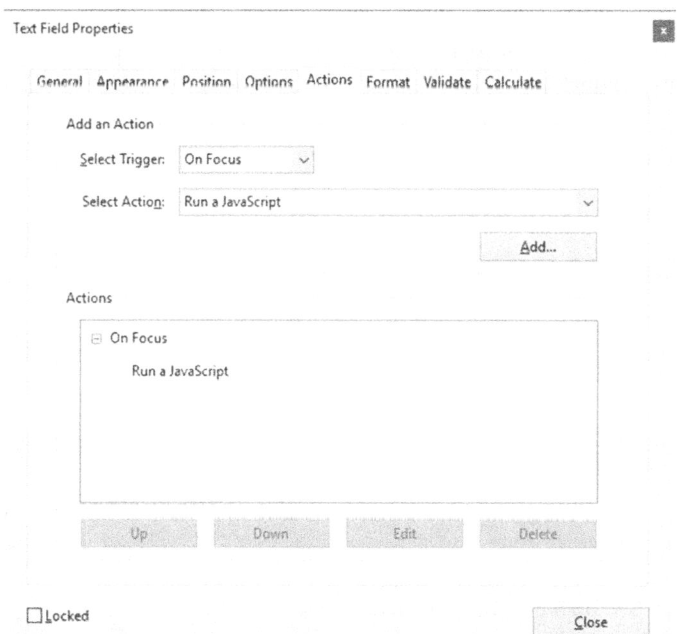

Figure 9-10. *Run a JavaScript in the Actions tab*

This is the code:

```
var t = event.target; // the target field
var cResponse = app.response({
    cQuestion: "Type your name First, Last",
    cTitle: "Name",
    cDefault: "Name not added",
    cLabel: "Type your name"});
{
    if (cResponse == null){ // if Cancel is selected
    app.alert ("You cancelled adding your name.");
    cResponse = "";
    }
    else{
    app.alert("You typed your name as: \""+cResponse+"\" \n\n Tab out of the
    field to register your name",3);
    }
}
t.value = cResponse; // places the data from the dialog to the target field
```

In Figure 9-11, you can see that the Alert creates a description and a space for the user to type their name as requested.

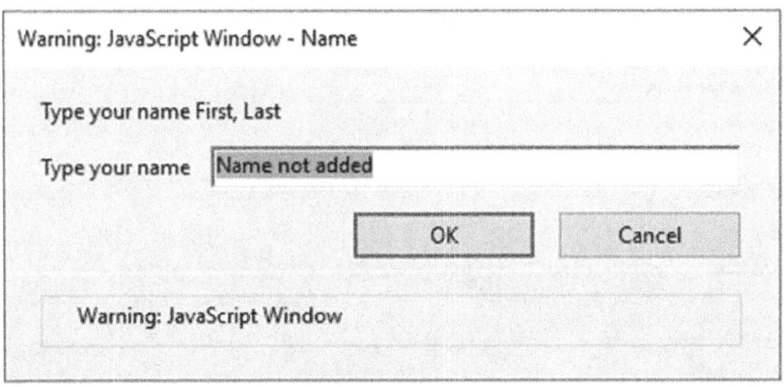

Figure 9-11. *The JavaScript help message*

If the user hits cancel, the warning they will get is “You cancelled adding your name.” And the text field will go back to blank. Refer to Figure 9-12.

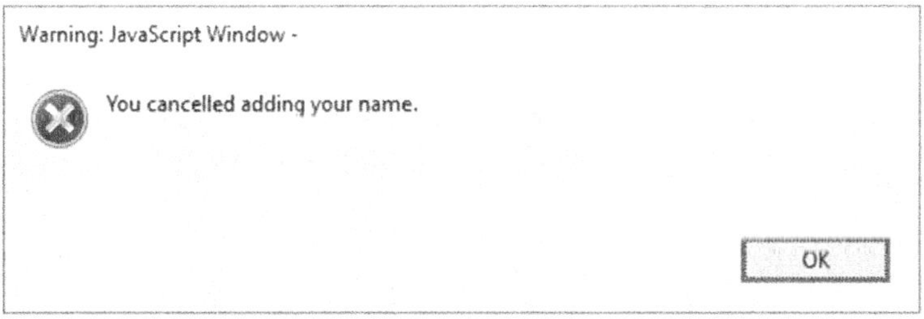

Figure 9-12. *The JavaScript warning when the user hits cancel*

If the user types in their name, they get "You typed your name as: [*client name*]". Once the client tabs out of that field, their name is confirmed. Refer to Figure 9-13.

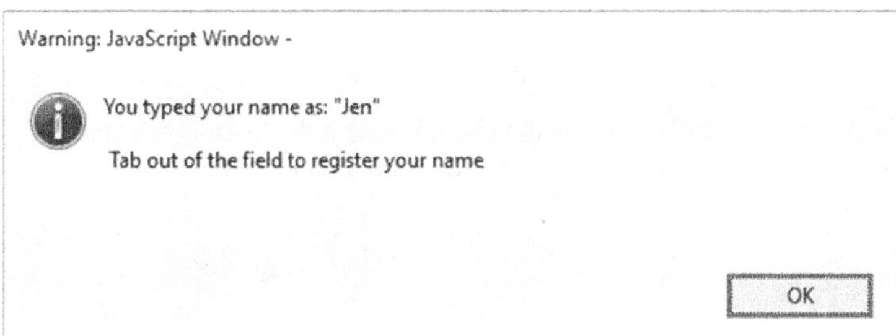

Figure 9-13. *The JavaScript confirmation after the user clicks OK*

Let's move to the next field. Notice how again you use the if/else condition to get two possible answers.

Date

The Date field behaves in a similar fashion. However, remember to make sure this field is formatted to a date that matches the text. Refer to Figure 9-14.

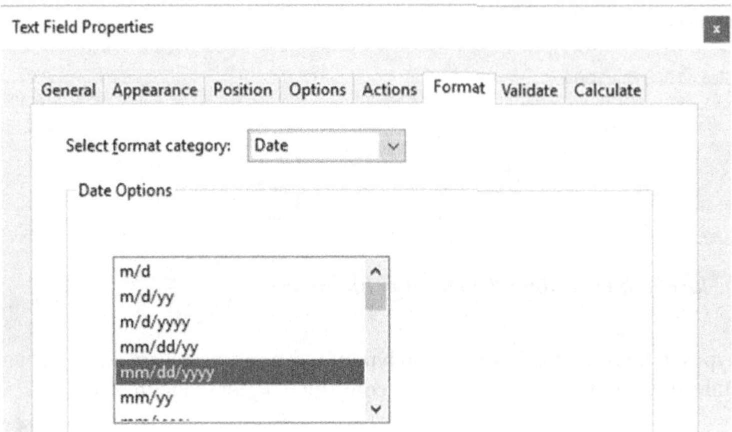

***Figure 9-14.** The Date Options menu in the Format tab*

Now go to the Actions tab and use the same setting as with the Customer's Full Name, altering the text to suit your needs. Refer to Figures 9-15 and 9-16.

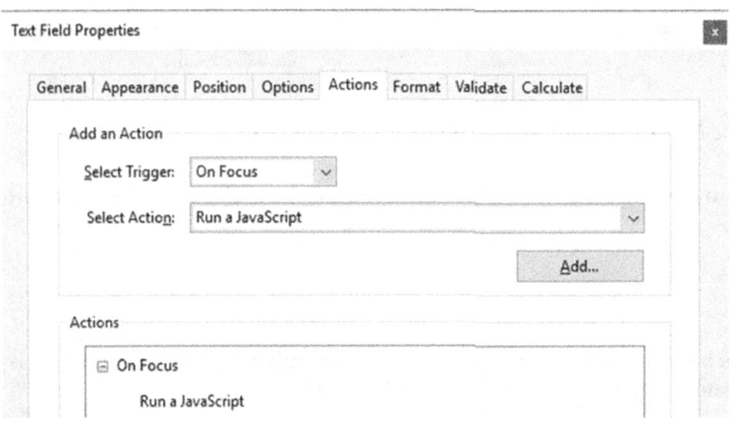

***Figure 9-15.** Run a JavaScript for the Date field*

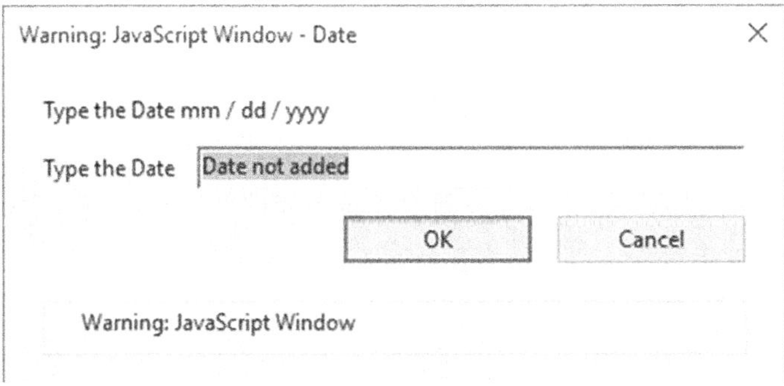

***Figure 9-16.** JavaScript help message for the Date field*

The code:

```
var t = event.target; // the target field
var cResponse = app.response({
    cQuestion: "Type the Date mm / dd / yyyy",
    cTitle: "Date",
    cDefault: "Date not added",
    cLabel: "Type the Date"});
{
    if ( cResponse == null){ // if Cancel is selected
        app.alert ("You cancelled adding the date.");
            cResponse = "";
    }
    else{
    app.alert("You typed the date as: \""+cResponse+"\" \n\n Tab out of the
    field to register the date",3);
    }
}
t.value = cResponse; // places the data from the dialog to the target field
```

Customer Order Code

You will construct the customer order code in the same way as the date, only the code will be different. Refer to Figure 9-17 to see the result.

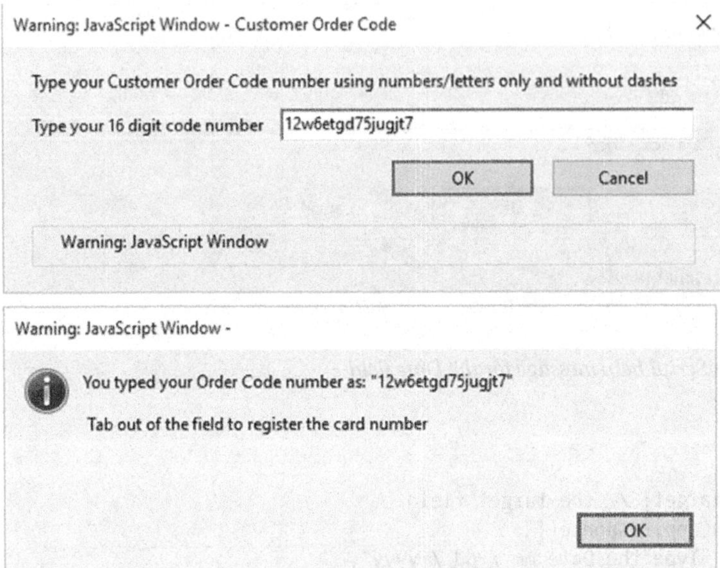

Figure 9-17. *JavaScript help message for customer order code and confirmation message*

The customer order code functions similarly and you could have set the format to number. However, you may want letters and numbers in your code, so leave the formatting to None.

```
// Customer Code or Credit Card Example
var t = event.target; // the target field
var cResponse = app.response({
    cQuestion: "Type your Customer Order Code number using numbers/letters
    only and without dashes",
    cTitle: "Customer Order Code",
    cLabel: "Type your 16 digit code number"});
{
    if ( cResponse == null){ // if Cancel is selected
    app.alert ("You cancelled adding your code.");
    cResponse = "";
}
    else {
    if (cResponse.length != 16){
    app.alert("Type the complete number/letters without dashes or there may
    be more or less than 16 digits.");
    cResponse = "";}
```

```
    else{
    app.alert("You typed your Order Code number as: \""+cResponse+"\" \n\n
    Tab out of the field to register the card number",3);}
    }
}
t.value = cResponse; // places the data from the dialog to the target field
```

Notice how the outer else statement does its own conditional check to make sure that there are 16 characters inside the field. If there are not, the alert might remind you to type without dashes or that there are not 16 characters typed in, if you decide to adjust the message.

Customer's Company Name

This code is similar to the Customer's Full Name field. Refer to Figure 9-18.

```
// Company name
var t = event.target; // the target field
var cResponse = app.response({
    cQuestion: "Type your Company's Name",
    cTitle: "Company Name",
    cDefault: "Company Name not added",
    cLabel: "Type your Company name"});
{
    if ( cResponse == null){ // if Cancel is selected
    app.alert ("You cancelled adding your Company's name.");
    cResponse = "";
    }
    else{
    app.alert("You typed your Company name as: \""+cResponse+"\" \n\n Tab
    out of the field to register your name",3);}
}
t.value = cResponse; // places the data from the dialog to the target field
```

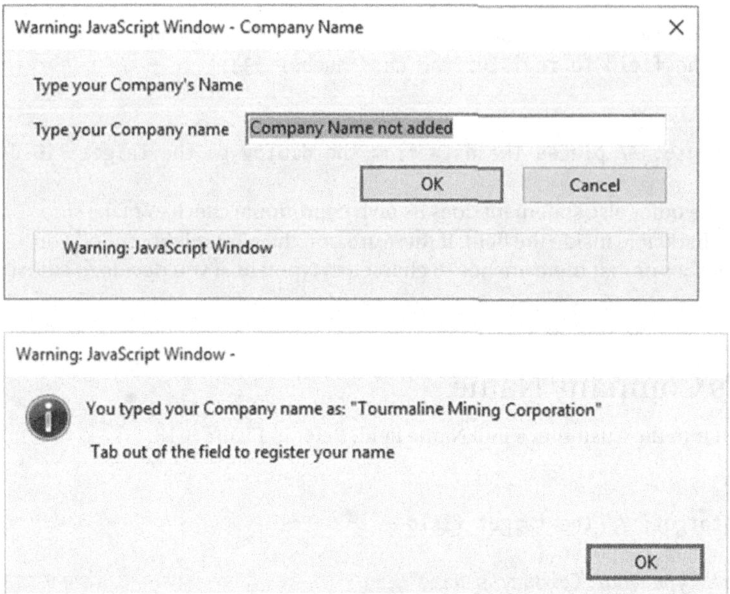

Figure 9-18. *JavaScript help message for company name and the confirmation message*

Final Thoughts

As you can see, there are several ways that you can help your customers fill out forms. Not all fields must offer help. Some are unmistakable and self-explanatory. However, if your client is not familiar with a word or maybe needs a translation because their English is not the best, this might be a possible workaround. If your form is one page, a rollover may be just fine. However, on forms with two pages or more where the help is spread out, I recommend the alert method.

■ **Note** Recently Adobe Acrobat DC added the Popup menu for Date. So adding the alert method to the Date is optional since when the user chooses a date, it formats itself automatically. In this case, you may choose to alter or remove the alert altogether. Refer to Figure 9-19.

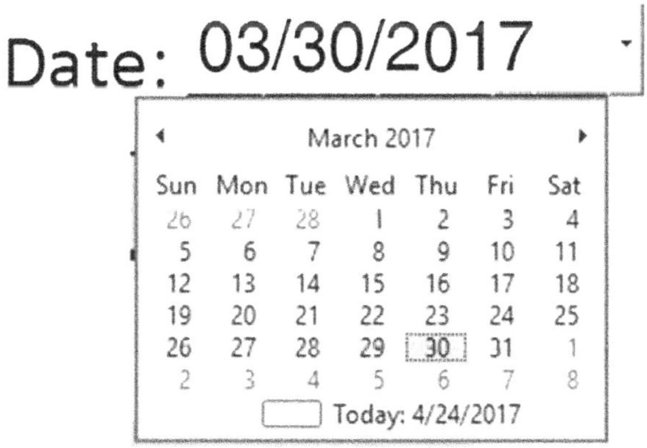

Figure 9-19. *The new Date Popup menu that appears in the latest version of Acrobat*

Summary

In this chapter, you learned about three possible methods for creating help for your clients when they work with text fields. You also saw how to reuse document JavaScript in many fields and how you can apply custom formatting to text fields.

In the next chapter, you are going to see what other options you have to alter the text within your fields depending upon the numbers that are entered.

CHAPTER 10

Various Types of Formatting with JavaScript

In the last chapter, you looked at creating various alerts that could assist your clients in knowing when they entered incorrect information. In this chapter, you will explore ways that you can globally and individually alter the appearance of various fields so that they conform to a set format you choose. You will also alter the appearance of the resultant value depending on what radio buttons or check boxes are chosen. Other topics you will tackle are

- Buttons that allow their label to run onto more than one line
- How to allow a client's text in a multi-line text field to flow into another text field when there is not enough room in the current field
- Using JavaScript and a button to print only one page or range of pages rather than printing the entire document

Adding Global Formatting to Text Fields

With forms, formatting font or field colors can be accomplished quite easily using the properties in the Appearance and Option tabs. Refer here to Figure 10-1.

J. Harder, *Enhancing Adobe Acrobat DC Forms with JavaScript*,
DOI 10.1007/978-1-4842-2893-7_10

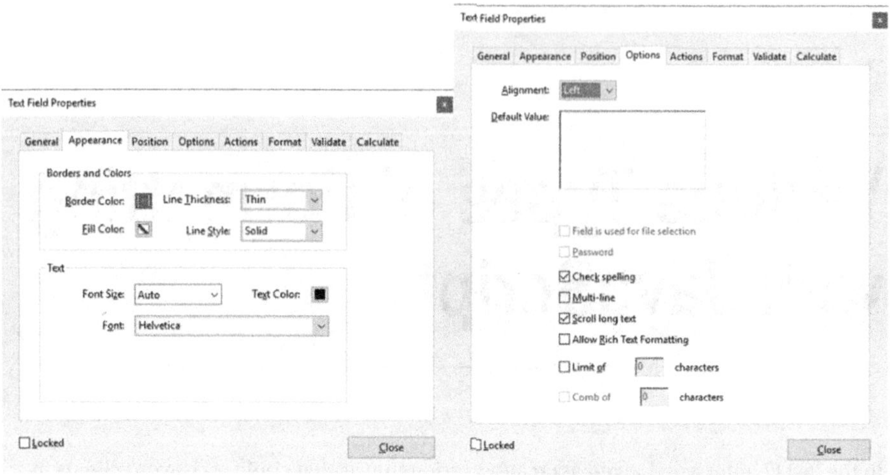

***Figure 10-1.** The Appearance and Options tabs showing formatting choices*

On other occasions, you may want all the fields to have the same color or font. You could select all the fields and then right-click Properties and set the Appearance tab. Refer here to Figure 10-2.

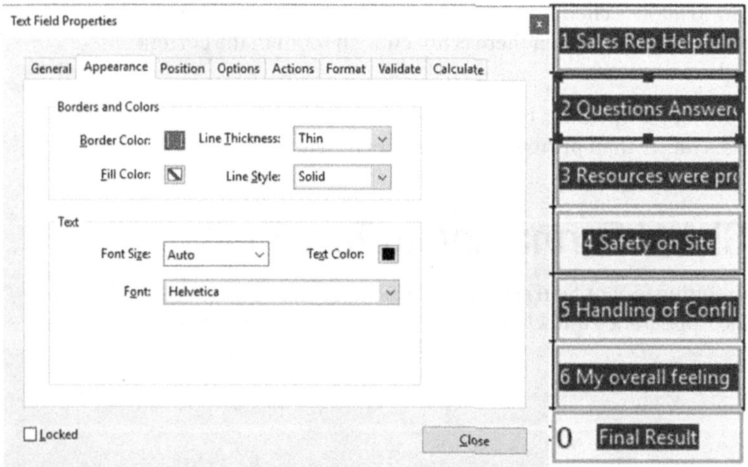

***Figure 10-2.** The Appearance tab with multiple fields highlighted at the same time*

However, this might lead to errors, and you might not get the result you intended especially if you forgot to select something.

■ **Note** If you want to work along in this lesson or review the final result, download the Chapter 10 files from `www.apress.com/9781484228920`. The file with the label "Start" is the file without the code and the file with the label "End" is the final result. You will also find a folder containing the original scripts if you would like to add them to your own PDF forms.

If you are creating your form from an original PDF, refer to the "Forms Review" section in Chapter 1.

Remember that to view the properties of a field you must select the Prepare Form tool; only then can you right-click or double-click a field to review its properties.

Using JavaScript, you can change the color quickly. To do things globally you need to go into your document JavaScript. See the Customer Survey PDF End Part 2 in this chapter's file folder. Refer to Figure 10-3 for the formatting code.

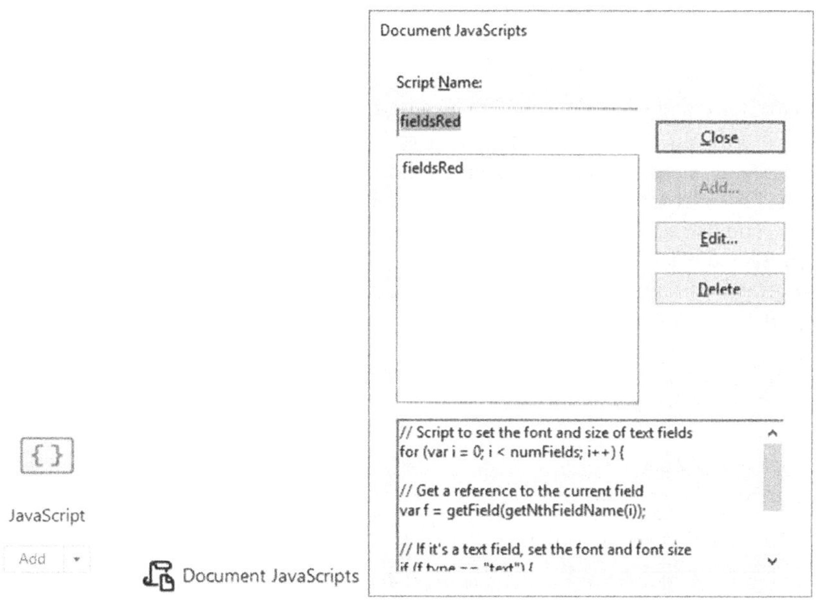

Figure 10-3. *The JavaScript tool inside the Document JavaScripts dialog box*

Here is a JavaScript called `fieldsRed`. Enter the following code:

```
// Script to set the font and size of text fields
for (var i = 0; i < numFields; i++) {
    // Get a reference to the current field
    var f = getField(getNthFieldName(i));
```

```
    // If it's a text field, set the font and font size
    if (f.type == "text") {
    f.strokeColor = color.red;
    }
}
```

To find just the text fields and apply a stroke color of red to them, use a JavaScript for() loop. Refer to Figure 10-4 to see the result.

Figure 10-4. *The result of adding the for() loop to the code*

Loops are not seen very often in Acrobat JavaScript. The most commonly used is the for() loop. There are other loops used in JavaScript, like while and do while. For the sake of simplification, let's just focus on the for() loop.

The for() loop contains three statements:

```
"var i = 0; i < numFields; i++"
```

The variable `var i = 0;` is executed before the loop (the code block) starts. The 0 field, like the array example earlier, is the starting point.

`i < numFields;` defines the condition for running the loop (the code block). `var i` is less than (<) `numFields`. Your form may be very large. You don't know how many fields there are, so you use `numFields` instead of an actual number. You want the loop to keep on going until you reach the end of the form.

i++ is executed each time after the loop (the code block) has been executed. This keeps the loop going until the end is reached.

This middle section acts as the control:

```
var f = getField(getNthFieldName(i));
  // If it's a text field, set the font and font size
if (f.type == "text") {
f.strokeColor = color.red;
}
```

When the amount of fields has been collected, you check using a conditional if statement that they are indeed strictly text fields. If they are, then a stoke color of red can be applied. Notice how the button fields didn't have a red stroke applied to them; they were canceled out during the loop.

To format other fields instead of text, format these lines:

- `if (f.type == "checkbox")`
- `if (f.type == "radio")`
- `if (f.type == "button")`
- `if (f.type == "signature")`

- `if (f.type == "combobox")`
- `if (f.type == "listbox")`

Or with this loop, if you want to change the stroke color to blue, you can change this line:

```
f.strokeColor = color.blue;
```

All the fields that had a red colored stroke will all become blue instantly and you didn't have to worry about selecting them all.

Color Properties

Other colors you could try are defined in Table 10-1.

Table 10-1. *Color Properties*

Color Object	Keyword	Equivalent JavaScript
Transparent	`color.transparent`	`[ "T" ]`
Black	`color.black`	`[ "G", 0 ]`
White	`color.white`	`[ "G", 1 ]`
Red	`color.red`	`[ "RGB", 1,0,0 ]`
Green	`color.green`	`[ "RGB", 0,1,0 ]`
Blue	`color.blue`	`[ "RGB", 0, 0, 1 ]`
Cyan	`color.cyan`	`[ "CMYK", 1,0,0,0 ]`
Magenta	`color.magenta`	`[ "CMYK", 0,1 0,0 ]`
Yellow	`color.yellow`	`[ "CMYK", 0,0,1,0 ]`
Dark Gray	`color.dkGray`	`[ "G", 0.25 ]`
Gray	`color.gray`	`[ "G", 0.5 ]`
Light Gray	`color.ltGray`	`[ "G", 0.75 ]`

Multi-Line Buttons

Another type of formatting that you may want to add is having the text of buttons on two or more lines. Buttons without this type of formatting often have the text on one line. There is no automatic way to tell the text to spread on to two lines, as you can see in Figure 10-5.

Figure 10-5. *A reset button with the text spreading on one line*

The button becomes longer and longer. An option is to make the text smaller. Unfortunately, it then becomes difficult to read. You could create an icon graphic, but then the text won't be editable if you need to change it quickly. Refer here to Figure 10-6 to see the current properties of the button.

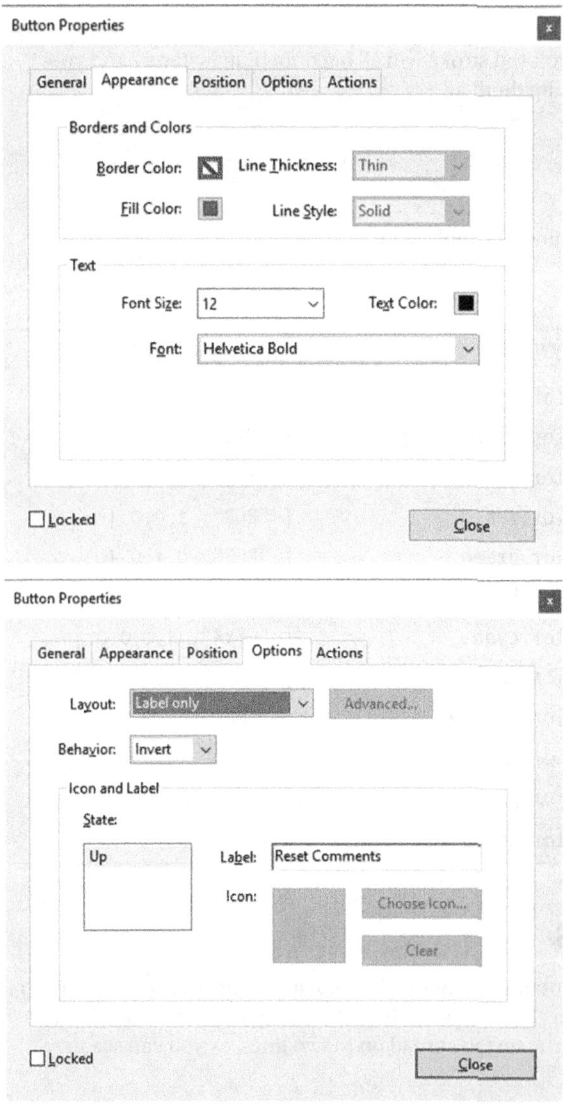

***Figure 10-6.** Button Properties Appearance and Option tabs with the label of Reset Comments*

Once again JavaScript has a solution. Refer here to Figure 10-7.

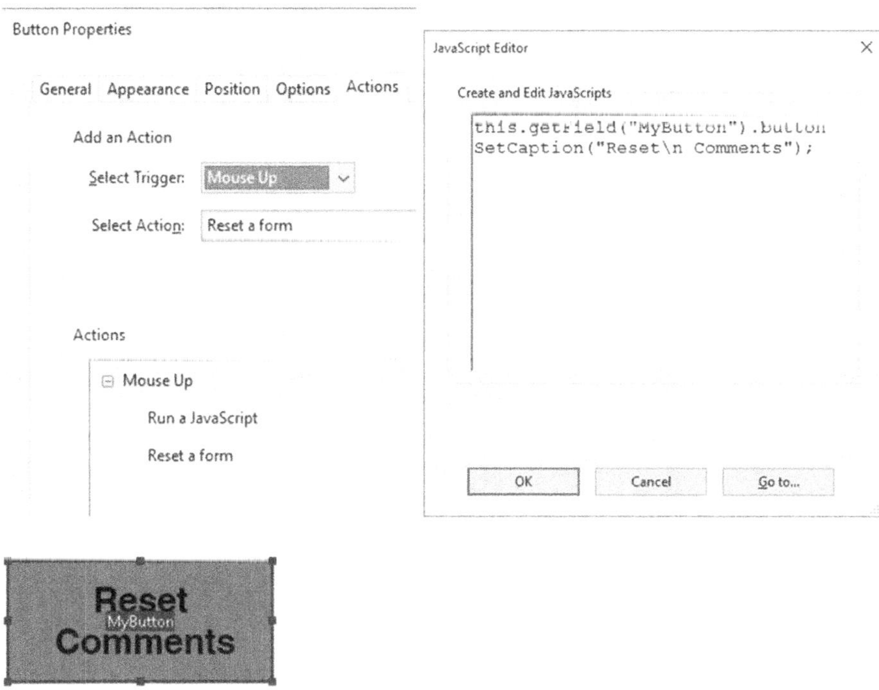

Figure 10-7. *Run a JavaScript to make the text multi-line*

Besides resetting the comment field, this adds a JavaScript to the button.
Here is the code:

```
this.getField("MyButton").buttonSetCaption("Reset\n Comments");
```

Just one line does what you need. Call upon the name of the button, "MyButton", and tell it that you want to set a caption same as label in the Option tab. To make the words on two lines, use the invisible character, " \n". Another name for this is a metacharacter. Basically what it means is a new line, so the word Comments goes onto the second line. This is very handy when the button requires several lines of text.

■ **Note** You may have noticed that you used the metacharacter `\n` in Chapter 9 when you were creating alert boxes and needed line breaks. In Chapter 11, you will look at some regular expressions where metacharacters can be use with other patterns.

Multi-Line Text

Buttons aren't the only fields that require multiple lines. Text fields that require a lot of text such as comments can be made multi-line as well. If you've reviewed your form basics you'll know that you can make a text field multi-line simply by selecting the multi-line check box. Refer here to Figure 10-8 to see an example of this.

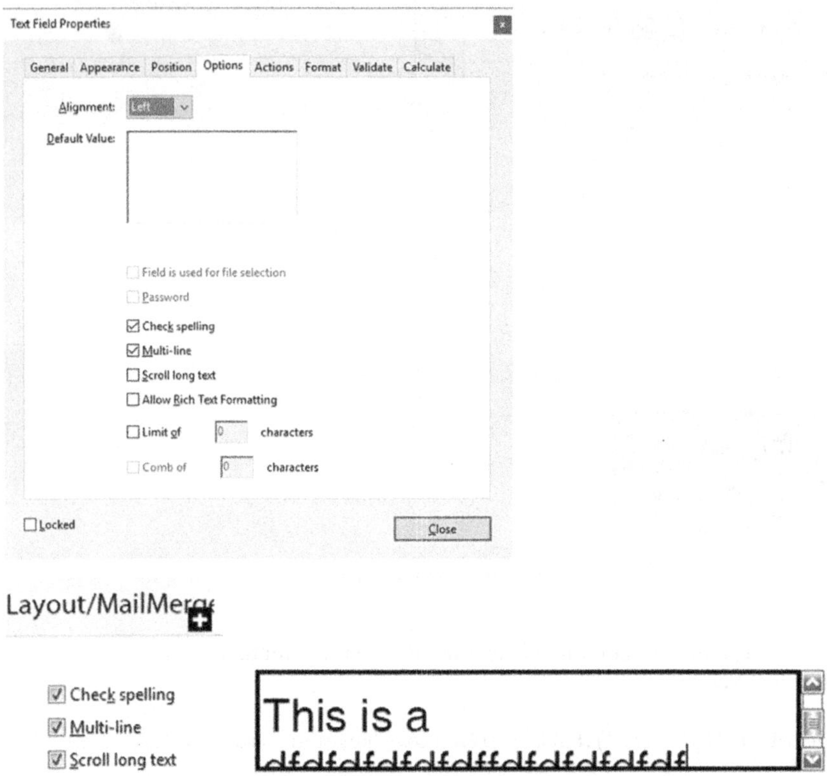

***Figure 10-8.** In the Options tab, the Multi-line box is checked so you get a scroll box*

When creating a text comments field, a plus symbol appears at the end of the field once it's filled with type. Refer to Figure 10-8.

With comments, if you want to read them on your computer, you might check the "Scroll long text" box.

While this makes it easier to read on the computer, when you go to print you may not see all of the text that was in the box.

Unfortunately, Acrobat does not have expandable boxes. This is a problem if your form requires that a client write a lengthy statement and you only have a small amount of room at the end of the page.

Here is a workaround. Create a second page and allow the text to flow into a second comment text field.

Rather than using the Actions tab this time, let's add a custom format in the Format tab. Refer here to Figure 10-9.

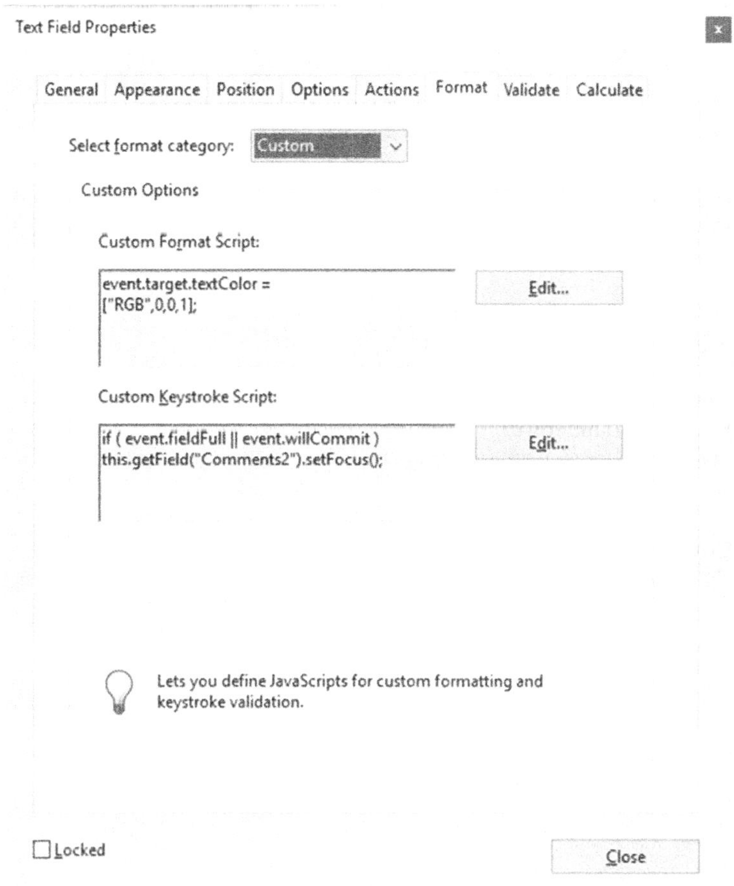

***Figure 10-9.** The Custom Keystroke Script settings applied*

On the first field, Comments1, put the following code:
Custom Format Script

```
event.target.textColor = ["RGB",0,0,1];
```

I did not have to write this line, but I wanted to show how you can adjust the color of text, as you saw in the stroke example earlier. I want this `textColor` to be different than the other fields. I could have just as easily set it over in the Appearance tab. Refer here to Figure 10-10.

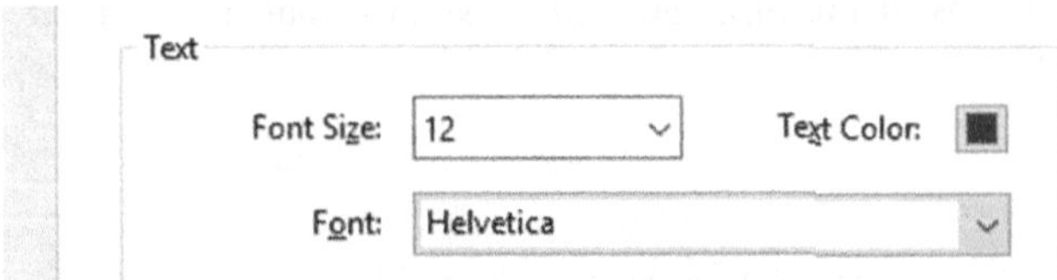

Figure 10-10. *The Apperance tab showing the set font size, text color, and font*

However, later in Chapter 11, you will see a more complex example where this is not always what you want to do; there, formatting color with JavaScript is a better option.

The Custom Keystroke Script

```
if ( event.fieldFull || event.willCommit )
    this.getField("Comments2").setFocus();
```

This code allows the user to type. When the script senses that the box is full, it moves onto the next box named Comments2.

If you need a third box for some reason, you can add the following lines in the Comments2 box:

```
//Second to 3rd box if required
var t2=this.getField("Comments2");
if (event.fieldFull)
{
    getField("Comments3").setFocus();
}
```

The final field, Comments3, does not require any JavaScript and the Format tab can be set to None. Refer here to Figure 10-11.

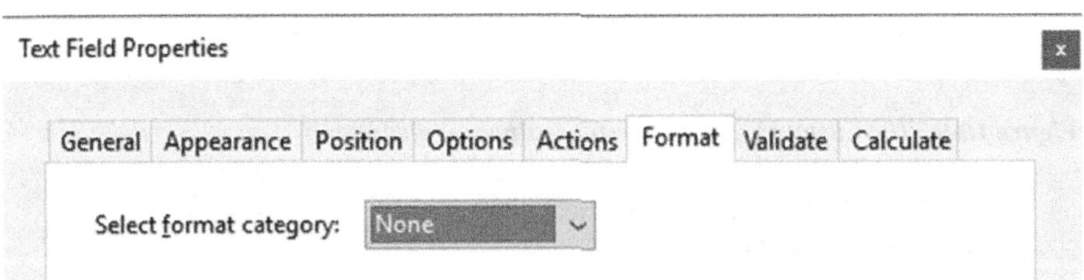

Figure 10-11. *In the Format tab, the category is set to None*

This example is a good workaround. One note of caution: Only use this flow method for typing directly into the field. I found that pasting text in does not always flow into the second and subsequent boxes.

Complex Formatting Using Check Boxes and Text Fields

In Figure 10-12, you can see how check boxes can be used for addition and subtraction ratings. Like with radio buttons, you don't need JavaScript to do this. See the Survey End Part 2b PDF file.

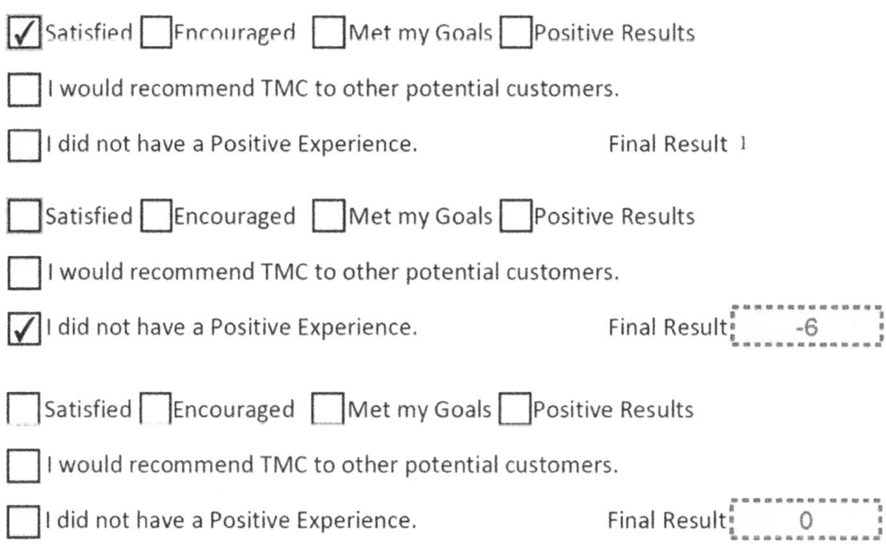

Figure 10-12. *A survey where the font style and color of the box changes depending upon the rating*

All you need to do is give the check boxes a negative or positive value in the Options tab. Refer here to Figure 10-13.

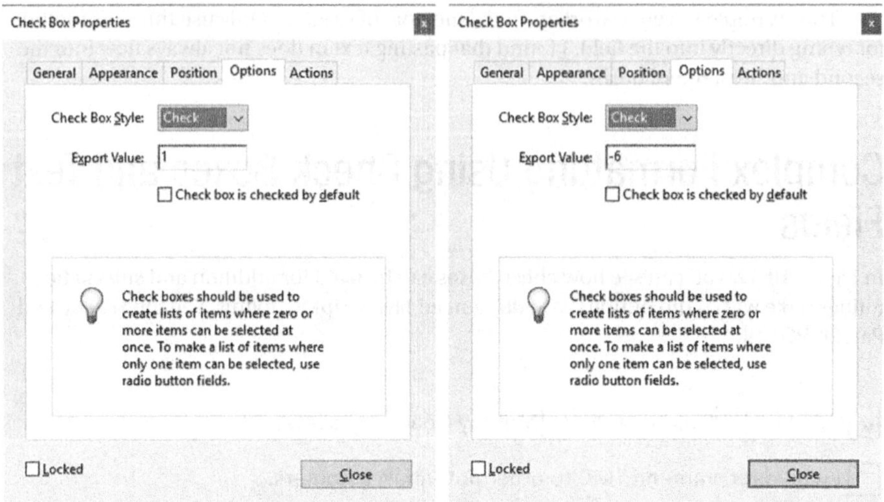

***Figure 10-13.** Check box properties in the Options tab set to positive and negative export values*

In the Calculate tab of text field Final Result_4, you can use the value of sum (+) to add them all up. Refer here to Figure 10-14.

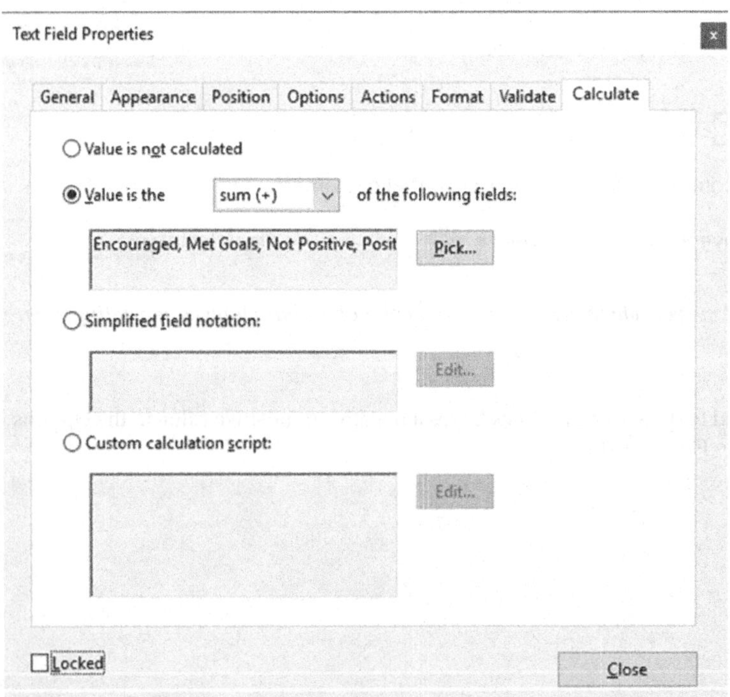

***Figure 10-14.** Set the value to sum (+) in the Calculate tab in the Text Field Properties window*

However, sometimes you may want to alert yourself to the fact that the rating is becoming negative.

You can format your appearance of the box and text once in the Appearance tab without JavaScript. Unfortunately, if the number changes from positive to negative, its appearance will not change without adding a conditional script into the Validate tab section. Refer here to Figure 10-15.

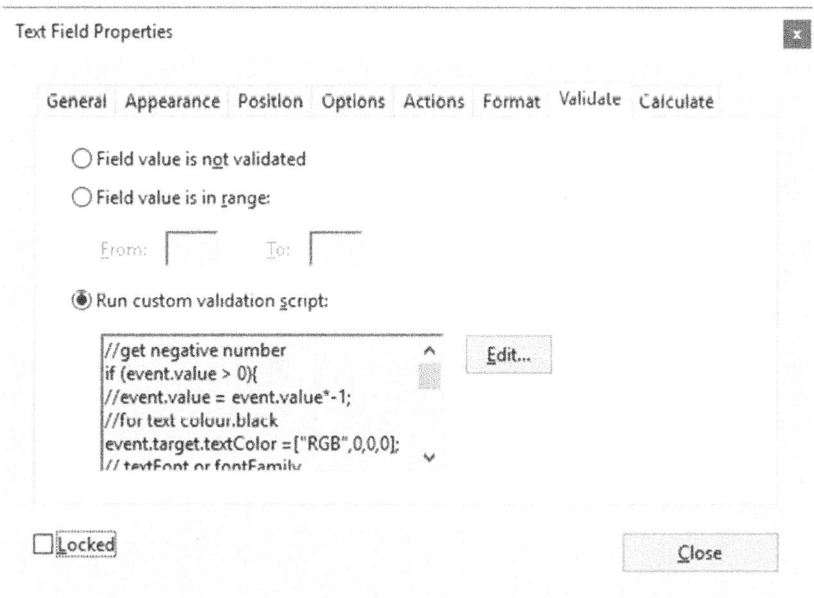

Figure 10-15. *The Validate tab with a custom validation script*

Here is the code:

```
//get negative number
if (event.value > 0){
    //event.value - event.value*-1;
    //for text color.black
    event.target.textColor =["RGB",0,0,0];
    // textFont or fontFamily
    event.target.textFont =font.Times;
    //Size
    event.target.textSize = 11;

    //for field color.none
    event.target.strokeColor = ["T"];
    event.target.fillColor = color.transparent;
    //left=0, centered=1, right=2
    event.target.alignment ="left";
}
```

```
else{
    event.target.textColor = ["RGB",1,0,0];
    // textFont or fontFamily
    event.target.textFont =font.Helv;
    //Size
    event.target.textSize = 14;
    //for field color.red
    event.target.strokeColor = ["RGB",1,0,0];
    //fill of field
    event.target.fillColor = color.yellow;
    // Borders 0=none, 1=thin, 2=medium, 3 = thick
    event.target.lineWidth =2;
    // Border Style border.s= solid, border.b= beveled, border.d = dashed,
    border.i = inset, border.u = underline
    event.target.borderStyle = border.d;
    //left=0, centered=1, right=2
    event.target.alignment ="center";
}
```

While this might seem very complex at first glance, in reality it is not. You are merely changing your formatting as the number changes.

Here is a simplified breakdown:

```
if (event.value > 0){
    // Change my formatting
}
else {
    //Change my formatting to something else
}
```

When the number is greater than (>) 0, please change the format of the fonts, color, and field to something defined. When it is less than (<) 0, change it to something else defined.

The formats affected are

Text color or `textColor`: This effects the color of the text. You could say `color.black` or `["RGB",0,0,0];`.

```
event.target.textColor = ["RGB",0,0,0];
event.target.textColor = ["RGB",1,0,0];
//this is a  red color
```

Text font or `textFont`:

```
event.target.textFont =font.Times;
event.target.textFont =font.Helv;
```

■ **Note** For bold, italic, or bold italic font styles:

`event.target.textFont=font.TimesBI;` or `font.HelvBI;`

`event.target.textFont=font.TimesI;` or `font.HelvI;`

`event.target.textFont=font.TimesB;` or `font.HelvB;`

Text size or `textSize`: To change the size of the text

```
event.target.textSize = 11;
event.target.textSize = 14;
```

Stroke color or `strokeColor`: The stroke around the field

```
event.target.strokeColor = ["T"]; // transparent
event.target.strokeColor = ["RGB",1,0,0]; // red
```

Fill color or `fillColor`: The fill of the field

```
event.target.fillColor = color.transparent;
event.target.fillColor = color.yellow;
```

Border width or `lineWidth`: The width of the field

```
// Borders 0=none, 1=thin, 2=medium, 3 = thick
event.target.lineWidth =2;
```

Border style or `borderStyle`: The style of the border field

```
// Border Style border.s= solid, border.b= beveled, border.d = dashed,
border.i = inset, border.u = underline
event.target.borderStyle = border.d;
```

Text alignment or the alignment within the field

```
//left=0, centered=1, right=2
event.target.alignment ="left";
event.target.alignment ="center";
```

You don't have to use all of these. However, with if/else conditionals you need to make sure you have in most cases an on or off state (when "if" formats like this, then "else" formats like that).

Some other formatting you can use with some PDF tools, but not form fields, are the following:

Font family or `fontFamily`: Used for an array (many fonts listed) when you are trying to make sure that the user font will display similar on all computers.

Font style or `fontStyle`: There are two styles: normal or italic.

```
event.target.fontStyle = "italic";
```

Font stretch or `fontStretch`: There are several styles to choose from: normal (default), ultra-condensed, extra-condensed, condensed, semi-condensed, semi-expanded, expanded, extra-expanded, ultra-expanded.

```
event.target.fontStretch= "expanded";
```

Font weight or `fontWeight`: This takes over for bold fonts. Normal is anything under 700 and bold is anything over 700. The options are 100, 200, 300, 400, 500, 600, 700, 800, 900.

```
event.target.fontWeight= 400;
```

`strikethrough`**:** Draws a line through the words. It can either be true or false.

```
event.target.strikethrough=true;
event.target.strikethrough=false;
```

`subscript`: The text is subscripted, reduced point size, and lower baseline.

```
event.target.subscript=true;
event.target.subscript=false;
```

`superscript`: The text is superscripted, lowered point size, and raised baseline.

```
event.target.superscript=true;
event.target.superscript=false;
```

`underline`: The text is underlined.

```
event.target.underline=true;
event.target.underline=false;
```

`rotation`: This is used to rotate the field. Not used that often. Make sure that you test it in Reader first before you try this with a client, as it might have unexpected results. Numbers you might use are 0, 45, 90, 180, or 270 depending on the rotation.

```
event.target.rotation=0;
event.target.rotation=90;
```

Silent Printing

Refer to Figure 10-16 on how to print all pages in a document with a button.

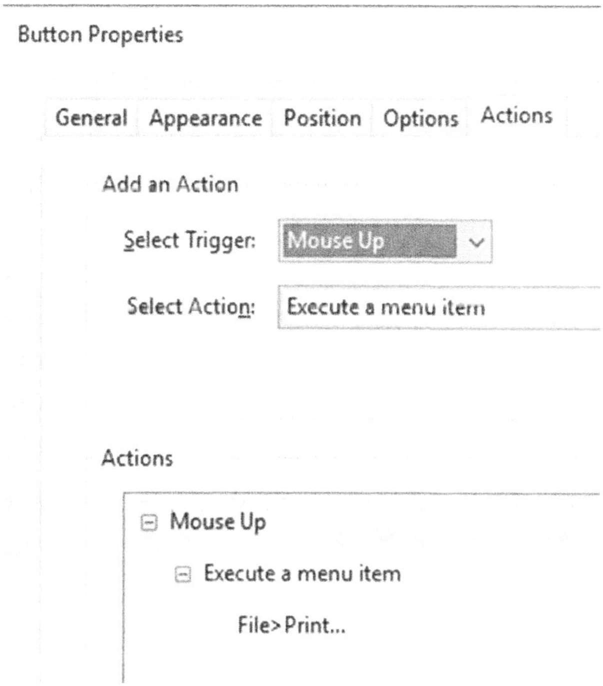

Figure 10-16. *The "Execute a menu item" action in the Actions tab. File ➤ Print to print the document.*

One final feature about this form is silent printing. In most cases, when you want to print a document in Acrobat, you just go to the menu and Choose File ➤ Print. As seen in Chapter 2, you can do this with a button and the Actions tab. However, this action prints the whole document, which may not be what you want to do. Maybe you want to print out just the form page(s). Refer here to Figure 10-17.

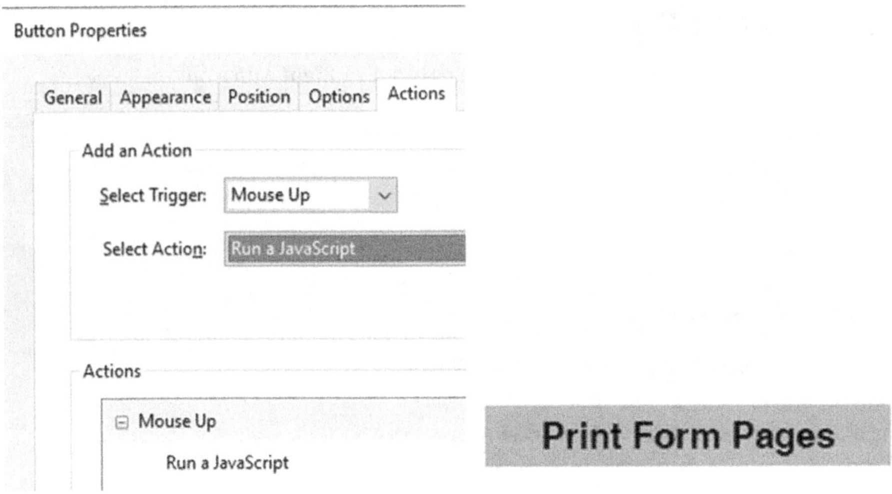

Figure 10-17. *Run a JavaScript to print specific pages*

Here is the code you can use to run an action in the Actions tab of the button:

```
// Print current page silently
this.print(false, this.pageNum, this.pageNum);
```

When you add the code to a button, only the page that this button is on will print.

If the user gets the message shown in Figure 10-18, they just press the Yes button and continue.

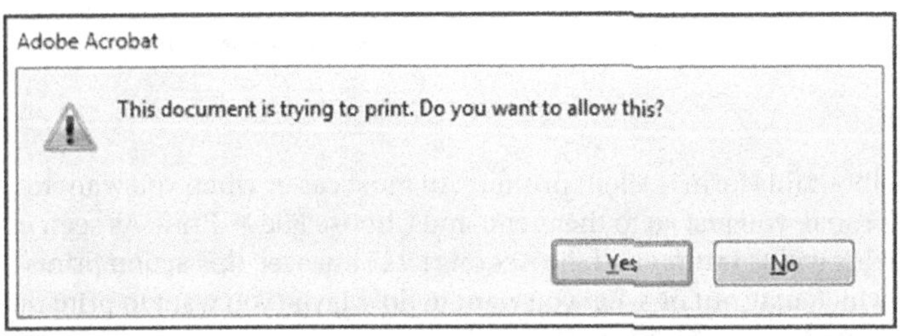

Figure 10-18. *Acrobat Alert message appears regarding printing*

When you need to print this form page and the ones below it, change the code to this:

```
// Print current page silently and the range below it
this.print(false, this.pageNum, this.pageNum+1);
```

If there are more pages in the range, `this.pageNum+1` becomes `this.pageNum+2` and so on.

Once again, this is like an array:

```
this.pageNum (0) = page 1
this.pageNum+1 = page 2
this.pageNum+2 = page 3
```

and so on.

Final Thoughts

As you can see, there are many useful ways you can customize forms with JavaScript to suit your needs.

- Custom text
- Fields
- Buttons
- Printing

A final note on formatting with `textFont`:
An alternate way of writing the line

```
event.target.textFont=font.Helv;
```

is to put the actual name in quote marks, like

```
event.target.textFont="Helvetica";
```

Here, the style is added with a dash:

```
event.target.textFont="Helvetica-Bold";
```

Another name for italic:

```
event.target.textFont="Helvetica-Oblique";
```

Two styles are often fused together:

```
event.target.textFont="Helvetica-BoldOblique";
```

A better method for uncommon names:

```
event.target.textFont="MinionPro-Regular";
```

Access to less traditional styles:

```
event.target.textFont="Arial-Black"; - event.target.textFont="ArialNarrow";
```

Not all styles use the dash. Refer to your computer's control panel area for the correct font names. For example: MinionPro-Italic is written as MinionPro-It. When you enter an incorrect name, you will not get the font or font style you require. Also, be aware that your client's computer may not have all specialized fonts so stick to safe names like Times, Courier, Arial, or Helvetica to avoid text field font issues.

Summary

As you saw in this chapter, there are many options you can use to format form fields and non-form items. Sometimes custom formatting is used and other times the Validation tab is a better option. You can add JavaScript globally to affect many fields or to the Actions tab to affect just one. I recommend spending some time reviewing this chapter before moving on to Part 3. Add some of this JavaScript to one of you own forms.

For most of Part 2, you have focused on adding JavaScript to text fields and buttons. However, as you will see in Part 3, PDF forms can be complex once you start adding JavaScript to radio buttons, check boxes, dropdown menus, and list boxes.

PART 3

Working with More Complex Forms

CHAPTER 11

Validation with Text Boxes, Alerts, and Radio Buttons

The JavaScript becomes more complex as multiple form fields work in tandem.

As you've seen in past examples, to avoid errors you need to create warnings or alerts so clients will enter the correct information.

Text boxes are not the only field item that alerts or choices can be applied to. You can also use radio buttons.

Note If you want to work along in this lesson or review the final result, download the Chapter 11 files from `www.apress.com/9781484228920`. The file with the label "Start" is the file without the code and the file with the label "End" is the final result. You will also find folders with original MS Word and PDF files if you would like to edit them and a folder containing the original scripts if you would like to add them to your own PDF forms.

If you are creating your form from an original PDF, refer to the "Forms Review" section in Chapter 1.

Remember that to view the properties of a field you must select the Prepare Form tool; only then can you right-click or double-click a field to review its properties.

Money Transfer Example

The money transfer example is a wonderful way to see how validation can be applied to fields that do not have the Validate tab in their Properties dialog box. Refer to Figure 11-1.

J. Harder, *Enhancing Adobe Acrobat DC Forms with JavaScript*,
DOI 10.1007/978-1-4842-2893-7_11

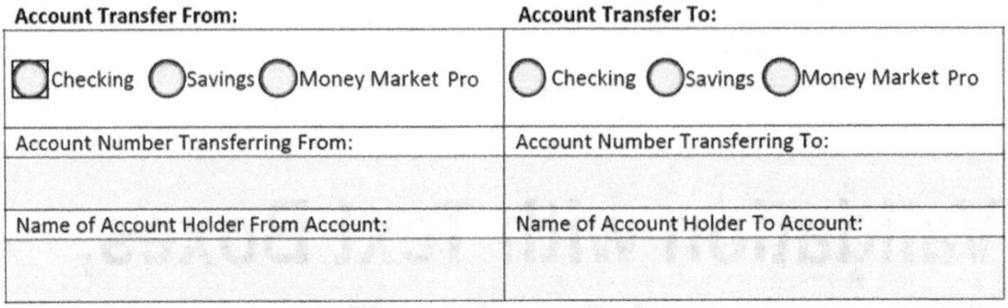

***Figure 11-1.** In this money transfer example you can choose to transfer your money to another account*

Sometimes you may want to transfer an amount of money into another type of account. See the TMC Account Transfer End PDF file. Refer to Figures 11-1, 11-2, and 11-3.

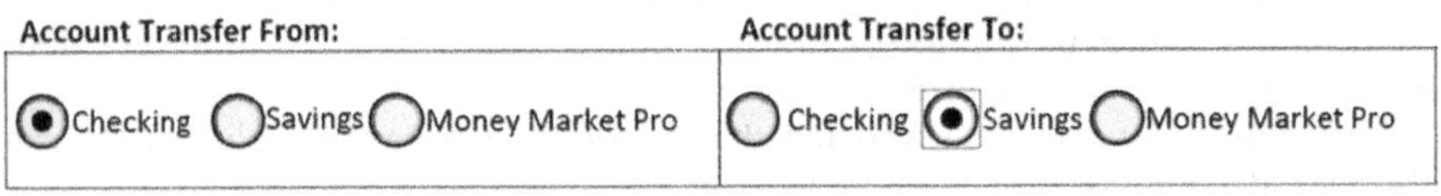

***Figure 11-2.** Checking to Savings or Money Market Pro is a possible transfer*

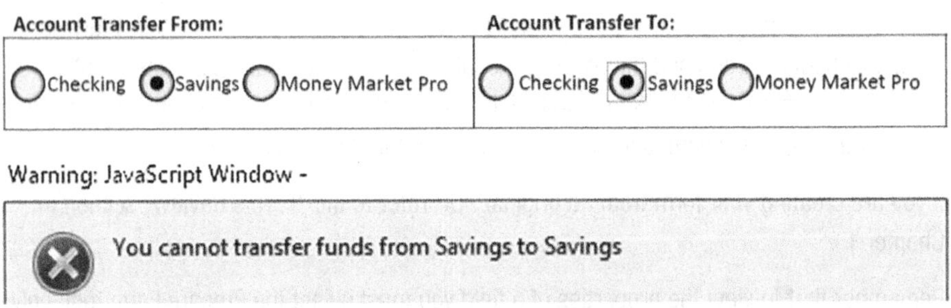

***Figure 11-3.** Savings to Savings account transfer with warning*

The choice in Figure 11-2 gives you no warning, because you are transferring money from Checking to Savings. However, if you want to transfer from Savings to Savings, you would get a warning; see Figure 11-3.

This type of transfer gives you a warning.

You would also get a warning if you transferred from Checking to Checking and Money Market Pro to Money Market Pro.

Figure 11-4 shows how the buttons are set up in the Form Edit mode.

***Figure 11-4.** Radio button layout: the left is the From group and the right is the To group*

As mentioned earlier, radio buttons must always be grouped to work together. They can have different values/choices but they need to be part of the same group. Refer here to Figure 11-5.

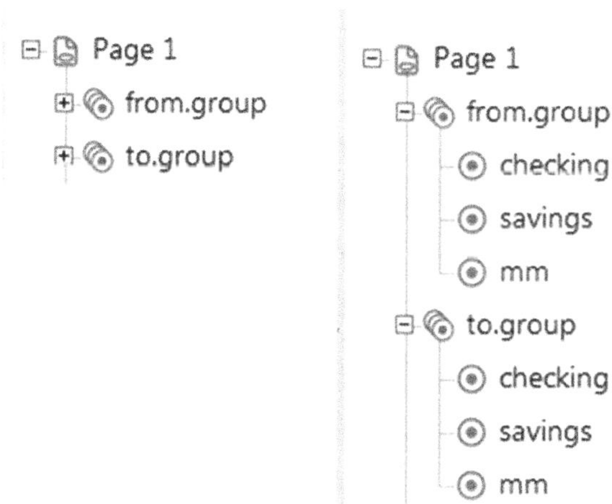

***Figure 11-5.** The Form tool shows the grouping of the radio buttons*

Here you can see the setup for the from.group radio buttons. In this case, I have selected just the one with the choice of checking so that you can see its properties. If you choose savings or mm, the only difference would be the choice in the Options tab. Refer here to Figure 11-6.

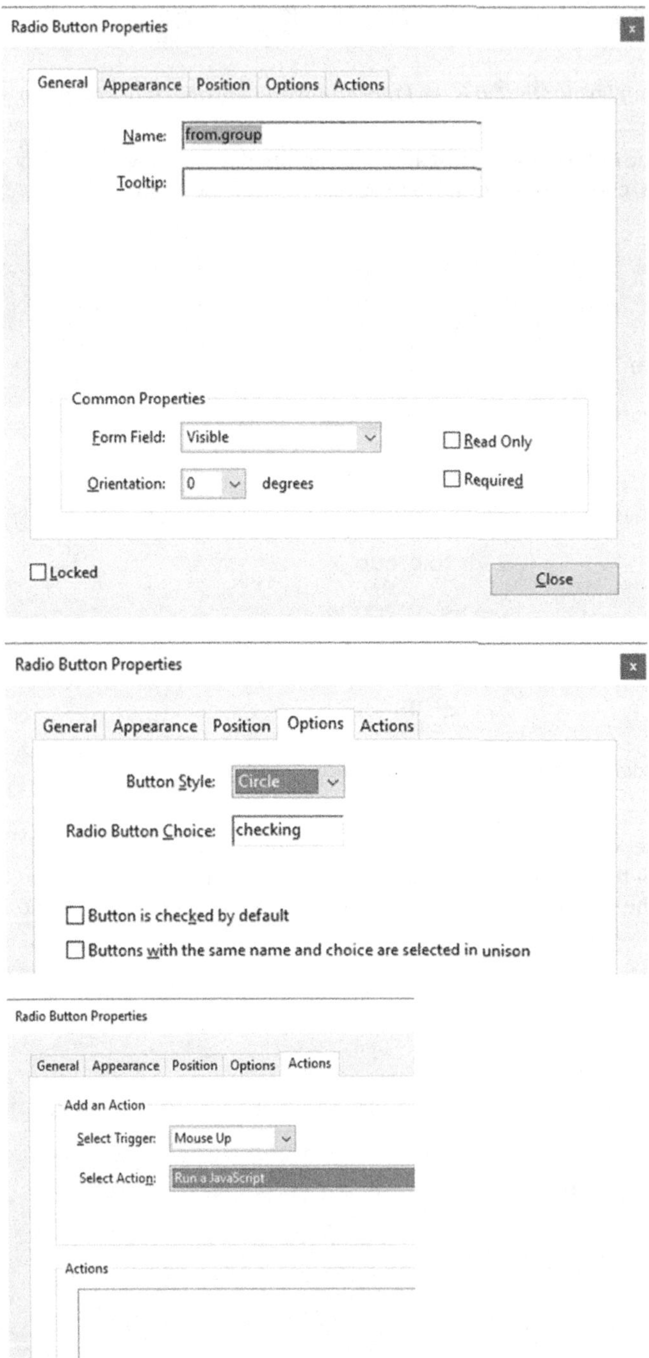

Figure 11-6. *Settings for the radio buttons in the from.group in the General, Options, and Actions tabs. The only difference is the radio button choice.*

On the left-hand side, the from.group radio buttons contain no actions.

However, the to.group radio buttons do contain an action because they are the second choice that may or may not trigger a warning based on whether its choice matches the first choice. Refer here to Figure 11-7.

***Figure 11-7.** Settings for the radio buttons in the to.group Actions tab. The code is for a transfer from Checking to Checking account.*

```
//to.group radio button 1 checking

var rfrom = this.getField("from.group");
var rtrans = event.target;
var msg = "You cannot transfer funds from Checking to Checking";
```

```
if (rfrom.value == "checking"){
        app.alert(msg);
        rfrom.value = "";
        rtrans.value = "";
}
```

Here you have two variables: `rfrom` and `rtrans`. The first variable, `var rfrom`, represents the whole radio button group from.group. The second variable, `var rtrans`, represents the current field, which is part of to.group and has a choice of checking. An alert message is written and appears if the two choices do match exactly:

```
var msg = "You cannot transfer funds from Checking to Checking";
```

Once the alert's OK button is pressed, the if statement also resets the two variables.

```
rfrom.value = "";
rtrans.value = "";
```

They become blank as if never checked.

Similar code can be written for the savings and money market pro radio buttons:

Savings Code

```
//to.group radio button 2 savings
var rfrom = this.getField("from.group");
var rtrans = event.target;
var msg = "You cannot transfer funds from Savings to Savings";

if (rfrom.value == "savings"){
                app.alert(msg);
                rfrom.value = "";
                rtrans.value = "";
}
```

Money Market Pro Code

```
//to.group radio button 3 mm
var rfrom = this.getField("from.group");
var rtrans = event.target;
var msg = "You cannot transfer funds from Money Market Pro to Money Market
Pro";

if (rfrom.value == "mm"){
                app.alert(msg);
                rfrom.value = "";
                rtrans.value = "";
}
```

As you can see, when two fields' choices match, an alert can be triggered.

Changing the Shipping Price Using Radio Buttons

As you've seen in past projects, check boxes and radio buttons can be used to adjust numbers in text boxes. Let's look at another example of how this can be done with prices. See the Invoice Form Shipping Change End PDF file. Refer here to Figure 11-8.

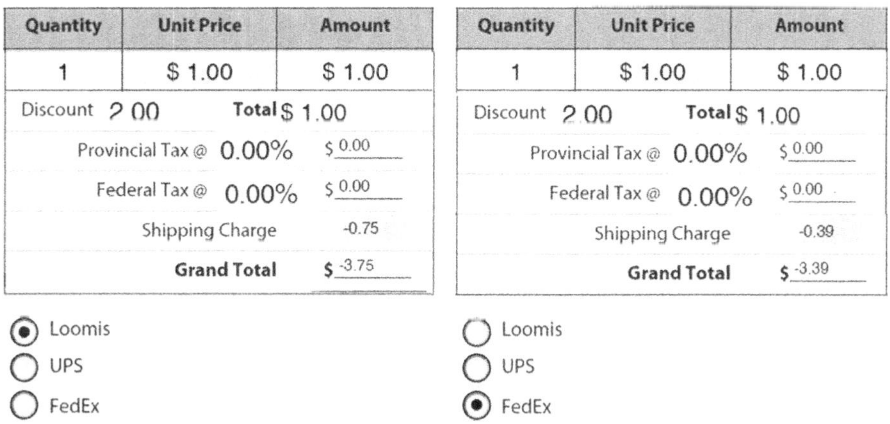

Figure 11-8. *Invoice form for adjusting the shipping price using radio buttons*

These numbers will vary depending on what you input. If you choose a different company like FedEx, the shipping charge changes again.

How does this work?

Most of this form is set up like most invoice forms, which use a combination of Value and simplified field notation (SFN) and very little JavaScript. However, this example contains a new field called discount and the radio buttons to the lower left.

The field called discount is just formatted as a number and has no action applied to it. However, you are going to call upon it once you start using the radio buttons. The buttons are as one group, each with their own choices. Refer here to Figure 11-9.

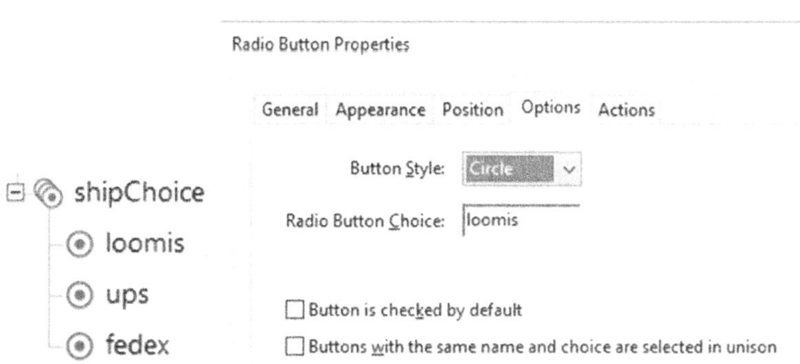

Figure 11-9. *Radio button properties in the Options tab*

The panel on the left of the Prepare Form tool shows how the buttons are grouped. Then you add a JavaScript to each radio button. Refer here to Figure 11-10.

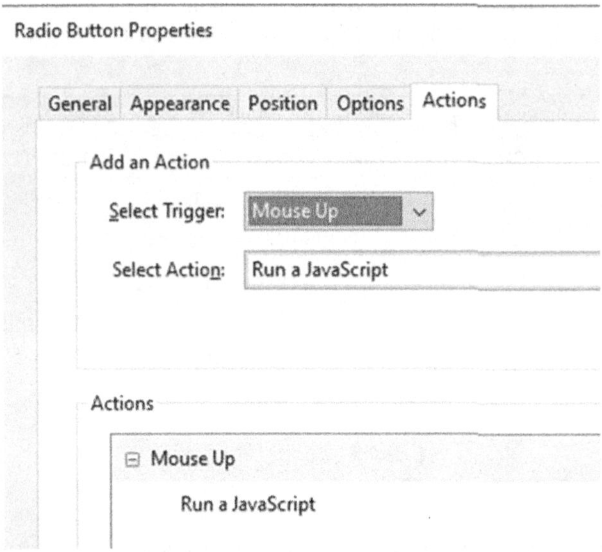

Figure 11-10. *The Radio Button Properties screen in the Actions tab, with the action of "Run a JavaScript"*

This is similar code for each radio button:

```
//Shipping Price Charge
var oShip = this.getField("Shipping");
var oSub = this.getField("Total");
var oDiscount = this.getField("discount");

if(oSub.value <200)
    var oRate = (oSub.value - oDiscount.value)*.25;
else
    var oRate =0;
    oShip.value = oRate;
```

The code says that if the subtotal before or after the discount is under or less than $200, then add a shipping (that is the Total Price *.25) to get the shipping price. However, if the price is over $200 even with the discount (else statement), the shipping is 0 dollars, or free.

As you can see, you can apply this function to other couriers like this:

```
var oShip = this.getField("Shipping");
var oSub = this.getField("Total");
var oDiscount = this.getField("discount");

if(oSub.value <200)
    var oRate = (oSub.value - oDiscount.value)*.17;
else
    var oRate =0;
    oShip.value = oRate;
```

You could change the price from

```
var oRate = (oSub.value - oDiscount.value)*.17;
```

to

```
(oSub.value - oDiscount.value)*.13;
```

Or you could change the dollar limit from

```
if (oSub.value <200)
```

to

```
if (oSub.value <300)
```

depending on the preferences of the courier company.

■ **Note** You could have written the conditional part of the code with the added brackets ({}).

```
if(oSub.value <200){
    var oRate = (oSub.value - oDiscount.value)*.17;
}
else{
    var oRate =0;
    oShip.value = oRate;
}
```

■ **Note** In this case, it was a very small and uncomplicated conditional script and I left some brackets sets out. JavaScript will sometimes let you do that to make code less complicated. However, in other cases, if you leave them out, you may get an error warning or the script will not function correctly. If you are unsure or want to keep the code accurate, I recommend leaving the brackets in complex examples in order to avoid confusion.

One final item you add to each radio button is the ability to reset/refresh the shipping when you click the radio button again rather than having click another radio button (On Mouse Down ➤ Reset form). Check off only for the Shipping field. Refer here to Figure 11-11.

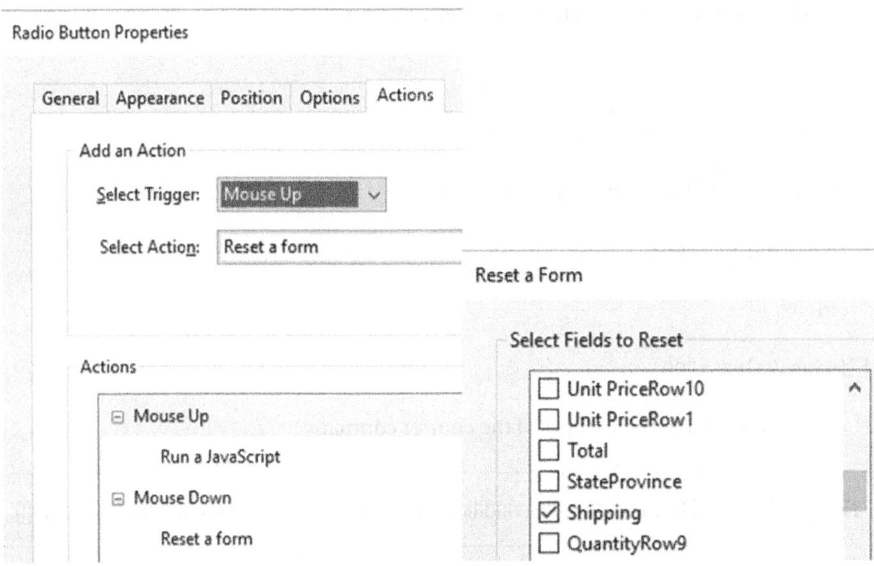

Figure 11-11. Radio button settings in the Actions tab to refresh the shipping

Text Field Validation with Regular Expressions

Another feature to try in this form (see the Invoice Form Shipping Change End r2 PDF file) is a telephone validation script. Refer here to Figure 11-12.

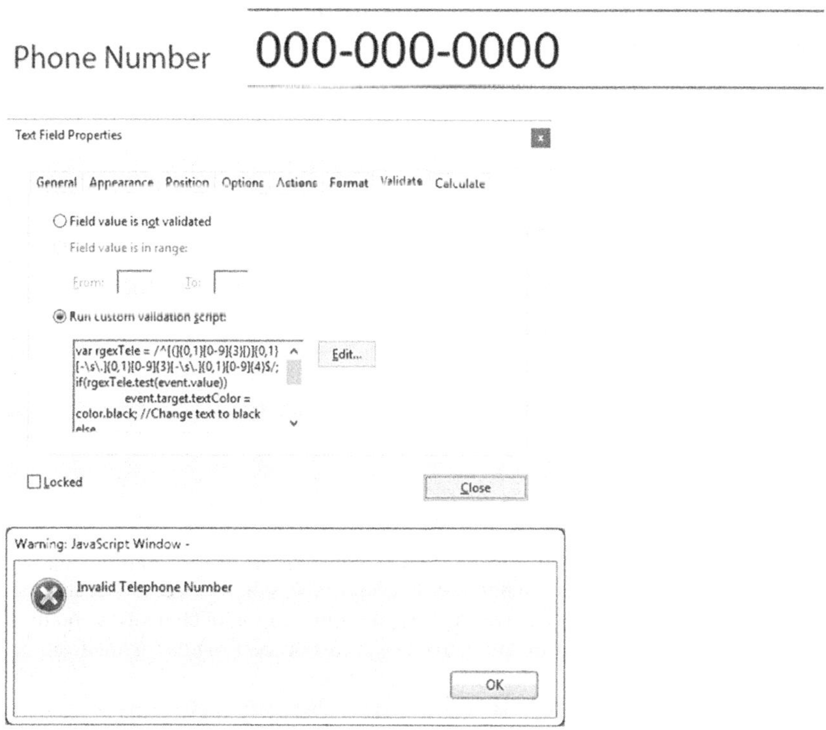

Figure 11-12. *Telephone text field validation in the Validate tab and the alert that is produced when the input is incorrect*

If the client does not type in the text field the correct way, an alert will happen. The correct format is displayed in Figure 11-13.

Figure 11-13. *Top: Incorrectly entered information appears red. Bottom: Correctly entered information in the Telephone text field.*

After the OK button in the alert is clicked, the text in the text field turns red and will not change back to black until the user types in the correct format.

Telephone Validation

Here is the JavaScript:

```
var rgexTele = /^[(]{0,1}[0-9]{3}[)]{0,1}[-\s\.]{0,1}[0-9]{3}[-\s\.]{0,1}
[0-9]{4}$/;
if(rgexTele.test(event.value)){
    event.target.textColor = color.black; //Change text to black
{
else{
    event.target.textColor = ["RGB",1,0,0]; //Change text to red
    app.alert("Invalid Telephone Number");
}
```

In order to accomplish this, you use a form of JavaScript called a regular expression. You saw a very simple example of this when you created your multi-line button using \n, the new line, and you created a metacharacter in Chapter 10. When you combine more than one metacharacter you create a pattern and this combination of characters creates a regular expression. This time you are going to use a more complex regular expression.

```
/^[(]{0,1}[0-9]{3}[)]{0,1}[-\s\.]{0,1}[0-9]{3}[-\s\.]{0,1}[0-9]{4}$/
```

This portion of the expression is saying that the code must be

- Three digits ranging within parenthesis from 0 to 9 in the first section that can be separated by either a dash, space, or dot
- Three digits ranging from 0 to 9 in the second section that can be separated by either a dash, space, or dot
- Four digits ranging from 0 to 9 in the last section

The following examples are acceptable:

- (123) 456-7890
- 123-456-7890
- 123.456.7890
- 123 456 7890
- 1234567890

Anything more or less than 10 digits is unacceptable.

You could have used the format Special Phone Number or Arbitrary Mask if you did not want to write this. Refer to Figure 11-14.

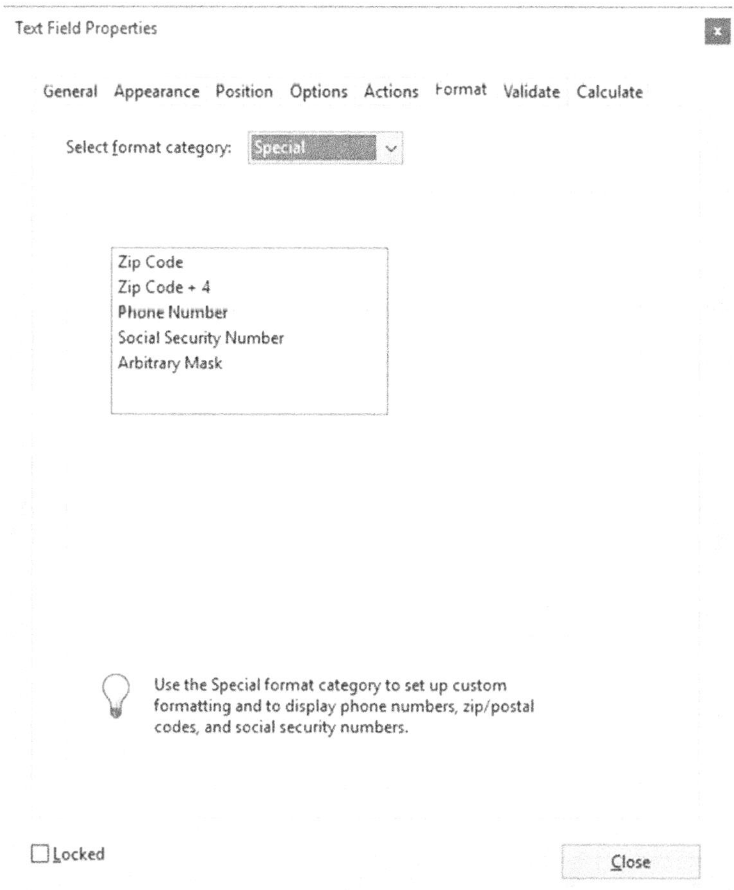

Figure 11-14. *The Special Phone Number format can only format as one option*

However, doing so would not have given you the custom number and color formatting, used to show the difference between correct and incorrect. So, leave format as None and enter the following code into the Validate tab:

```
if(rgexTele.test(event.value)){
    event.target.textColor = color.black;
//Change text to black
}
else{
event.target.textColor = ["RGB",1,0,0]; //Change text to red
app.alert("Invalid Telephone Number"); }
```

If the text matches the regular expression format, leave it as black. If not (else), send out a warning and change the text to red until it is corrected and matches the regular expression.

There are a lot of good regular expressions that can be used and I recommend exploring them.

■ **Note** According to Adobe documentation, the format of Special Arbitrary Mask will allow you to use some basic regular expressions such as

A: Accepts only letters (A-Z, a-z)

X: Accepts spaces and printable characters, including all characters available on a standard keyboard and ANSI characters in the ranges of 32-126 and 128-255

O: Letter accepts alphanumeric characters (A-Z, a-z, and 0-9)

9: Accepts only numeric characters (0-9)

For example, a mask setting `AAA- -q#999` accepts the input of BRT- -q#123 and `OOO@XXX` accepts the input of v12@2up. However, as you'll see, regular expressions with JavaScript offer a wider range of possibilities.

See the Text Field Validation End PDF file. Refer here to Figure 11-15.

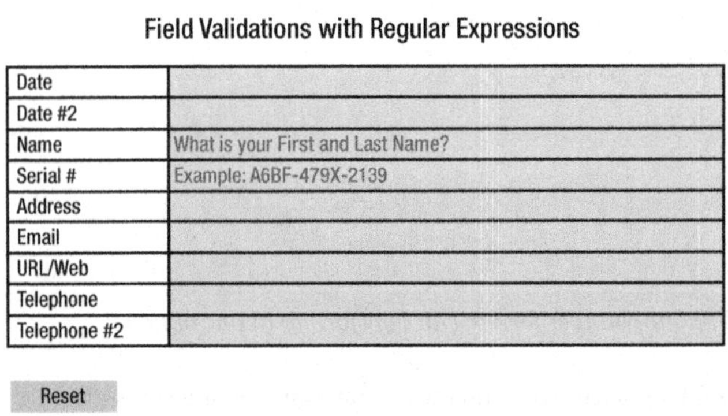

Field Validations with Regular Expressions

Date	
Date #2	
Name	What is your First and Last Name?
Serial #	Example: A6BF-479X-2139
Address	
Email	
URL/Web	
Telephone	
Telephone #2	

Reset

Figure 11-15. *Text field examples to which you can add regular expressions*

Name Validation

Use this script if you want to have a first and last name in the same field. Refer here to Figure 11-16.

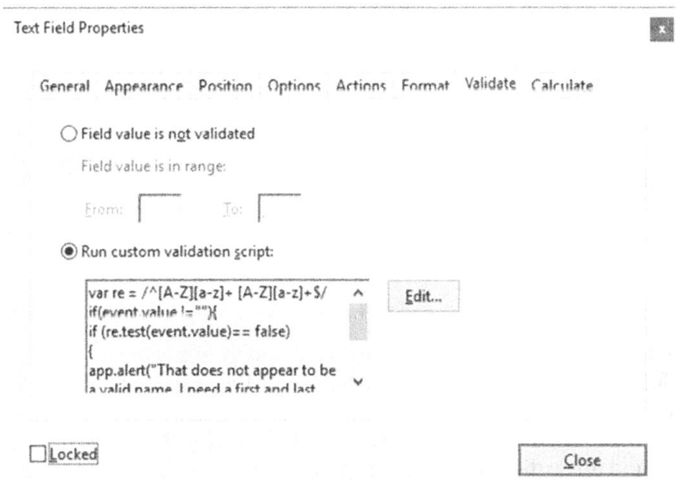

Figure 11-16. *Running a custom validation script*

```
// Custom Validation of Name
var re = /^[A-Z][a-z]+ [A-Z][a-z]+$/
if(event.value !=""){
    if (re.test(event.value)== false){
    app.alert("That does not appear to be a valid name. I need a first and
    last name.");
    event.rc = false;
    }
}
```

■ **Note** The following are basic examples of regular expression metacharacters:

`[abc]`: Find any character between the brackets

`[A-Z]`: Any character from uppercase A to uppercase Z

`[a-z]`: Any character from lowercase a to lowercase z

`[A-z]`: Any character from uppercase A to lowercase z

`[0-9]`: Find any digit between the brackets

`.`: Find a single character, except newline or line terminator

\d: Find a digit

\n: Find a newline character

\s: Find a whitespace character

\w: Find a word character

For more detailed information on regular expressions, visit www.w3schools.com/jsref/jsref_obj_regexp.asp.

In this field, the name needs a first and last name that contains uppercase and lowercase letters, like John Smith. If the user types in JS or just J, they will get the error alert **"That does not appear to be a valid name. I need a first and last name."** When they click the OK button on the error alert, the field returns to blank (event.rc = false;) and they must try again and no further information is processed.

Account Number Validation

Use this script if you want to create a field where a person must enter a special account number or serial number. Refer to Figures 11-15 and 11-16 for where to enter the code.

```
//account number
//A6BF-479X-2139
var re = /^[A-Z]\d[A-Z]{2}-\d{3}[A-Z]-\d{4}$/
//prevent alert if field is blank
if(event.value !=""){
    if (re.test(event.value)== false){
        app.alert("I'm sorry. That is not a valid account number.");
        event.rc = false;
    }
}
```

In this field, the code must be uppercase letter, number digit, two uppercase letters, then a dash, three number digits, uppercase letter, then another dash, four number digits. This must be correct or an error alert will happen and the field will be returned to blank.

Email and URL Validation

Use the following script if you want to create a field where a person must enter an email or a URL. Refer to Figures 11-15 and 11-16 for where to enter the code.

```
 //email
var re = /^\w+([\.-]?\w+)*@\w+([\.-]?\w+)*(\.\w{2,3})+$/;
//prevent alert if field is blank
if(event.value !=""){
```

```
    if (re.test(event.value)== false){
    app.alert("I'm sorry. That is not a valid email address.");
    event.rc = false;
    }
}
```

As you can see, the code is like the others except that this time you need to use the following format to check for the email names and the @ symbol. So jennifer@email.com would be correct, but excluding the @ symbol would trigger an alert. If you were creating a validation for a URL website, you would need to adjust the code to perhaps something like this.

```
var re = /^(http:\/\/www\.|https:\/\/www\.|http:\/\/|https:\/\/)[a-z0-9]+
([\-\.]{1}[a-z0-9]+)*\.[a-z]{2,5}(:[0-9]{1,5})?(\/.*)?$/;
```

And then you could add an alert to reflect if there was an error (example: `http://www.mysite.com`).

```
app.alert("I'm sorry. That is not a valid URL address.");
```

Another Phone and Date Example with Two Variables

Use this script if you want to create a field where a person must enter a phone number or date with two options. Refer to Figures 11-15 and 11-16 for where to enter the code. For the alert warning message, see Figure 11-17.

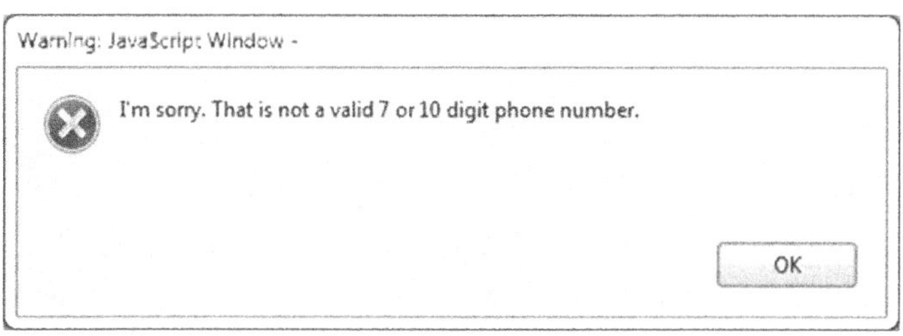

Figure 11-17. *The alert warning when a telephone number is added incorrectly*

```
//phone validation alert
var re7Digits = /^(\d{3})-(\d{4})$/;
var re10Digits = /^(\d{3})-(\d{3})-(\d{4})$/;
//prevent alert if field is blank
if(event.value !=""){
    if (re7Digits.test(event.value)== false && re10Digits.test(event.
    value)== false){
```

```
app.alert("I'm sorry. That is not a valid 7 or 10 digit phone number. ");
    event.rc = false;
    }
}
```

This final example deals with the option to enter a 7-digit or 10-digit code. While not as complex as the first phone example, it does show how to have two formatting options inside one validation. By using the && you are asking for two conditions to be false or true. If true, no alert warning will happen; if false, the alert will happen and the fields will be set back to blank.

You could also use this example with a Date text field, if you set the variables to something like this:

```
var re6Date = /^(\d{1,2})\/(\d{1,2})\/(\d{2})$/;
var re8Date = /^(\d{1,2})\/(\d{1,2})\/(\d{4})$/;
```

Make a few adjustments to the variable names in the conditional statement so they match. You would have two options (12/31/05 or 12/31/2005) for date formats for a person to enter. However, be aware that if this is something that is going into the database, it might cause errors, so check with the people who oversee the database before you set an alternate date entry.

■ **Note** With the update of Acrobat DC you can alternately set your formatting of the date field to Date to access the popup menu. Refer to Chapter 1 if you need to see a screen shot. However, when you have two alternate date options, you must set the Format tab to None and place the code in the Validate tab. Doing this does not give you access to the popup menu.

Final Thoughts

As you can see, errors in typing and selection can be avoided if you have the correct warnings and validations in place. You can assist yourself and your clients when you take the guesswork out of a form.

If you are planning to work with the gray default text method from Chapter 9 and combine it with the regular expression examples from this chapter, it can easily be done by adding this custom format under the Format tab. (See the Invoice Form Shipping Change End r2 PDF and Field Validations End files). Refer here to Figure 11-18.

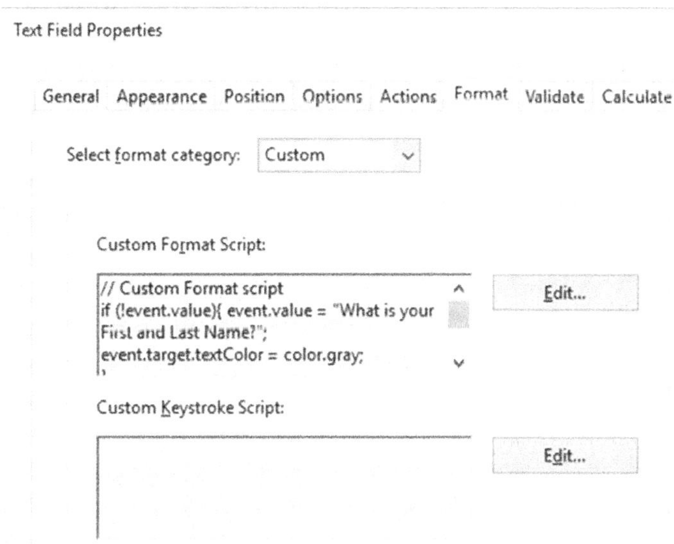

Figure 11-18. *A custom format script can be added if you want default text*

```
if (!event.value){ event.value = "What is your First and Last Name?";
    event.target.textColor = color.gray;
}else{
    event.target.textColor = color.black;
}
```

Remember to use the validation code for each field from earlier in this chapter if it is not already applied. Refer here to Figure 11-19.

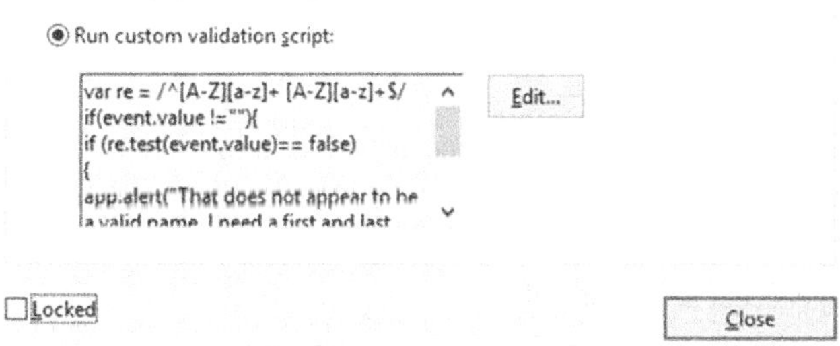

Figure 11-19. *Run the custom validation script*

However, for the telephone validation in this file, a minor adjustment needs to be made to the custom format script to work with three colors rather than two and still get an alert message. Refer here to Figure 11-20.

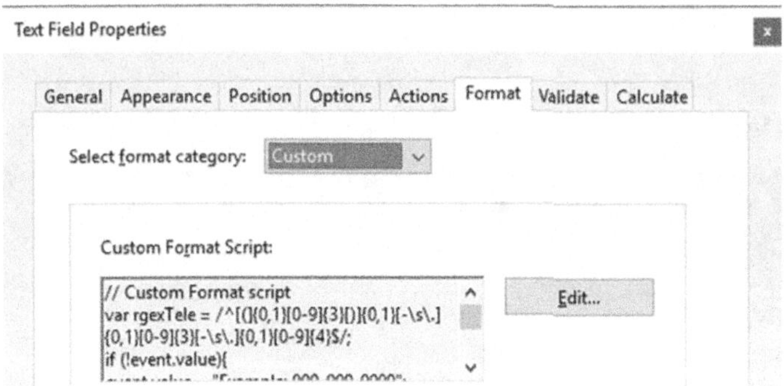

Figure 11-20. *Changing the custom format script*

The code:

```
var rgexTele = /^[(]{0,1}[0-9]{3}[)]{0,1}[-\s\.]{0,1}[0-9]{3}[-\s\.]{0,1}
[0-9]{4}$/;
if (!event.value){
    event.value = "Example: 999-999-9999";
    event.target.textColor = color.gray;
}
else if(rgexTele.test(event.value)){
    event.target.textColor = color.black;
}
else{
    event.target.textColor = ["RGB",1,0,0]; //Change text to red
}
```

■ **Note** Be cautious using this method with the phone number with two variables because it could cause an issue and may not display correctly. Also, don't use default text when a field is formatted to Date, to avoid errors and warnings in Acrobat; when a field is formatted to Date, it cannot accept any other text.

Summary

In this chapter, you learned several ways to add validation to radio buttons and text fields. You also saw a variety of ways to use the validation in combination with formatting to create fields that will alert clients when they chose or typed incorrect information into a field.

Besides warning clients, radio buttons can be used to adjust shipping rates when used in an invoice or order form. They can also be used to refresh or reset a value so your client sees the correct information.

Finally, you also explored a variety of regular expressions which can be used in the Text Field Properties Format and Validation tabs rather than just relying on the formatting that comes with Acrobat, such as Special.

In the next chapter, you will be working with dropdown menus. You'll see how they can interact with text fields and other dropdown menus.

CHAPTER 12

Working with Dropdown Menus

So far you have looked at ways to improve text boxes, buttons, radio buttons, and check boxes with JavaScript. However, there are other types of fields that can be dynamic as well. In this chapter, you are going to take a look at incorporating JavaScript with dropdown menus so that information will be accurately entered or calculated in order to avoid clients entering incorrect information.

Note If you want to work along in this lesson or review the final result, download the Chapter 12 files from `www.apress.com/9781484228920`. The file with the label "Start" is the file without the code and the file with the label "End" is the final result. You will also find folders with original MS Word and PDF files if you would like to edit them and a folder containing the original scripts if you would like to add them to your own PDF forms.

If you are creating your form from an original PDF, refer to the "Forms Review" section in Chapter 1.

Remember that to view the properties of a field you must select the Prepare Form tool; only then can you right-click or double-click a field to review its properties.

Current Skills Request Form

In a small company, an employer may want to ask their employees to submit a form to HR that informs them of the employee's current skill set. In this example, an employee selects the name of their department from the dropdown menu, and their name and some of their information is automatically entered in. If their department is not on the list, they can still type that information in themselves. See the Request Form End PDF. Refer here to Figure 12-1.

J. Harder, *Enhancing Adobe Acrobat DC Forms with JavaScript*,
DOI 10.1007/978-1-4842-2893-7_12

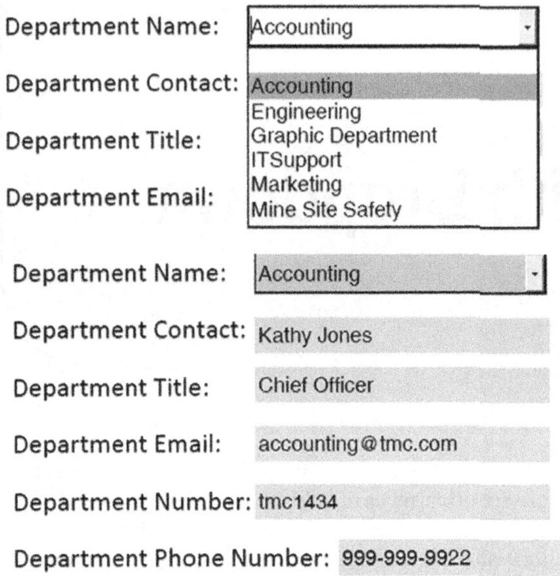

Figure 12-1. *The Current Skills Request Form project*

This automatic action has two parts: a document JavaScript and a script attached to the dropdown menu. Refer here to Figures 12-2 and 12-3.

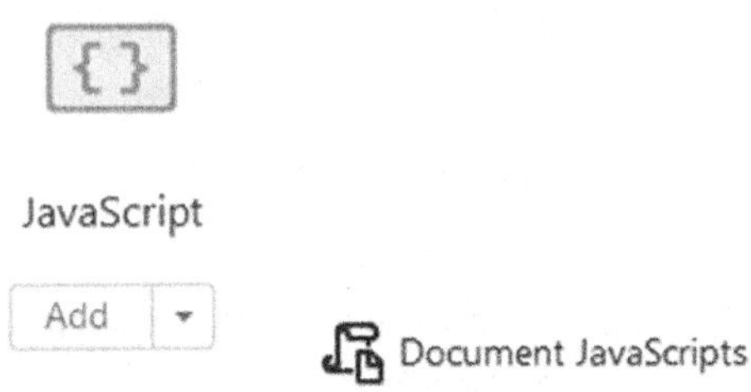

Figure 12-2. *Enter the JavaScript tool and choose the Document JavaScripts tool*

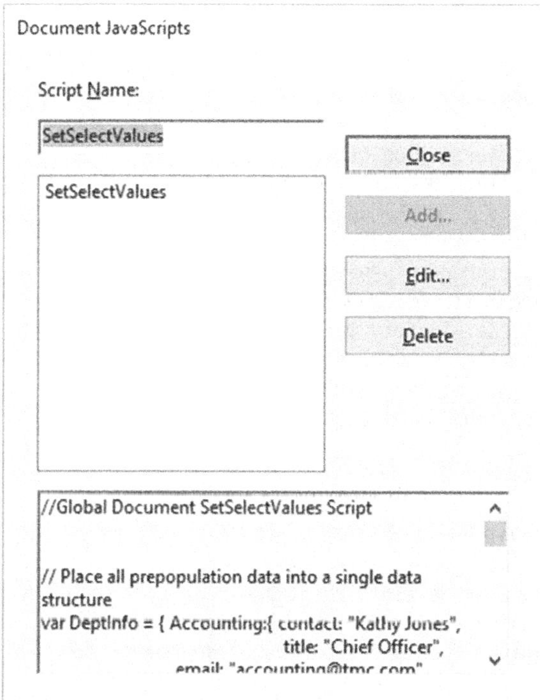

Figure 12-3. *Inside the document JavaScripts dialog box with the script SetSelectValues entered with the Add button*

The Document JavaScript I've created is called `SetSelectValues`:

```
//Global Document SetSelectValues Script

// Place all prepopulation data into a single data structure
var DeptInfo = { Accounting:{ contact: "Kathy Jones",
                              title: "Chief Officer",
                              email: "accounting@tmc.com",
                              deptnum: "tmc1434",
                              deptphone: "999-999-9922"},
                Engineering:{ contact: "Frank R. Smith",
                              title: "Senior Specialist",
                              email: "engineering@tmc.com",
                              deptnum: "tmc1435",
                              deptphone: "999-999-9921" },
       "Graphic Department":{ contact: "Nancy Smith",
                              title: "Artwork Planner",
                              email: "graphics@tmc.com",
                              deptnum: "tmc1436",
                              deptphone: "999-999-9923" },
```

```
                ITSupport:{ contact: "Troy  Carson",
                            title: "Official Coder",
                            email: "it@tmc.com",
                            deptnum: "tmc1437",
                            deptphone: "999-999-9927" },
                Marketing:{ contact: "Janice Walker",
                            title: "Marketing Advisor ",
                            email: "marketing@tmc.com",
                            deptnum: "tmc1438",
                            deptphone: "999-999-9925" },
        "Mine Site Safety":{ contact: "Rick James",
                            title: "Safety Officer",
                            email: "mss@tmc.com",
                            deptnum: "tmc1439",
                            deptphone: "999-999-9924"},
                };
function SetSelectValues(cDeptName)
{
  this.getField("DeptContact").value = DeptInfo[cDeptName].contact;
  this.getField("DeptTitle").value = DeptInfo[cDeptName].title;
  this.getField("DeptEmail").value = DeptInfo[cDeptName].email;
  this.getField("DeptNumber").value = DeptInfo[cDeptName].deptnum;
  this.getField("DeptPhone").value = DeptInfo[cDeptName].deptphone;
}
```

`SetSelectValues` is a function that is calling upon an array variable called `DeptInfo`. Remember that an array is a complex variable that can hold multiple pieces of information. In the array above there are six departments:

- Accounting
- Engineering
- Graphic Department
- Marketing
- IT Support
- Mine Site Safety

Each department has five text fields that must be filled in:

- Contact
- Title
- Email
- Department Number
- Department Phone

In a sense, this has become an array within an array, or a nested array.

■ **Note** This type of array is, as mentioned in Chapter 9, called an associative array. A better term is an associative syntax, in the case of JavaScript when referring to these object literals with in the square brackets []. Rather than using indexes or numbers 0-3 to call upon a variable, it uses words to call up information or object literals/variables. It is also nested in that it can hold another object literal within an object literal. Later in this chapter you will see another example that is also nested.

The last part the function `SetSelectValues` must now draw in each of these parts from the associative syntax so that when a selection from the dropdown menu is chosen the correct information is filtered in the correct order.

Notice how each field is calling for an item called `cDeptName`; however, you don't see it anywhere in the global function as a variable or part of the associative syntax. What is this? `cDeptName` refers to the dropdown field DepartmentNames. Refer to Figure 12-4.

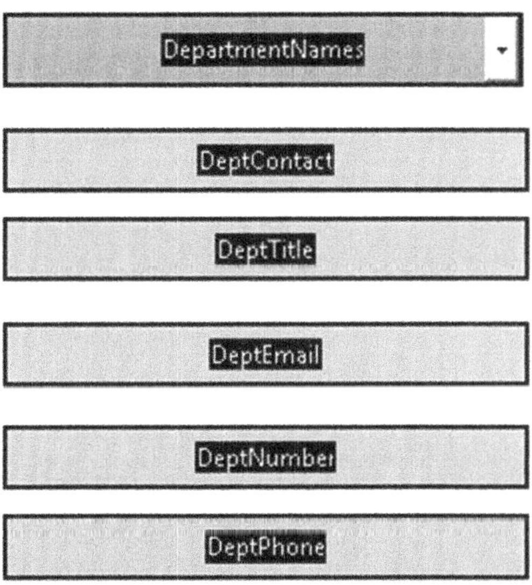

***Figure 12-4.** The dropdown and text fields in Prepare Form Tool view*

Check "Allow user to enter custom text" in the Dropdown Options tab. This way if a department is not on the list, the user can enter the information themselves. Also check "Commit selected values immediately" to allow the text to fill the other fields as soon as the dropdown selection is released. It is optional to check the "Check spelling" box. Refer to Figure 12-5.

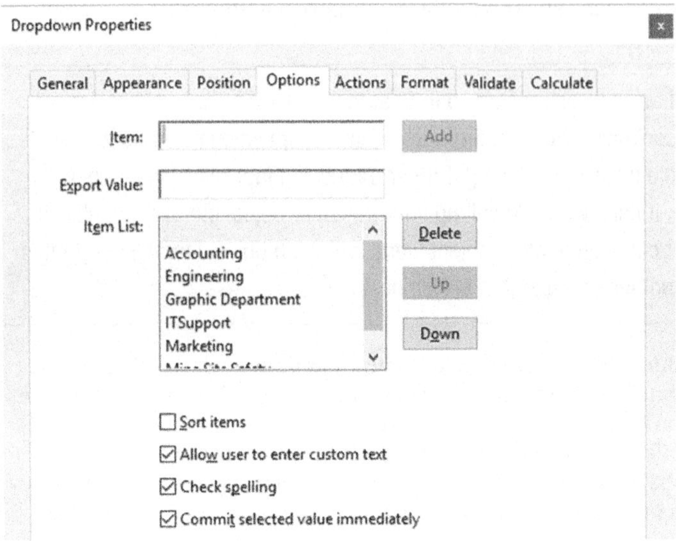

Figure 12-5. *The Dropdown Properties Options tab that is referenced in the document JavaScript*

Now go to the Format tab. Refer to Figure 12-6.

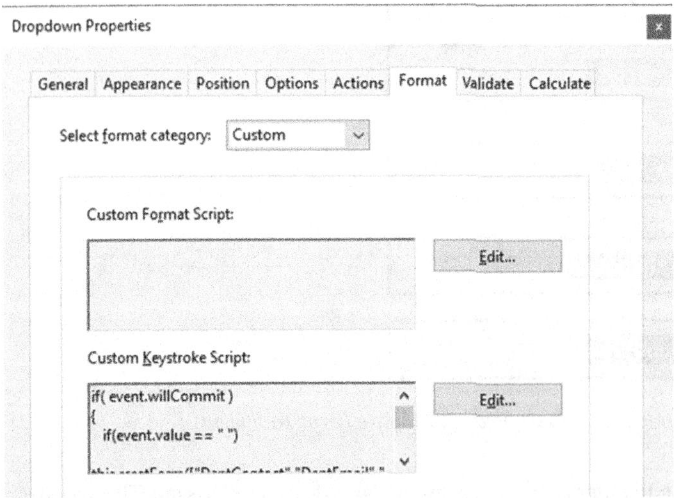

Figure 12-6. *The Format tab with a custom setting and a custom keystroke script*

Enter the following JavaScript into the Format tab's custom keystroke script section:

```
// Custom Format Script
if( event.willCommit ){
   if(event.value == " "){
     this.resetForm(["DeptContact","DeptTitle","DeptEmail","DeptNumber",
     "DeptPhone"]);
}
   else{
     SetSelectValues(event.value);
}
}
```

Now you have created this field and applied JavaScript to the custom keystroke script area (See Figure 12-6). The script "will commit" because this was also checked in the Options tab (See Figure 12-5) and do one of two things:

- If you set the dropdown menu to blank, all the text fields will become blank or " " and it will reset these form fields.
- Otherwise (else) it will make a connection with the function `SetSelectValue` found within the document JavaScript so that the information or values will flow through to the text fields.

Without this trigger to the function, the dropdown field would not be able to place any data in the dropdown list. Note that if the selection is set back to blank information in the dropdown menu, then the fields will reset themselves immediately because it is part of the `willCommit` event. And as mentioned earlier, a person who could not find their information in the list could enter their own data in the blank area.

■ **Note** No JavaScript code was applied to the text fields.

Parts Order Form

Somctimes a client has to search through multiple items and then through multiple subitems in order to find the exact information or item they are looking for. For instance, in a job setting, there may be more than one type of screw, in retail more than one size of T-shirt or more than one color. In just about any job, you can find items that have several variations, and those variations might have different prices depending upon their size and material.

The parts order form is a simplified example of this scenario. See the Parts Order Form End PDF. Refer here to Figure 12-7.

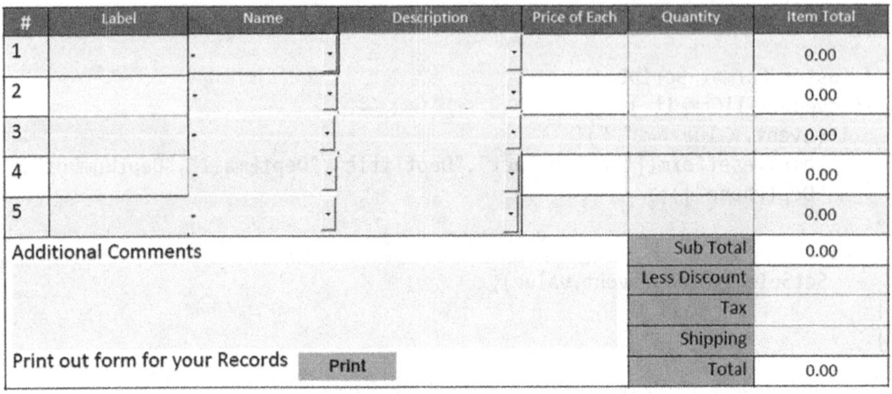

Figure 12-7. *Dropdown menus in the parts order form project*

This time the form contains two connecting dropdown menus: Name and Description. Refer to Figure 12-8.

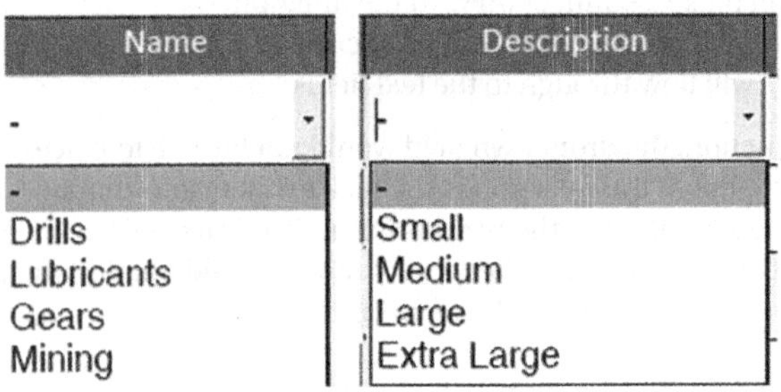

Figure 12-8. *The two connecting dropdown menus found in the current project*

Once the user chooses a name, they can choose a description. Once the description is chosen, a price is then set for the part. Refer here to Figure 12-9.

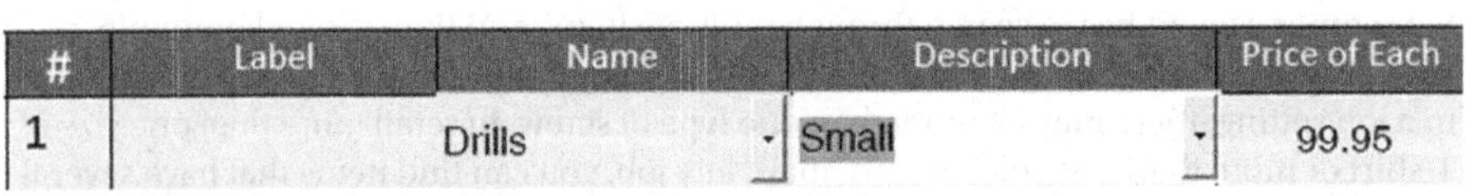

Figure 12-9. *The Description dropdown menu changes the Price field*

All the customer has to do is decide how many parts he wants to buy, and the order form prices start to fill in. Refer here to Figure 12-10.

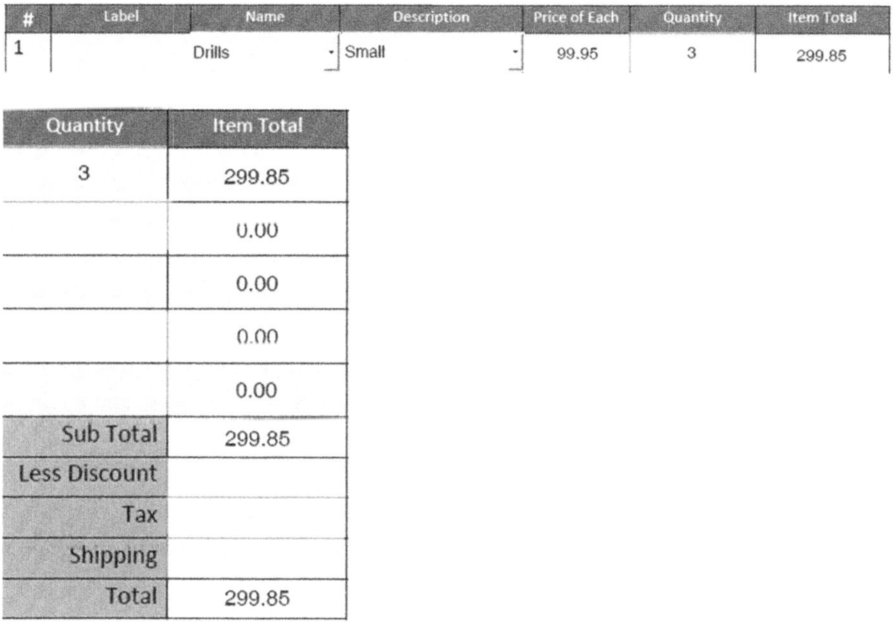

#	Label	Name	Description	Price of Each	Quantity	Item Total
1		Drills	Small	99.95	3	299.85

Quantity	Item Total
3	299.85
	0.00
	0.00
	0.00
	0.00
Sub Total	299.85
Less Discount	
Tax	
Shipping	
Total	299.85

Figure 12-10. *When a client enters a quantity, this changes the total price*

Let's look at this in depth. Once again you will need to create some global document JavaScript. Refer here to Figure 12-11.

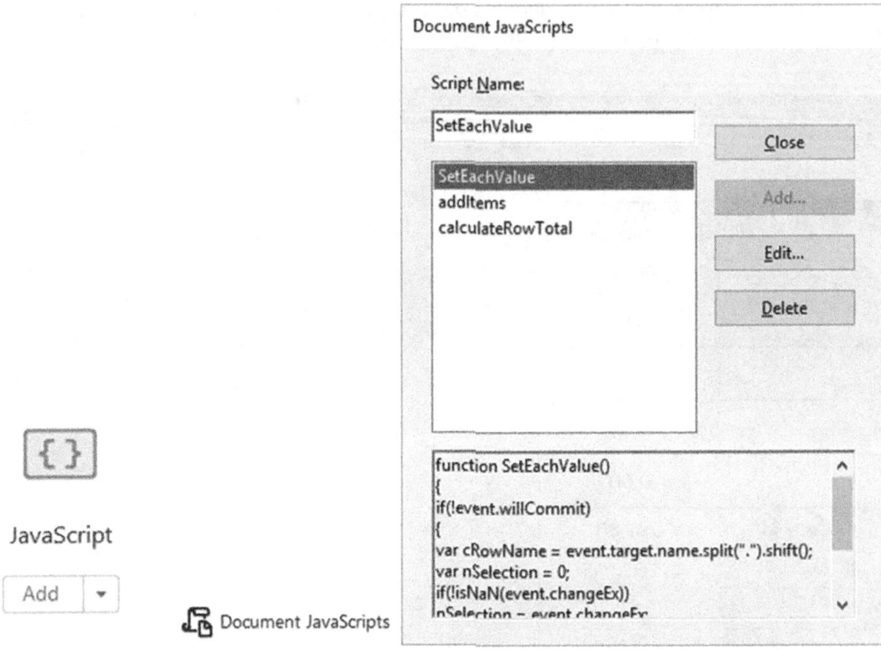

Figure 12-11. *Document JavaScripts that will affect various fields in the project*

As you can see, with the addition of another dropdown, more JavaScript is required.

The first thing you need to do is create your associative syntax/object literal array and the function `addItems`. Each associative syntax `oArray` is separated with a comma.

```
// Global Document addItems
var oArray = {
    Drills: [ ["-","None"], ["Small",19.95], ["Medium",29.95],
    ["Large",39.95], ["Extra Large",44.95]],
    Lubricants: [ ["-","None"], ["Oil",69.95], ["Grease",49.95], ["Super
    Smooth",79.95],["Averge",139.95]],
    Gears:  [ ["-","None"], ["Small",149.95], ["Medium",159.95],
    ["Large",219.95], ["Very Large",339.95]],
    Mining:[ ["-","None"], ["Hard Hat",39.95], ["Pick",29.95], ["Axe",19.95],
    ["Shovel",49.95]]
};
function SetDescriptionEntries(){
if(event.willCommit){
    var cRowName = event.target.name.split(".").shift();
    var list = oArray[event.value];
    if( (list != null) && (list.length > 0) ){
    this.getField(cRowName + ".Description").setItems(list);
    }
```

```
    else{
    this.getField(cRowName + ".Description").clearItems();
    }
    this.getField(cRowName + ".Each").value = 0;
  }
}
```

■ **Note** If for some reason on another page you need to add a separate set of dropdown menus, you must create another document JavaScript like `addItems2` and then change the associative syntax/object's name and the function's name to avoid a clash.

In the previous single dropdown example, you had to take the data from the item in the dropdown and copy it to other text fields. This time you have to copy the subitems to another dropdown menu called description. Again, if no value is found in the name dropdown, the description value remains blank and no choice is available. In this example, for array (`oArray`), the associative syntax is divided into four item names:

- Drills
- Lubricants
- Gears
- Mining

Each part of the associative syntax name divides into another dropdown for a subitem `description` and a text field that contains the price/each item. You will see shortly how this function to separate the price is called upon.

Then you need to add `SetEachValue` in the document JavaScript:

```
function SetEachValue(){
    if(!event.willCommit){
    var cRowName = event.target.name.split(".").shift();
    var nSelection = 0;
    if(!isNaN(event.changeEx))
    nSelection = event.changeEx;
    this.getField(cRowName + ".Each").value = nSelection;
    }
}
```

The fields have like `Row1.Item`, `Row2.item`, and so on. Using this type of order or schema allows the document JavaScript to easily call each item through the function. Because this type of form is so complex, using ordered and meaningful names is crucial.

If the event will not commit, this refers to the exclamation point (!) override, then the value is 0. This takes care of any missing numbers in the object array. If a non-number (NaN) like a word was entered instead, the value will remain 0. Otherwise, the function `SetDescriptionEnteries` will enter the value found in the associative syntax for price/each item.

This is the setting for the price of each item that was chosen from the `description` dropdown menu. The description and price are split here into their respective fields using the `split` method. You can see this because of the methods called `.split()` and `.shift()`. The `shift` method removes the first item in the associative example `["Oil",69.95]` and leaves only the price that will now go into the price of each item field.

There are other methods that you can use to add or remove elements or object literals from the associative syntax. Here are a few explained for your reference:

- `pop()`: Removes the last element from the array and returns the remaining elements. Example: `["Oil",69.95]` = `Oil`
- `push()`: Adds a new element to the end of an array and gives a new length count
- `unshift()`: Adds new elements to the beginning an array and gives a new length count
- `splice()`: Adds/removes elements from an array anywhere

For more information on methods and what else they can do, visit these links:

- `www.w3schools.com/js/js_array_methods.asp`
- `www.w3schools.com/jsref/jsref_split.asp`
- `www.w3schools.com/jsref/jsref_obj_array.asp`

I created the function `SetEachValue` here in the Document JavaScript because I will be using it multiple times and I want to be able to call on it as many times as I like depending on how many dropdowns I have. Also, I do not have to rewrite this code for each field, which could lead to errors.

The last function is used to calculate the item total (`calculateRowTotal`) of the row. This is not the Subtotal or Final Total fields, which can only be found out when you have finished adding up multiple items. Refer to the Parts Order Form End PDF.

```
// Global Document calculateRowTotal
function CalculateRowTotal()
{
    var cRowName = event.target.name.split(".").shift();
    event.value = this.getField(cRowName + ".Each").value * this.
    getField(cRowName + ".Qty").value;
}
```

This function once again uses the `shift` method. However, only the price is calculated against the quantity field so that the Item Row Total price is now calculated.

Like the `SetEachValue()` function, this will be used multiple times so you create it the Document JavaScripts tool. Whenever you have a function that you think you will use many times, it's good to set it up in the Document JavaScripts tool.

Now you will take a look at the first row of your parts order form to see where it all fits. You will skip the Label field since it is not part of the project.

The first dropdown, `Row1.item`, is set up like Figure 12-12 so that it can reference the associative syntax/object called `oArray`. In the Options tab, you do not put anything in the value Export Value; this needs to remain blank.

***Figure 12-12.** Dropdown properties in the Options tab in the first dropdown menu*

In the Format tab's Custom field, you call upon the `SetDescriptionEntries` function, which is found in the Document JavaScript `addItems`. This references the associative syntax `oArray` and lets the next dropdown fields of Row1.Description and Row1.each fill with information. Refer to Figure 12-13.

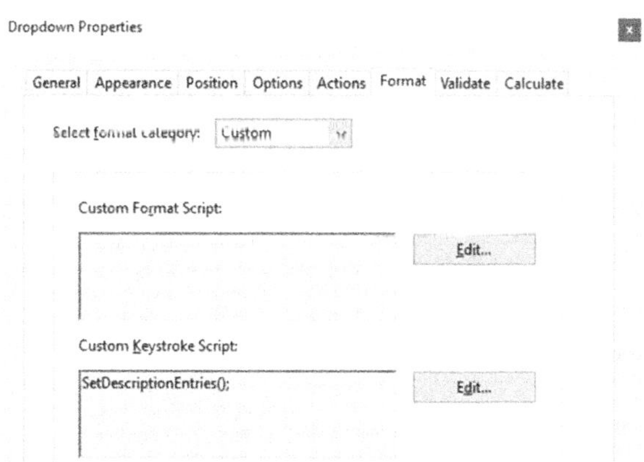

***Figure 12-13.** The custom keystroke script in the first dropdown menu*

```
// Format Custom Keystroke for Name
SetDescriptionEntries();
```

For all the other item dropdowns, you repeat these steps in the Option and Format tabs. To see how you use this same function in the other dropdown fields, refer to Figure 12-14.

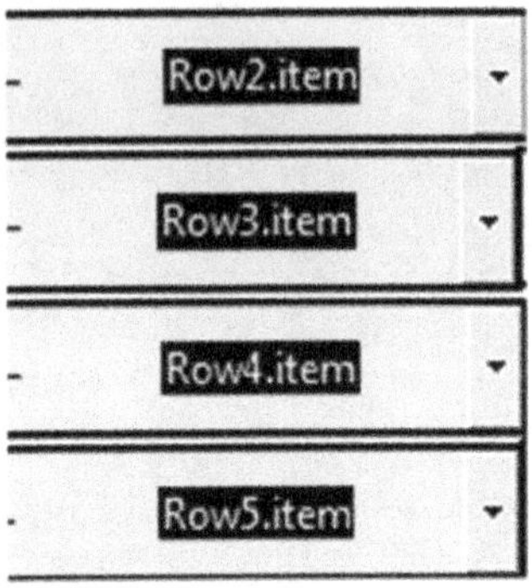

Figure 12-14. *Dropdown fields requiring same options and format settings*

The description dropdown Row1.Description is left blank like this and you do not preset in its Options tab. JavaScript will do that work for you. Refer to Figure 12-15.

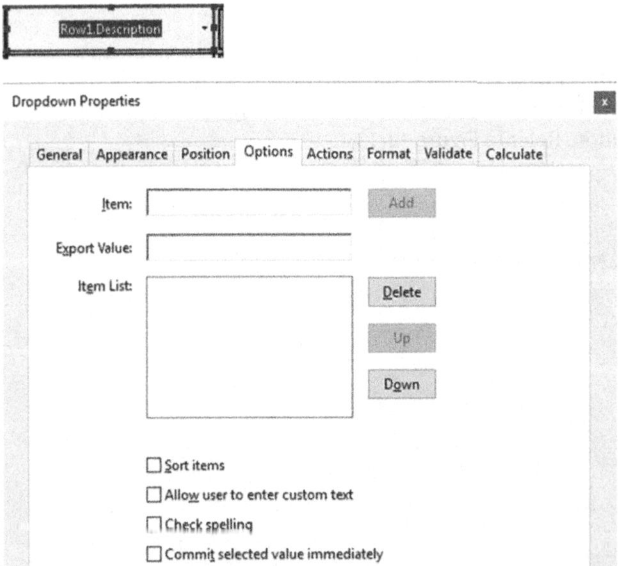

Figure 12-15. *Dropdown properties in the Options tab in the second dropdown menu*

The `SetEachValue` function is now called upon in the Format tab's Custom field to get the value into the price of each field and can be added to the other description fields. See Figure 12-17. Remember, if the price was left out of the associative syntax or was text, the price will come in as 0 or $0.00. Refer to Figure 12-16.

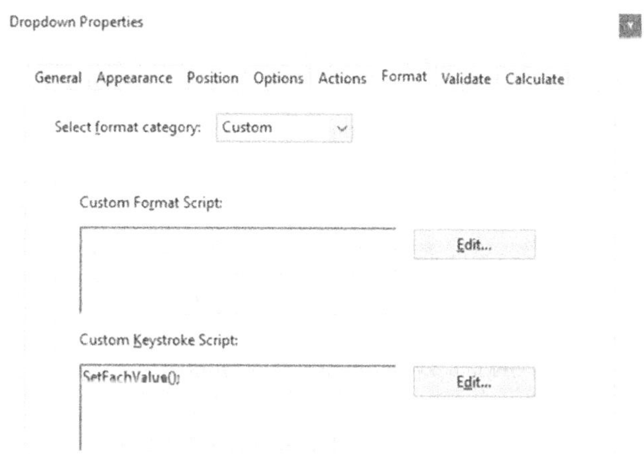

Figure 12-16. *The custom keystroke script for the second dropdown menu*

```
// Format Custom Keystroke for Description
SetEachValue();
```

This code is entered into each description drop-down menu. Refer to Figure 12-17.

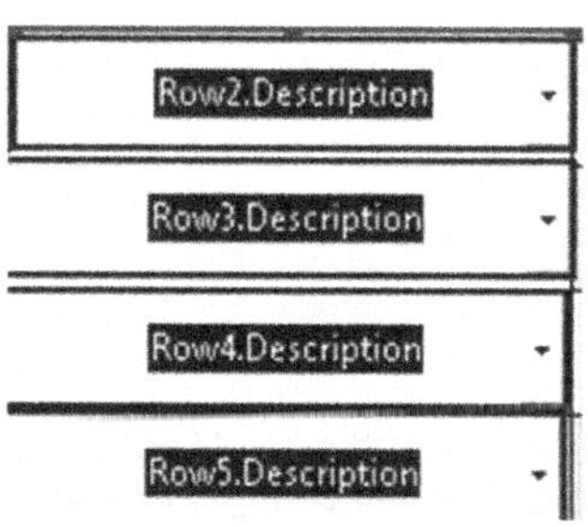

Figure 12-17. *Dropdown fields requiring same options and format settings*

The price of each field Row1.Each has no JavaScript in it. Its settings come from the `SetEachValue` function in the previous dropdown menu. However, it has been formatted to Number with a currency symbol. Refer to Figure 12-18.

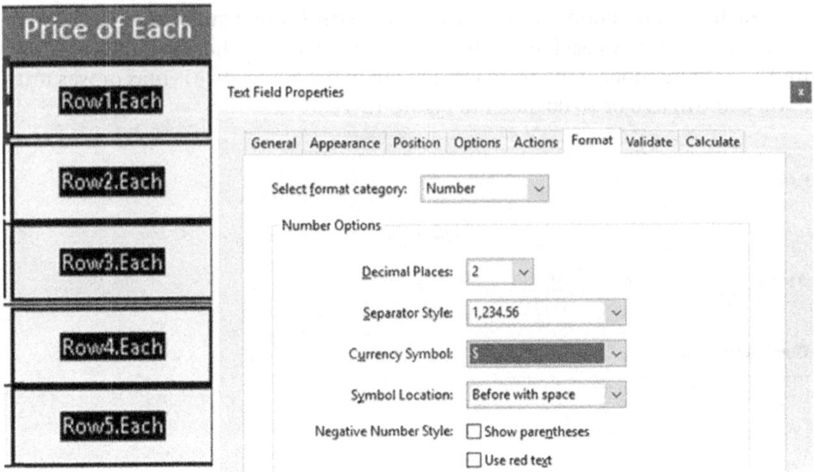

***Figure 12-18.** The text field properties in the Format tab are set to Number*

The same is true of the quantity column, Row1.Qty. It contains no JavaScript. It just needs to be formatted to Number with no currency symbol and the decimal place set to 0. This field will be referenced shortly. Refer to Figure 12-19.

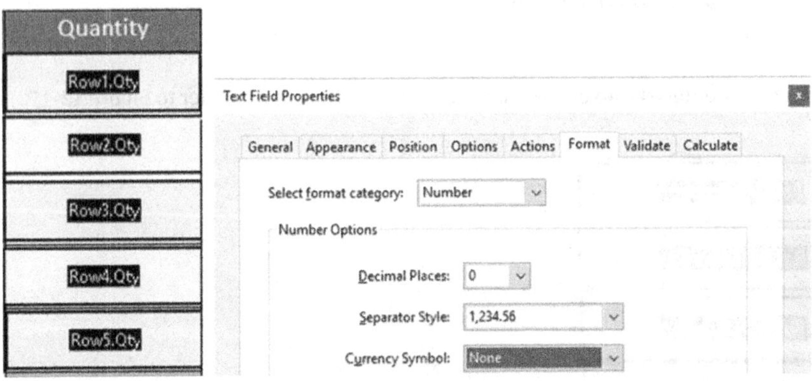

***Figure 12-19.** The text field properties in the Format tab are set to Number without a currency symbol*

The final area, Item Total (formatted to Number with currency symbol), now multiplies the information from the Price of Each and Quantity fields. Again, the calculation function was reference from the document JavaScript section and can be applied to multiple fields. Refer to Figure 12-20.

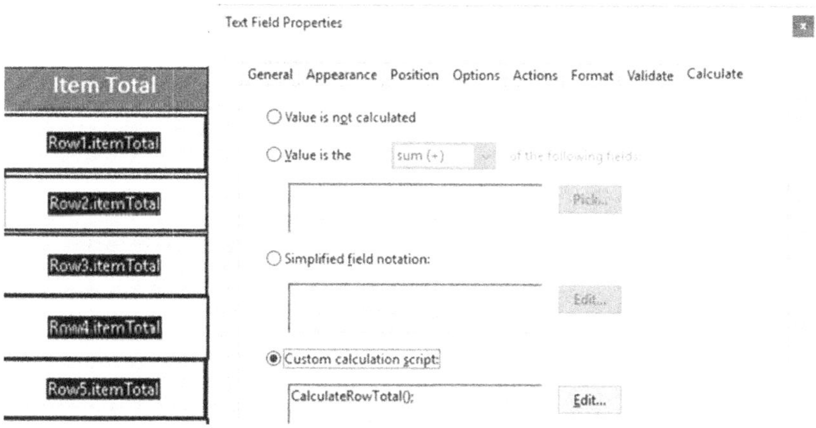

Figure 12-20. *Text field properties in the Calculate tab's custom calculation script*

```
// Calculate Script Items
CalculateRowTotal();
```

Set the itemTotal fields to read-only in the General tab.

Now make sure that your fields, SubTotal, Discount, Tax, Shipping and Total, are all formatted to Number with a currency symbol. SubTotal and Total should be set to read-only in the General tab so that the client does not overwrite a number. Refer to Figure 12-21.

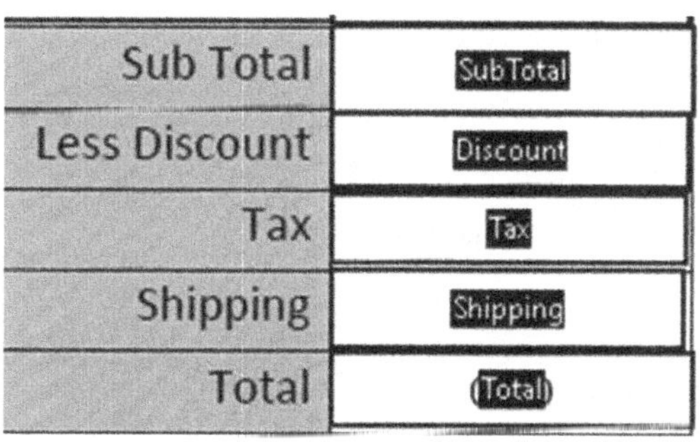

Figure 12-21. *Final text fields that need to be calculated in the project*

In past Invoice forms, you used Value or Simplified Field Notation. Here you might be tempted to use these options to add up your subtotal and final total. Refer here to Figure 12-22.

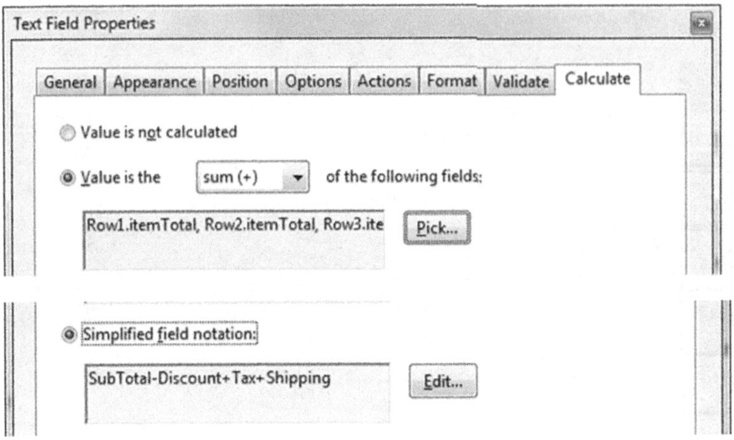

Figure 12-22. *Some field calculations do not require JavaScript*

While the above examples do work, I found them to be a bit buggy and they did not refresh well. We don't want users of our form to get frustrated and confused as to why their inputs are not working smoothly. In the end, what I discovered was that you need to add or subtract everything with JavaScript and then the form will run smoothly. In the Subtotal field, I placed the following script into the Calculate tab's Custom Calculation Script field. Refer to Figure 12-23.

```
//Subtotal Script
var a = this.getField("Row1.itemTotal");
var b = this.getField("Row2.itemTotal");
var c = this.getField("Row3.itemTotal");
var d = this.getField("Row4.itemTotal");
var f = this.getField("Row5.itemTotal");
event.value =a.value + b.value + c.value + d.value + f.value;
```

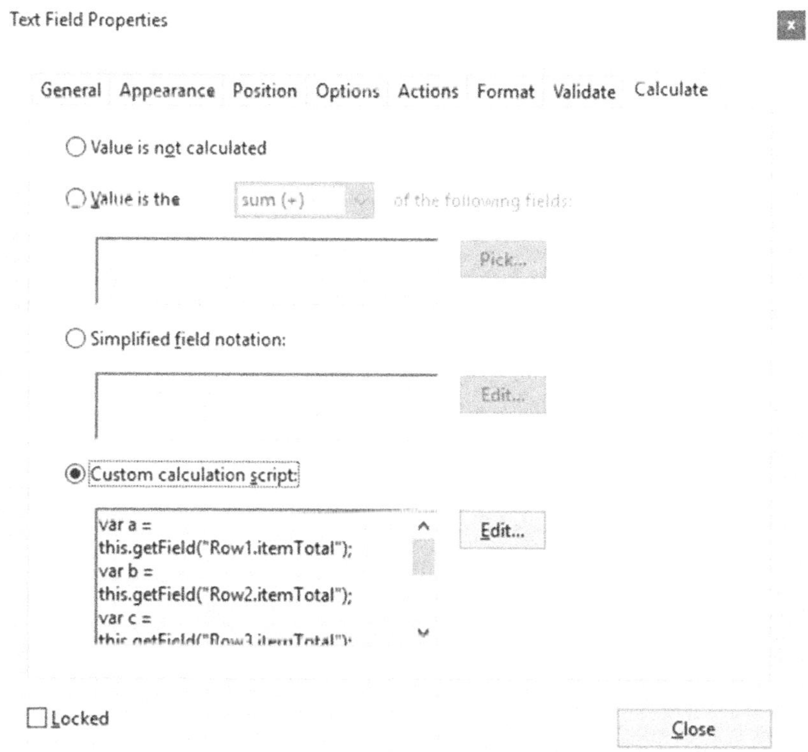

Figure 12-23. *Text field properties in the Calculate tab for the SubTotal field*

As you can see, it is like an example you tried in earlier lessons such as Chapter 6. Refer to Figure 12-24.

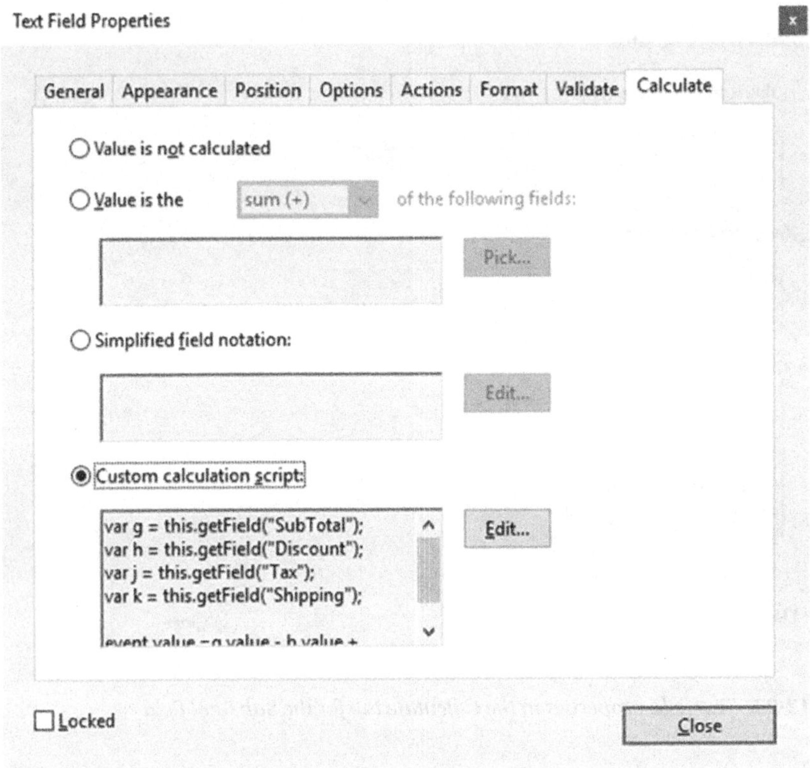

***Figure 12-24.** Text field properties in the Calculate tab for the Total field*

Then for the Grand Total or Total Field, I used this script:

```
//Total Script
var g = this.getField("SubTotal");
var h = this.getField("Discount");
var j = this.getField("Tax");
var k = this.getField("Shipping");
event.value =g.value - h.value + j.value + k.value;
```

This worked the best for me for this example.

Final Thoughts

When making a complex form with multiple dropdowns, it's best to plan it out on paper or a drawing program first and decide what you would like to do. You may need an associative syntax with object literals or a global function, but write it all out first.

Once you've built the form, similar to what I have done, make sure that number areas are formatted to Number correctly, and then add the JavaScript. Test the form or maybe get others to test it. It's important to work out all the bugs before your customers use it. The focus here is to avoid client errors and frustration and to get the results you want when working with fields in a form.

Load a Lengthy Single Dropdown or List Menu

While not as complex as the examples above, occasionally you may need to load only a single dropdown menu with 30 or more items that don't affect other fields or menus in the form. See the Load Single Menu folder.

Having to enter this into a dropdown or list menu can be labor intensive: you must select the Options tab, enter a name, enter a value, and then click the Add button for each item. Also, you may want the same information in multiple menus that change often (see the Time Sheet PDF example). To save time for lengthy single menus, I have included extra files where I have put all my code for the menu into the global Document JavaScript area. I call this function `LoadOptions`. You can view the code on the following pages and will find it in the supplied text file as well. As always, make sure that your fields have the same name as what is written in the JavaScript so that the connection will work correctly. Refer to Figure 12-25.

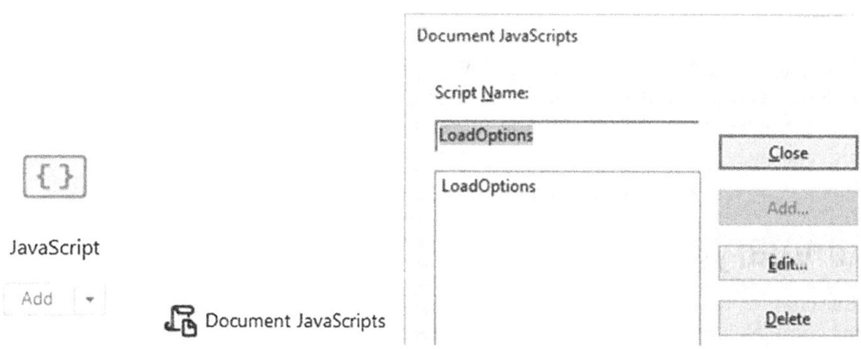

Figure 12-25. *The LoadOptions script*

The following code is added to the Document JavaScripts tool:

```
// define array of entries and export values for dropdown array
// define array of states and abbreviations
var aMinerals = new Array(["Select Mineral", ""],
                          ["Diamond", "DI"],
                          ["Emerald", "EM"],
                          ["Garnet", "GA"],
                          ["Opal", "OP"],
                          ["Ruby", "RB"],
                          ["Sapphire", "SP"]);
// function to load a combo/list box with an array of values
function LoadOptions(oField, aValues) {
    var bResult = false;
// load array of values into field object
    if(oField.type != "combobox" && oField.type != "listbox") {
    app.alert("Load Options function requires a combobox or listbox", 0, 0);
    bResult = false;
}
    else{
    oField.setItems(aValues); // set values
    bResult = true;
}
return bResult;
} // end LoadOptions
// load the data - comment out after updating when only doing array changes
LoadOptions(this.getField('Dropdown1'), aMinerals);
LoadOptions(this.getField('ListBox1'), aMinerals);
```

The above example works for dropdown or list box menus. If you are not using a list box, you can comment that line out or add more `LoadOptions` if other dropdowns require the same object literals that may change often. Remember to give all dropdown fields a distinct name.

Summary

In this chapter, while working with dropdown menus and text boxes, you encountered some complex JavaScript. You learned how nested associative/object literals work and how you can extract information from those associative syntax functions. You also saw the benefit of document JavaScript and how writing the script in one location saved you time so you didn't have to write multiple edits in several locations, only reference the script or other fields.

In the next chapter, you are going to take a more detailed look at probably one of the most underused fields: the list box. You've just seen as with dropdown menus that you can load text into them using document JavaScript. However, they're not as compact as a dropdown, so what else can you do with them?

CHAPTER 13

Working with List Boxes

The last main type of form field you are going to explore is list boxes. In my experience, list boxes are the most underused of form fields. While they may not be as compact as dropdowns, they are great for helping organize a list of priorities. Refer to Figure 13-1.

Note If you want to work along in this lesson or review the final result, download the Chapter 13 files from `www.apress.com/9781484228920`. The file with the label "Start" is the file without the code and the file with the label "End" is the final result. You will also find folders with original MS Word and PDF files if you would like to edit them and a folder containing the original scripts if you would like to add them to your own PDF forms.

If you are creating your form from an original PDF that contains no form fields, refer to the "Forms Review" section in Chapter 1.

Remember that to view the properties of a field you must select the Prepare Form tool; only then can you right-click or double-click a field to review its properties.

J. Harder, *Enhancing Adobe Acrobat DC Forms with JavaScript*,
DOI 10.1007/978-1-4842-2893-7_13

List Box Priority List with Control Buttons

Figure 13-1 shows list boxes (see the Priority List End PDF file). As you can see, there are list boxes and five buttons. I'll discuss the lower text field and button later.

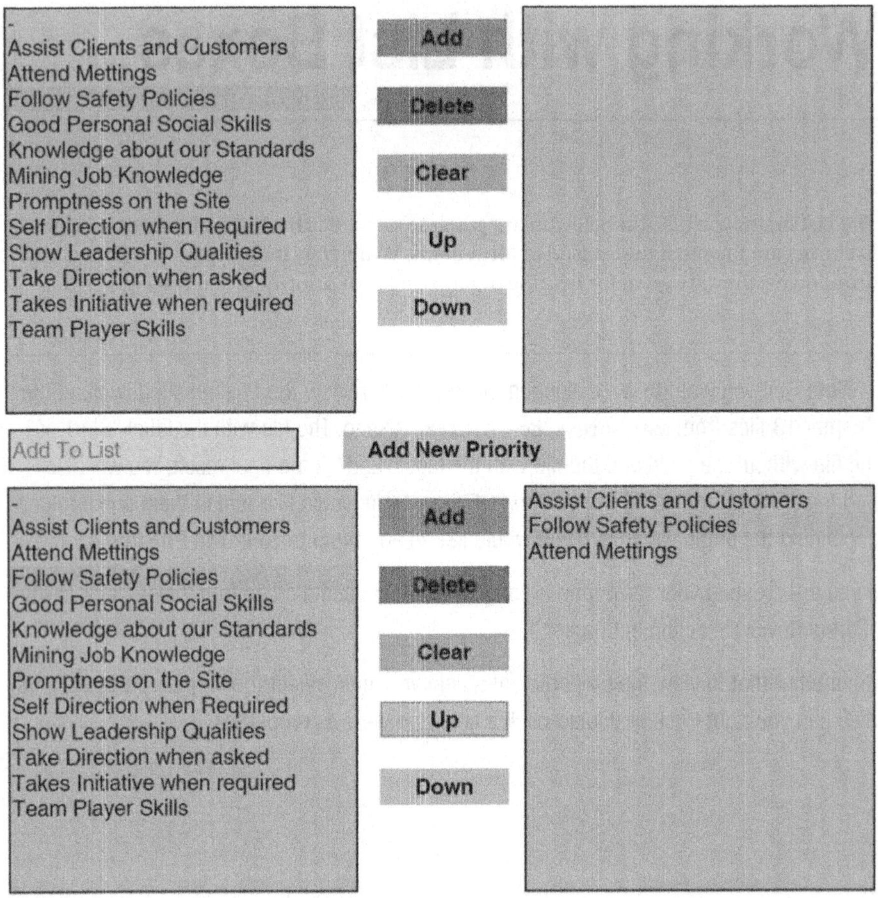

Figure 13-1. *List Box Priory project with buttons and a custom form field with a button that allows you to add your own priority to the final list*

The Add button transfers the selected phrase one at a time over to the right list box. The Delete button deletes a selected phrase from the right list. The Clear button resets the whole form. The Up and Down buttons reorder the selected phrase either up or down. You have complete control over your list of priorities.

Here's how it works. You start with some global document JavaScript. Refer to Figure 13-2.

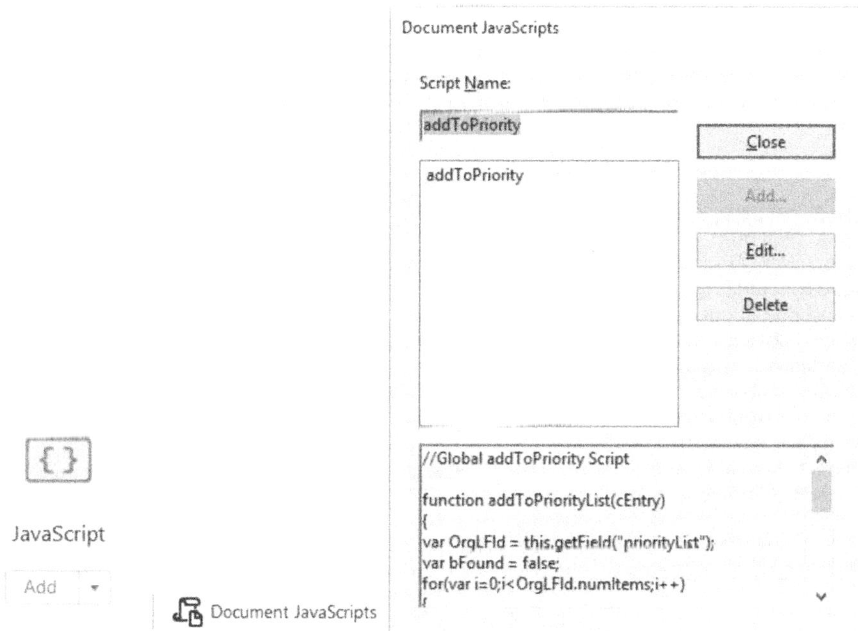

Figure 13-2. *The document JavaScript added to the PDF project*

This JavaScript is called `addToPriority`:

```
//Global addToPriority Script

function addToPriorityList(cEntry){
    var OrgLFld = this.getField("priorityList");
    var bFound = false;
for(var i=0;i<OrgLFld.numItems;i++){
        if(OrgLFld.getItemAt(i,false) == cEntry){
            bFound = true;
            break;
        }
    }
    if(!bFound){
    OrgLFld.insertItemAt({cName:cEntry, nIdx:-1});}
}
```

In this `addToPriorityList` function you are selecting items from the qualityList list box form field and using the buttons to move those items over to the priorityList list box form field. Notice that you are using a for loop to loop through all of the object literals found with the associative syntax (see Chapters 9 and 12) that are found in the qualityList.

When an item is found that will be added by the Add button, it will be broken out and inserted into the priorityList but only once. You can see this with the variable `bFound`; it's set to true and then false if an attempt is made to enter it again. You can only enter it again if it is cleared or deleted from the priorityList.

The qualityList list box form field has been set up like this. No script is directly applied to it; it is only called upon. The same is true for the priorityList; it, however, contains no entries. Refer here to Figures 13-3, 13-4, and 13-5.

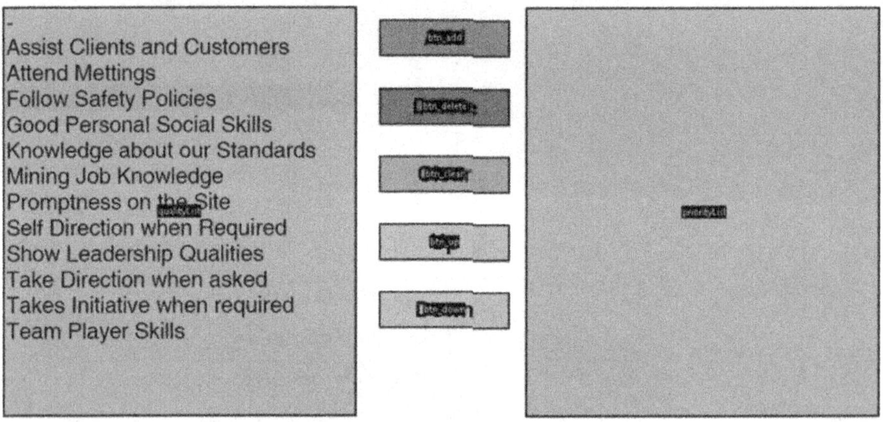

***Figure 13-3.** List boxes and buttons in the Prepare Form view*

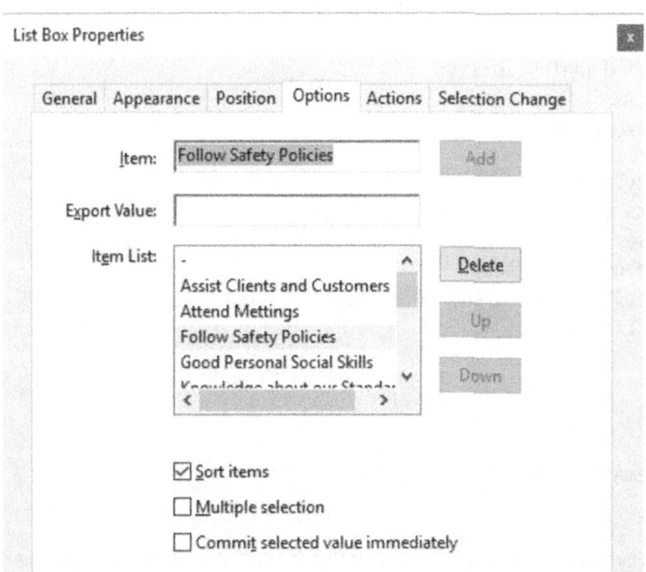

***Figure 13-4.** The list box properties in the Options tab for qualityList*

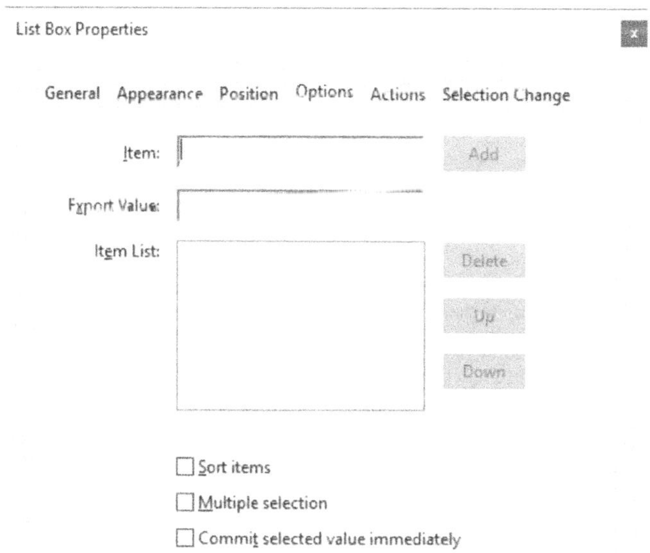

Figure 13-5. *The list box properties in the Options tab for priorityList*

Only the buttons contain the actions. Refer to Figure 13-6.

Figure 13-6. *The list box properties in the Actions tab for buttons and how the buttons appear in the Prepare Form view and normally*

The Add Button

Refer to Figure 13-7.

Figure 13-7. *The Add button*

```
// Add Button
var OrgLFld = this.getField("qualityList");
if(OrgLFld){
var cEntry = OrgLFld.getItemAt(OrgLFld.currentValueIndices,false);
addToPriorityList(cEntry);
}
```

Notice how it calls on the function `addToPriorityList` and gets the items from the `qualityList` and adds the item to the `priorityList` field only once.

The Delete Button

Refer to Figure 13-8.

Figure 13-8. *The Delete button deletes list items from the priority list*

```
// Delete Button

var OrgLFld = this.getField("priorityList");
var prev = OrgLFld.currentValueIndices;
if(OrgLFld.currentValueIndices > -1){
   OrgLFld.deleteItemAt(OrgLFld.currentValueIndices);
      if(OrgLFld.numItems > prev){
      OrgLFld.currentValueIndices = prev;}
   else if(OrgLFld.numItems > 0){
     OrgLFld.currentValueIndices = prev-1;}
}
```

The Delete button's script looks at what was previously added or just selected. Whatever is currently selected when the delete button is pressed is removed from the priortyList list box form field.

The Clear or Reset Button

Refer to Figure 13-9.

Figure 13-9. *The Clear Button resets/clears the priority list*

You could have simply used your actions to reset the form with no code. However, sometimes you just want to clear a specific list, and reset alone is not enough.

```
// Clear Button
this.getField("priorityList").clearItems();
```

The `.clearItems()` acts as a reset for the priortyList.

The Up Button

The Up button moves items up in the list. Refer to Figure 13-10.

Figure 13-10. *The Up button moves an item up in the list*

```
//Up Button
OrgLFld = this.getField("priorityList");
if(OrgLFld){
    var prevIdx = OrgLFld.currentValueIndices;
    if(prevIdx > 0){
        var curValue = OrgLFld.getItemAt(prevIdx);
        OrgLFld.deleteItemAt(prevIdx);
        OrgLFld.insertItemAt({cName:curValue, nIdx:prevIdx-1});
        OrgLFld.currentValueIndices = prevIdx - 1;
    }
}
```

It acts like an organizer or index. For instance, in an array or associative syntax, the first item or object literal is 0, then 1, then 2, and so on. In order for an item that is a 2 rank in the list to move upwards, it must become rank 1 or the highest rank, which is 0. By using `prevIdx - 1` you are telling the button to move this item one back or one higher.

The Down Button

The Down button works in reverse, moving items down the list. Refer to Figure 13-11.

Figure 13-11. *The Down button moves a priority down in the list*

```
//Down Button
OrgLFld = this.getField("priorityList");
if(OrgLFld){
 var prevIdx = OrgLFld.currentValueIndices;
    if( (prevIdx >= 0) && (prevIdx < (OrgLFld.numItems -1)) ){
    var curValue = OrgLFld.getItemAt(prevIdx);
    OrgLFld.deleteItemAt(prevIdx);
    OrgLFld.insertItemAt({cName:curValue, nIdx:prevIdx+1});
    OrgLFld.currentValueIndices = prevIdx + 1;
    }
}
```

This time, if an item is a rank of 2, it will become a rank 3 if that is possible. In the if conditional statement, a check is made: is the item greater (>) or equal (=) to zero, and (&&) is it less than (<) but not already the last item. By using `prevIdx + 1`, you are telling the button to move this item one forward or one lower in the priorityList list box.

The Add New Priority button allows the user to add a custom priority that might not be on the original list. Unlike dropdown menus, you cannot add text directly to a list box. Like any list item, it can be deleted. Noticed that, as in earlier lessons like Chapter 9, you can add a default text format to the text field so that it will always be filled. The same word will not enter twice. The button has the following code and resets the text field after an addition. Refer to Figure 13-12.

Figure 13-12. *This text field allows you to enter a new priority and the Add New Priority button allows you to add that priority to the list*

```
var textValue = this.getField("customAdd").value;
    var listField = this.getField("priorityList");
    if (textValue) {
        listField.insertItemAt(textValue, textValue, -1);
    }
```

List boxes are useful and creative way to organize priorities. You will improve upon this list later in the chapter.

Check Box, Dropdown, and List Box Example 1

A single list box can be used in combination with other form field items as well. See the TMC Free Newsletter End Option 1 file. Refer to Figure 13-13.

Figure 13-13. *This project allows you to chose a free newsletter after making a selection from the dropdown menu. The menu only appears if you check the check box.*

This example uses a check box to reveal a dropdown menu. When an item in the dropdown is selected, it reveals a secondary choice in the list box. Refer to Figure 13-14.

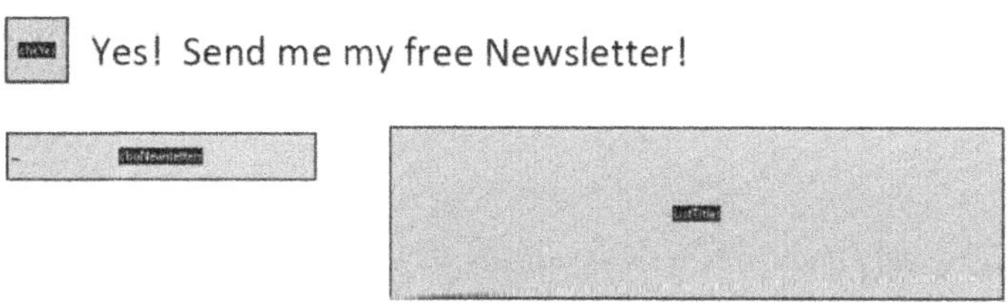

Figure 13-14. *Choice of a free newsletter fields in the Prepare Form view*

Here you begin with a global document JavaScript called `SetTitleEntries`. Refer to Figure 13-15.

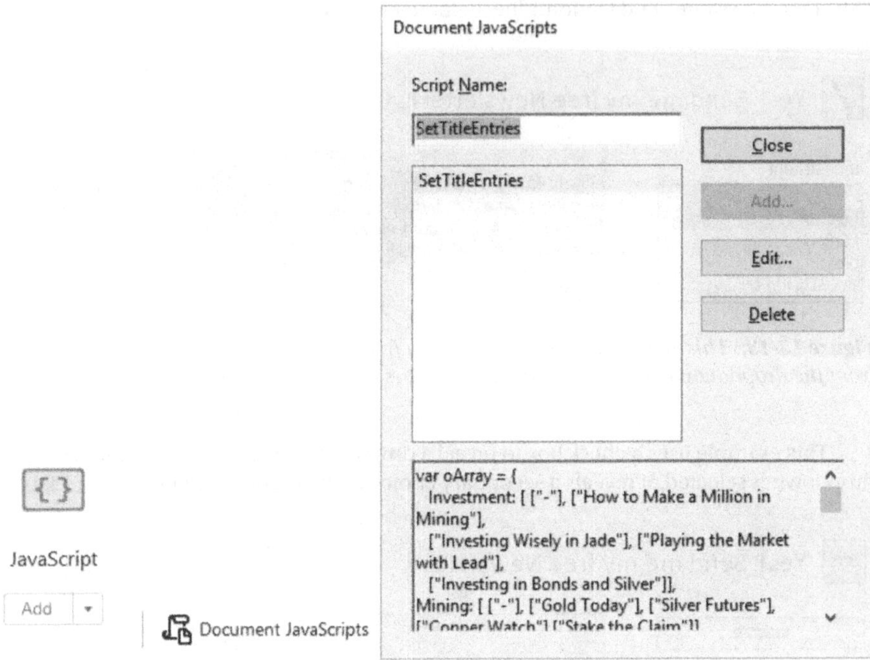

Figure 13-15. *The document JavaScript for the newsletter PDF file*

Enter the following code:

```
//Set Title Enteries
var oArray = {
     Investment: [ ["-"], ["How to Make a Million in Mining"],
   ["Investing Wisely in Jade"], ["Playing the Market with Lead"],
   ["Investing in Bonds and Silver"]],
Mining: [ ["-"], ["Gold Today"], ["Silver Futures"], ["Copper
Watch"],["Stake the Claim"]],
Gold:  [ ["-"], ["Global Annual Gold Festival"],
   ["Gold Watch"], ["All that Glitters"],
   ["Fool's Gold"]],
"Tourmaline Mining":  [ ["-"], ["Tourmaline Queen"],
    ["Waltermelon Gem"], ["Pick and Shovel"],
   ["Rocks and Gems"]],
};
```

```
function SetTitleEntries(){
    if(event.willCommit){
    var list = oArray[event.value];
        if( (list != null) && (list.length > 0) ){
        this.getField("ListTitles").setItems(list);
        }
    else{
    this.getField("ListTitles").clearItems();
    }
  }
}
```

Notice how, as in the previous dropdown examples, you are using an associative syntax/object called `oArray` to contain all your dropdown items in the cboNewsletters dropdown field and subitems that will go into the list box field called ListTiles. Different subselection items appear in the list box based the selection made in the dropdown. It's important that the names in the associative syntax match the names in the dropdown; otherwise, errors can result and these fields will not work correctly. Always double-check your work for errors. When you have a name in your associative syntax that is two words, always put quotes around it, like `"Tourmaline Mining"`; if it is one word, it needs no quotes, like `Mining`. If no item is selected in the dropdown, the list box is cleared.

The check box has a script applied to it to show and hide fields. You could have used the no script action to show and hide as well. However, in some cases you need to write JavaScript to confirm you are getting the results you want when doing on and off actions. Refer to Figure 13-16.

```
//Check Box JavaScript
var topicFld = this.getField("cboNewsletters");
var clistT = this.getField("ListTitles");

if (event.target.value == "Yes"){
    topicFld.display = display.visible;
    clistT.display = display.visible;
    }
else {
    topicFld.display = display.hidden;
    clistT.display = display.hidden;
}
```

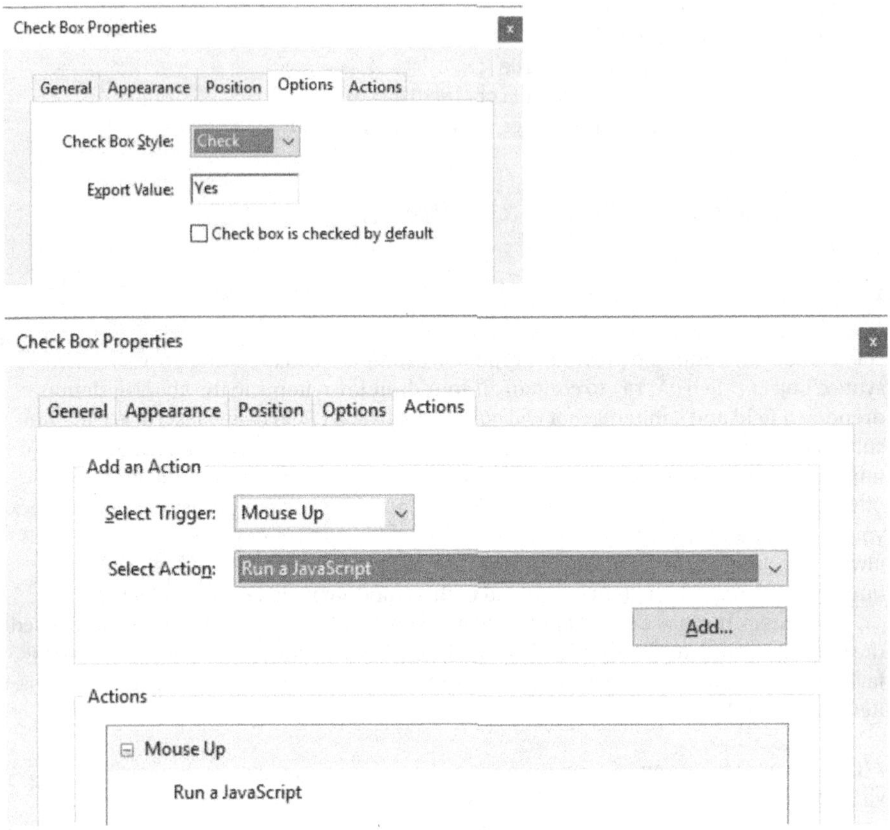

Figure 13-16. *The Check Box Properties screen showing the Actions tab*

For the dropdown menu, make sure to check "Commit selected value immediately" in the Options tab so that the items for the list box will appear once the selection is made.

The final part of the script is called in the dropdown in the Format area as a custom script. Refer to Figure 13-17.

```
//dropdown script custom format script
SetTitleEntries()
```

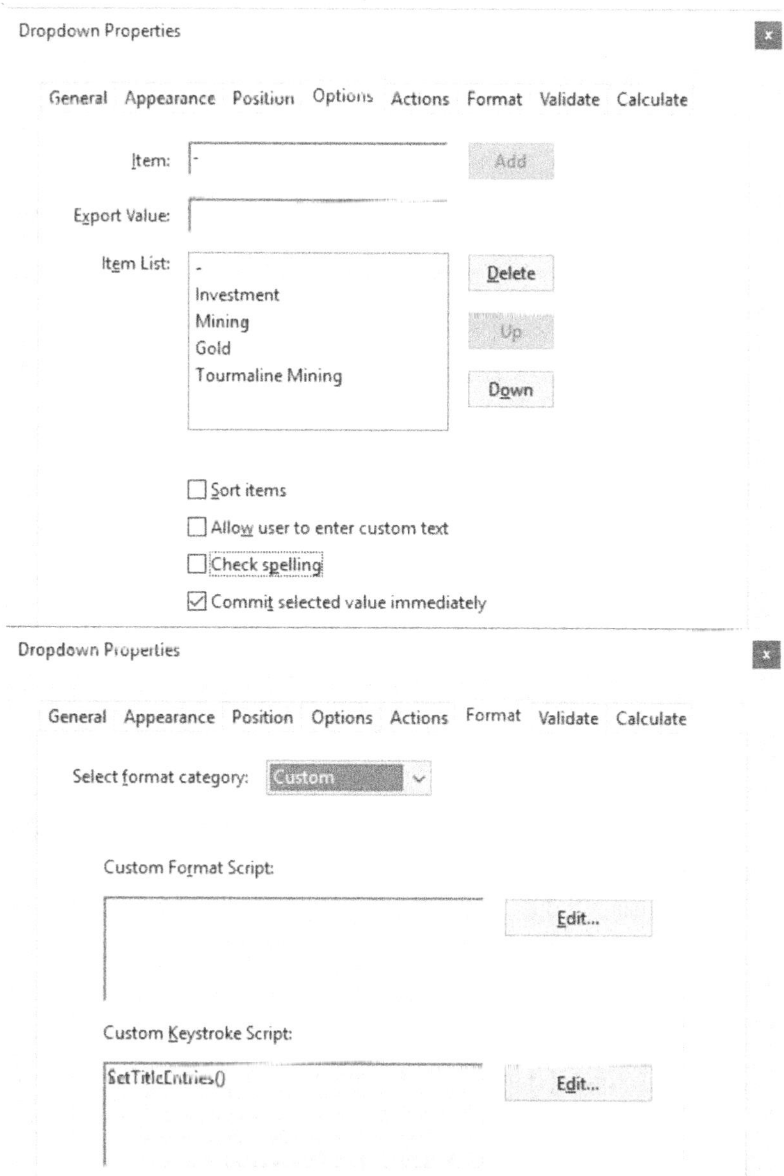

Figure 13-17. *The dropdown menu properties in the Options and Format tabs*

Here it calls upon the document JavaScript to help it populate the list box correctly.

Until called upon, the list box will remain blank. Also, no script is applied to the list box; it is only called upon when required. Refer to Figure 13-18.

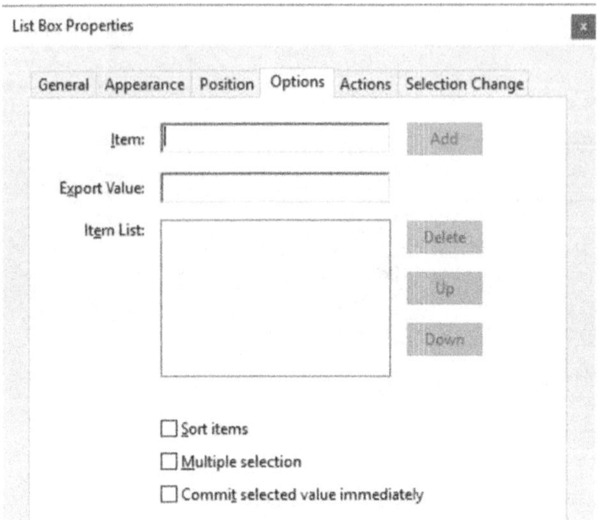

Figure 13-18. *The properties in the Options tab are blank*

■ **Important Note** Prior to 2006 if you wanted to show or hide a field you would write.

```
genreFld.hidden = false;
genreFld.hidden = true;
```

This method has been deprecated and should be written as shown in the following examples. Refer also to Figure 13-30.

```
genreFld.display = display.visible;
genreFld.display = display.hidden;
a.display = display.noPrint //field text visible on screen, but does not print
a.display = display.noView // field text hidden on screen, but prints
```

Check Box, List Box, and Multi-Dropdown Example 2

For a variation on this theme, you could try it in reverse order. Previously, you started off with a dropdown menu, so now start with a list box. The list box, depending upon which selection is made, reveals various dropdown menus that contain selections. You may prefer one option over the other so I am showing both. See the TMC Free Newsletter Option 2 PDF file. Refer to Figure 13-19.

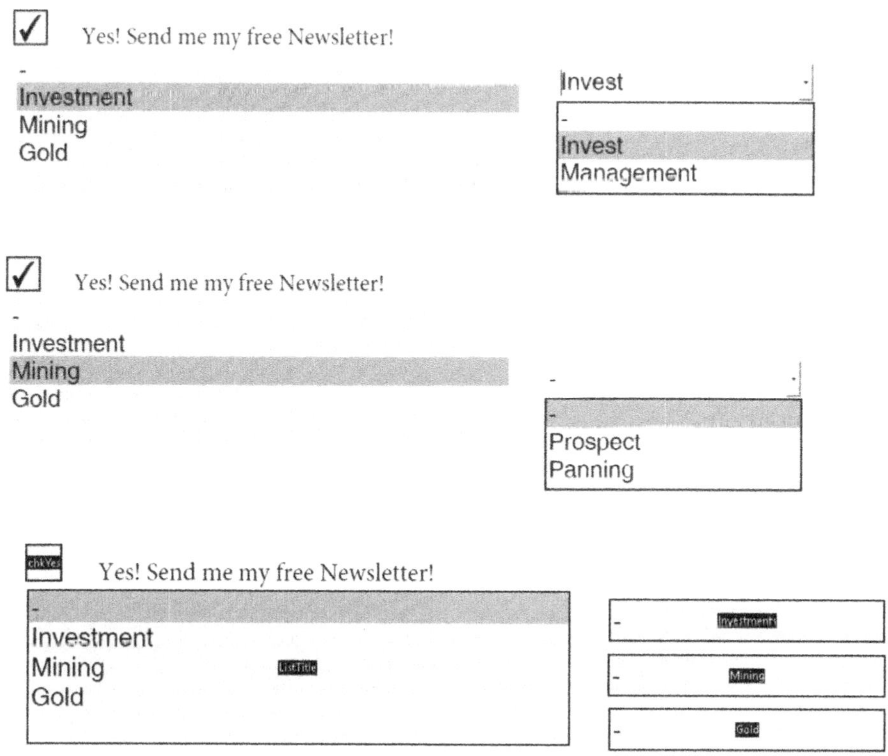

Figure 13-19. *The list box and dropdown menu options for the second free newsletter project*

This time there is no document JavaScript, based on the way that I set up the file. Refer to Figure 13-20.

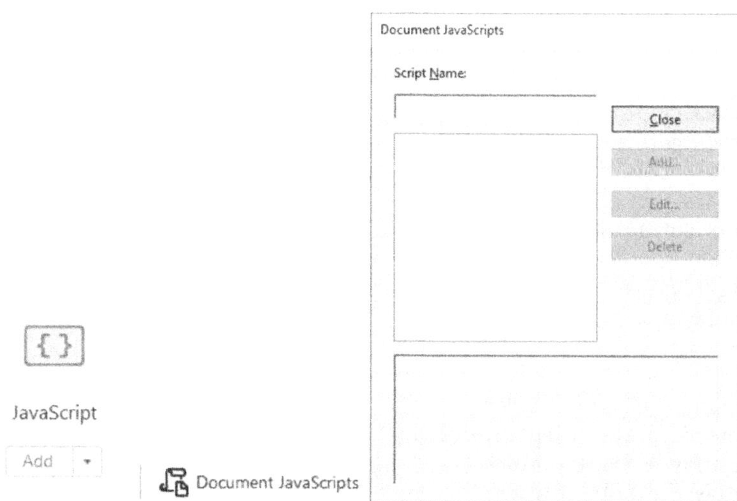

Figure 13-20. *This project contains no document JavaScript*

The check box contains this script to show and hide items. Refer to Figure 13-21.

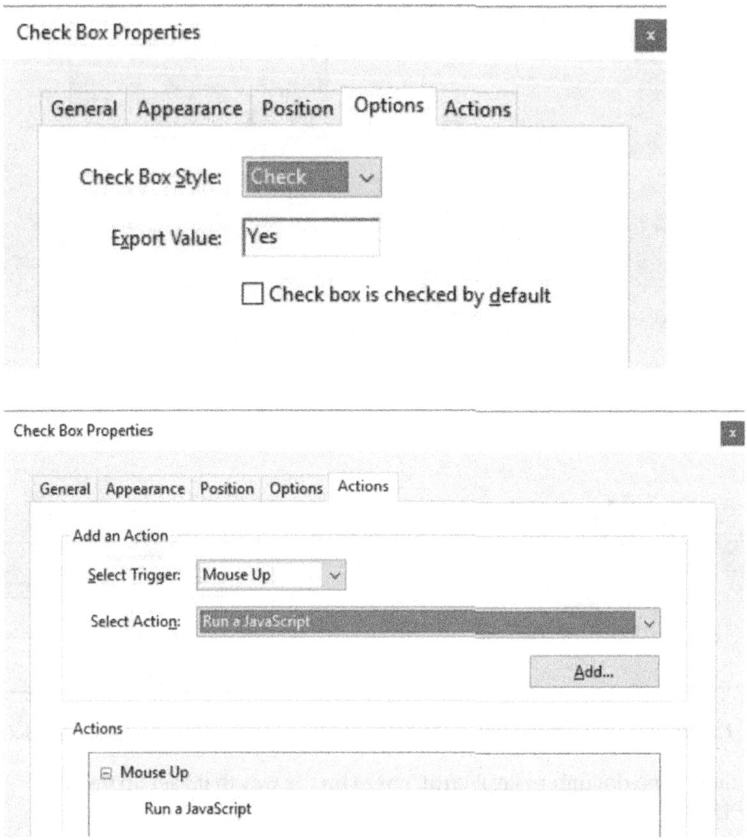

Figure 13-21. *The check box properties in the Options and Actions tabs*

```
//Check Box JavaScript
var listT = this.getField("ListTitle");
var investments = this.getField("Investments");
var mining = this.getField("Mining");
var gold = this.getField("Gold");

if (event.target.value == "Yes"){
    listT.display = display.visible;
}
else {
    listT.display = display.hidden;
    investments.display = display.hidden;
    mining.display = display.hidden;
    gold.display = display.hidden;
}
```

Notice how there are more items to show or hide depending upon what is happening. You can choose what you want to see or hide using the if/else conditional statements. See Part 2 of this book if you need to review if/else statements.

Now let's move on to the list box field.

Unlike the earlier dropdown, the items in the list box named ListTitle do have export values, as you'll see shortly. Refer to Figures 13-22 and 13-23.

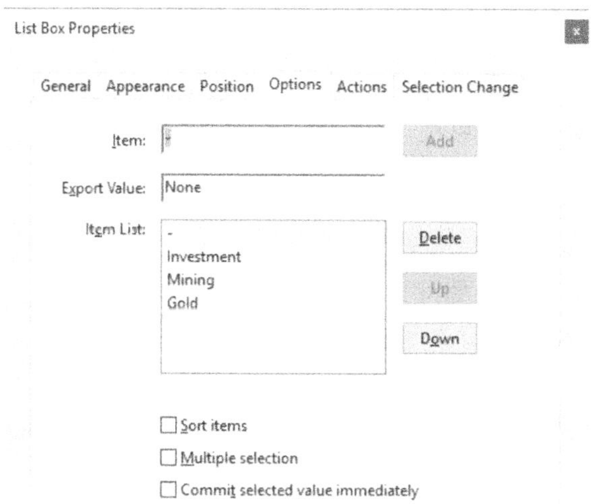

Figure 13-22. *The Options tab in the List Box Properties dialog box*

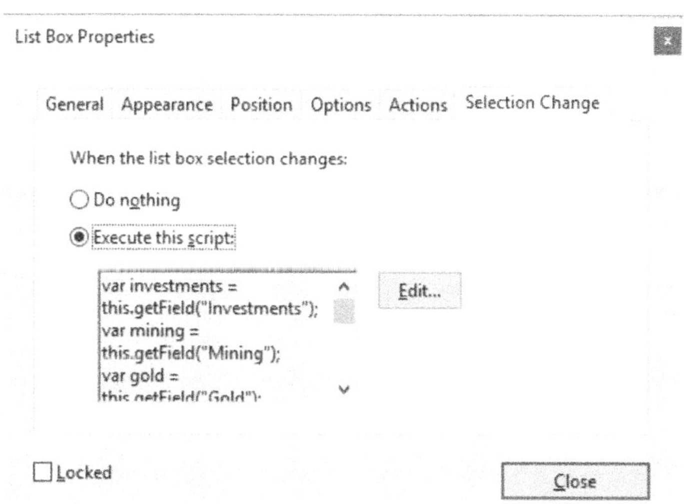

Figure 13-23. *The Selection Change tab in the List Box Properties dialog box*

This time the script is added to a different tab. It is controlled in the Selection Change tab.

List boxes do not have a Format tab and a setting of Custom is not an option; they must be controlled here.

Execute this script:

```
// Combo Box Selection Change Text Example
var investments = this.getField("Investments");
var mining = this.getField("Mining");
var gold = this.getField("Gold");
if (event.changeEx == "IV"){
    investments.display = display.visible;
    mining.display = display.hidden;
    gold.display = display.hidden;
}
else if (event.changeEx == "MN"){
    investments.display = display.hidden;
    mining.display = display.visible;
    gold.display = display.hidden;
}
else if (event.changeEx == "GD"){
    investments.display = display.hidden;
    mining.display = display.hidden;
    gold.display = display.visible;
}
else if (event.changeEx == "None"){
    investments.display = display.hidden;
    mining.display = display.hidden;
    gold.display = display.hidden;
    }
```

Once again, you add more if/else conditional statements. Notice how this code is all about the hiding or showing of dropdowns based on their value in the list box and the dropdown menu's name. Refer to Figure 13-24.

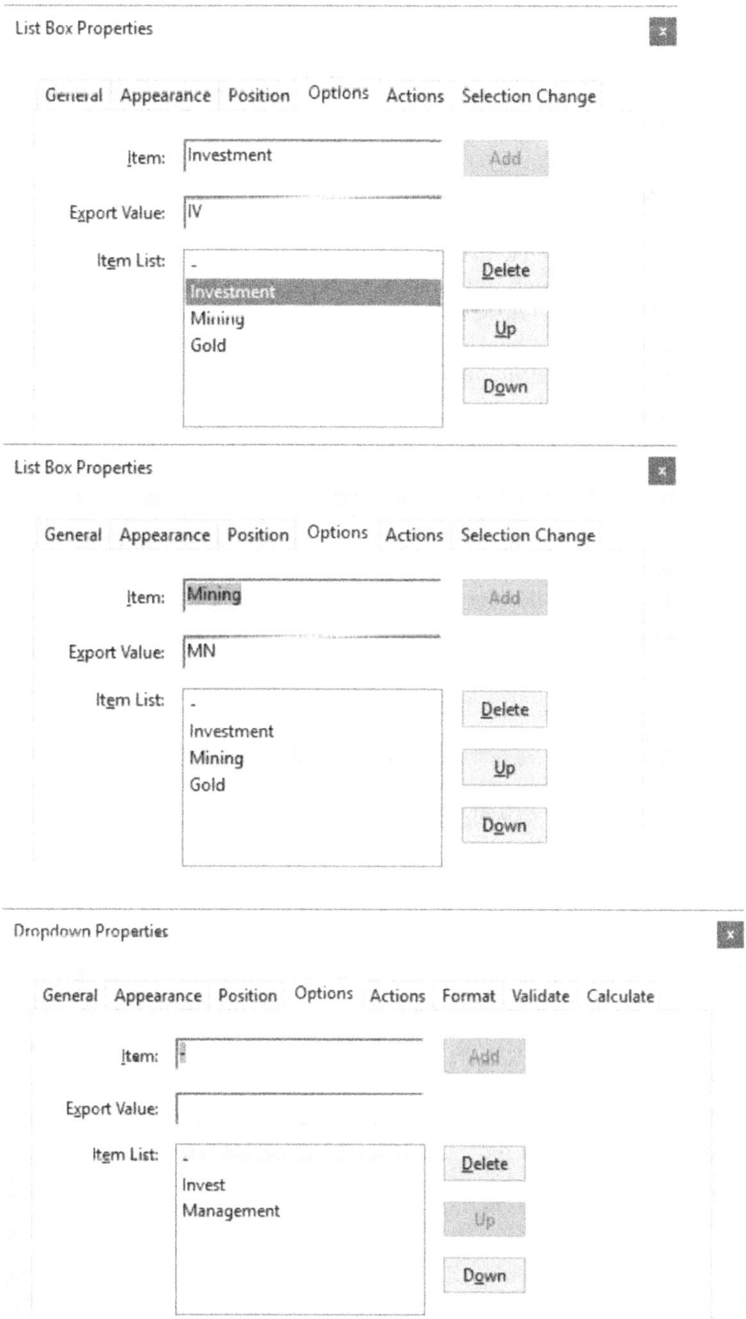

Figure 13-24. *The list box properties in the Options tab compared to the dropdown properties in the Options tab*

This time the dropdown menus have no actions applied to them; they are only called upon. However, rather than using a document JavaScript and creating an associative syntax, they do contain their items with no values preset, only referenced by the selection change of the list box.

Button Slide Show Variation

This last example could also be used with buttons that contain images if you want to create a type of slide show for a client. You can find a sample of this in the extra slide show project folder called `Mineral Identifier`. Explore this file further on your own and format it to suit your needs. For long lists, the order of the JavaScript variables should always match the same order as the options in the Options tab from top to bottom; otherwise, errors are likely to occur.

Extra Example Priority List Improved

Now that you've discovered a few things about list boxes, let's look at how you can improve the priority list earlier in this project. You can see how this interaction might work and you can add a text box below for an added description of a speaker's topic to assist your organization. To see the full code, go to the Priority List End Guest Speaker PDF file. Refer to Figure 13-25.

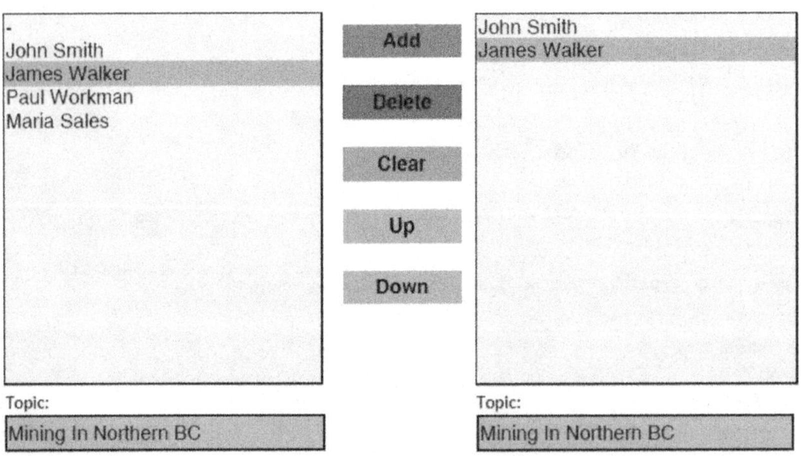

***Figure 13-25.** A list box project with guest speakers and text fields containing their topics below*

The buttons' code will remain the same except for the names of the list boxes; speakerList replaces qualityList, and orderTalkList replaces priorityList. However, the document JavaScript will be altered. Now it is called `talkExport`. Refer to Figure 13-26.

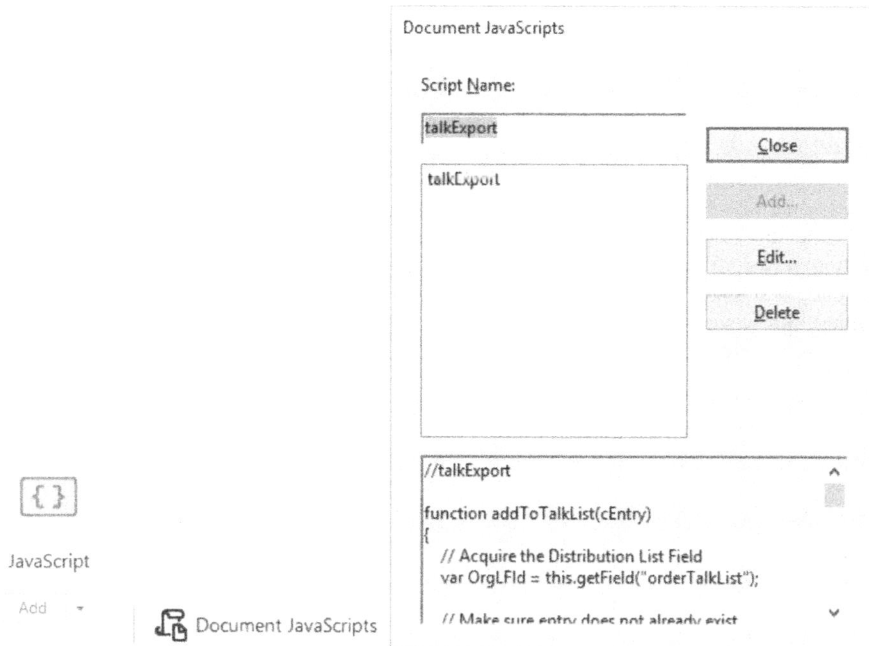

Figure 13-26. *Document JavaScript added to the PDF file*

```
function addToTalkList(cEntry){
    // Acquire the Distribution List Field
    var OrgLFld = this.getField("orderTalkList");

    // Make sure entry does not already exist
    // by comparing it to all of the existing entries
    var bFound = false;
    for(var i=0;i<OrgLFld.numItems;i++){
       if(OrgLFld.getItemAt(i,false) == cEntry){
          bFound = true;
          break;
       }
    }
    if(!bFound){
      // Insert entry at end of list
      OrgLFld.insertItemAt({cName:cEntry, nIdx:-1});
    }
}
```

```
function GetMasterExport(cEntry){
   // Acquire the Master List Field
   var OrgLFld = this.getField("speakerList");
   for(var i=0;i<OrgLFld.numItems;i++){
// If item matches, then return the export value
      if(OrgLFld.getItemAt(i,false) == cEntry){
        return OrgLFld.getItemAt(i,true);
      }
   }
   return null;
}
```

You add an extra script to deal with values that will act as the speakers' topics. You want to transfer this information as well to the right, so you add the GetMasterExport function which, if everything is correct or true, will help display the value or speaker topic. Otherwise, it will not display.

Figure 13-27 shows what this looks like in the left list box. Notice how each name has a value.

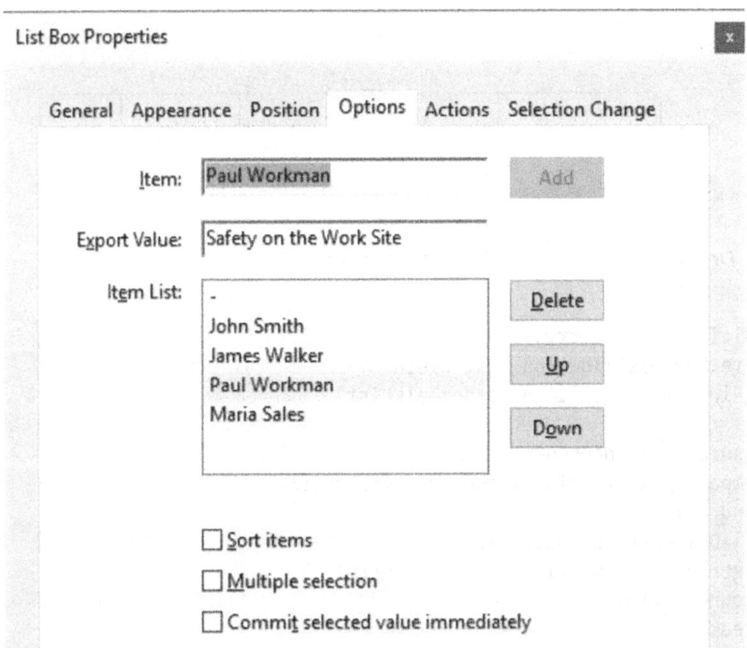

***Figure 13-27.** The list box properties in the Options tab for the left list box*

The list box on the right should remain blank. However, only here make sure to check "Commit selected value immediately" in the Options tab or the values will not commit properly in the text box below. Refer to Figure 13-28.

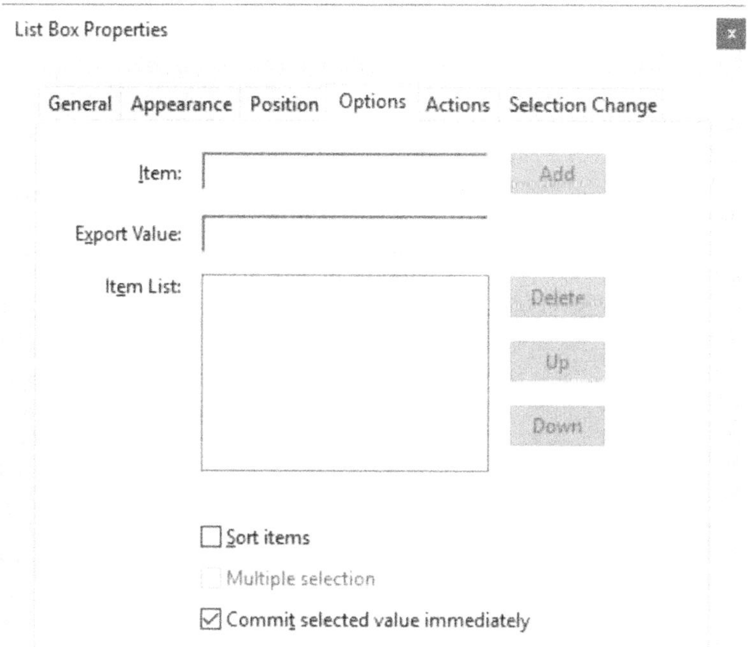

***Figure 13-28.** The list box properties in the Options tab on the right list box*

The final script is this time found in the list boxes in the Selection Change tab. For the left list box:

```
//Selection Change for First List box

if(event.willCommit){
  addToTalkList(event.value, this.cLastValEx);
  this.cLastValEx = null;
}
else{
  this.getField("Topic1").value = event.changeEx;
}
```

This adds the value as text to text field Topic1.

For the right list box:

```
//Selection Change for Second List Box
if(event.willCommit){
  if(event.value){
    this.getField("Topic2").value = GetMasterExport(event.value);}
  else{
    this.getField("Topic2").value = "";}
}
```

This adds the value as text to text field Topic2 after it has been exported over to the left.

In the extra example, you also add a text field and buttons to this file in case the user wants to add a last-minute guest speaker with their topic. See the Guestspeakers Extra PDF file for details. Refer to Figure 13-29.

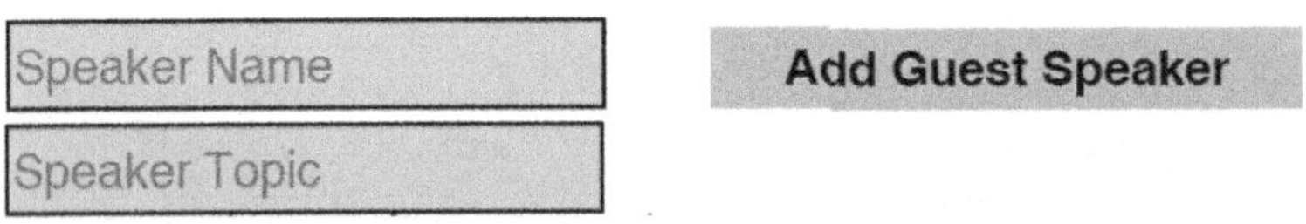

Figure 13-29. *Adding a guest speaker and their topic to the left list box and text field, which can later be added to the right list box and text field and then reordered*

Final Thoughts

As you can see, there is no right or wrong way to organize your list boxes. You can also use them to interact with text boxes or even in combination with check boxes or radio buttons. Depending upon the form, one way or another will help you accomplish your goal.

Hidden Fields

■ **Note** For those of you who are more familiar with JavaScript, buttons and text fields can also be used as a hidden object field if an extra calculation in a form needs a hidden function. While there are no examples in this chapter, things like double-clicking on a list item to transfer it or a complex calculation that you don't want the client to see (see the Invoice Form in an earlier lesson), those fields can be set to hidden in the General tab or set or no color in the Appearance tab to avoid form clutter for the client. Refer to Figure 13-30.

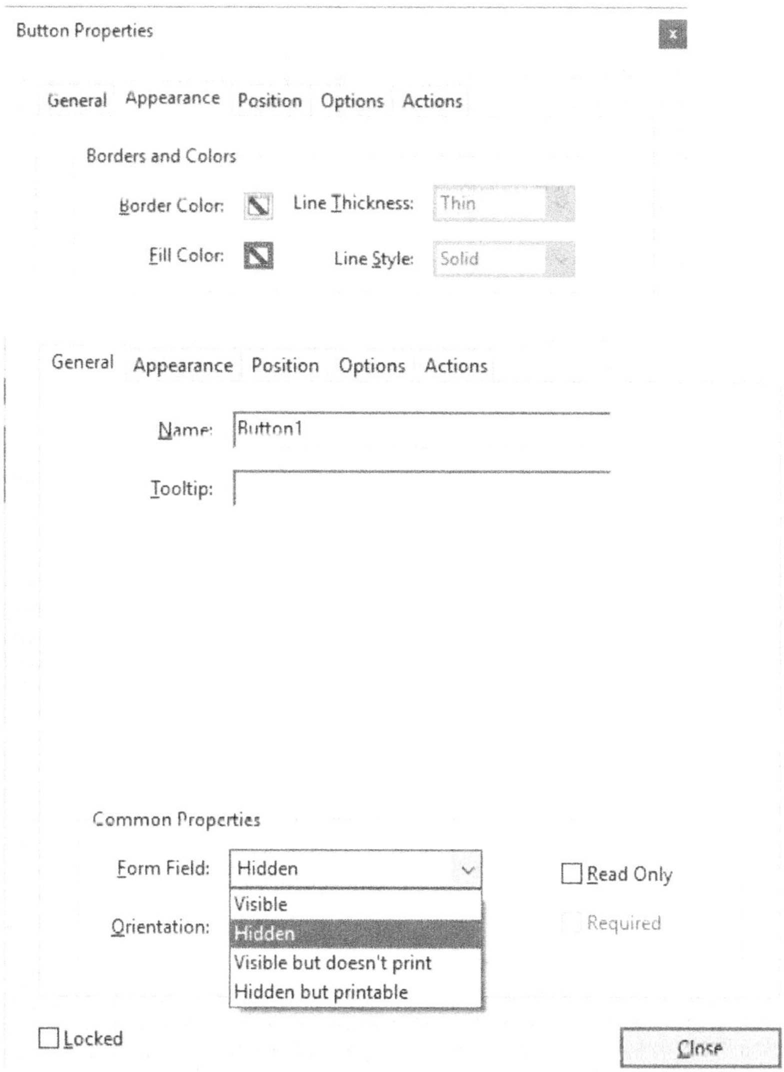

Figure 13-30. *A hidden button can have a fill and border color of none in the Appearance tab or set to Hidden in the General tab*

Using List Boxes for Number Rating

It is possible to use two or more list boxes to add values together in a final text field. However, I find this method to be buggy and it does not allow for multiple selection values to be added together. List boxes, as mentioned earlier, do not contain a Format tab so the final text field can only control the calculation output of the value as a true number. When working with specific multiple number selections, a dropdown menu or text field should be used instead of a list box.

Summary

As you can see, list boxes can be used in combination with other types of form fields. You can use them to transfer information from one list box to another or to a dropdown menu or a text field. You can even use them with buttons to create a slide show of images.

In the next chapter, you are going to look at a type of dropdown menu that you might not have heard of before in Acrobat: the popup menu.

CHAPTER 14

Advanced Navigation: The Popup Menu

In this chapter, you'll look at the final example on buttons and navigation: a popup menu. Popups are great non-form way to get from one page to another in a document and can act like a Table of Contents, as shown in Figure 14-1. The files can be found in the Gem Show Booklet PDF in this chapter's download folder.

Note If you want to work along in this lesson or review the final result, download the Chapter 14 files from `www.apress.com/9781484228920`. The file with the label "Start" is the file without the code and the file with the label "End" is the final result. You will also find folders with original PDF files if you would like to edit them and a folder containing the original scripts if you would like to add them to your own PDF forms.

Remember that to view the properties of a field you must select the Prepare Form tool; only then can you right-click or double-click a field to review its properties.

J. Harder, *Enhancing Adobe Acrobat DC Forms with JavaScript*,
DOI 10.1007/978-1-4842-2893-7_14

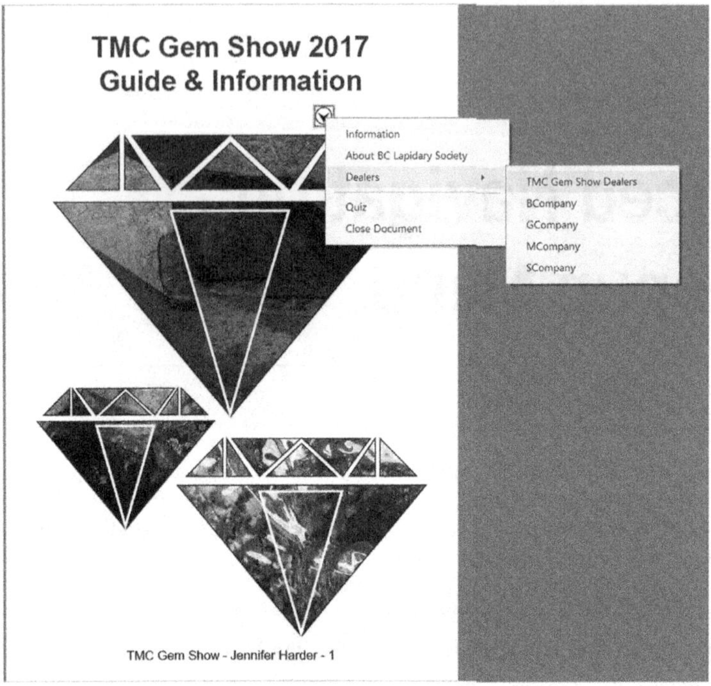

Figure 14-1. *An example of a Popup Menu in the PDF file*

The Popup Menu Example

In this example, you'll use a similar conditional statement to the if/else. This one is easier to write and is called the switch case break. Like the previous example, it works well for running through the associative syntax and its objects with in the square brackets ([]). To begin, add a document JavaScript called `CloseWarning. Refer to` Figure 14-2.

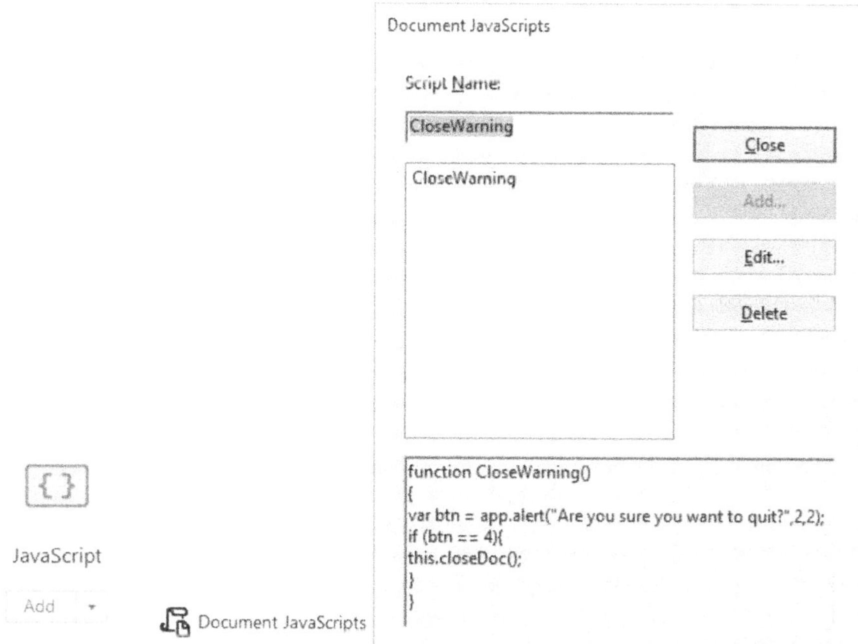

Figure 14-2. *The document JavaScript with the close warning*

Now add the following JavaScript:

```
// Global CloseWarning

function CloseWarning(){
var btn = app.alert("Are you sure you want to quit?",2,2);
    if (btn == 4){
    this.closeDoc();
    }
}
```

This JavaScript creates an option in the dropdown menu to close the document. Depending on where you want it to be within the associative syntax, it is based on the number. In this case, I chose 4 but you may have to adjust this in your list. You can also attach an alert message to it. Refer to Figure 14-3.

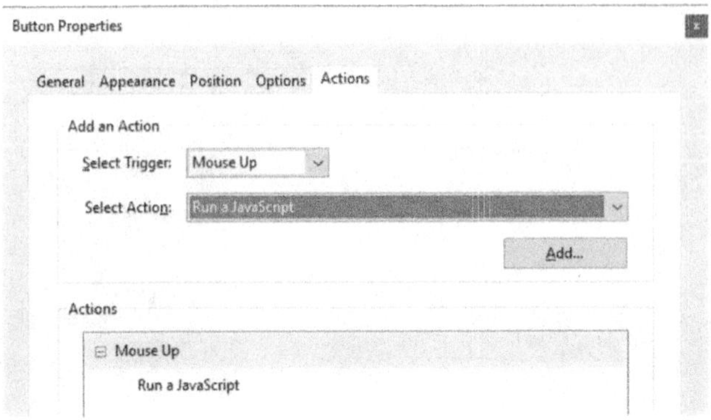

Figure 14-3. *Button properties in the Actions tab*

The button itself has the following JavaScript and associative syntax:

```
var itemPicked = app.popUpMenu("Information","About BC Lapidary Society",
["Dealers","TMC Gem Show Dealers","BCompany","GCompany","MCompany",
"SCompany"] ,"-","Quiz", "Close Document");

switch(itemPicked){
case "Information":
this.pageNum = 1;
break;

case "About BC Lapidary Society":
this.pageNum = 3;
break;

case "TMC Gem Show Dealers":
this.pageNum = 5;
break;

case "BCompany":
this.pageNum = 6;
break;

case "GCompany":
this.pageNum = 7;
break;

case "MCompany":
this.pageNum = 8;
break;
```

```
case "SCompany":
this.pageNum = 9;
break;

case "Quiz":
this.pageNum = 10;
break;

case "Close Document":
CloseWarning();
break;

//optional
 default:
app.alert("Not found here.");
break;
}
```

The script helps you navigate `app.popUpMenu`. The associative syntax helps you navigate to the page you want. Remember that 5 is actually page 6. Like arrays, they start at 0 so page 1 is actually page 0. So, make sure that you test your popup menu as you go along to make sure you can navigate to the page you want. Subitems are placed in brackets ([]) and you must make a horizontal divider using a dash (-). However, do not include it as part of the conditional switch case break statement.

```
case "Close Document":
CloseWarning();
break;
```

This calls upon the function rather than a number, like the others. You want the document to close when this is pressed.

You can add a default statement as an option. If nothing is found in the list, an alert comes up:

```
app.alert("Not found here.");
```

You do not have to add this part to the switch expression; it's optional.

On the final page, create a Back button to get back to the top. You can put an item like this on other pages if you want to. Refer to Figure 14-4.

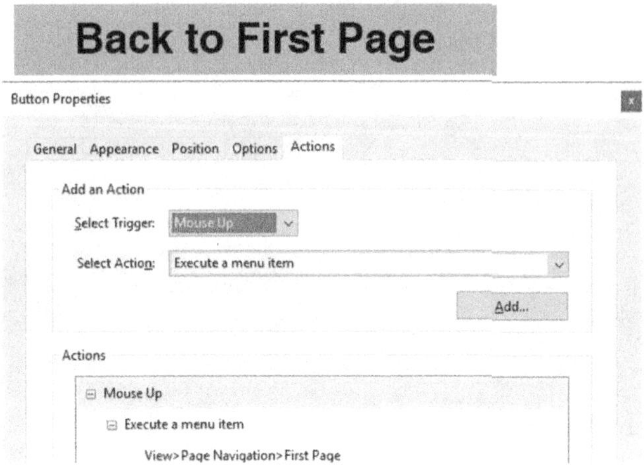

Figure 14-4. *Button properties in the Actions tab for the Back to First Page button. Execute a menu item ➤ View ➤ Page Navigation ➤ First Page.*

As you can see, it requires no JavaScript, but it is nice to have for navigation purposes.

■ **Note** Beyond the customization shown with the `app.popUpMenu`, you can't alter its color or fonts like `the app.Alert`; it's hardwired into the application.

Final Thoughts

I hope that you have enjoyed these lessons. I have also included the following extra lessons in Part 4:

- Action Wizard: Create a task using JavaScript
- Faux multi-state check boxes
- 5-star rating button
- Import an image into a button
- Mass formatting of numbers
- Digital signatures and barcodes

In the meantime, practice the previous lessons first to build up your JavaScript knowledge. If you want some extra practice, you can also jump to Part 5 (Chapter 20) where there are four assignments that reference Chapters 1-12 of this book.

Summary

In this chapter, you looked at the popup menu and how it can improve navigation in a document. You also learned about JavaScript's switch case break statement.

PART 4

Beyond the Basics

CHAPTER 15

Action Wizard and JavaScript

This chapter is a collection of extra lessons that I added to the end of the book for those who are more advanced users of JavaScript.

The Action Wizard is another tool that is available to us in Adobe Acrobat. With it you can create tasks or repetitive actions that you can save and then later use in multiple PDF files (Figure 15-1).

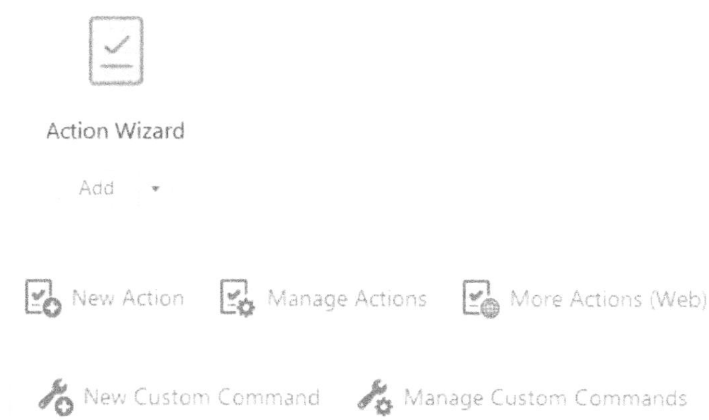

Figure 15-1. *These are tools you can find in the Action Wizard menu*

Working with Action Wizard

Action Wizard comes with some precreated actions already available. However, you can use the Create New Action dialog box to create new actions by adding an action from a choice of available tools like the ones you saw in the Form Properties Actions tab. And just like in that tab you can create a JavaScript action when you choose "Execute a JavaScript." Refer here to Figures 15-3 and 15-4.

J. Harder, *Enhancing Adobe Acrobat DC Forms with JavaScript*,
DOI 10.1007/978-1-4842-2893-7_15

■ **Note** If you want to work along in this lesson or review the final result, download the Chapter 15 files from `www.apress.com/978148422892`. You will find a folder containing the original script and `.sequ` files if you would like to add them to your own Action Wizard files.

Let's look at an example of this. Here's how to auto-add the name of the PDF file in Acrobat Wizard for Acrobat Pro:

1. Begin by opening a file you want to apply this action to (File ➤ Open).
2. Go to Tools ➤ Action Wizard ➤ New Action, as seen in Figure 15-2.

Figure 15-2. *Go to Action Wizard ➤ New Action to begin the project*

3. Choose More Tools ➤ Execute JavaScript. Refer here to Figure 15-3 and Figure 15-4.

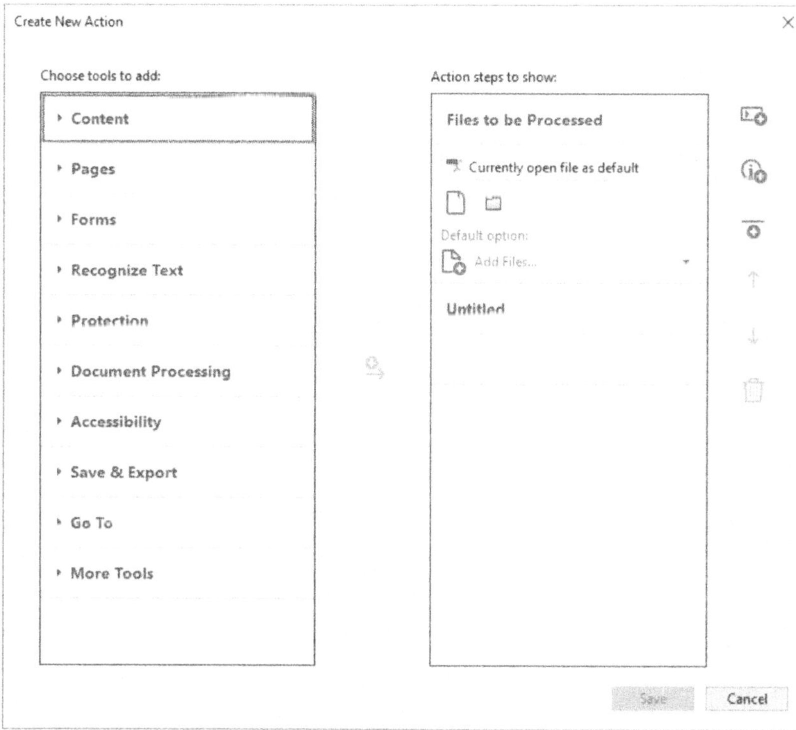

__Figure 15-3.__ The Create New Action selections; there are many to choose from

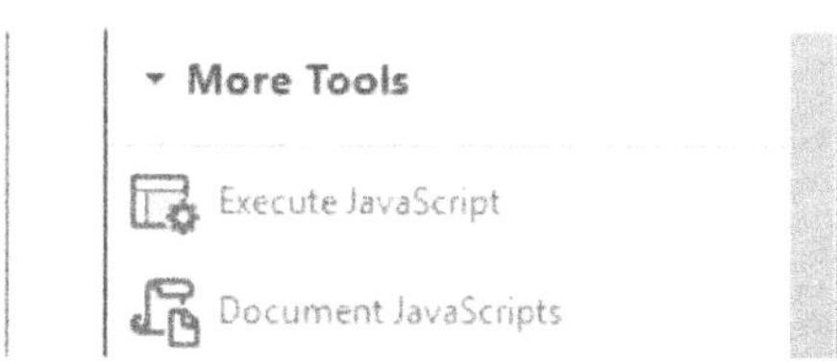

__Figure 15-4.__ More Tools ➤ Execute JavaScript

4. Once selected, click the "Add to Right-Hand Pane" button to move the tool over to the "Actions steps to show" side. Refer here to Figure 15-5.

__Figure 15-5.__ The "Add to Right-Hand Pane" button

5. Once the Execute JavaScript option is on the right-hand side, double-click Specified Settings to enter the JavaScript Editor. Refer here to Figure 15-6.

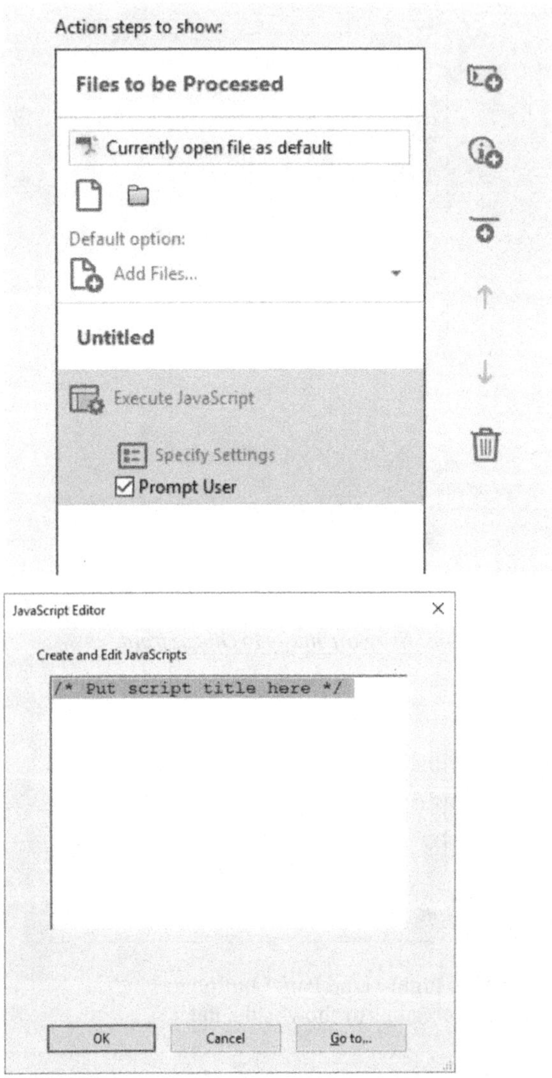

Figure 15-6. *Enter the JavaScript Editor upon opening the specified settings*

The Editor appears and allows you to begin to type.

6. Enter the following code:

```
/* Put script title here */
this.addWatermarkFromText({
    cText: this.documentFileName.replace(/\.pdf$/i, ""),
    nFontSize: 12,
    cFont: "Arial,Bold",
    aColor: color.red,
    nOpacity: 0.4,
    nVertAlign: app.constants.align.bottom,
    nHorizAlign:app.constants.align.left,
    nVertValue: 18
});
```

This script is using a regular expression, which you saw in Chapter 11. You are removing or replacing the `.pdf` extension with a blank area. The `/i` acts as modifier so that the `.pdf` is made blank. You are also requesting that the script add the name of this file at the bottom of the page in a font size of 12 and a vertical value or position of 18. You're also making the font red with an opacity of 40%. If you just want the text to be a default of black, you can remove the `aColor` and `nOpacity` lines.

It should look something like this file name.

For more information on regular expressions, go to `www.w3schools.com/jsref/jsref_obj_regexp.asp`.

■ **Note** If you want to keep the `.pdf` at the end of the watermark, remove the command of `.replace(/\.pdf$/i, "")`.

`nVertAlign: app.constants.align.` can be `top`, `center`, or `bottom`.

`nHorizAlign:app.constants.align.` can be `left`, `center`, or `right`.

---

7. When you are done, click the OK button to close the JavaScript Editor.

8. Now click the Save button. Refer here to Figure 15-7.

Figure 15-7. *The Save button that allows you to save the action*

9. Then give it a title in the Action Name box and a description in the Save Action dialog box. Refer here to Figure 15-8.

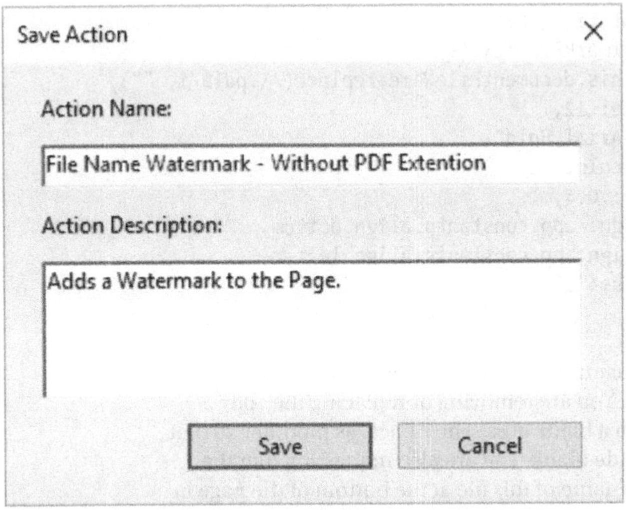

Figure 15-8. Add a name and description to the action

10. When done, click Save and the action is added to the Actions List on the right-hand side. Refer here to Figure 15-9.

Figure 15-9. The action is added to the Actions List

If you want to make adjustments/edits or remove this action, you can do so under Manage Actions. Refer to Figure 15-10.

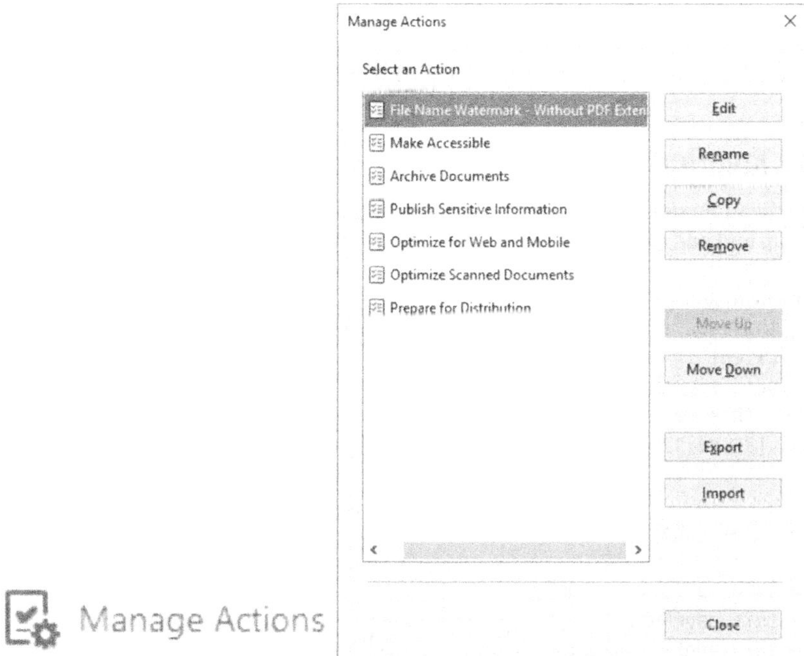

Figure 15-10. *The Manage Actions tool*

11. To execute, click the action. Click Start and then OK to the action when the editor appears, and it will add the text to the bottom of the file. If you like what you see, save the file. Refer here to Figure 15-11.

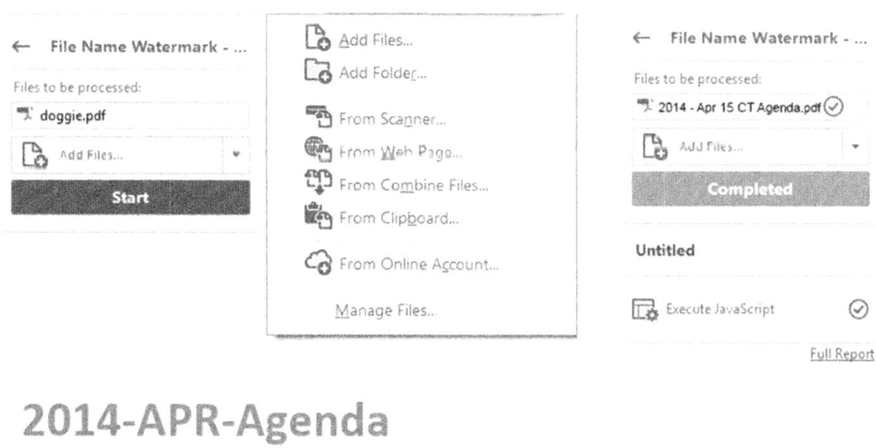

Figure 15-11. *The Action Wizard adds a watermark to the file*

JavaScript actions can be imported and exported if you want to share your actions with your friends and coworkers. Refer to Figure 15-10. They are saved as a `.sequ` file, as is the one for this example in the folder. You can also find more actions on the Web.

Reuse JavaScript from Chapter 8

By using the same steps above, you can also use some of the JavaScript code to create a time stamp and add a signature field to multiple documents.

```
//Adding a signature field automatically
var c = this.addField({
cName: "clientSignature",
cFieldType: "signature",
nPageNum: this.pageNum,
oCoords: [35,74,176,112]
})

//script that creates the text field
{
var r = [200, 200, 400, 300];
var i = this.pageNum;
var f = this.addField(String("completeDate."+i),"text",i,r);
f.textSize = 10;
f.alignment = "right";
f.textColor = color.blue;
f.fillColor = color.transparent;
f.textfont = font.HelvB;
f.strokeColor = color.transparent;
f.value = String("This page was reviewed on: " + util.printd("mmm dd, yyyy",
new Date()));
f.readonly = true;

}
```

■ **Note** You can also access document JavaScripts as well. Refer to Figure 15-12.

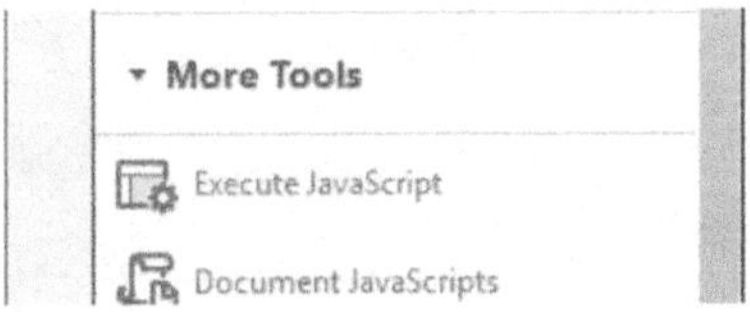

***Figure 15-12.** The JavaScript options*

Is It a Custom Action or a Custom Command?

Custom commands in Figure 15-13 are single-step and applicable to the current document, while actions are multi-step sequences and applicable to multiple files. Refer here to Figure 15-14.

Figure 15-13. *Action and command options*

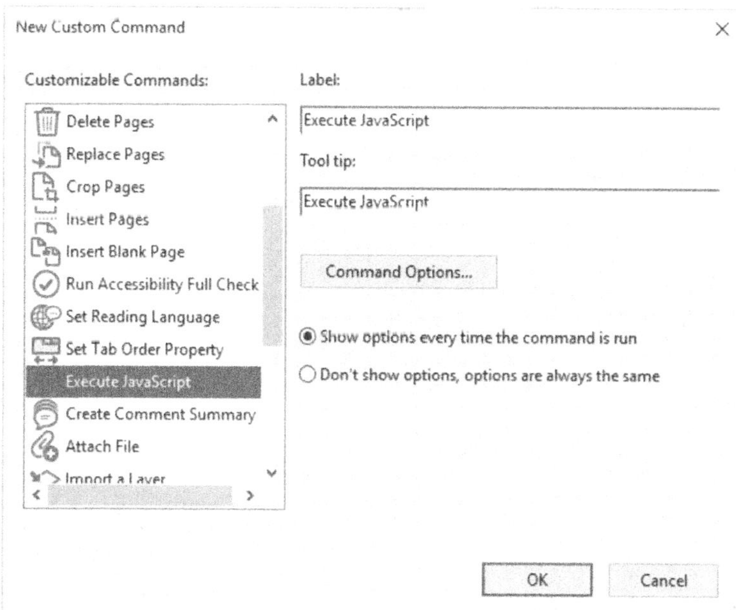

Figure 15-14. *The New Custom Command dialog box*

Create and Manage Custom Commands

Custom commands allow you to preconfigure commands such as watermark, header, and footer to reduce the amount of time each command takes to set up. This saves time for repetitive tasks.

Whether an action or command, either one can use JavaScript. Refer to Figure 15-14.

Summary

In this chapter, you looked at a tool known as the Action Wizard. This versatile tool allows you to apply your JavaScript actions in multiple documents and saves you time. You can also share these actions with other Acrobat Pro users and they can use the code as well. Take some time to add a few new actions to your Action Wizard tools and PDF documents.

CHAPTER 16

Multi-State Check Boxes

When space is limited in a document it is often helpful to be able to combine multiple states into one field. For example, suppose that you have a form and in it you would like to be able to change the setting from blank to a check symbol (representing yes) to an X or cross symbol (representing no or wrong). Or maybe you have multiple symbols that represent distinct levels. As the user who fills out the form advances in skill, they require a frequent update to their status in a specific order. In this chapter, you'll see how to create a type of multi-state check box using a button field.

The Problem of Multi-State Check Boxes

If you had lots of room, you could do the following with radio buttons:

Do you like our newsletter? • `Yes` ❍ `No` ❍ `Undecided`

• `Level 1` ❍ `Level 2` ❍ `Level 3`

As you have discovered with Acrobat, radio buttons come in groups and you can only choose one option. They also appear in one state (`On` • or `Off` ❍); there is no third or fourth option.

You can also use check boxes to save space. Yes could mean checked and No could be unchecked. However, once again there is no third option and the person filling in the form may not be sure if not checking means No or Undecided.

Do you like our newsletter? ❏ `Yes` ❏ `No` or ✓ `Yes` ✓ `No (I like it however...)`.

✓ `Level 1` ✓ `Level 2` ❏ `Level 3` - Here I might want people to know I am Level 2 now but this takes up a lot of space.

To save space, a more visual clue with a check box would be the following:

Do you like our newsletter?

❏ - This means I have not answered yet

✔ - This means Yes, I do

✘ - This means No, I don't

Or current level ❶
❷
❸

J. Harder, *Enhancing Adobe Acrobat DC Forms with JavaScript*,
DOI 10.1007/978-1-4842-2893-7_16

With Acrobat check boxes, you can choose more than one. Unfortunately, they are not able to have three or more states, only on or off.

The best way to achieve a multi-state goal is to mimic a check box with a button field and some JavaScript actions. Refer to Figure 16-1.

Figure 16-1. *The Prepare Form tool for making a button look like a check box*

■ **Note** If you want to work along in this lesson or review the final result, download the Chapter 16 files from `www.apress.com/9781484228920`. The file with the label "Start" is the file without the code and the file with the label "End" is the final result. You will also find folders with original MS Word and PDF files if you would like to edit them and a folder containing the original scripts if you would like to add them to your own PDF forms.

If you are creating your form from an original PDF, refer to the "Forms Review" section in Chapter 1.

Remember that to view the properties of a field you must select the Prepare Form tool; only then can you right-click or double-click a field to review its properties.

Let's begin by altering the Appearance tab of the button so that it will look like a check box. You can also adjust the size further if you need to fill a certain area. Refer to the TMC Mineral Checklist PDF file in this chapter's file folder. Refer here to Figure 16-2.

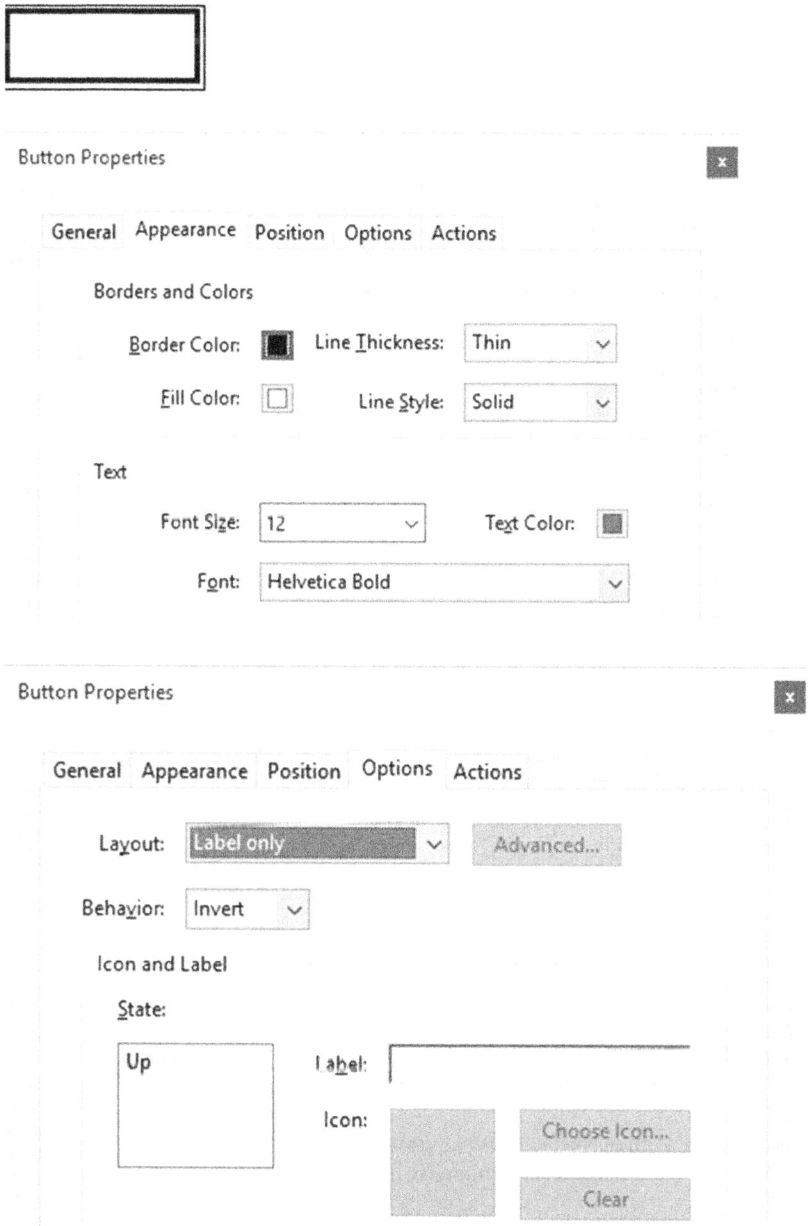

Figure 16-2. *The button properties in the Appearance and Options tabs*

The button has a border to make it look like a check box and currently has no text. The Options tab remains at default and you do not give the button a label name; you will let the JavaScript actions handle this.

The final step is to choose Mouse Up and the action of "Run a JavaScript" and enter the following script. Refer to Figure 16-3.

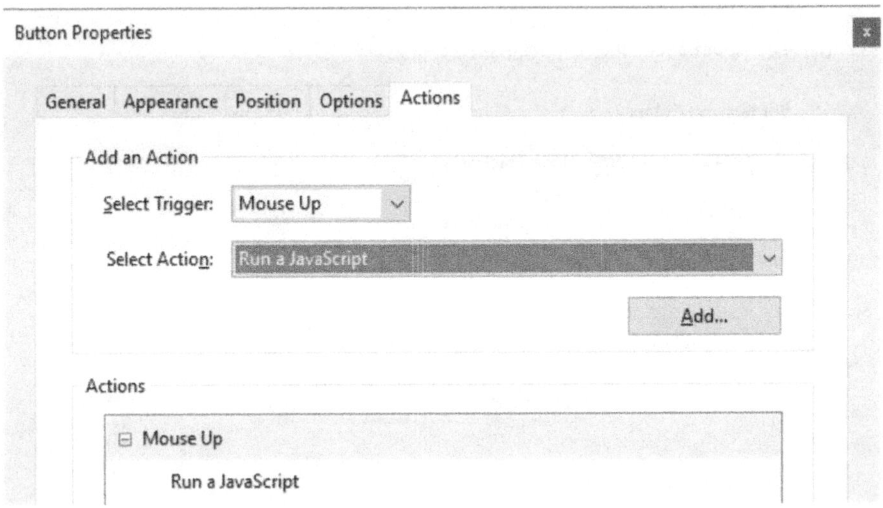

Figure 16-3. *The Mouse Up trigger and the "Run a JavaScript" action*

```
if (event.target.buttonGetCaption()=="\u2714"){
    event.target.buttonSetCaption("X");
    event.target.textColor = color.red;
}
 else if (event.target.buttonGetCaption()=="X"){
    event.target.buttonSetCaption("");
}
 else if (event.target.buttonGetCaption()==""){
    event.target.buttonSetCaption("\u2714");
    event.target.textColor = color.green;
}
```

When you test it with each click on the button, you see now that you have the states shown in Figure 16-4 and it looks very much like a check box.

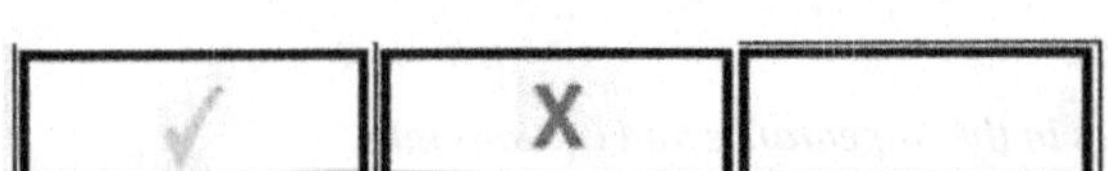

Figure 16-4. *Three button states: a check, an X, and a blank that mimics a check box*

Three conditions were used in the following if/else conditional statements:

- The symbol or Unicode for the check shape, \u2714
- The symbol for the cross or X
- A blank state

The reason for the blank state is that unlike other form fields, Acrobat does not allow you to use a Reset button to reset another button's field state and so within each button a cleared state must be created as part of the toggle.

The code moves through a cycle of `buttonGetCaption` to `buttonSetCaption`. After one caption appears (`Get`), you click to `Set` the next caption and so on.

■ **Note** You cannot select or deselect a button field. It doesn't show up as a field you can reset. Refer to Figure 16-5.

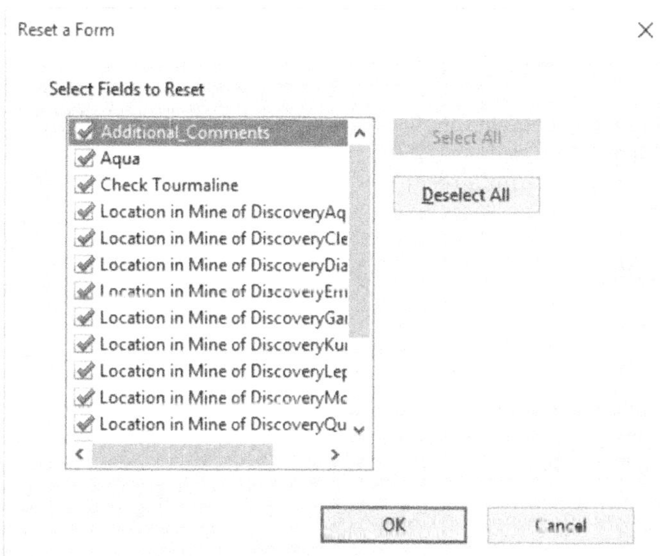

Figure 16-5. *No reset selection for a Button field can be found when you try to add the action in your Actions tab of the "Reset a Form" screen*

As each if/else condition is met on a click, you toggle to the next state and cycle back to the beginning.

```
event.target.buttonSetCaption("X");
event.target.buttonSetCaption("");
event.target.buttonSetCaption("\u2714");
```

You also differentiate the check from the cross by color.

```
event.target.textColor = color.red;
event.target.textColor = color.green;
```

The blank state required no color because nothing is in the field.

As a final note, let's see what the code looks like with the level symbols.

In Forms, if you're just using regular numbers, text fields or dropdowns are fine. However, when using special symbols that have a precise order, this might be a better solution for toggling to the correct choice:

```
if (event.target.buttonGetCaption()=="\u2776"){
    event.target.buttonSetCaption("\u2777");
    event.target.textColor = color.red;
}
else if (event.target.buttonGetCaption()=="\u2777"){
    event.target.buttonSetCaption("\u2778");
    event.target.textColor = color.blue;
}
else if (event.target.buttonGetCaption()=="\u2778"){
    event.target.buttonSetCaption("");
}
else if (event.target.buttonGetCaption()==""){
    event.target.buttonSetCaption("\u2776");
    event.target.textColor = color.green;
}
```

- ❶ uses `\u2776`
- ❷ uses `\u2777`
- ❸ uses `\u2778`

In the Appearance tab, adjust the font size to Auto, which will center the symbol better if it appears to be chopped off or not centered on the button. You can also resize the field slightly. Refer to Figure 16-6.

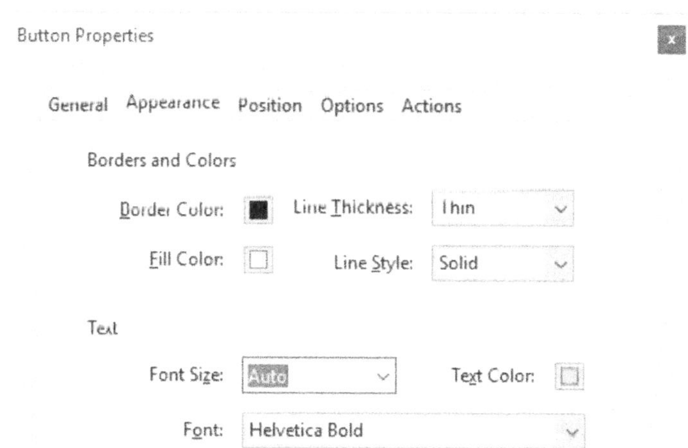

Figure 16-6. *The font size is set to Auto*

Bonus Star Rating Idea

Maybe you want to rate an idea or a product. Figure 16-7 shows the button.

Figure 16-7. *A button with a 5-star rating option*

Here is what a star rating button could look like using Unicode symbols:

```
if (event.target.buttonGetCaption()=="\u2605 \u2606 \u2606 \u2606 \u2606") {
    event.target.buttonSetCaption("\u2605 \u2605 \u2606 \u2606 \u2606");
    event.target.textColor = color.yellow;
//1 star
}
else if (event.target.buttonGetCaption()=="\u2605 \u2605 \u2606 \u2606
\u2606") {
    event.target.buttonSetCaption("\u2605 \u2605 \u2605 \u2606 \u2606");
    event.target.textColor = color.yellow;
//2 star
}
```

```
else if (event.target.buttonGetCaption()=="\u2605 \u2605 \u2605 \u2606
\u2606") {
    event.target.buttonSetCaption("\u2605 \u2605 \u2605 \u2605 \u2606");
    event.target.textColor = color.yellow;
//3 star
}
else if (event.target.buttonGetCaption()=="\u2605 \u2605 \u2605 \u2605
\u2606") {
    event.target.buttonSetCaption("\u2605 \u2605 \u2605 \u2605 \u2605");
    event.target.textColor = color.yellow;
// 4 star
}
else if (event.target.buttonGetCaption()=="\u2605 \u2605 \u2605 \u2605
\u2605") {
    event.target.buttonSetCaption("Rate Me");
// 5 back to blank
}
else if (event.target.buttonGetCaption()=="Rate Me") {
    event.target.buttonSetCaption("\u2605 \u2606 \u2606 \u2606 \u2606");
    event.target.textColor = color.yellow;
}
```

Always test your form before submitting it to others.

For more on Unicode symbols, see `https://en.wikipedia.org/wiki/Dingbat`.

Select All or Deselect All Check Boxes at Once

If you have a lot of check boxes that need to be checked in your form, wouldn't it be great to check them all at once? Refer to Figure 16-8 and the following text.

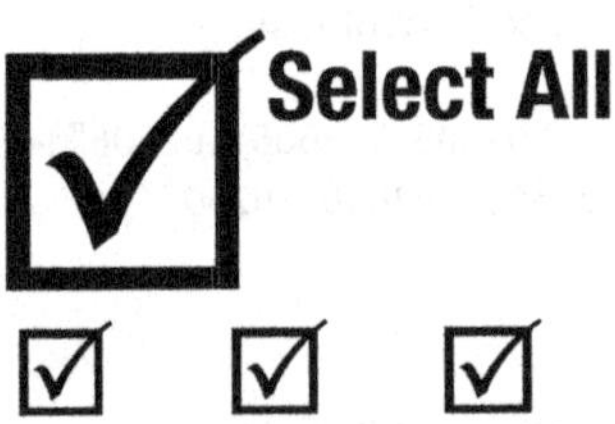

Figure 16-8. *Select all check boxes at once with one master check box*

You may have noticed that Acrobat does not have an option to create a check box that will select all the other check boxes in a set. You can use the code included in the PDF file TMC Mineral Check List Select All found in the downloaded folder for this chapter. The following is the code for the "Select All" check box in the Actions tab with a Mouse Up trigger:

```
/*Check Box Select All*/
var otherCheckBoxes = ["CheckBox1", "CheckBox2", "CheckBox3"];  // etc.
if (getField("Select All").value!="Off") {
    for (var i in otherCheckBoxes) getField(otherCheckBoxes[i]).
checkThisBox(0,true);
    }
else{
    for (var i in otherCheckBoxes) getField(otherCheckBoxes[i]).
checkThisBox(0,false);
    }
```

The code states that when the main checkbox, Select All, is not off (which would be on), then all the other checkboxes within its group should check.

Each of the check boxes are numbered in order (1, 2, 3); this is so that the for() loop will find all the check boxes so they can be selected or deselected. Refer to Chapters 10 and 13 for examples of for() loops.

Make sure that your check box names match the names that are in the associative syntax/object (square brackets, []) `otherCheckBoxes` . If they do not, they will not select and deselect.

Summary

In this chapter, you looked at a way to create a type of multi-state check box using a button field. You also discovered that a single check box field can select other check boxes when JavaScript is added. With slight alterations to the code you can cause one type of field to mimic another.

CHAPTER 17

Importing an Image into a Button

In this chapter, you'll create a button that will import an icon image using a script. This could be useful for clients who want to attach an image or photo to the form.

While you can do all the steps in this chapter with Acrobat XI, be aware that you will not have access the new Add an Image Field icon, which is only available in the latest version of Acrobat DC, shown in Figure 17-1.

Figure 17-1. *The new Add an Image Field icon found in the Prepare Form tool*

Note If you want to work along in this lesson or review the final result, download the Chapter 17 files from `www.apress.com/9781484228920`. The file with the label "Start" is the file without the code and the file with the label "End" is the final result. You will also find a folder containing the original scripts if you would like to add them to your own PDF forms.

If you are creating your form from an original PDF, refer to the "Forms Review" section in Chapter 1.

Remember that to view the properties of a field you must select the Prepare Form tool; only then can you right-click or double-click a field to review its properties.

J. Harder, *Enhancing Adobe Acrobat DC Forms with JavaScript*,
DOI 10.1007/978-1-4842-2893-7_17

Creating the Button

Insert either a Button icon or the Add an Image Field icon on your page. Refer here to Figure 17-1.

Make sure the Layout field in the Options tab is set to "Icon only," as shown in Figure 17-2.

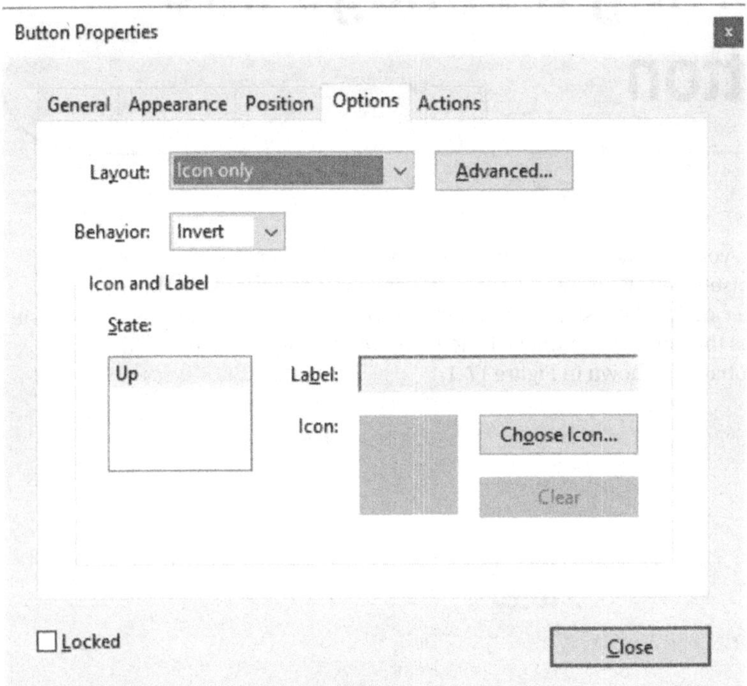

Figure 17-2. *Select "Icon only" for the Layout field in the Options tab*

Note that it will look the same for the Add an Image Field icon; both will default to button properties. Refer to Figure 17-3. However, the Image field will have the JavaScript already added.

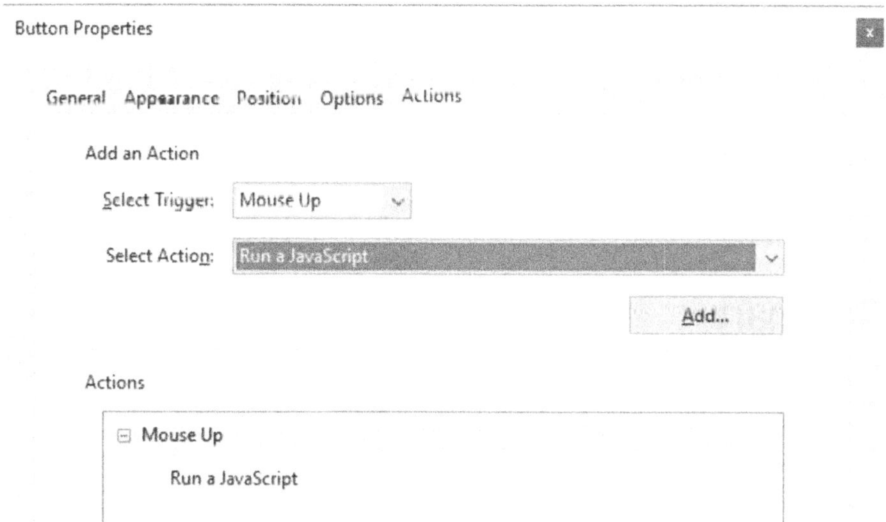

Figure 17-3. *Run a Javascript action in the Actions tab*

Then add the following code, if it is not already added:

```
// Mouse Up script for a button
event.target.buttonImportIcon();
```

When the user clicks on the blank button, the Select Icon box appears. Refer to Figure 17-4.

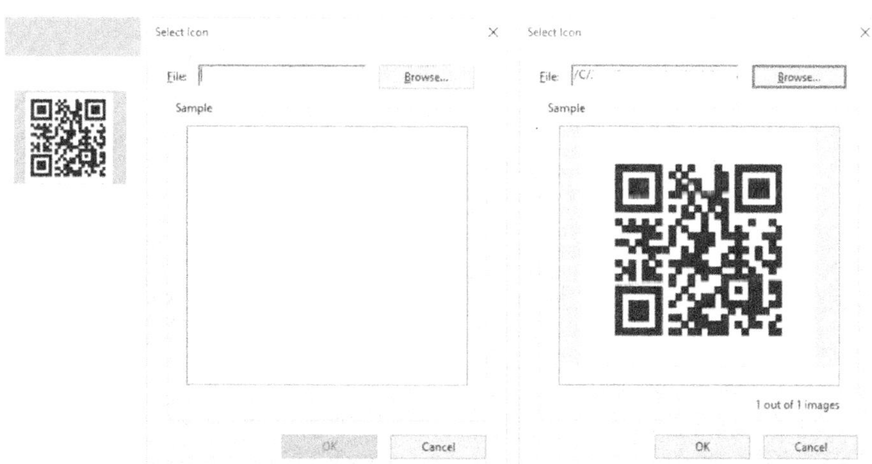

Figure 17-4. *When the button is clicked, an image or icon of your choice can be imported*

The user can then browse for the image and, depending on what file formats are available to them, select the correct image.

Click the OK button and the image will be imported as an image within the button.

■ **Note** The button may need to be presized if you know a client will be importing a specific sized image so that it can be seen clearly.

Summary

In this chapter, you looked at how to import an image into a button. You also discovered the new Add an Image Field icon, which is new to Acrobat DC.

CHAPTER 18

Multiple Formatting

One of the most laborious tasks that I have found when creating forms in Acrobat is formatting many fields to Numbers. Wouldn't it be nice if Acrobat were like MS Excel, and you could format the fields all at once? And what if you need to format them all again? Do you want to go through them one at a time? What if you could update them quickly?

Until the day that Acrobat comes up with a solution, there are two possible ways to deal with this problem: do it yourself or call a professional. This chapter discusses both options.

The Problem of Multiple Formatting

You can select each field, one at time, and perform this task, as shown in Figure 18-1.

J. Harder, *Enhancing Adobe Acrobat DC Forms with JavaScript*,
DOI 10.1007/978-1-4842-2893-7_18

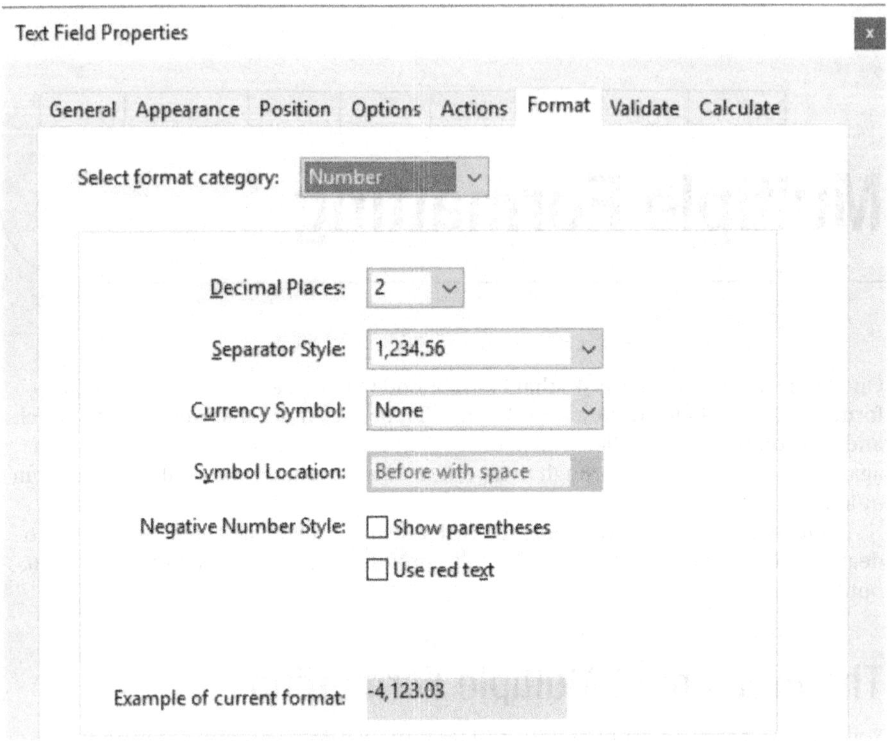

Figure 18-1. *Text field properties in the Format tab*

However, when you select multiple text fields and choose Properties, this is the result you get: the Format, Validate and Calculate tabs disappear. Refer here to Figure 18-2.

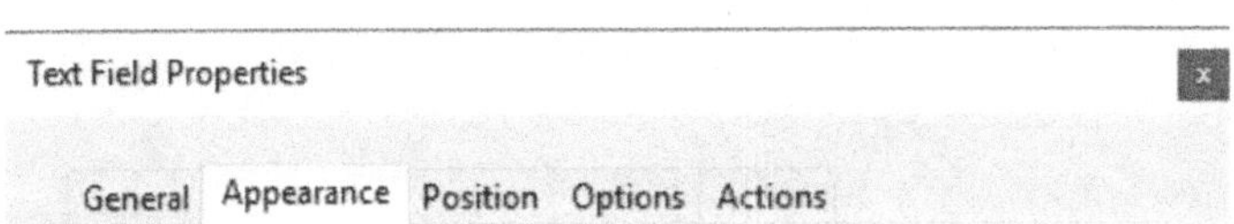

Figure 18-2. *The Text Field Properties screen where three tabs have disappeared because multiple fields are selected*

So, you're stuck with the task of formatting them one at a time. Refer here to Figure 18-3.

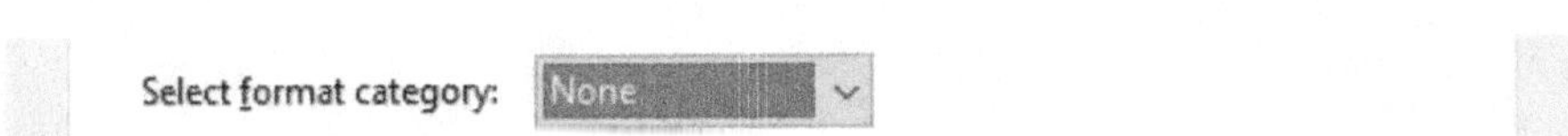

Figure 18-3. *Text Field Properties Format tab is only available through single field selection*

I can understand why the Acrobat developers might remove the Validate and Calculate tabs, since these areas would contain custom scripts that you would not want to overwrite in a mass conversion.

As in all cases, it is important to give your fields unique names. Refer here to Figure 18-4 and to the Testing Form Format PDF file.

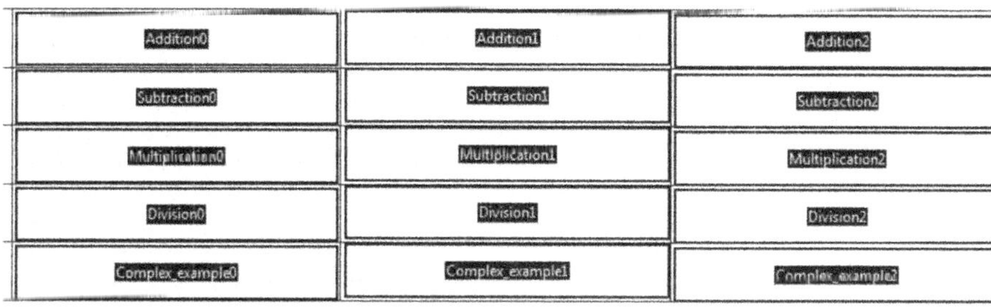

Figure 18-4. *The text fields in form mode with their unique names*

■ **Note** If you want to work along in this lesson or review the final result, download the Chapter 18 files from `www.apress.com/9781484228920`. The file with the label "Start" is the file without the code and the file with the label "End" is the final result. You will also find a folder containing the original scripts if you would like to add them to your own PDF forms.

If you are creating your form from an original PDF, refer to the "Forms Review" section in Chapter 1.

Remember that to view the properties of a field you must select the Prepare Form tool; only then can you right-click or double-click a field to review its properties.

Option 1: Do It Yourself

As mentioned in previous chapters, when you want to affect something globally, you need to create document JavaScripts. Refer here to Figure 18-5.

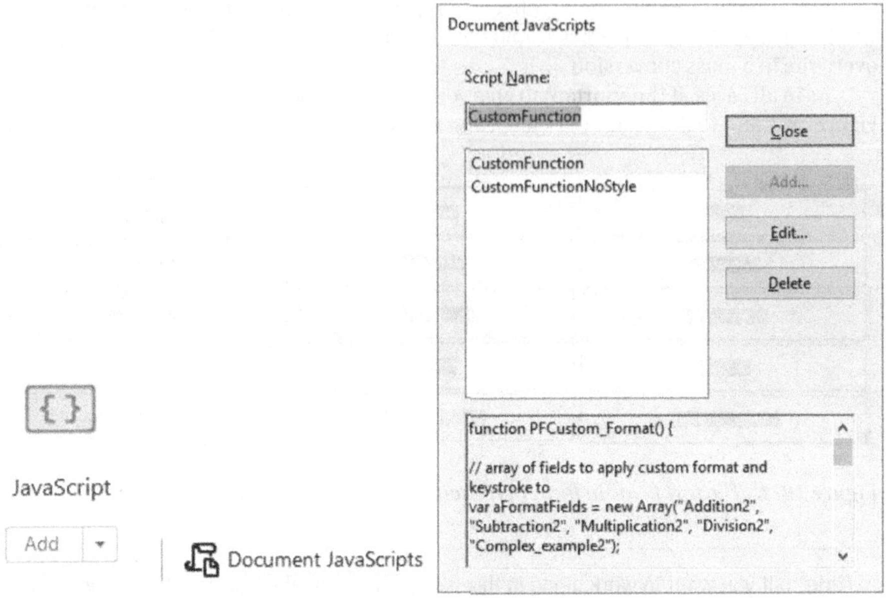

Figure 18-5. *The document JavaScripts used for formatting the numbers*

In this case there are two. The first makes sure the number has a ($) price sign and the second has no price sign.

Here are the scripts used for both.

Price Script

```
function PFCustom_Format() {

// array of fields to apply custom format and keystroke to
var aFormatFields = new Array("Addition2", "Subtraction2",
"Multiplication2", "Division2", "Complex_example2");

// define the varibles for the custom number formatting and keystroke
    var nDecimal = "2"; // number of decimals
    var separStyle = "0"; // separator style
    var negativeStyle = "0"; // negative display style
    var currencyStyle = "0"; // currency style
    var symCurrency = "\"$\""; // currency symbol
    var symCurrencyPrepend = "true"; // logical to prepend (add before)
    currency symbol
// build the format string
var strFormat = nDecimal + ", " + separStyle + ", " + negativeStyle + ", " +
currencyStyle +", " + symCurrency + ", " + symCurrencyPrepend;
```

```
// set the custom format and keystroke for the fields
    for (i = 0; i < aFormatFields.length; i++) {
        this.getField(aFormatFields[i]).setAction("Format",
        "AFNumber_Format(" + strFormat + ")");
        this.getField(aFormatFields[i]).setAction("Keystroke",
        "AFNumber_Keystroke("+ strFormat + ")");
    } // end for loop
return;
} // end custom format function
```

No Price Script

```
function PFCustom_Format2() {

// array of fields to apply custom format and keystroke to
var aFormatFields2 = new Array("Addition0", "Addition1","Subtraction0",
"Subtraction1", "Multiplication0", "Multiplication1", "Division0",
"Division1","Complex_example0", "Complex_example1");

// define the varibles for the custom number formatting and keystroke
    var nDecimal = "2"; // number of decimals
    var separStyle = "0"; // separator style
    var negativeStyle = "0"; // negative display style
    var currencyStyle = "0"; // currency style
    var symCurrency = "\"\""; // currency symbol
    var symCurrencyPrepend = "false"; // logical to prepend(add before)
    currency symbol, not required here.
// build the format string
var strFormat2 = nDecimal + ", " + separStyle + ", " + negativeStyle + ", "
+ currencyStyle +", " + symCurrency + ", " + symCurrencyPrepend;
// set the custom format and keystroke for the fields
    for (i = 0; i < aFormatFields2.length; i++) {
        this.getField(aFormatFields2[i]).setAction("Format",
        "AFNumber_Format(" + strFormat2 + ")");
        this.getField(aFormatFields2[i]).setAction("Keystroke",
        "AFNumber_Keystroke("+ strFormat2 + ")");
    } // end for loop
return;
} // end custom format function
```

The second script shows the areas that are different from the first script in bold. I changed the names of some of the variables as a precaution so that the two functions would not become conflicted.

The following variables are all prebuilt into the inner format scripts (`AFNumber_Format` and `AFNumber_Keystroke`) that are controlling this Format tab:

- `var nDecimal = "2"; // number of decimals`
- `var separStyle = "0"; // separator style`
- `var negativeStyle = "0"; // negative display style`
- `var currencyStyle = "0"; // currency style`
- `var symCurrency = "\"\""; // currency symbol`
- `var symCurrencyPrepend = "false"; // logical to prepend (add before) append(after) currency symbol`

`nDecimal` controls the number of decimal places. Refer here to Figure 18-6.

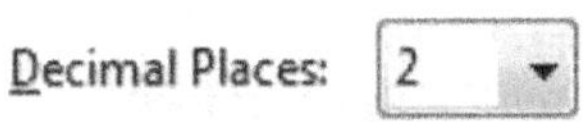

***Figure 18-6.** Format the number of decimal places*

`separStyle` is the separator style for the 000s and decimal point. Refer here to Figure 18-7.

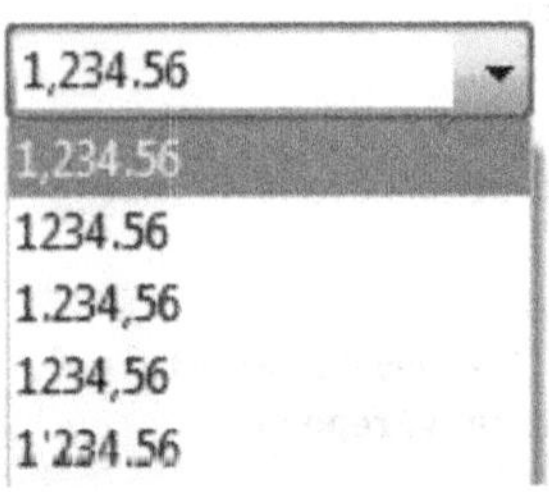

***Figure 18-7.** Format the separator style*

```
0 ="," Thousands and "." decimal point Example: 1,000.00
1= "." Decimals only Example: 1000.00
2 = "."Decimal point and "," Thousands Example: 1.000,00
3 = "," Thousands Only Example: 1000,00
4 =" ‘ " quote mark and decimal "." Example: 1’000.00
```

negativeStyle controls the negative style. Refer here to Figure 18-8.

Figure 18-8. *Format the negative number style*

```
0 = "-"
1 = red text
2 = parentheses black
3 = parentheses red
```

currencyStyle refers to currency style set to 0 (in most cases it is unused; it is a reserved feature).

symCurrency refers to the type of symbol used for currency. Refer here to Figure 18-9.

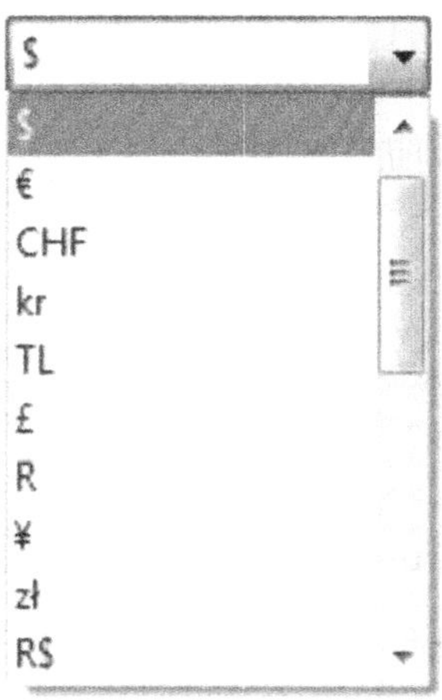

Figure 18-9. *Format the currency symbols*

In this example, you use \"$\" for dollar sign and \"\" for none. If you had a foreign currency, you might need to look up the Unicode code for how to create the symbol. Some examples are shown here:

- Euro sign € \u20AC
- Pound £ \u00A3
- Yen ¥ \u00A5
- Won ₩ \u20A9

See `http://en.wikipedia.org/wiki/Currency_Symbols_(Unicode_block)`.

Other Unicode codes you may need to look up and test if you are doing a custom symbol.

`symCurrencyPrepend` is either set to true ($1.00) or false (1.00$) depending on where you want the symbol to be placed. Refer here to Figure 18-10.

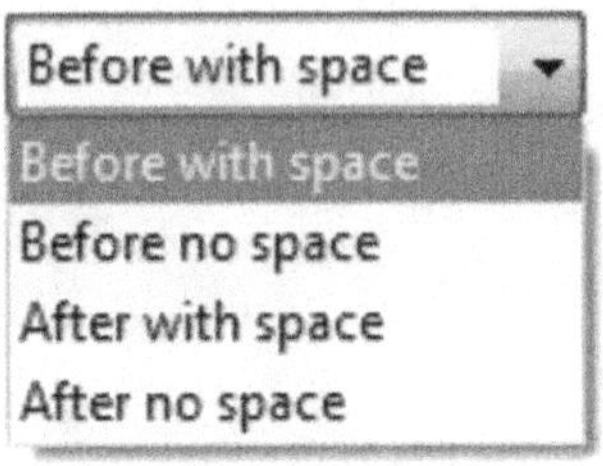

Figure 18-10. *Format the prepend space*

■ **Note** While this is visually correct, you may notice that the Format tab might say "After with space" rather than "Before no space." Do not alter this formatting here, only in the document JavaScript, because it will unlink the global formatting to this field.

In both functions, you separate your associative syntax and object literals in the square brackets ([]) with the fields that you want formatted into two functions, with or without dollar signs. This avoids confusion and keeps it organized.

Next, the variable string sets the order.

```
var strFormat2 = nDecimal + ", " + separStyle + ", " + negativeStyle + ", "
+ currencyStyle +", " + symCurrency + ", " + symCurrencyPrepend;
```

The for loop of each function then runs through the arrays, distributing the information in the correct order. Refer to the for loop in Chapters 10, 13, and 16.

```
for (i = 0; i < aFormatFields2.length; i++) {
this.getField(aFormatFields2[i]).setAction("Format", "AFNumber_Format(" +
strFormat2 + ")");
this.getField(aFormatFields2[i]).setAction("Keystroke", "AFNumber_
Keystroke("+ strFormat2 + ")");
}
```

The final word `return` allows the information to display properly from the associative syntax/objects for the various fields.

If you were to test the form at this point, you might notice a bug. The fields for some reason remain at a format of None. Refer here to Figure 18-11.

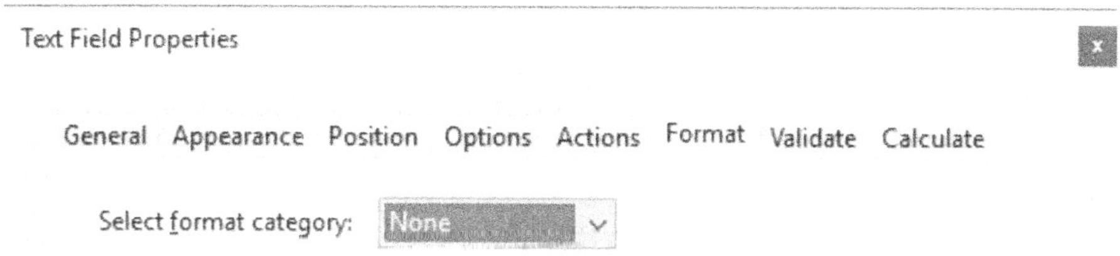

Figure 18-11. *The format category is set to a category of None*

Why is this happening?

In order to get the form working, in this case you need to "kick start" the format. However, you only need to do it once for each function so that the other fields accessing the associative syntax in their functions will work properly. If you make a major change to the function, always remember that it needs a "kick start" to affect the other fields. Choose a field that you know is part of the function `PFCustom_Format`. Choose Custom in the Format tab, not the Number option. Refer here to Figure 18-12.

Figure 18-12. *Choose Custom in the Format tab*

Click Edit. Then in the Custom Format Script area, click Enter.

```
PFCustom_Format();
```

Confirm by pressing the OK Button. The formatting will then automatically switch over to Number. Refer here to Figure 18-13.

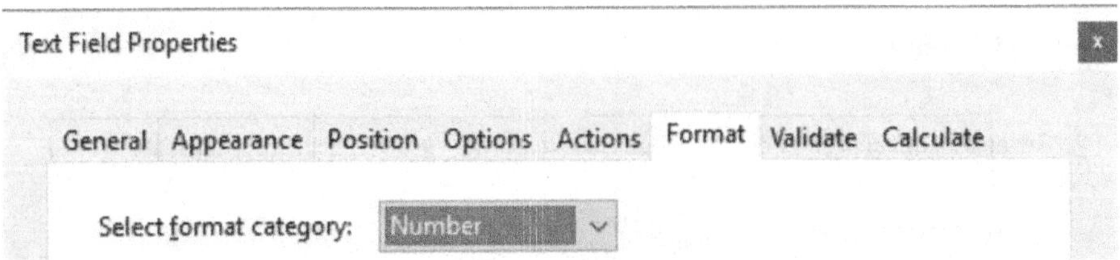

Figure 18-13. *In the Format tab, the category automatically changes to Number*

The other function you may have to apply once to an appropriate field is

```
PFCustom_Format2();
```

Once this is accomplished, all the fields that use these two functions should be set automatically and you don't have to go into each one.

Option 2: Call a Professional

While this example is faster to work with and eliminates errors, it would be nice if there was an even faster way that maybe included a dialog box. Thankfully after a lot of research, I found a JavaScript developer who has devoted a lot of time to figuring out this very issue.

His name is Gilad Denneboom. (try67). He has created a plug-in extension for Acrobat on his website that is called "Apply Format to Multiple Text Fields." You can get it at `http://try67.blogspot.com/2012/06/acrobat-apply-format-to-multiple-fields.html`.

Figure 18-14 shows what it looks like.

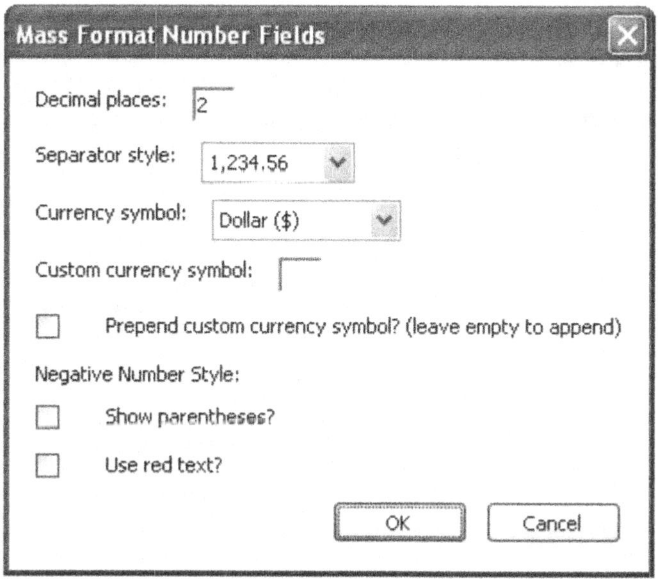

Figure 18-14. *The Mass Format Number Fields plug-in example*

His formatting also allows you to mass format

- Percentage
- Date
- Time
- Special

If you think you will be doing a lot of this type of formatting, I think his $60 product is worth it.

He also has other offers such as `"Acrobat - Mass Edit Fields Actions"` at `http://try67.blogspot.com/2014/11/acrobat-mass-edit-fields-actions.html`. This one allows you to even apply formatting to areas like the Validate and Calculate tabs through his dialog boxes.

Before you buy, if you have questions about the programs like which is the best product or how to install it, ask him first. He is very helpful; he assisted me on a few questions that I had as I wrote this book. He also often answers questions in the Adobe and Acrobat user forums.

Summary

In this chapter, you looked at ways to format multiple text fields with Number formatting. While you could format this easily for one document, it's important to find the best option if you must create a lot of forms with Number formatting. Your choices are do it yourself or call a professional.

CHAPTER 19

Digital Signatures and Barcodes

Throughout this book two form fields were not discussed in great detail in regards to JavaScript: digital signatures and barcodes. Thus, this chapter focuses on them. Let's first look at how they and other fields relate to security.

Note If you want to work along in this lesson or review the final result, download the Chapter 19 files from (`www.apress.com/9781484228892`). The file with the label "Start" is the file without the code and the file with the label "End" is the final result. You will also find a folder containing the original scripts if you would like to add them to your own PDF forms.

If you are creating your form from an original PDF, refer to the "Forms Review" section in Chapter 1.

Remember that to view the properties of a field you must select the Prepare Form tool; only then can you right-click or double-click a field to review its properties.

Digital Signatures and Security

Basic security can be added to text fields. See file `TMC Password Access.pdf` for an example. Refer to Figures 19-1 and 19-2.

J. Harder, *Enhancing Adobe Acrobat DC Forms with JavaScript*,
DOI 10.1007/978-1-4842-2893-7_19

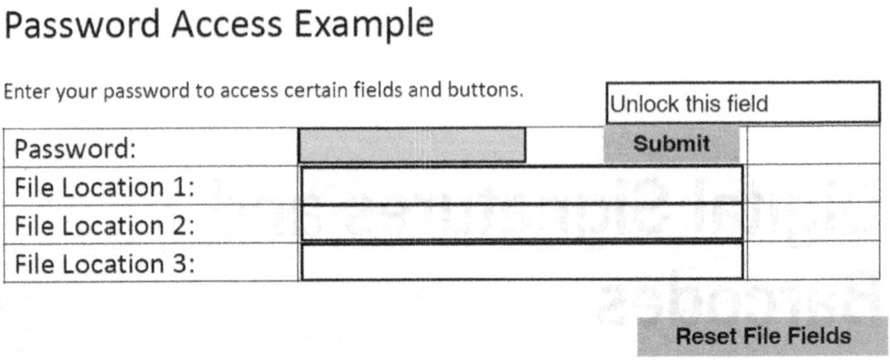

Figure 19-1. *If you don't know the password, you can't unlock the fields and buttons that allow you to add file location links*

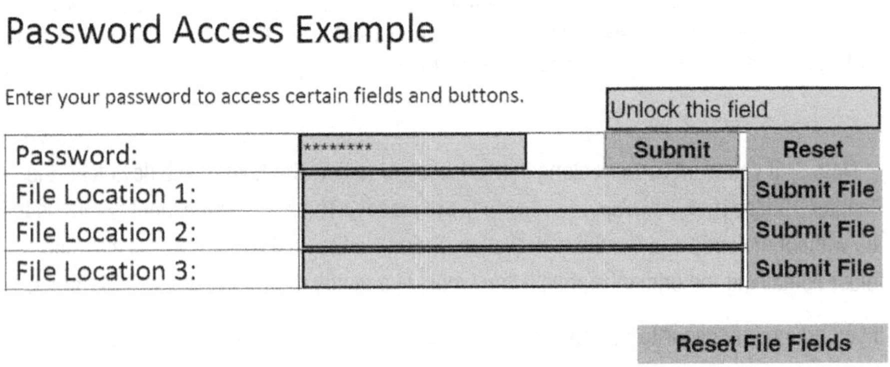

Figure 19-2. *Entering the correct password unlocks the fields and buttons. You can also reset all the fields back to read-only.*

All text fields except the password field have a setting of read-only in the General tab.

The Text1Password field has a setting of Password in the Options tab. Refer to Figure 19-3. This setting will display only a series of asterisks (***); the actual text will remain hidden.

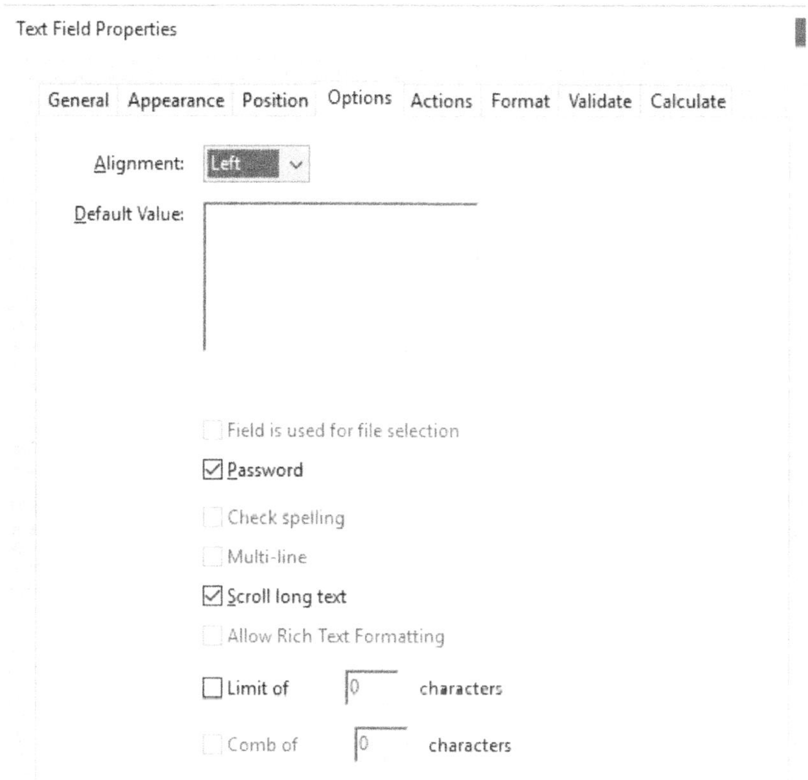

Figure 19-3. *The Options tab has a setting of Password so that the actual text is hidden*

Here is the JavaScript code for the Submit button in the Actions tab ➤ Run a JavaScript:

```
//Submit Password Button
var b=this.getField("Text1Password");
var c=this.getField("Text2");
var file1=this.getField("SubmitFile");
var btn1=this.getField("Submitfilebtn");
var d=this.getField("Reset");
if(b.value=="password"){
    c.readonly =false;
    file1.readonly=false;
    btn1.display=display.visible;
    d.display=display.visible;
    app.alert("Fields are Unlocked",3,0);
}
else{
    app.alert("Wrong Password");
    b.value="";
}
```

Only if you enter the value of "password" will you be able to access the other fields and buttons. Upon clicking the Submit button, if the value is correct, the read-only fields will change to editable and the hidden buttons will display. You will also get an alert that the fields are unlocked. However, if you enter the wrong value, you will get an alert that you entered the wrong password and the field will reset itself so you must try again. Refer to Figure 19-4.

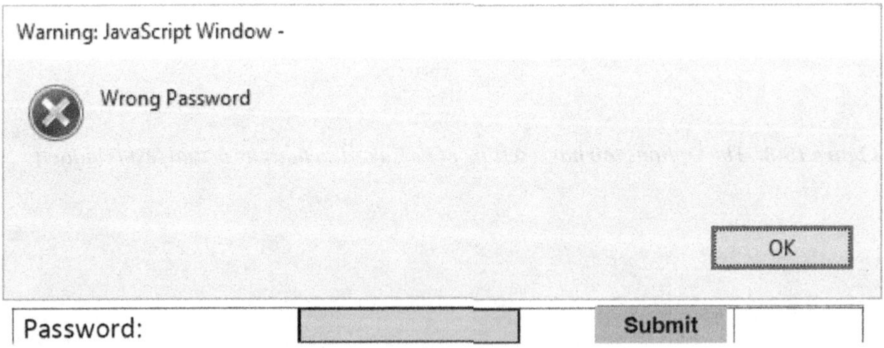

Figure 19-4. *The Password field returns to blank if the password is incorrect*

The Reset button will reset the form and make the text fields read-only and hide some of the buttons. Refer to Figure 19-5.

***Figure 19-5.** The Reset button has two actions in the Actions tab*

For the Reset button, besides resetting the form, you can add the following code:

```
//Reset Password Field, File Fields and Button
var b=this.getField("Text1Password");
var c=this.getField("Text2");
var file1=this.getField("SubmitFile");
var btn1=this.getField("Submitfilebtn");
var d= this.getField("Reset");
```

```
if(b.value==""){
    c.readonly =true;
    file1.readonly =true;
    btn1.display =display.hidden;
    app.alert("Fields are Locked again",3,0);
    d.display= display.hidden;

}
```

Not only does this lock (read-only), hide, and reset fields, but you also get an alert message saying that the fields are locked again.

While not part of security, you can add this code to the Submit File buttons in the Actions tab ➤ Run a JavaScript:

Submitfilebtn.1

```
// Additional Script for Submit a File Button
var file1 = this.getField("SubmitFile.1");
file1.browseForFileToSubmit();
```

Submitfilebtn.2

```
var file2 = this.getField("SubmitFile.2");
file2.browseForFileToSubmit();
```

Submitfilebtn.3

```
var file3 = this.getField("SubmitFile.3");
file3.browseForFileToSubmit();
```

The fields that correspond to these buttons have this setting added in the Options tab "Field is used for file selection." When the Submit File button is clicked, a dialog box will open, allowing you to enter a text version of the location of a specific file on your computer's drive. Without these action settings for the buttons and these specific text field settings in the Options tab, the Open dialog box will not appear. Refer to Figure 19-6.

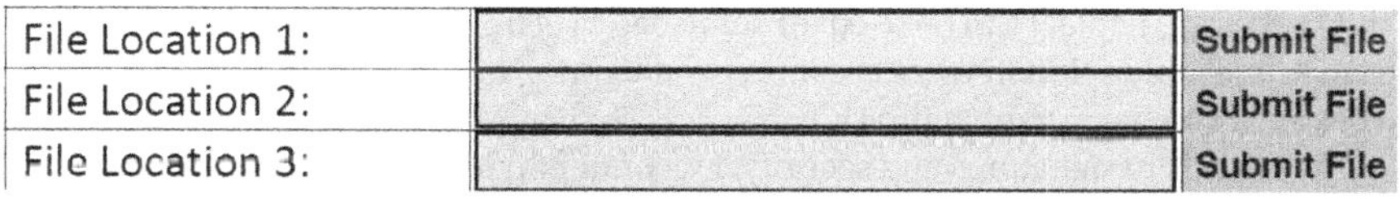

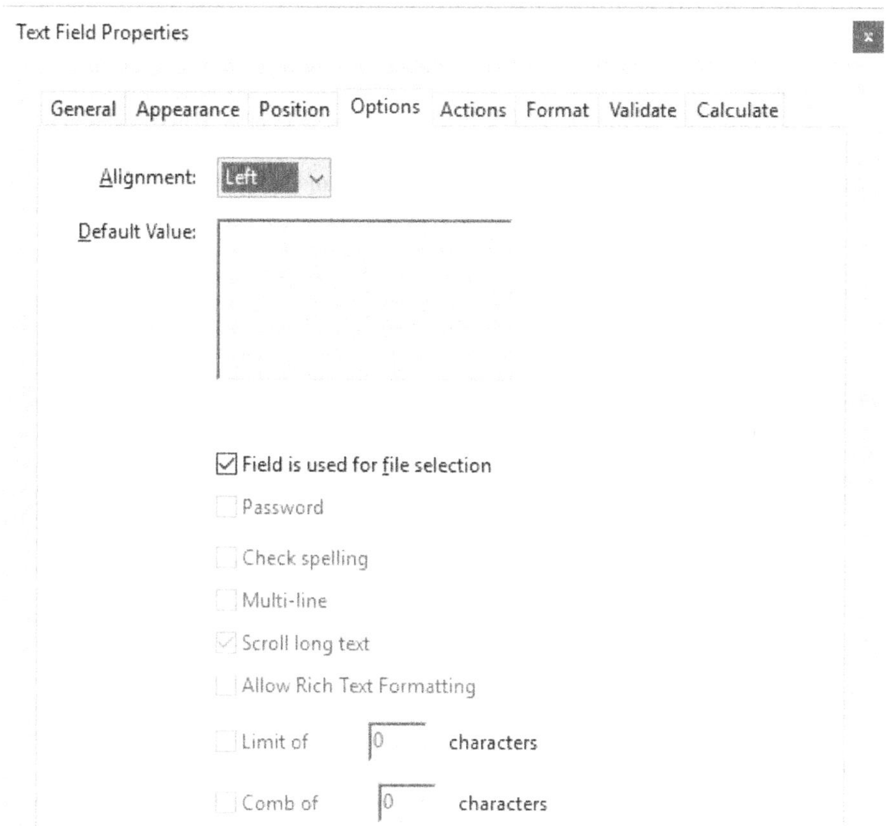

Figure 19-6. *The properties in the Options tab so that this field will work with the Submit File button*

JavaScript, while it can be used for some basic security, is not always the most secure or reliable solution when it comes to encryption because these areas can be easily accessed if you have Acrobat Pro DC.

In regards to signatures and security, I recommend reading *Adobe Acrobat DC Classroom in a Book* by Lisa Fridsma and Brie Gyncild, especially Chapter 8 on signatures and security. I find it has the most up-to-date PDF information in regards to secure encrypted signatures that should be used in a company that requires professional certification and IDs. Likewise, you can also contact Adobe if you need certificates or any similar security.

For interest sake, I've included a file (TMC Signature Agreement) in this chapter's folder that does have JavaScript applied to the digital signatures, which you may want to explore. This file uses a combination of signature fields and buttons to

- Make the signature fields read-only
- To show or hide
- To reset part or the entire form

In the Digital Signature Properties screen, take a moment to look at the Signed tab, which is only available to digital signatures. Unlike other text fields, digital signatures do not have Format, Validate, and Calculate tabs so the only places you can add actions are the Actions and Signed tabs. Refer to Figure 19-7.

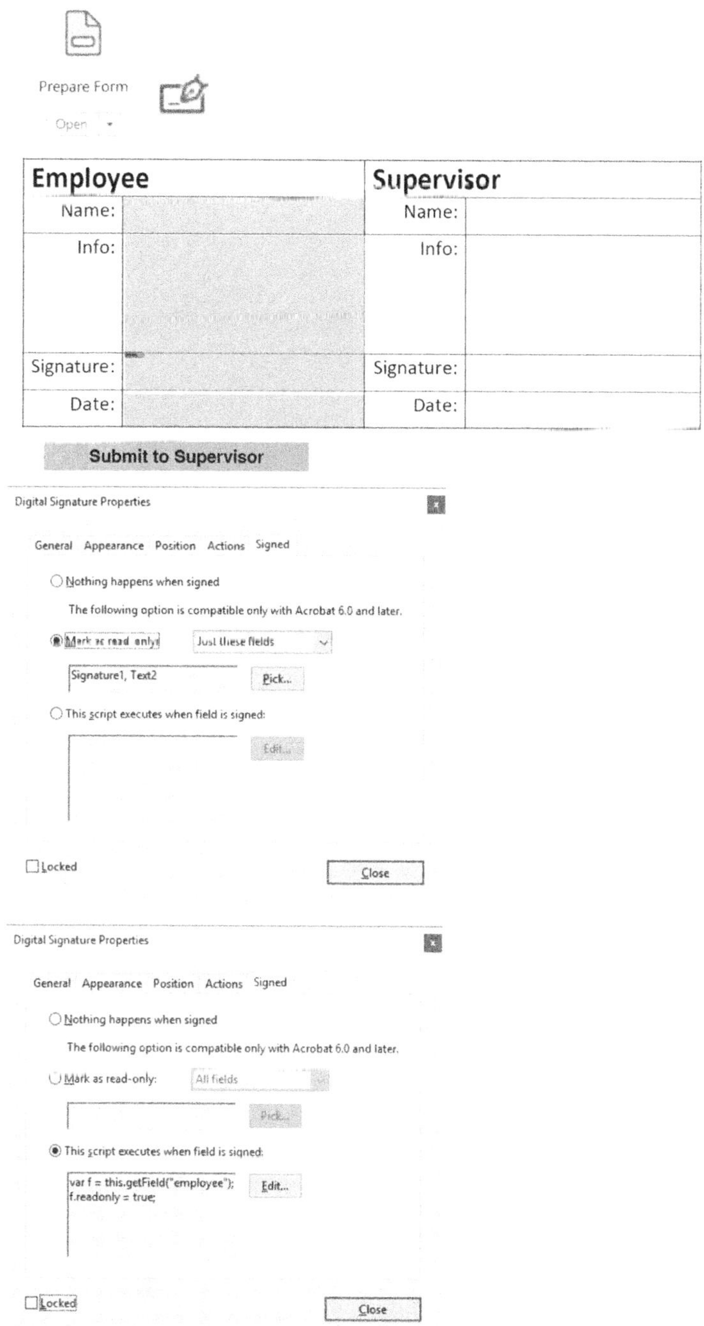

Figure 19-7. *Digital signature properties found in the Signed tab when you either use the option of "Mark as read-only" or "This script executes when a field is signed"*

Basically, as one signature is filled by the employee, the next signature becomes available to the next supervisor. The example is the same as show and hide using fields and a combination of buttons. At the very least, it provides a way to make sure files are signed off in the correct order. It also places a restriction on who can reset what fields. This method is more precise than simply choosing "Mark as read-only." Refer to Figures 19-7 and 19-8.

Code examples used in signatures and buttons:

```
//Employee Signature Field
var a = this.getField("employee");
a.readonly = true;

//Submit to Supervisor button
var a = this.getField("supervisor");
a.display = display.visible;

//Employee Reset Button
var a = this.getField("employee");
this.resetForm(a);

//Submit to HR Button
var a = this.getField("supervisor");
var b = this.getField("employee.submitForm");
a.display = display.visible;
b.display = display.hidden;

// Supervisor Reset Button
var a = this.getField("supervisor");
this.resetForm(a);

//Reset the whole form Button
var a = this.getField("supervisor");
var b = this.getField("employee.submitForm");
var c = this.getField("employee.resetForm");
a.display = display.hidden;
b.display = display.visible;
c.display = display.visible;
```

Figure 19-8. *A Digital Signature field in the Signature Agreement PDF file*

Notice how, as in Chapter 13, you are using display hidden and visible to hide and show certain fields. Read only (`.readonly`) is a Boolean that can be set to either true or false and determines whether the field is read-only or not. This script only executes once the field has been signed and can't be undone by the employee.

Barcodes

Finally, in regards to barcodes, this custom JavaScript influences how the barcode is visually displayed when it refers to the various fields in the form. When the barcode is scanned, this information is collected by a software program and entered into a database for later viewing. If you are planning on buying a barcode reader/scanner or fax to use with Acrobat PDF files, contact the company first and ask what types of JavaScript codes its reader can decipher in regards to PDF barcodes. The company may be able to supply documentation or allow you to test the scanner before buying. Also, to refer to Adobe's Barcoded Paper Forms Solution you may have to contact Adobe directly. Refer to Figure 19-9.

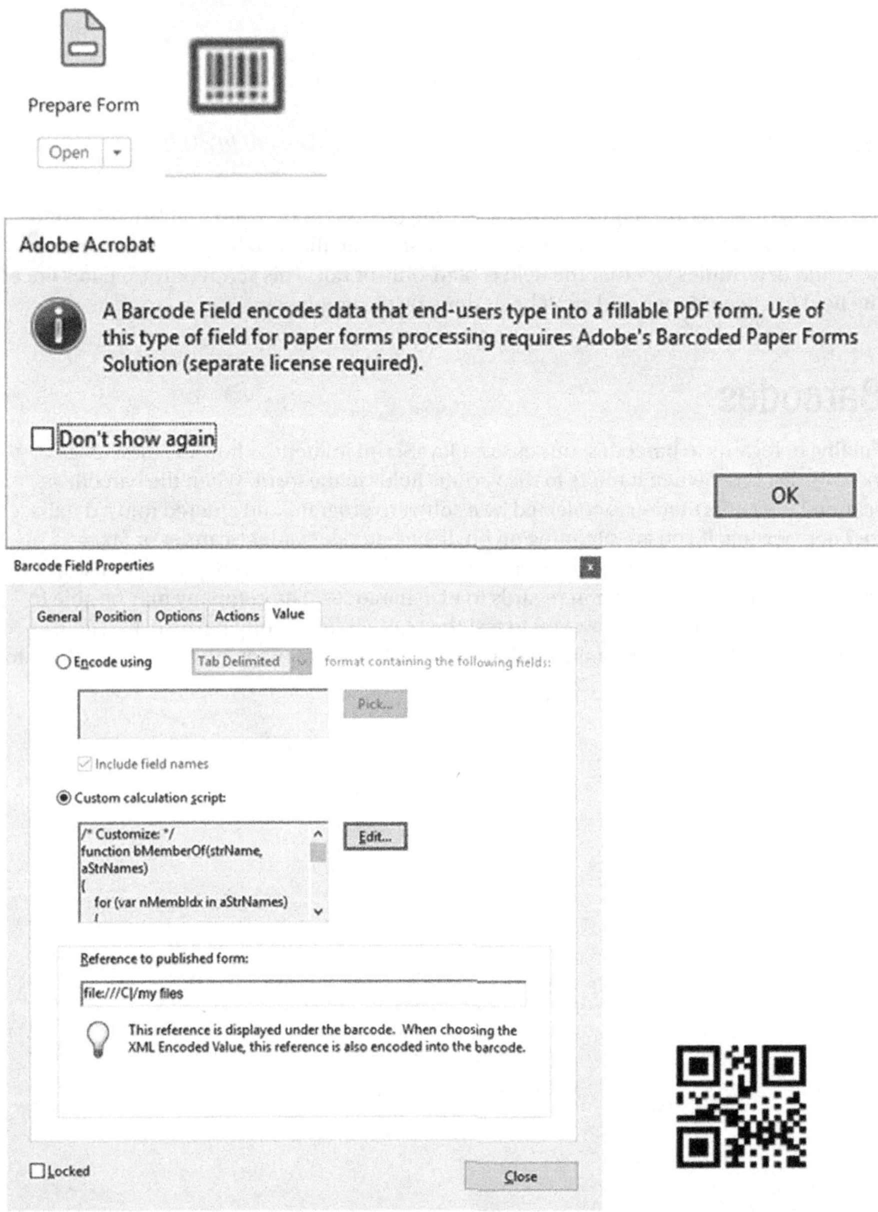

Figure 19-9. *Barcode field properties are found in the Prepare Form tool. When you choose the Barcode field, you may get the alert shown here. You can add or edit JavaScript in the Value tab in the custom calculation script field.*

JavaScript for barcodes is entered into the Actions or Value tabs. Unlike other form fields, the barcode fields do not possess an Appearance tab. Changes to the type of barcode need to be made in the Options tab symbology; however, if you are considering adding a non-form related QR or barcode code to a document or form, refer to Chapter 3 of this book.

More information on Acrobat PDF barcodes can be found at `https://helpx.adobe.com/acrobat/using/pdf-barcode-form-fields.html`.

Summary

In this chapter, you looked at signature fields and barcodes. Signature fields with JavaScript can be used for basic security; however, they are not the most secure PDF options unless combined with other security IDs and certifications. To use barcodes properly requires a barcode reader or scanner.

The concluding chapter is a collection of homework assignments you can use to practice and test the knowledge that you have gained from previous chapters.

Summary

PART 5

Putting It into Practice

CHAPTER 20

Homework Assignments

To complete the assignments in this chapter, be sure to download the Chapter 20 folder at `www.apress.com/9781484228920`.

Homework Assignment 1: Show and Hide

Review Chapters 1, 2, and 4.

Use file Assignment1_showhide_start_2.

This assignment will be a review of the show and hide actions. However, this time you will use yes and no radio buttons rather than a check box and a regular button. It's good to try similar projects in different ways to see which solution you are more comfortable with. Depending on the form you create, one way may be better than another. Remember that radio buttons are always found in groups. Most of the fields have already been created for you. All you need to do is add the correct actions to them.

1. Go to the Prepare Form tool. Refer to Figure 20-1.

Figure 20-1. *Add a button to page 1*

On page 1 of the document, add a button called "Go to Form" in the blank area at the bottom of the page. This will help the reader to jump to the page that has the form. Helpful navigation is useful when a document contains many pages and you want the reader to get to the exact page quickly.

J. Harder, *Enhancing Adobe Acrobat DC Forms with JavaScript*,
DOI 10.1007/978-1-4842-2893-7_20

2. Add the following properties to the General and Options tabs. Refer to Figure 20-2.

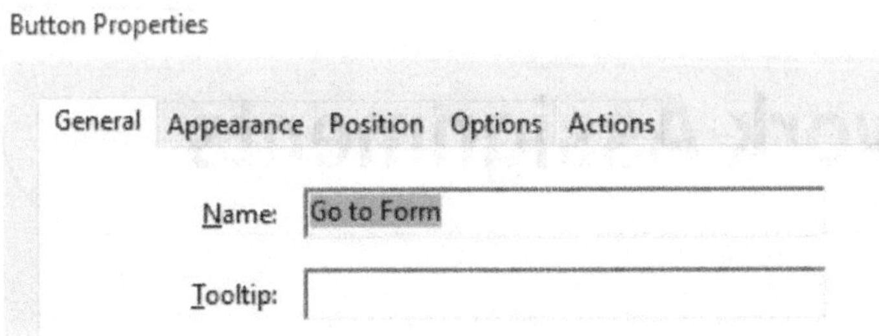

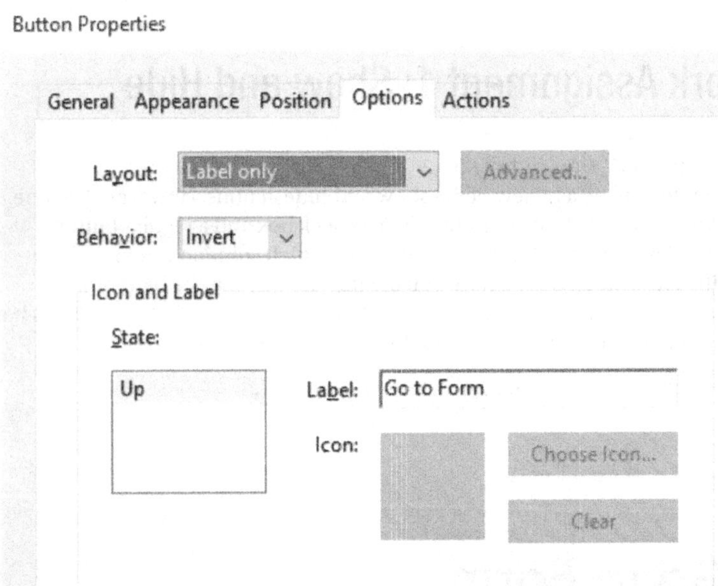

Figure 20-2. *The button properties in the General and Options tabs. You can also add tooltip text. The label layout is "Label only" and the label is named "Go to Form".*

3. For the Actions tab, do the following:
   Select Trigger: Mouse Up
   Select Action: Go to a page view
   Refer to Figure 20-3.

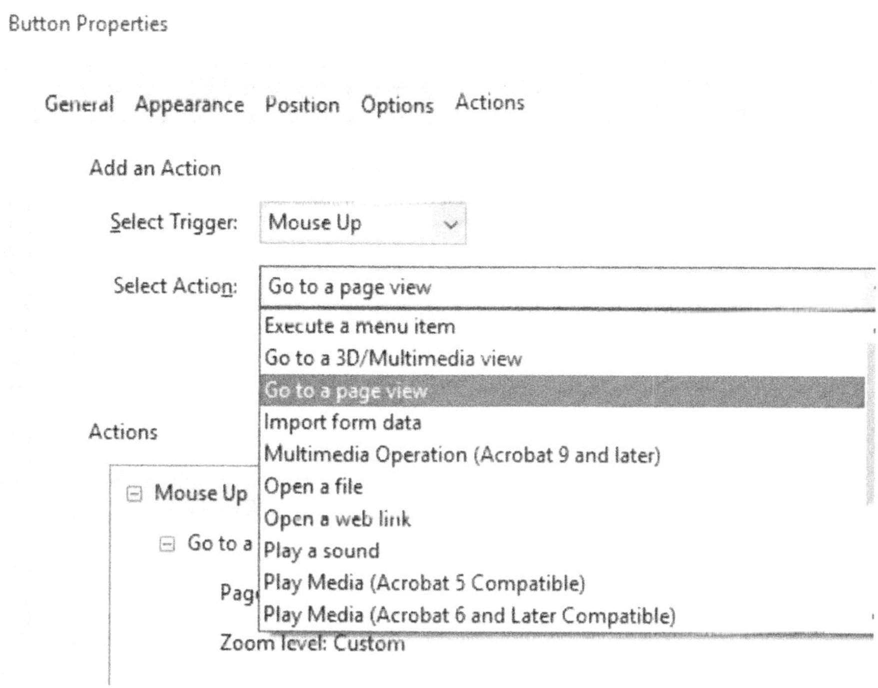

Figure 20-3. *The button properties in the Actions tab*

4. Now click the Add button. Refer to Figure 20-4.

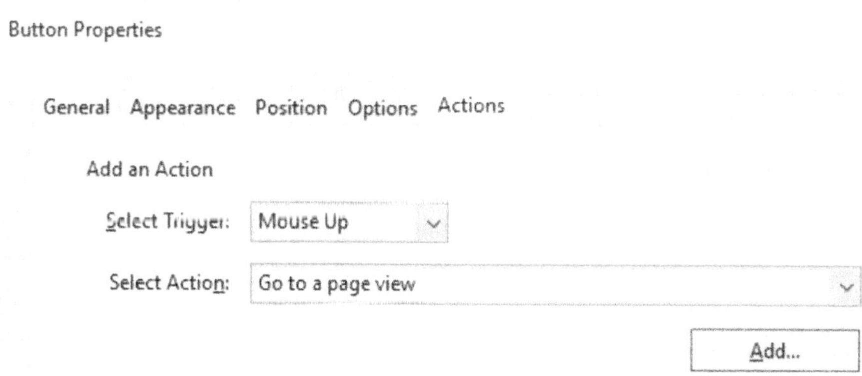

Figure 20-4. *In the Action tab, click the Add button*

5. While these instructions are on the screen, go to page 2 of the document. Make sure the form is at least 75% so you can see the entire form. When you are happy with the size, press the Set Link button. Refer to Figure 20-5.

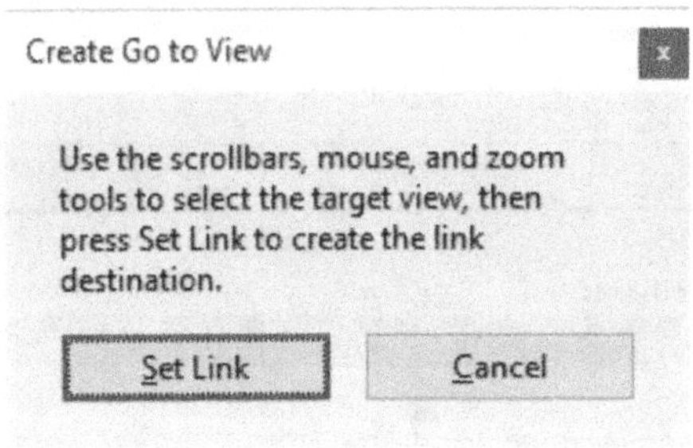

Figure 20-5. *Click the Set Link button when you have gone to page 2*

6. When you are done, your Actions properties should look like Figure 20-6.

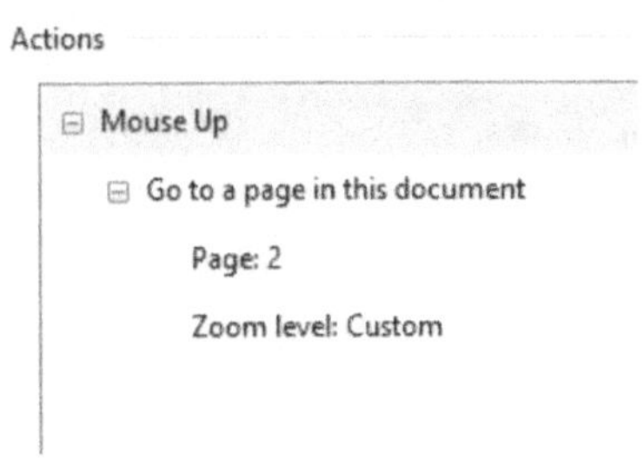

Figure 20-6. *The final set of actions is added to the Actions tab*

7. Click the Close button in the properties dialog box when done.

8. Click the Preview button in the upper right area of the Prepare Form tool to make sure the Go to Form button is working. Refer to Figure 20-7.

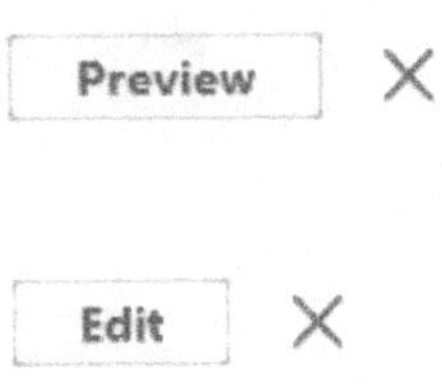

Figure 20-7. *The Edit and Preview buttons*

9. To return to editing, click the Edit button. Refer to Figure 20-7.

   Now you'll work on page 2. Refer to Figure 20-8.

Assignment 1 Show & Hide

Customer's Full Name: ____________________ Date: ____________

Customer Order Code: ___________________________________

Customer's Company Name:

____

Figure 20-8. The upper half of page 2 of Assignment 1

10. In the upper right area for a review, make sure the Date field is formatted to mm/dd/yyyy. Otherwise, leave this area alone and not apply any additional changes or actions. Refer to Figure 20-9.

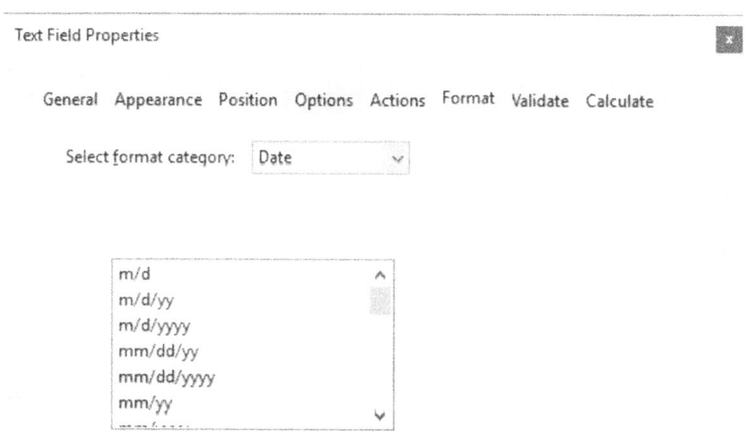

Figure 20-9. The Format tab with a specific date setting

Let's look at the next area of the form you want to work on. Refer to Figure 20-10.

Ship To:

Home Address

Shipping Address Different? ◯Yes ◯ No

First Name		First Name	
Last Name		Last Name	
Address		Address	
City		City	
Province	Select a Province	Province	Select a Province
Country	Canada	Country	Canada
Postal Code		Postal Code	

Figure 20-10. *The lower half of page 2 Assignment 1, Shipping Info*

What you want to do, as in Chapter 4, is when the No radio button is selected, the fields on the right will be hidden. When the Yes radio button is selected, you want the fields on the right to be visible. As in the button example, if you realize afterwards that the addresses are the same, you can click the No radio button again to hide all the right-hand fields and reset them to blank. Refer to Figure 20-11.

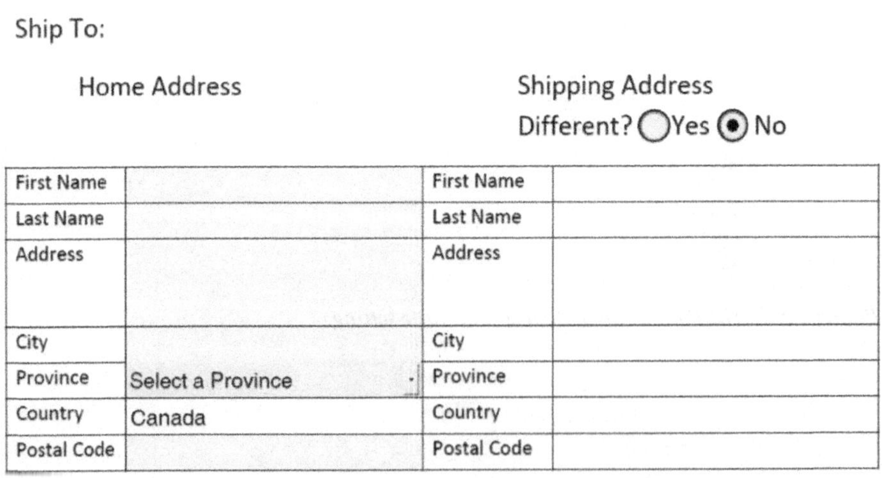
Ship To:

Home Address

Shipping Address Different? ◯Yes ◉ No

First Name		First Name	
Last Name		Last Name	
Address		Address	
City		City	
Province	Select a Province	Province	
Country	Canada	Country	
Postal Code		Postal Code	

Figure 20-11. *The lower half of page 2 Assignment 1, Shipping Info with No selected*

11. Begin with the right-hand fields and make sure that their General tab property is set to Form Field: Hidden. Refer to Figure 20-12.

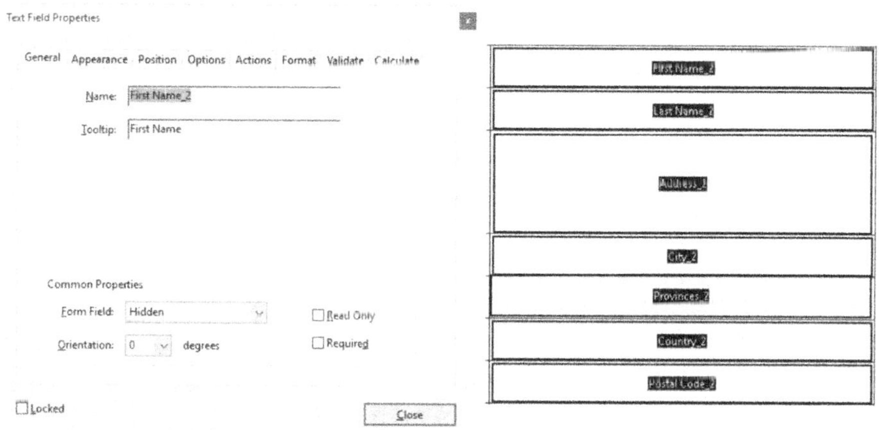

Figure 20-12. *The text fields on the right in the shipping info are set to Hidden*

12. Only the Country field should be checked to "Read Only." Refer to Figure 20-13.

Figure 20-13. *The Country field on the right is set to hidden and read-only*

You do not need to make any other adjustments to these fields.

Now focus on the radio button group, which will do the show/hide and reset. Refer to Figure 20-14.

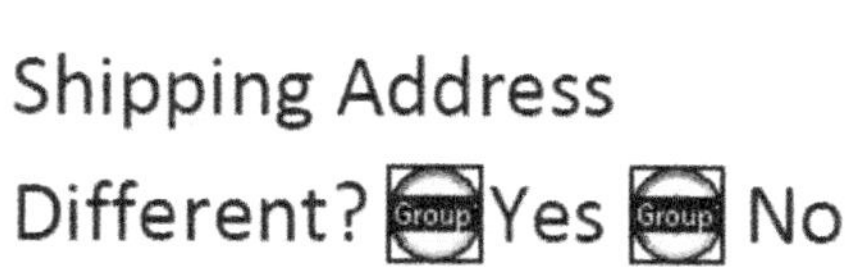

Figure 20-14. *Yes and No radio buttons in the upper right of the shipping info*

13. Go to the Options tab of the Yes radio button. Refer to Figure 20-15.

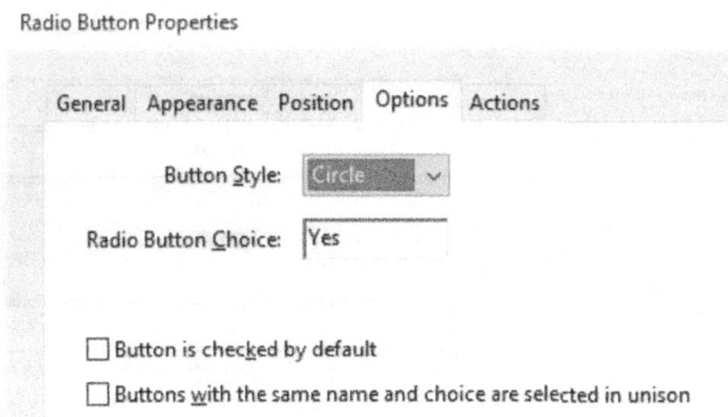

Figure 20-15. *The Options tab with a choice of Yes*

14. Now go to the Options tab of the No radio button.

    Refer to Figure 20-16.

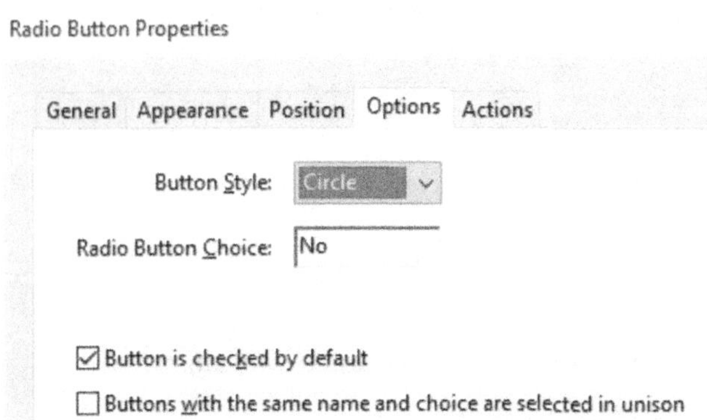

Figure 20-16. *The Options tab with a choice of No*

15. For the actions for Yes and No, refer to Chapter 4 and apply them to the Radio buttons. Refer to Figure 20-17.

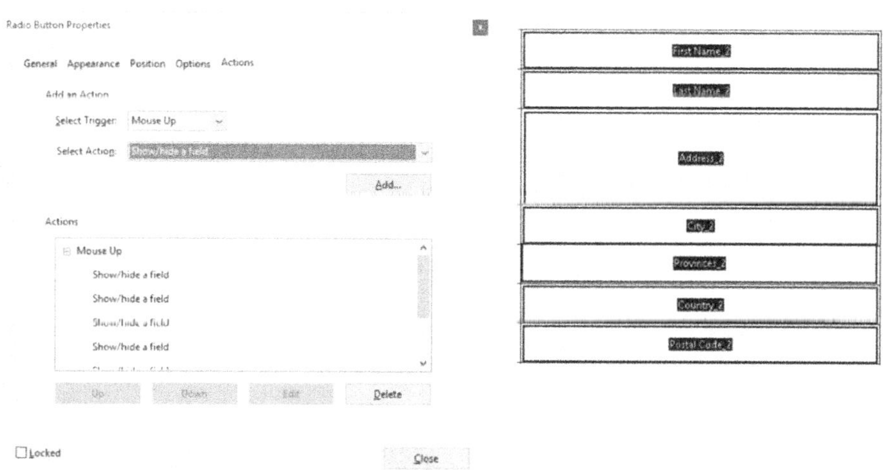

Figure 20-17. *The actions for the radio buttons that will effect the text fields on the right*

Remember that Yes radio button will show the fields.

16. Make sure to add actions to show these fields:

    - First Name_2
    - Last Name_2
    - Address_2
    - City_2
    - Provinces_2
    - Country_2
    - PostalCode_2

Refer to Figure 20-18.

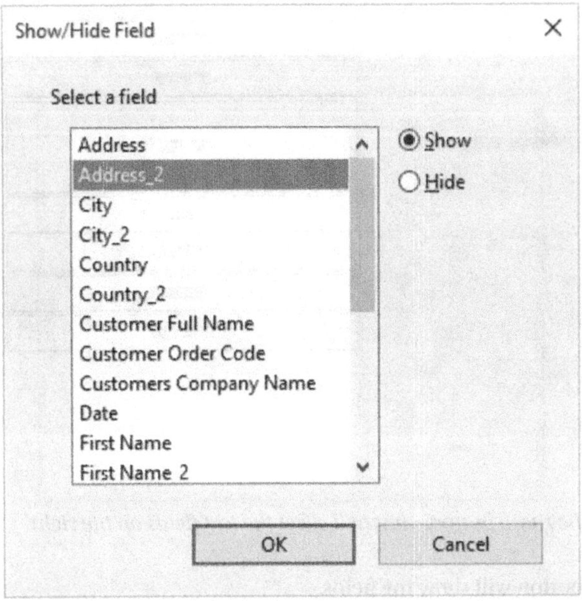

Figure 20-18. *The actions for radio buttons: show or hide. Change the toggle to show or hide a specific field.*

■ **Note** You will need to show and add these one at a time because you cannot select more than one at a time.

The No radio button will hide and reset the form fields.

17. Make sure to add actions to hide these fields:
    - First Name_2
    - Last Name_2
    - Address_2
    - City_2
    - Provinces_2
    - Country_2
    - PostalCode_2

■ **Note** You will need to hide and add these one at a time because you cannot select more than one at a time.

---

18. Finally, you will need to select and add the action called "Reset a Form." Refer to Figure 20-19.

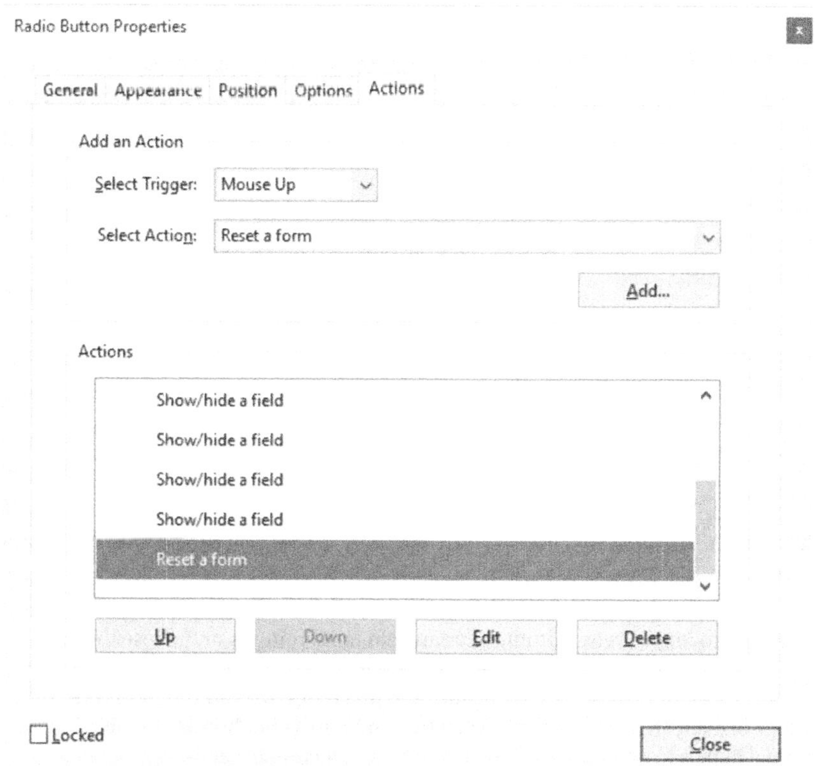

Figure 20-19. *The Actions tab for the No radio button with a reset added last*

19. You will then select the items you need to reset, which you can do in one action. Refer to Figure 20-20.

    - First Name_2
    - Last Name_2
    - Address_2
    - City_2
    - Provinces_2
    - Country_2
    - PostalCode_2
    - Group1

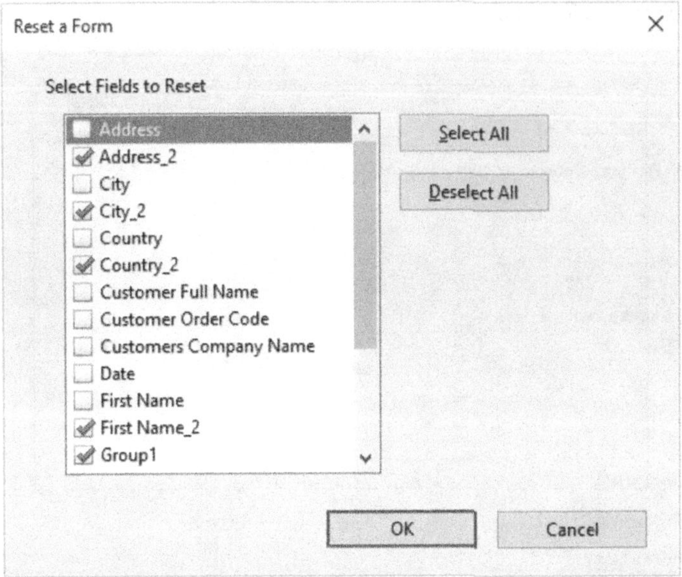

Figure 20-20. *The Actions tab for the No radio button and the field choices that will be reset*

Remember to include your Group 1 Yes and No radio buttons in the reset because they need to refresh if set back to the original settings.

When you are done, preview your results and make sure the radio buttons are functioning correctly. Refer to Figure 20-7 if you can't remember how to do this.

The final item is to add a button called "Print This Document" at the bottom of page 2. Refer to Figure 20-21.

Figure 20-21. *The Print This Document button*

20. Make sure to give the button a name of Print in the General tab. And give the label in the Options tab as you see in Figure 20-21.

21. For the Actions tab, choose "Execute a Menu Item" and Select File ➤ Print. Refer to Figure 20-22.

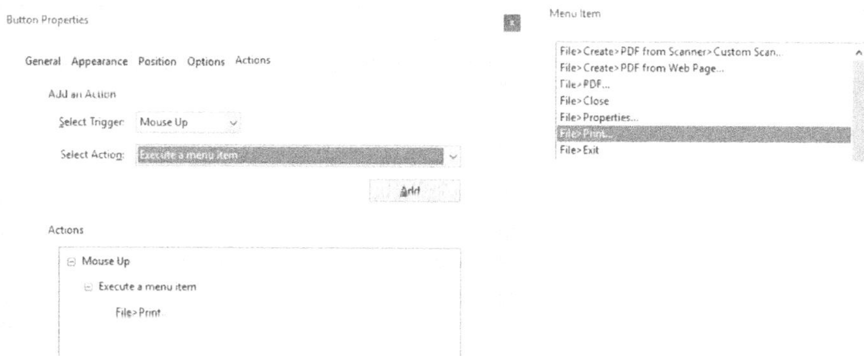

***Figure 20-22.** The actions for the Print button*

This will print both pages. To print just one page, you will need the JavaScript coding from Chapter 10.

22. Test the button. When the user clicks Print, they will go automatically to the Print dialog box.

Save the document. You are now finished with Assignment 1.

Homework Assignment 2: Working with JavaScript to Create Formulas

Review Chapters 5, 6, 7, and 10.

Use the file Start with file Assignment_2_Formulas_start_2.

Refer to Figure 20-23 to open your form with the Prepare Form tool.

***Figure 20-23.** The Prepare Form tool*

For this assignment, you will complete five formulas using JavaScript. The actual formulas have been given above each field. The fields have already been created for you and formatted to Number in the Format tab. The fields on the right are also set to read-only in the General tab so that that these fields cannot be tampered with by clients during the calculation. Refer to Figure 20-24.

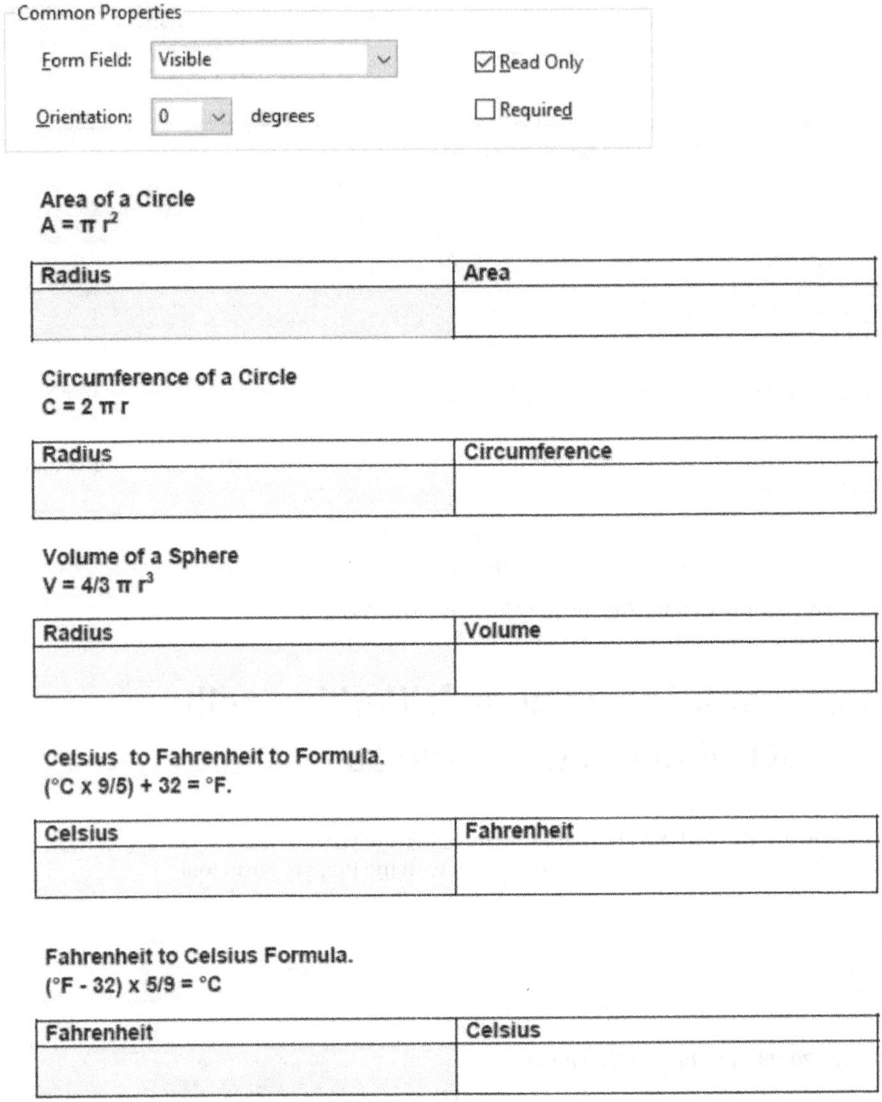

Figure 20-24. *Assignment 2 has five formulas you can use to create the calculations for the fields on the right. Note that the fields have been set to read-only.*

The fields on the left side require no extra JavaScript. You will only call to them through variables as required using the fields on the right.

The first formula must be written as

Area of a Circle

$$A = \pi r^2$$

In the field AreaRow 1, enter the following script in the custom calculation script area in the Calculate tab and refer to Figure 20-25:

```
var radius1 = this.getField("RadiusRow1");
event.value = Math.PI * Math.pow(radius1.value, 2);
```

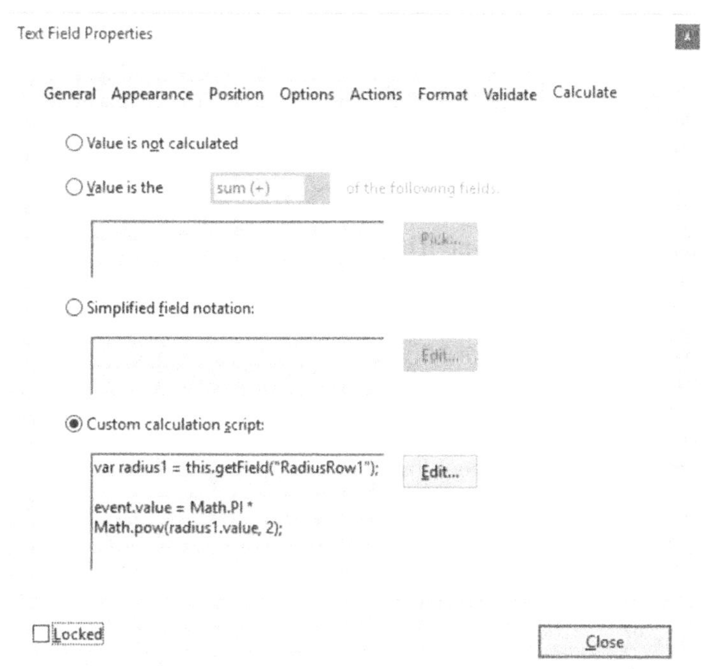

***Figure 20-25.** Assignment 2 in the Calculate tab*

The number 2 in `Math.pow(radius1.value, 2);` is equivalent to writing r^2.

Test it to make sure that the formula is working and then proceed to the other four calculations.

If you're not sure where to start, here is a hint:

Field: CircumferenceRow1

Circumference of a Circle

$$C = 2 \pi r$$

```
var radius2 = this.getField("RadiusRow1_2");
event.value = 2 * ______ * radius2.value;
```

What value from the above example should go here to complete the formula? What does the JavaScript equivalent look like?

Field: VolumeRow1
Volume of a Sphere
$V = 4/3\ \pi\ r^3$

```
var radius3 = this.getField("RadiusRow1_3");
event.value = (4/3)* ______ * Math.pow(radius3.value, _____);
```

What two values from the above example should go here to complete the formula? What does the JavaScript equivalent look like?

Field: FahrenheitRow1
Celsius to Fahrenheit to Formula.
(°C x 9/5) + 32 = °F.

```
var celsius = this.getField("CelsiusRow1");
event.value = (celsius.value* 9/5)+ ______;
```

What value from the above example should go here to complete the formula? What does the JavaScript equivalent look like?

Field: CelsiusRow1_2
Fahrenheit to Celsius Formula.
(°F - 32) x 5/9 = °C

```
var fahrenheit = this.getField("FahrenheitRow1_2");
event.value = (fahrenheit.value-______)*(5/9);
```

What value from the above example should go here to complete the formula? What does the JavaScript equivalent look like?

Once you have entered the correct formulas into the Calculation tab area, refer to Figure 20-26.

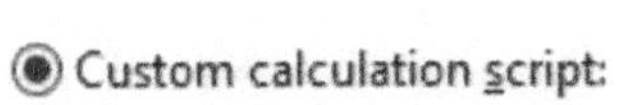

Figure 20-26. *Assignment 2 in the Calculate tab ➤ Custom Calculation Script*

Test them to make sure they are working. Sometimes you need to save the file, close it, and then open it again so that it takes effect.

If it is functioning correctly, continue on to the next part of the assignment.

For the next part of the assignment, you will add a JavaScript to the Validation tab of these fields. Refer to Chapter 6 and Figure 20-27.

- AreaRow1
- CircumferenceRow1
- VolumeRow1

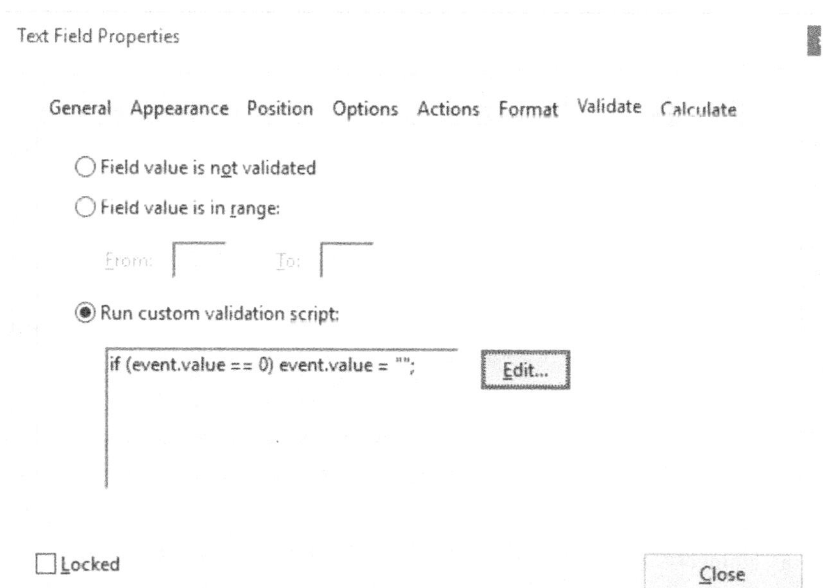

Figure 20-27. *The Validate tab with a custom validation script*

Select "Run custom validation script, "

Enter the following code:

```
if (event.value == 0) event.value = "";
```

This is to ensure that the field remains blank if nothing is entered in the radius fields.

Click OK after entering the script.

For the fields

- FahrenheitRow1
- CelsiusRow1_2

enter this validation script:

```
if (event.value > 0){
    event.target.textColor = color.black;
}
else{
    event.target.textColor = color.red;
}
```

If the calculation is greater than zero, the text will be black; if less than zero, the text will be red. As mentioned in Chapter 10, without JavaScript you could not have given these numbers a two-color option.

Save your file. You have finished Assignment 2.

Homework Assignment 3: Custom Validation and Regular Expressions

Refer to Chapters 8, 9, 10, and 11.

Use file Assignment_3_validation_start_2.

Refer to Figure 20-28 to open your form with the Prepare Form tool.

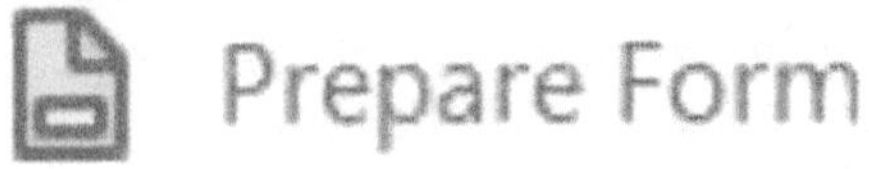

Figure 20-28. *Prepare Form tool*

This assignment is a review of custom validations and regular expressions. Refer to Figure 20-29.

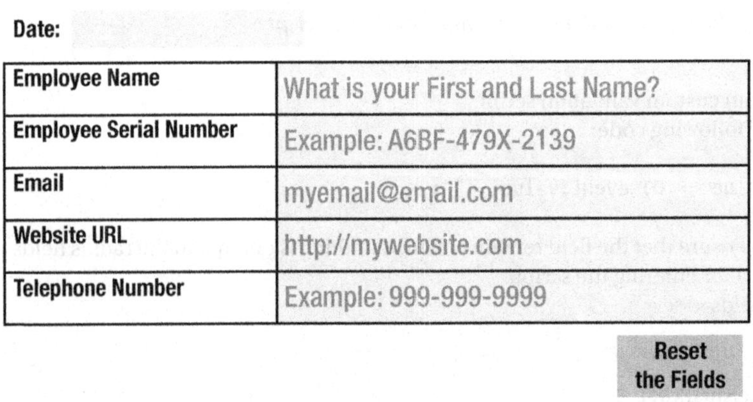

Figure 20-29. *Assignment 3 contains regular expressions and default text in the Format tab*

For the Date field, leave the format to None since you will try two format options. Refer to Figure 20-30 for the next step.

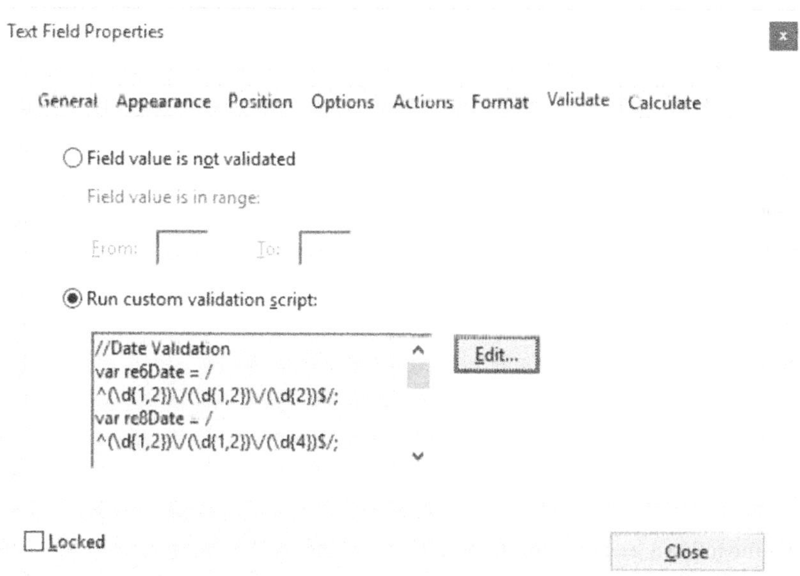

Figure 20-30. *Run a custom validation script*

Instead, add the following validation under the Validate tab:

```
//Date Validation
var re6Date = /^(\d{1,2})\/(\d{1,2})\/(\d{2})$/;
var re8Date = /^(\d{1,2})\/(\d{1,2})\/(\d{4})$/;
//prevent alert if field is blank
if(event.value !=""){
     if(re6Date.test(event.value)== false && re8Date.test(event.value)==
     false){
     app.alert("I'm sorry. That is not a valid format. It must be mm/dd/yy
     or mm/dd/yyyy. ");
event.rc = false;
     }
}
```

For the Employee Name field, set the Format tab to Custom. Refer to Figure 20-31.

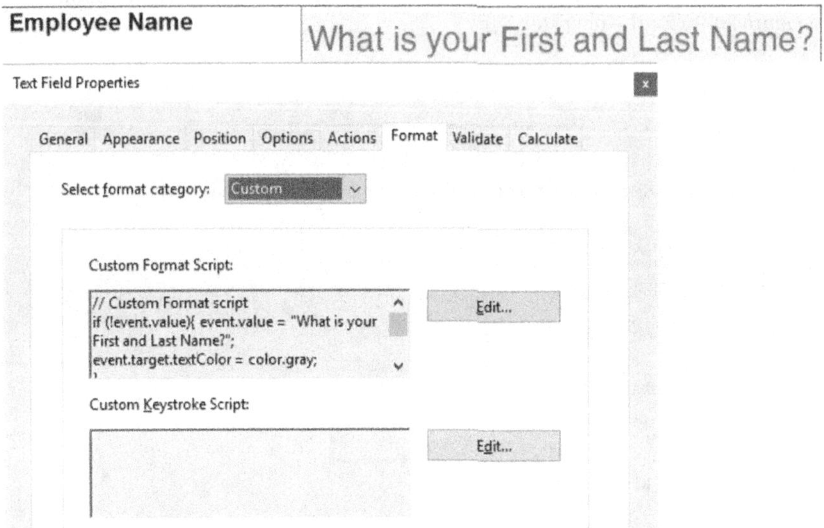

Figure 20-31. *Apply a custom format category*

Enter the following custom format script:

```
// Custom Format script
if (!event.value){ event.value = "What is your First and Last Name?";
     event.target.textColor = color.gray;
}
else{
     event.target.textColor = color.black;
}
```

Then select the "Run custom validation script" button in the Validate tab and enter the following code. Refer to Figure 20-32.

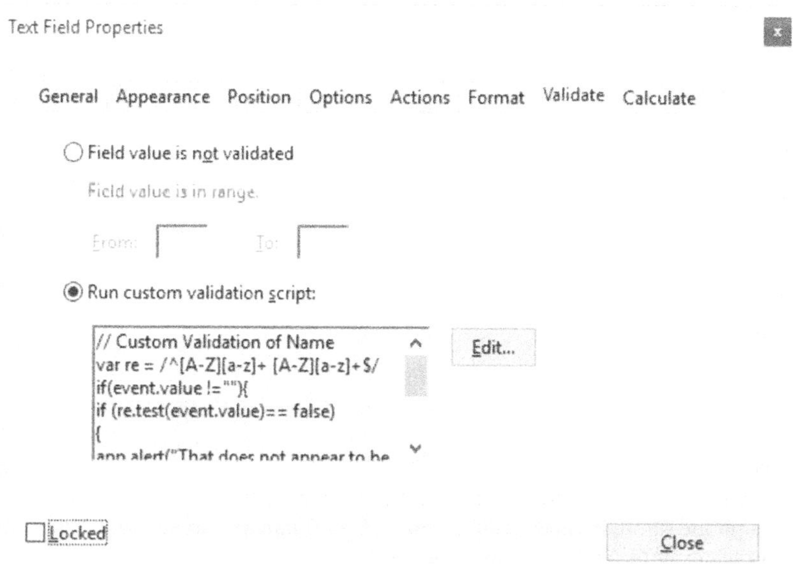

Figure 20-32. *Apply validation in the Validate tab for the Employee Name field*

```
// Custom Validation of Name
var re = /^[A-Z][a-z]+ [A-Z][a-z]+$/
if(event.value !=""){
     if (re.test(event.value)== false){
     app.alert("That does not appear to be a valid name. I need a first and
     last name.");
     event.rc = false;
     }
}
```

Looking at JavaScript, think about how you could modify this code for the other fields in the Format and Validate tabs. This script is covered in Chapters 9 and 10 (the default method).

- Employee Serial Number
- Email
- Website URL
- Telephone Number

For the telephone number, alter the script in the Custom Format tab slightly for three colors since the original only had two colors in the example.

```
// Custom Format script
var rgexTele = /^[(]{0,1}[0-9]{3}[)]{0,1}[-\s\.]{0,1}[0-9]{3}[-\s\.]{0,1}
[0-9]{4}$/;
if (!event.value){
     event.value = "Example: 999-999-9999";
     event.target.textColor = color.gray;
}
else if(rgexTele.test(event.value)){
     event.target.textColor = color.black;
}
else{
     event.target.textColor = ["RGB",1,0,0]; //Change text to red
}
```

For the Employee Serial Number Validate tab script, refer to Chapter 11 (text field validation with regular expressions).

For the Email Validate tab script, refer to Chapter 11.

For the Website URL Validate tab script, refer to Chapter 11.

For Telephone Number Validate tab script, refer to Chapter 11 for correct script; use only the 10-digit example at the beginning of the chapter.

Alerts such as the one in Figure 20-33 should appear if the data is not entered correctly.

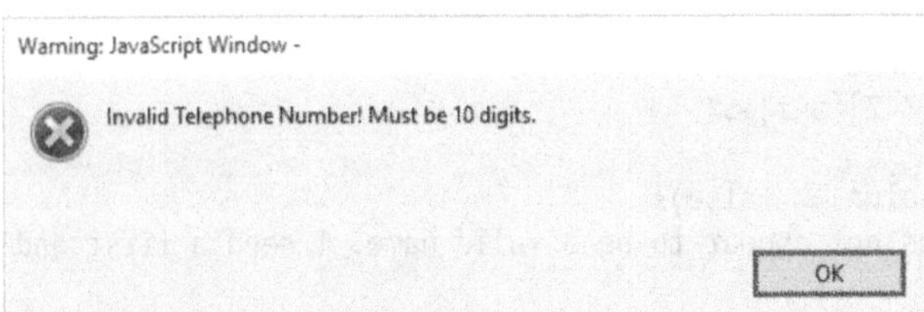

Figure 20-33. *An alert from a custom validation script*

At the end of the assignment make sure to add a reset action to all the fields with a button.

A final thing to add to the button is to make it multi-line. Refer to Chapter 10 for an example. Refer to Figure 20-34 for how to set up the button.

Figure 20-34. *Various properties in the General, Options and Actions tabs for the Reset button. Add "Run a JavaScript" to make the button multi-line.*

Choose "Run a JavaScript" and enter this code:

```
this.getField("Reset").buttonSetCaption("Reset\n the Fields");
```

Then reset all the form fields. Click OK and close the button properties.
When done, save your file. You have completed Assignment 3.

Homework Assignment 4: Personal Dropdown Menu and Definitions Text Box

Review Chapters 11 and 12.
Use file Assignment_4_multiline_dropdown_start_2.
Refer to Figure 20-35 to open your form with the Prepare Form tool.

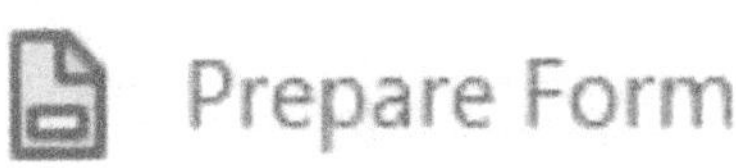

Figure 20-35. The Prepare Form tool

This final assignment is useful when you have a topic, but you need to see more information on the topic such as a definition. Dropdown menus can only be single line, and a multi-line menu is a nice option to have. Refer to Figure 20-36.

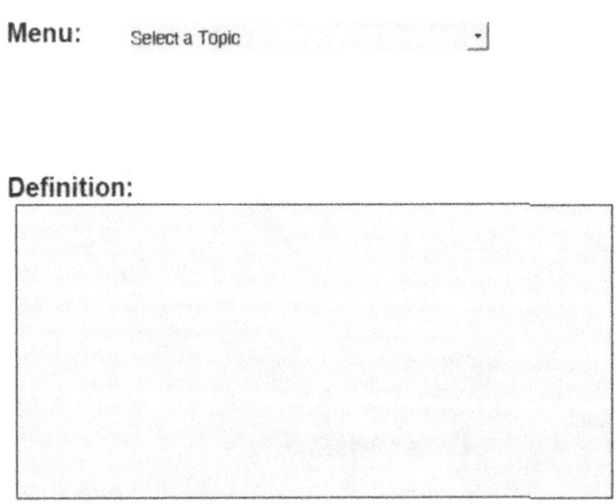

Figure 20-36. The final assignment is to create a dropdown that has extra information appear in a text box

The dropdown and the text field have already been set up. Refer to Figure 20-37.

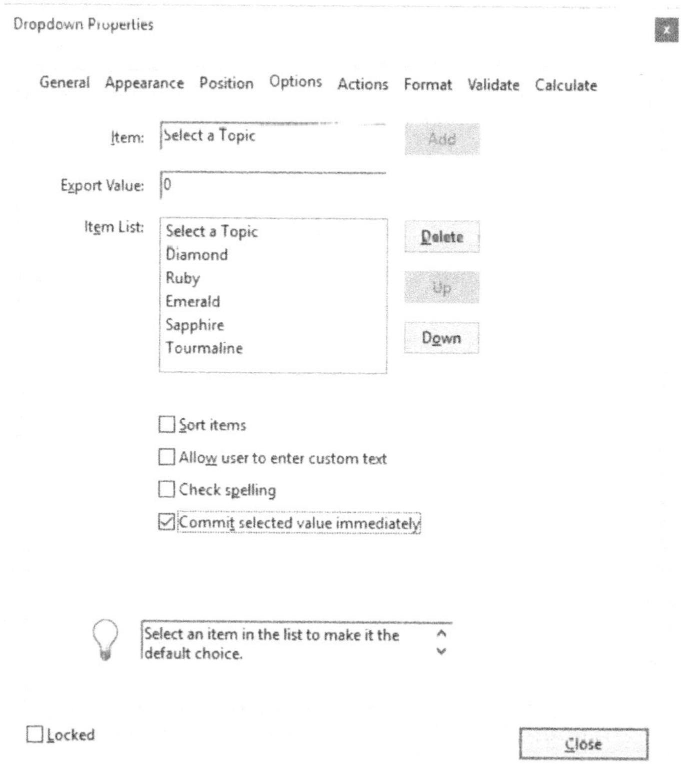

Figure 20-37. The Options tab of the Dropdown Properties dialog box

The Options tab offers these options:

- Diamond
- Ruby
- Emerald
- Sapphire
- Tourmaline

Leave the export value blank, so it will not mess with the JavaScript. Remember to check "Commit selected value immediately" so the script will load right away into the text box.

For the Option tab of the text field Text2, make sure it is set to multi-line in case the comments become longer. As in Figure 20-38, you can uncheck "Check spelling" because this option is not required.

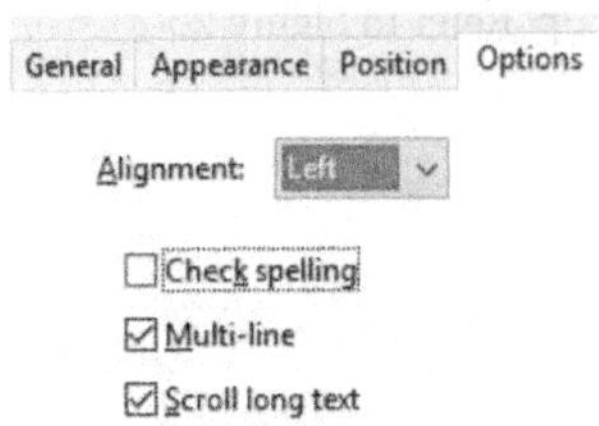

***Figure 20-38.** The properties in the Options tab with "Check spelling" not selected*

In the General tab, give the text field a setting of read-only.

Do not alter anything else in the text field and only focus on the dropdown menu and document JavaScript. Refer to Figure 20-39.

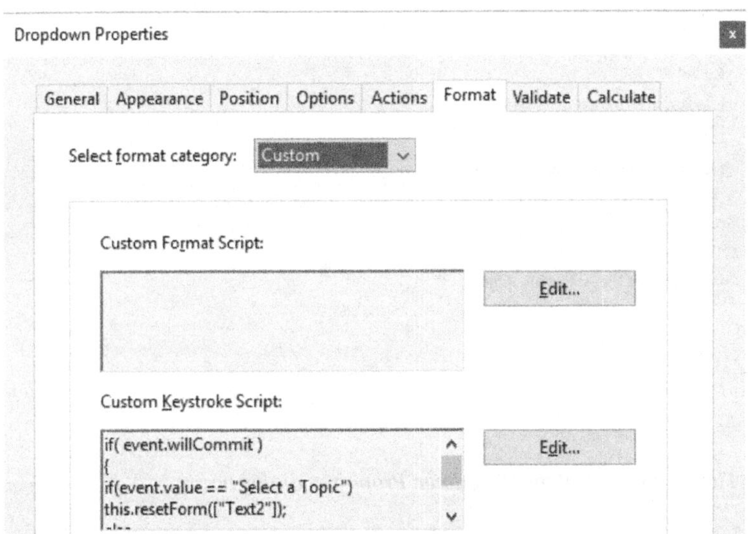

***Figure 20-39.** The Dropdown Properties Format tab with a custom keystroke script*

In the dropdown menu under the Format tab, set it to Custom and add the following JavaScript to the custom keystroke script area:

```
if(event.willCommit)
{
    if(event.value == "Select a Topic")
            this.resetForm(["Text2"]);
    else
    SetFieldValues(event.value);
}
```

You don't need to do anything else to the dropdown menu.

Now exit from the Prepare Form tool and go to Tools ➤ JavaScript. Refer to Figures 20-40 and 20-41.

Figure 20-40. *From the Prepare Form tool, switch to the JavaScript tool*

Select the Document JavaScripts tool. Refer to Figure 20-41.

Figure 20-41. *Select the Document JavaScripts tool to enter the dialog box*

Give it the script a name of `SetFieldValue` and click the Add button. Refer to Figure 20-42.

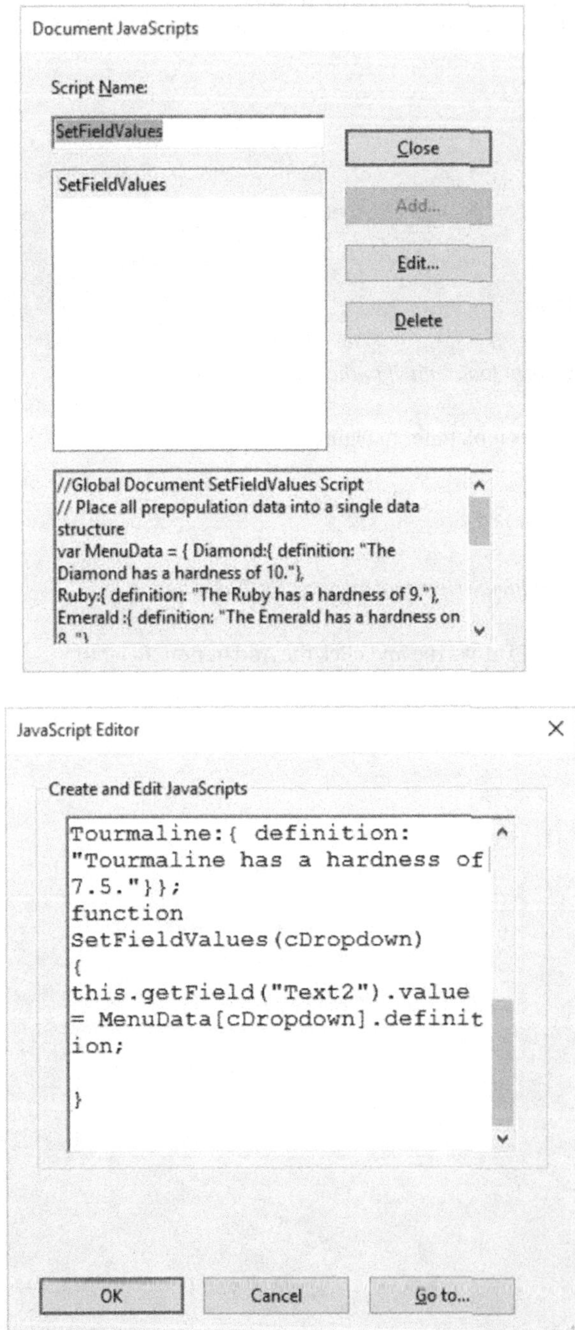

Figure 20-42. *The Document JavaScripts dialog box with the SetField values script. The text is entered into the JavaScript Editor.*

Enter only this script:

```
//Global Document SetFieldValues Script
// Place all prepopulation data into a single data structure
var MenuData = { Diamond:{ definition: "The Diamond has a hardness of 10."},
     Ruby:{ definition: "The Ruby has a hardness of 9."},
     Emerald :{ definition: "The Emerald has a hardness on 8. "},
     Sapphire:{ definition: "The Sapphire has a hardness of 9."},
     Tourmaline:{ definition: "Tourmaline has a hardness of 7.5."}};
function SetFieldValues(cDropdown)
{
     this.getField("Text2").value = MenuData[cDropdown].definition;

}
```

Once entered, click OK to confirm and click Close to close the Document JavaScript dialog box. Refer to Figure 20-42.

Exit out of the JavaScript tools and test the dropdown menu by selecting a name from the menu.

As you let go of the selection from the dropdown menu, the definition text should appear in the text box.

When you select the top value, it should reset itself to blank.

Make sure to test the file to confirm that all parts of the menu are functioning.

Refer to Figure 20-43.

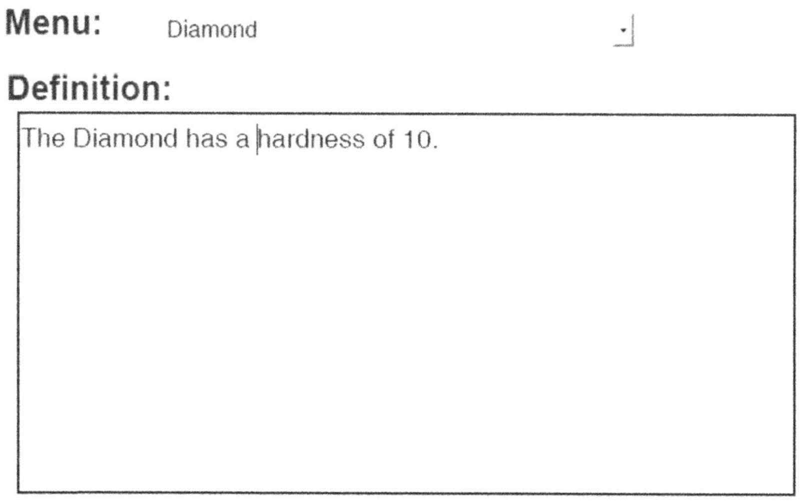

Figure 20-43. *This is what the final assignment should look like*

Save your file. You have completed the final assignment.

Summary

To help apply what you've learned throughout the book, this chapter presented you with four assignments.

Index

A

B

J. Harder, *Enhancing Adobe Acrobat DC Forms with JavaScript*,
DOI 10.1007/978-1-4842-2893-7

C

D

E

F, G, H

I, J, K

L

M

N, O

P

T, U

V, W, X, Y, Z

Made in the USA
Monee, IL
14 September 2026

63190911R00216